Trust and the Islamic Advantage

In much of the Muslim world, Islamic political and economic movements appear to have a comparative advantage. Relative to similar secular groups, they are better able to mobilize supporters and sustain their cooperation long term. Nowhere is this more apparent than in Turkey, a historically secular country that has experienced a sharp rise in Islamic-based political and economic activity. Drawing on rich data sources and econometric methods, Avital Livny challenges existing explanations – such as personal faith – for the success of these movements. Instead, Livny shows that the Islamic advantage is rooted in feelings of trust among individuals with a shared, religious group identity. This group-based trust serves as an effective substitute for more generalized feelings of interpersonal trust, which are largely absent in many Muslim-plurality countries. The book presents a new argument for conceptualizing religion as both a personal belief system and a collective identity.

Avital Livny is Assistant Professor in the Department of Political Science, University of Illinois at Urbana-Champaign. She is the recipient of several awards from the National Science Foundation, the US Department of Education, and the Andrew W. Mellon Foundation. Her dissertation research also received the Juan Linz Award from the APSA Comparative Democratization Section.

Trust and the Islamic Advantage

Religious-Based Movements in Turkey and the Muslim World

AVITAL LIVNY
University of Illinois at Urbana-Champaign

CAMBRIDGE
UNIVERSITY PRESS

University Printing House, Cambridge CB2 8BS, United Kingdom

One Liberty Plaza, 20th Floor, New York, NY 10006, USA

477 Williamstown Road, Port Melbourne, VIC 3207, Australia

314-321, 3rd Floor, Plot 3, Splendor Forum, Jasola District Centre, New Delhi - 110025, India

103 Penang Road, #05-06/07, Visioncrest Commercial, Singapore 238467

Cambridge University Press is part of the University of Cambridge.

It furthers the University's mission by disseminating knowledge in the pursuit of education, learning and research at the highest international levels of excellence.

www.cambridge.org
Information on this title: www.cambridge.org/9781108707237
DOI: 10.1017/9781108751667

© Avital Livny 2020

This publication is in copyright. Subject to statutory exception and to the provisions of relevant collective licensing agreements, no reproduction of any part may take place without the written permission of Cambridge University Press.

First published 2020
First paperback edition 2022

A catalogue record for this publication is available from the British Library

ISBN 978-1-108-48552-4 Hardback
ISBN 978-1-108-70723-7 Paperback

Cambridge University Press has no responsibility for the persistence or accuracy of URLs for external or third-party internet websites referred to in this publication, and does not guarantee that any content on such websites is, or will remain, accurate or appropriate.

To my family

Contents

List of Figures	*page* ix
List of Tables	xi
Acknowledgments	xii

1	Introduction	1
	Lessons from the Turkish Case	4
	A Trust-Based Theory of Islamic-Based Movements	5
	Existing Theories of Islamic Politics and Economics	11
	Preview of Findings	13
	Plan of the Book	14

PART I   Theoretical Development

2	Understanding the Rise of Islamic-Based Movements in the Muslim World	21
	2.1 Political and Economic Activity in the Muslim World	24
	2.2 Existing Theories of Islamic-Based Mobilization	29
	2.3 A Theoretical Evaluation of Existing Explanations	35
3	Evaluating Existing Theories of the Islamic Advantage	37
	3.1 Empirical Implications of the Grievance Theory	38
	3.2 Assessing the Faith-Based Theory of "Transvaluation"	45
	3.3 The Role of Information in Islamic Politics	59
	3.4 The Puzzle of the Islamic Advantage	64
4	Generalized Distrust and the Participation Gap in the Muslim World	65
	4.1 The Value of Interpersonal Trust	67
	4.2 Trust and Trustworthiness in the Muslim World	78
	4.3 Can Trust Expectations Be Improved?	84
	4.4 The Trust Problem in the Muslim World	91

5	Muslim Identity and Group-Based Trust	94
	5.1 Trust within Identity Groups	96
	5.2 Islam as a Group Identity	105
	5.3 Conclusion	121

PART II Applications and Empirics

6	Explaining the Islamic Advantage in Political Participation	125
	6.1 The Trust Problem in Mass Political Movements	126
	6.2 The Trust-Based Islamic Advantage in Mass Politics	132
	6.3 State Repression and the Islamic Advantage	140
	6.4 Conclusion	145
7	Islam, Trust, and Strategic Voting in Turkey	148
	7.1 The Complexities of the Turkish Electoral System	150
	7.2 The Trust Problem in Voter Coordination	158
	7.3 Trust and the Success of Turkey's Islamic Parties	166
	7.4 Conclusion	178
8	The Quasi-Integration of Firms in an Islamic Community: The Case of MÜSİAD	181
	8.1 The Trust Problem in Economic Relations	183
	8.2 Estimating MÜSİAD's Comparative Advantage	195
	8.3 Conclusion	203

PART III Conclusion

9	Conclusion	209
Appendix		222
Bibliography		225
Index		251

Figures

1.1	Map of the Muslim World	page 12
2.1	Participation in Collective Political Activities in the Muslim World	25
2.2	Saving Activity, In and Outside of the Muslim World	27
3.1	Political and Economic Grievances in the Muslim World	41
3.2	Income and Political Participation in the Muslim World	43
3.3	Income and Bank Savings in the Muslim World	44
3.4	Obstacles to Political and Economic Participation	47
3.5	Political Participation and Religious Faith	50
3.6	Faith and Bank Assets across the Muslim World	53
3.7	Faith and Islamic Party Vote Share in Turkey	55
3.8	Faith and Support for the AKP	56
3.9	Faith and Support for Islamic Parties, Cross-Nationally	58
3.10	Policy Positions of Turkish Political Parties	62
4.1	Determinants of Generalized Trust	84
4.2	The Effect of Islam on Trust across Individuals	86
4.3	Trust among Migrants	90
5.1	Relationships between Markers of Religion in Turkey	114
5.2	Relationships between Markers of Religion, Cross-Nationally	115
5.3	Self-Reported Religiosity and Mosque Attendance	116
5.4	Religious Identity, Efficacy, and Trust	120
6.1	Political Participation and Generalized Distrust	134
6.2	Political Participation and Mosque Attendance	137
6.3	Distrust and Political Participation, across Mosque Attendance	139
6.4	Distrust, Identity, and Participation, across Levels of Repression	143
6.5	The Substitution Effect under Repression	145
7.1	Party-System Fractionalization in Turkey (1961–2018)	151
7.2	Vote Volatility in Turkey (1965–2018)	152
7.3	Turkish Parties' Left–Right Orientation, over Time	154
7.4	Wasted Votes, across Electoral Districts (1961–2002)	156
7.5	Distrust and Wasted Votes, across Turkish Provinces over Time	170

7.6	Islamic Identity and Wasted Votes	173
7.7	Distrust and Wasted Votes, across Levels of Islamic Identity	174
8.1	Changes in MÜSİAD Membership over Time	192
8.2	Marginal Effect of Vertical Integration, across Levels of Volatility	198
8.3	Marginal Effect of MÜSİAD Membership	199
8.4	Effect of MÜSİAD Membership, by Level of Volatility	201
9.1	The Substitution Effect across Religious Denominations	212
9.2	Generalized Distrust and Vote Volatility, across Countries	214
9.3	Generalized Distrust and Islamic Group Identity, across the Muslim World	215
9.4	Trust and Honesty, across Countries	216
9.5	Trust and Honesty, across Levels of Regulation	218
A6.1	Turkish Parties' Left–Right Orientation, over Time	223
A6.2	Bank Savings as Trust Proxy	224

Tables

3.1	Comparing Existing Theories of Islamic-Based Mobilization	*page* 38
4.1	Heterogeneous Preferences in a Public Goods Game	72
5.1	Personal Religiosity and Islamic Identity Factor Loadings	117

Acknowledgments

This project began as my doctoral dissertation, completed in the Department of Political Science at Stanford University. As such, the work presented here would not have been possible without the mentorship of some remarkable people. David Laitin, Jeremy Weinstein, and Lisa Blaydes helped guide this project along, each offering their own variety of sage advice. At times, they (rightly) pushed me back to the field; at others, they (wisely) reminded me to just get on with it and put pen to paper. Along the way, they advocated for me and this project, even when we disagreed about a given twist and turn. In so doing, they led by the very best example, modeling behavior that I now seek to emulate with my own students.

Beyond the courses and advising, a great many of the lessons learned in graduate school were those taught by friends and colleagues. For the always-thoughtful feedback on various iterations of this project, I thank Jessica Gottlieb, Grant Gordon, Avner Greif, Justin Grimmer, Eric Kramon, Beatriz Magaloni, Aila Matanock, Ramya Parthasarathy, Tomer Perry, Amanda Robinson, Jonathan Rodden, and Mike Tomz. An especially heartfelt thank you goes to the members of my weekly working group – Rachel Gillum, Mackenzie Israel-Trummel, Lauren Prather – whose thoughtful contributions appear throughout this manuscript. I am also grateful to Ayça Alemdaroğlu, Joel Beinin, Burcu Karahan, Burçak Keskin-Kozat, Uğur Peçe, and Ali Yaycıoğlu for their warm embrace of my different methodology and for their friendship. Work aside, I am not sure I would have survived graduate school without Alex Blackman, Jessica Gottlieb, Bob Henig, Sara Mrsny, Ramya Parthasarathy, Tomer Perry, Lauren Prather, Amanda Robinson, Luke Stein, and Eliana Vasquez.

During fieldwork, I was privileged to spend my time with an incredible group of colleagues who became fast friends: Elizabeth Angell, Josh Carney, Sarah El-Kazaz, Gail Godbey, Timur Hammond, Hikmet Kocamaner, Özlem Özgür, Danielle van Dobben Schoon, Brian Silverstein, Vedica Kant, Elizabeth Williams, and Mark Wyers. And to those who always make the field feel like home, welcoming me back upon each return, I thank Alexios Menexiadis,

Acknowledgments

Seçil Öznur Yakan, and Veysel Öztürk. I am also forever grateful to members of the Peçe family for their endless warmth and hospitality. Finally, special thanks go to my collaborators and interlocutors: Ali Çarkoğlu; Seda Ertaç; Yılmaz Esmer; Eren Pultar and Aydın Erdem at KONDA Research and Consultancy; Eyüp Aydın and Nail Olpak at MÜSİAD; the fine folks at the American Research Institute in Turkey; and all those I encountered around my neighborhood and in my travels who, eager to share in a conversation, opened up their world to me.

Since graduating, my work has been generously supported by new colleagues, first, at the Carlos III-Juan March Institute of Social Sciences and, now, at the University of Illinois at Urbana-Champaign. In Madrid, I was lucky to spend my time learning from and laughing with María José Hierro Hernandez, Luis Fernando Medina, Magdalena Nebreda, Dídac Queralt, Andrew Richards, Pedro Riera, Ignacio Sánchez-Cuenca, Rick Sandell, Sarah Valdez, and Tod Van Gunten. Since arriving in Champaign-Urbana, I have been generously supported by a tremendous group of colleagues, many of whom read parts or all of this manuscript in preparation for my book conference. I thank Scott Althaus, Jake Bowers, Damarys Canache, Stephen Chaudoin, Hadi Esfahani, Brian Gaines, Sarah Hummel, Kostas Kourtikakis, Jim Kuklinski, Carol Leff, Jeff Mondak, Bob Pahre, Tom Rudolph, Gisela Sin, Matt Winters, and Cara Wong for their comments and suggestions. A special thanks to Kelly Senters for her participation in the conference, and to Kristin Bail for her comments on the final manuscript.

Outside my department at the University of Illinois, I have been honored to be so supported by the incredible team at the Cline Center for Advanced Social Research. This project would not have been completed without the physical and intellectual space provided to me by Scott Althaus, Dan Shalmon, and Sheila Roberts. I also appreciate the support from other units at UIUC, from the Center for Advanced Study, the Center for Global Studies, the Center for South Asian and Middle Eastern Studies, the European Union Center, and the Initiative in Holocaust, Genocide, and Memory Studies. I am also privileged to have found a tremendous community of friends in Urbana, whose support is hard-baked into everything I have accomplished while here: Nir Ben-Moshe, Jake Bowers, Eric Calderwood, Jennifer Carr, Alison Carter, Catharine Fairbairn, Nick Grossman, Verena Hoefig, Sarah Hummel, Jamie Jones, Aleks Ksiazkiewicz, Pendar Paul Madavi, John Meyers, Andrea Miller, Alyssa Prorok, Nate Schmitz, Gisela Sin, and Cara Wong. Outside of my Urbana community, I am very lucky to call Artemis Brod, Mark Budolfson, Federica Carugati my friends.

I have also enjoyed considerable support and encouragement from members of the Association for Analytic Learning about Islam and Muslim Societies (AALIMS), the Association for the Study of Religion, Economics, and Culture (ASREC), and from the Institute for the Study of Religion, Economics and Society (IRES). A special thanks to Jean-Paul Carvalho, Larry Iannaccone, Amaney Jamal, Saumitra Jha, Mark Koyama, Timur Kuran, Tarek Masoud, Rich Nielsen, Liz Nugent, Chris Paik, Tom Pepinsky, and Jared

Rubin. Portions of this book were written while I was in-residence at the Institute for Futures Studies (Institutet för Framtidsstudier), supporting meetings with members of the Stockholm University Institute for Turkish Studies. For that special opportunity, I thank Gustaf Arrhenius, Hans Ingvar Roth, and Folke Tersman. In addition, this project has been generously supported by the Stanford University Graduate Fund, the Stanford Institute for Innovation in Developing Economies, the Stanford Humanities Center, the Abbasi Program in Islamic Studies, the Center for Russian, East European and Eurasian Studies at Stanford University, the Stanford University Graduate Research Opportunity Grant, the United States Department of Education, the United States Department of State, and the Andrew W. Mellon Fellowship of Scholars in the Humanities Program. It has also been vastly improved based on comments from two anonymous reviewers and my editor, Sara Dostow.

Last, but by no means least, this book is dedicated to my family. In my application to graduate school, I described what it was like to be raised by my father, Miron, a computer scientist, and my mother, Efrat, an artist and healer. Together, they nurtured a curiosity in me that was at once precise and sensitive. If, at the end of this process, I have managed to produce a book that is both precise and sensitive, it is in no small part because of them and my step-parents, Ken and Marina. My brother, Jon, and his wife, Ayala, have also played an invaluable role in this, as have Talia and Dani, my niece and nephew. Thank you for proving to me that family members can become true friends. My dear extended family in Israel, Massachusetts, Michigan, and California has never wavered in supporting my academic pursuits, and I am grateful for every visit and every conversation. Finally, to Ben, my love and partner in crime: you have jumped into every adventure right alongside me, and each moment has been made infinitely better for your part in it. I cannot imagine what lies ahead for us, and I cannot wait.

1

Introduction

In 2006, political scientists Ali Çarkoğlu and Binnaz Toprak teamed up with the Turkish Economic and Social Studies Foundation (TESEV) to assess the role of religion in contemporary Turkish politics. Çarkoğlu and Toprak titled their study "Religion, Society, and Politics in a Changing Turkey," designing it as a follow-up to their earlier survey fielded in 1999. Their choice of title, with its focus on change, was a nod to recent events: despite deep secular (and secularist) roots derived from Kemalist *laïcité* (*laiklik*), Turkey was now led by the Justice and Development Party (Adalet ve Kalkınma Partisi, AKP), a party that made clear and repeated references to religion.

The right-of-center AKP won a surprisingly easy victory in the 2002 general election and were able to form a single-party government. Both the party's dominance at the polls and its use of Islamic themes were remarkable: on the one hand, Turkey's fractionalized electoral system had almost always resulted in coalition governments; on the other, the Turkish constitution explicitly prohibits the use of religious language in politics. In succeeding as an explicitly Islamic-based political movement, the AKP seemed to be part of a broader phenomenon taking place across the Muslim world: a growing set of large, mostly mainstream and increasingly successful Islamic social, political, and economic organizations, a group that includes the Muslim Brothers in Egypt, the Malaysian Islamic Party, and the Islamic Corporation for Development of the Private Sector, among others.

What defines all these organizations as "Islamic-based" is more about means than ends. They couch their appeals to supporters in Islamic terms, making regular and explicit use of religious language and symbols. For example, at a large rally leading up to the 2019 local election, AKP leader Recep Tayyip Erdoğan told the crowd that his party is "determined to keep Istanbul as a city of Islam and as a city of Turks until eternity" (Hürriyet Daily News 2019).[1] And in courting Kurdish voters in Diyarbakır just before the 2011

---

[1] Most notoriously, during the campaign, Erdoğan read aloud a poem, proclaiming "the mosques are our barracks, the domes our helmets, the minarets our bayonets, and the faithful our soldiers."

general elections, he implored that "the community in Istanbul's Süleymaniye Mosque turns to the same *qibla* as the community here in the Ulu Mosque. Our *qibla* is the same. Is there any difference? No" (Korkmaz 2015). This is little different than the traditional slogan of the Muslim Brothers – "Islam is the solution" – revived by Mohamed Morsi during his 2012 campaign for the Egyptian presidency (Kirkpatrick 2012).

For the AKP and its leadership, the 2002 victory proved to be the first of many successes. For decades, the Turkish electoral system had developed a reputation for instability in which political parties – especially those of the center-right – rose to prominence only to quickly lose hold on power (Hazama 2004). But the AKP, occupying a similar policy position to these other parties, but distinctive in its regular reference to Islam, was able to reverse this trend: it held on to its support base, maintaining and even expanding its vote share over time. Indeed, the party has managed to singularly rule the country ever since, ushering in a period of one-party dominance unparalleled in Turkish democratic history (Esen and Ciddi 2011; Müftüler-Baç and Keyman 2012).

Back in 2006, perhaps sensing the sociopolitical shift that was underway, Çarkoğlu and Toprak wanted to assess the causes of the AKP's dramatic rise and the consequences of its rule. In particular, they were interested in interrogating a widespread assumption that a religious resurgence within Turkish society could explain the party's initial success, as well as its remarkable staying power. On the morning following the 2002 election, the front page of *Sabah*, one of Turkey's largest newspapers, described the AKP win as an "Anatolian Revolution" (*Anadolu'nun İhtilali*), a nod to the country's more religiously conservative periphery, where support for the party was especially high. Similarly, international media outlets focused almost exclusively on the party's Islamic roots, proclaiming "Party Tied to Islam Wins Big in Turkey" (*Washington Post*) and "Islamic Party Sweeps Turkish Poll" (*Guardian*) (Christensen 2005). Two electoral cycles later, I myself witnessed a similar response among average citizens in the wake of an AKP win in 2011: the morning following that election, many residents of Istanbul's more secular neighborhoods donned black, half joking with me that they were attending a funeral for "secular Turkey" (*laik Türkiye*).

While the link between Islamic politics and religiosity in Turkey is commonly presumed, the connection between the two has not been established empirically. A paucity of data on religion and religiosity in Turkey is largely to blame: part of the Turkish state's commitment to Kemalist secularism dictates that the topic remain largely absent from official statistics, with questions about individuals' faith removed from the national census after 1965 (Dündar 2000). Çarkoğlu and Toprak wanted to fill this gap. By assessing patterns of behavior and preferences across individuals in their survey, and by comparing these to the results of their earlier study, they sought to unearth the real relationship between Islamic fundamentalism and the AKP in Turkey. To capture cross-temporal changes in religiosity, they repeated questions about religious practice posed in their first survey; and to gauge public perception of these changes, they asked respondents to comment on them directly.

Introduction

On a particularly hot-button issue, respondents were asked to estimate the change in popularity of head-covering among Turkish women over the previous decade (1996–2006). In line with the assumption of a religious resurgence in Turkey, an overwhelming majority of them – nearly 75 percent – said they noticed an increase over that time (p. 65). Further, those respondents who estimated an increase in head-covering were also more likely to note an increase in religious fundamentalism (p. 80). Indeed, when asked to explain why they perceived an uptick in fundamentalism, the most popular reason given was the rising popularity of the headscarf. In other words, the respondents' perceptions echoed the popular portrayal: the rise of Islamic-based politics reflected a change in the basic fabric of Turkish society, from secular to religious.

Despite these presumptions, when Çarkoğlu and Toprak examined the actual rates of head-covering among female respondents across their two studies, they found no evidence of an increase. Instead, they found that average levels of covering had *decreased* for nearly every demographic group: young and old, urban and rural, across all levels of education (p. 64).[2] In other words, the empirical pattern directly contradicted the common presumption. And some key concerns about measurement validity were unwarranted in this case. For example, social desirability bias towards feigned secularism would have weakened between the two studies, as years of AKP rule normalized public signs of piety (Özyürek 2006).[3]

In light of their results, Çarkoğlu and Toprak concluded that there is little evidence of a recent resurgence in religiosity in Turkey. In so doing, they challenged the widely held presumption to the contrary, bringing empirical evidence to bear on a topic of obvious social significance. This speaks directly to the power of the comparative method: examining variation across individuals, populations, or time, to identify patterns of change and covariation (Geddes 2003; King, Keohane, and Verba 1994). Whether based on qualitative or quantitative data, careful comparisons that leverage variation have the potential to confirm or upend even the most widely held assumption, including the supposed link between piety and Islamic politics, in Turkey and elsewhere in the Muslim world. Confronted with these empirical patterns, one is left with somewhat of a puzzle: on the one hand, the rise and sustained popularity of

---

[2] For an illustration of these cross-temporal trends, see Online Appendix Figure OA.1. Without disaggregated results or sample sizes within subgroups, it is impossible to know whether these changes are statistically significant, but the decline in head-covering among younger respondents appears to be particularly large in magnitude and importance. An ideal test of these changes would employ a panel survey – the same questions asked of the same respondents over time. Comparisons of two cross-sectional surveys could reflect differences in the samples rather than changes over time. Still, given that both samples were randomly selected and constructed using a very similar sampling method, this type of bias seems less likely.

[3] Social desirability bias pushes survey respondents to give the answer they think they should, rather than honestly reporting their beliefs, behaviors, and preferences (Fisher 1993; Maccoby and Maccoby 1954). In this case, the normalization of Islamic practice under AKP rule should have reduced any pressure women felt to hide their religiosity in this traditionally secular context.

the AKP is difficult to ignore, especially compared to the faltering of similar, but secular Turkish center-right parties; on the other, at least by one measure, there is little evidence of a religious resurgence to explain the comparative advantage of this Islamic-based party. So if the success of the AKP is not based on the religious faith of its supporters, what else could explain it?

It was precisely this question that led me to Turkey as I began pre-dissertation research in the summer of 2009. While there, I came to realize that the comparative advantage of Islamic-based movements extended well beyond party politics into other large-scale collective activities, including charitable giving (e.g., Sadakataşı Foundation), private education (e.g., *dershaneler*), and even business and finance (e.g., MÜSİAD). In other words, the rise of the AKP was remarkable in its own right, while also being a part of a broader phenomenon in Turkey, with potential implications beyond this single case into other parts of the Muslim world. More than identifying what organizational attributes made these different Islamic-based groups successful,[4] I sought to understand why they were so popular among their members and supporters, especially when similar but secular movements seemed unable to build or maintain such a steady base of support.

LESSONS FROM THE TURKISH CASE

Turkey represents a great opportunity for examining the broader phenomenon of Islamic-based politics and economics because the relative success of large-scale, mainstream Islamic movements is both clear and surprising. Clarity comes from the availability of different data sources, useful in tracing the popularity of these movements. Official statistics paint a clear picture of the social and economic realities of Turkey, across space and time. Similarly, representative surveys are able to assess changes in preferences and beliefs across individuals. In addition, almost seventy years of roughly competitive democratic elections allow one to gauge popular support for different political movements in various districts across decades. As the Muslim world's oldest democracy and one of the few with a long-standing bureau of statistics, Turkey is unmatched in terms of data quality and availability. And yet the Turkish case is not wholly unlike other countries in the Muslim world in terms of population, national income, and politics. Indeed, the AKP, in particular, has been explicitly used as a model by Islamic parties in other Muslim-majority contexts (Tepe 2005; Tuğal 2016).

In addition to being easier to identify in data, the success of Islamic-based movements in the Turkish case is also quite puzzling given the country's staunchly secularist history. The socio-political reforms led by Mustafa Kemal Atatürk in the 1920s effectively severed Turkey's ties with its more religious,

---

[4] Excellent work on Islamic-based politics and economics in Turkey has been done at the organizational level, examining networks of recruitment into the AKP (Ocaklı 2015) and how leaders of Islamic business organizations relate to the state (Buğra 1998).

Ottoman past. They removed key Islamic symbols and practices from everyday life and established a clear division between mosque and state, with the former strictly relegated to the private sphere (Berkes 1998; Çağaptay 2006; Kuru 2009; Yavuz 2009). More recently, an official commitment to maintaining these secularist policies led Turkey's Constitutional Court and its military to shut down a string of Islamic-based political groups in the 1970s, 1980s, and 1990s, making the subsequent success of the AKP even more unexpected.[5]

Given political obstacles to the success of Islamic politics in Turkey, it is easy to see why so many presume that the AKP's rise reflects a religious resurgence among the Turkish people. By this view, the popularity of the AKP and Turkey's other Islamic-based political and economic organizations reflects the support of pious Turks, whose relative share of the population has increased to roughly coincide with the support-base of each group. This link between faith, on the one hand, and the success of Islamic-based movements, on the other, is similar to those made in other Muslim contexts (Wickham 2002; Wiktorowicz and Kaltenhaler 2006). But over the course of my field research – in conversations with AKP field organizers and party supporters, with leaders of Islamic-based student organizations, and with members of Islamic-based business associations – I rarely heard anyone mention that they felt a religious duty to support these movements. Indeed, I found that many of the participants in these ostensibly Islamic groups freely admitted that they were not particularly motivated by God or their religious faith when it came to the practice of politics or economics.

Instead, they were much more likely to emphasize the group itself – the community of AKP supporters, the mass of Islamic-based student activists across the country, the set of firms that comprised the business association – and what they believed they were able to accomplish together: a sense of unity and efficacy that my interlocutors said they rarely felt in their other social endeavors. It was as though there was an obstacle to working together, more generally, in their local communities; and yet this obstacle had been addressed within their Islamic-based organizations. Although they rarely focused on the fact that their organization happened to make regular use of Islamic language and symbols, I wondered what role these religious references were playing in supporting the high levels of participation and cooperation among members of the Islamic-based groups.

A TRUST-BASED THEORY OF ISLAMIC-BASED MOVEMENTS

As a scholar, it was my challenge to translate these initial conversations into a falsifiable theory, to identify the obstacles to political and economic cooperation my interlocutors alluded to, and to explain why Islamic-based groups were particularly well-suited to overcome them. I would then need to design

---

[5] If anything, the frequent closure of Islamic-based parties by Turkey's Constitutional Court may serve to *under*-estimate the movement's appeal.

a test of my hypothesis, leveraging variation in the outcome I was trying to explain. The outcome I focused on first was individuals' willingness to join different political and economic movements; but I also became interested in how these individuals came to cooperate with one another and how this cooperation was sustained. I thought that, together, these could explain the success of Islamic-based organizations and their comparative advantage relative to their secular rivals. Overall, I wanted to be able to explain why Islamic-based parties, like the AKP, were able to outpace other center-right parties and why Islamic-based economic groups, like the Independent Industrialists' and Businessmen's Association (Müstakil Sanayici ve İşadamları Derneği, MÜSİAD), were able to support the growth of small- and medium-sized firms in Anatolia. In both cases, an Islamic-based group seemed to have reversed a decades-old pattern: electoral instability and an incumbency disadvantage, in the first instance, and the dominance of large, vertically integrated firms, in the second. To understand how they were able to do this, I wanted to look beyond the organizations themselves and their leaders, because I suspected that their comparative advantage rested in their individual members – specifically, in their superior willingness and ability to work together.[6]

My trust-based theory of Islamic-based politics and economics was sparked by what I observed during the course of my fieldwork. For example, I noticed that members of different Islamic-based groups spoke remarkably highly of each other, *even if they had never met one another or worked together before.* They emphasized that attendance rates at their events tended to be higher than at others' because their members tended to follow through on promises to attend. Similarly, business owners who were part of an Islamic-based association often mentioned that their organization was made up of "good people." When pressed for more details, they explained that this was not a reflection of their character but rather was based on their dedication to the group and to one another. Nowhere was mention made of a sanctioning system that helped

---

[6] Throughout the book, I use a number of terms interchangeably: "politics" and "economics" are meant to refer to political and economic activities that are *collective* by definition. As such, I often group the two types of activities together under the heading "collective action." At times, I focus on the decision by one individual to take part in the activity, in which case I discuss the phenomenon of "participation," although in collective economic activities, it can be described as a "transaction." At other times, I focus on the result of many individuals taking part in the same activity and working together, a phenomenon that I define as "cooperation" or, at times, "coordination." I emphasize that the decisions of individuals to participate and their collective capacity to cooperate and coordinate often serve the interests of entities that mobilize and organize these individuals towards a particular end. At times, I call these entities "movements" or "organizations," but they are often parties, interest groups, and associations, to be more specific. Similarly, I refer to their supporters, generically as "members," or "participants," although, in specific cases, they may be activists, voters, or investors. I often refer to attempts by the leaders of these collectivities to recruit and organize individual supporters as the act of "mobilization," although I am more concerned with the process through which individuals *become mobilized* – that is, the decision to participate in a collective activity, cooperating or coordinating with other individuals – than I am with the ways that organizers go about mobilizing, beyond their use of Islamic language and symbols.

Introduction

to uphold these behaviors and rationalize these positive expectations. Instead, it seemed that the expectations were self-fulfilling: each member showed up, in large part, because they knew that others were counting on them to do so.

This feeling – that others will follow through on their promises, even when they may have reasons not to – is the essence of trust. More technically, trust is the expectation of honesty or reciprocity in the face of incentives to be dishonest or to defect (Hardin 2002). In social situations, trust comes in a number of different forms. Particularized (or relational) trust reflects direct knowledge of the entrusted and her past behavior, while non-particularized forms of trust extend to individuals or groups with whom one has never interacted before. Best known of the different types of non-particularized trust is so-called "generalized" trust, which is extended to "most people," including to perfect strangers. Although related to other forms of trust – including to trust of politicians and in political institutions – particularized and non-particularized trust are decidedly *interpersonal*, an expectation that one individual has of another.

Trust is necessary to sustain cooperation in a diverse set of interpersonal interactions. Essentially, trust is needed whenever the behavior of the entrusted directly impacts the one who trusts and wherever there is an open question about what the entrusted is likely to do (Zand 1972). In other words, trust is required in the face of interdependence – that is, when the best outcome for any one is a function of what others do – and uncertainty – that is, when what others are likely to do is not immediately clear. Both interdependence and uncertainty are at play in many political and economic activities (e.g., everyday political activism, voting in local and national elections, investing in conventional banks and micro-financing institutions). Each of these activities is only successful when enough individuals take part and where most of these participants do not know each other personally.[7]

In these activities and in the organizations that support them – what Mancur Olson (2002) calls "latent" groups – uncertainty can be traced back to the so-called "free-rider problem." Because individuals benefit from a group's success irrespective of whether they actually contributed to it, they are incentivized to free ride off of others' efforts. The fact that there is heterogeneity in what individuals prefer to do – so that only rational egoists are incentivized to free ride, while more trustworthy "conditional cooperators" want to contribute to the group, as long as others will do the same – means that reciprocal cooperation is possible.[8] Ultimately, whether cooperation actually occurs depends on the expectations of those conditional cooperators: only if they feel confident that

---

[7] There are other types of political and economic movements – smaller, less mainstream, even violent – for which this trust-based model is less relevant. In contrast to the latent groups discussed here, these groups are "privileged" or "intermediate" in scope (Olson 2002, p. 50), and participation in them is better understood using a club-goods model (Berman and Laitin 2008; Carvalho 2016; Iannaccone 1992).

[8] In addition to "free riders" and "conditional cooperators" are a small number of "altruists" who strictly prefer to cooperate, under all circumstances.

other participants are trustworthy like them, will they opt in. In other words, they must expect that they are working with other conditional cooperators, who are worthy of being trusted.

For this reason, I argue that robust interpersonal trust expectations are a necessary condition for political and economic cooperation among individuals.[9] The need for trust is perhaps easiest to see in the case of mass politics: grassroots organizations and large-scale demonstrations of the type witnessed during the Arab Spring and the protests in and around Istanbul's Gezi Park in 2013. Here, there is safety (and success) in numbers, and the free-rider problem is also quite acute (Chong 1991). But I also posit that interpersonal trust is relevant for other political activities, including voting. In fractionalized electoral systems, where not every party is likely to win enough support to gain representation, voters may have to vote strategically, for a second- or third-best party, whenever they believe their most-preferred one will fail to win a seat (Cox 1994). Whether they are able to do so successfully, to make their votes count, hinges in large part on whether they trust what they hear about others' vote intentions (Myatt 2007). And beyond politics, there is an important role for trust in economic transactions: because the vast majority of trades and purchases are not simultaneous, there are opportunities for one party to defect on the other, especially when economic conditions are likely to change between agreement and delivery (Williamson 1985).

I contend that interpersonal trust is needed for cooperation and coordination in all these forms, and different types of trust are able to support collective action at different scales. Particularized trust – based on first hand knowledge of another's past behavior – is perhaps the strongest form, but is also most limited in its ability to support cooperation. In a latent movement, where participation is largely anonymous and extends well beyond any one participant's social circle, I would argue that *non-particularized* trust becomes necessary. This broader, more anonymous form of trust is also useful when beginning a long-term, repeated interaction through which particularized trust can eventually develop. Going back to my notes from the field, I came to realize that non-particularized trust was a common theme in my conversations with different interlocutors: they would emphasize how they expected that others in their group were "good people," who would do right by them, even if they had never met before; this was in sharp contrast to out-group members, who they deemed to be less reliable. I had a feeling that these robust interpersonal trust expectations could help explain why the members of the different Islamic-based groups I interviewed and observed were able to work together so effectively. But I had yet to identify the basis for this mutual trust and whether it could really account for the comparative advantage of these groups relative to their non-Islamic counterparts.

---

[9] This is in addition to sufficient information and motivation, which are both necessary though insufficient conditions for participation.

To explain the higher trust expectations among members of Islamic-based groups, I recalled the extensive literatures in social psychology, behavioral economics, and political science that emphasize the benefits of a shared group identity. Experimental evidence indicates that members of the same group are more likely to cooperate with one another (Tajfel 1974), in large part because they tend to trust (and be honest with) one another (Habyarimana et al. 2009). This "group-based trust" is especially prevalent when the shared identity is commonly recognized by everyone (Yamagishi, Jin, and Kiyonari 1999), in cases where individuals are actively encouraged to think about their shared identity through implicit or explicit priming (Pechar and Kranton 2017), and among those whose attachment to the group identity is especially salient (Charness, Rigotti, and Rustichini 2007). Unlike particularized trust, group-based trust does not depend on direct knowledge of, or experience with, other group members. Instead, it is a non-particularized form of trust, one conditioned on a shared identity. It appears that humans tend to react to group identities with this type of trust and trustworthiness, either as the result of an evolutionary process (Bowles and Gintis 2004) or simply because their trust expectations are reciprocal and therefore self-fulfilling (Hertel and Kerr 2001).

This concept of group-based trust seemed consistent with my observations from the field. It could bolster cooperation among members of Islamic-based organizations, whether or not they knew each other personally; and these trust expectations, based on a shared group identity, could be made salient by organization leaders through their use of Islamic language and symbols. A focus on Islamic identity, rather than piety, could also help explain why most members of the Islamic-based groups I spoke with were not particularly faithful and why few described working to serve God. Perhaps, instead, they had a salient *Islamic group identity*. Most of the existing research on in-group cooperation and group-based trust I was familiar with focused on ethnic groups rather than religious ones.[10] Meanwhile, studies of religion usually conceived of it as faith or piety – that is, a set of personal beliefs or preferences – rather than as a group identity (i.e., a social label that conditions individual behavior, especially as related to in-group and out-group members). But I could not see a reason why religion could not function as both.

The more I thought about it, and especially as I started to speak with my interlocutors, the difference between personal piety and a religious identity became increasingly clear. People could be deeply invested in their religious communities, irrespective of the intensity of their personal faith. For example, I met plenty of Turks who regularly attended mosque, particularly on Fridays, but who rarely prayed at home. For them, the point in attending mosque was the collective nature of the gathering, rather than the basic religious prescription or the individual connection they were forming with God. In other

---

[10] For notable exceptions to this general trend, see Ruffle and Sosis (2007) and Tan (2006).

words, it was about community more than faith. Based on this, I hypothesized that regular participation in religious group activities might serve as a good indicator of a salient religious group identity. (This was in contrast to personal religious beliefs and practices, which would speak more to the depth of personal piety.) If right, this would imply a different interpretation of the political significance of religious service attendance, which the existing literature usually sees as an opportunity for gathering information (Patel 2007), becoming more personally motivated (Wald, Owen, and Hill Jr. 1988), or developing the skills and resources needed to become politically active (Jones-Correa and Leal 2001). In contrast, I could argue that religious group activities of all types – including service attendance – supported political participation because they strengthened the salience of religious group identity.

If Islam could function as a group identity – bolstering trust expectations among those with an attachment to their religious community, especially when religious references primed them to think of themselves and others in terms of their shared identity – it could well explain the success of Islamic-based organizations. But to understand why these organizations succeeded where non-Islamic ones have struggled, there had to be some obstacle to political and economic cooperation, more generally, that Islamic-based groups were able to address via group-based trust. I wondered whether trust – part of the appeal of Islamic-based groups – might also be undermining cooperation and coordination in other organizations. In particular, if generalized trust expectations were low, this could pose a challenge for any organization unable to invoke a shared identity and prime group-based trust. While distrust would keep most participants sidelined, references to Islam could generate group-based trust among those with a salient religious identity, supporting cooperation and coordination, *even among those who generally distrust*.

My trust-based theory of Islamic-based politics and economics implies a number of patterns. Across individuals, those with low levels of generalized trust (in most people) should be less likely to participate in large-scale, latent political and economic movements, on average. At the same time, those with a salient religious identity, who have higher levels of in-group trust, should be more likely to participate, on average. Moreover, if group-based trust can indeed function as an effective substitute for generalized trust, a salient religious identity should support participation and cooperation even among those who generally distrust others. This substitution effect should be particularly effective when religious group identity is being actively primed. In the aggregate, this would imply that political and economic movements that do not reference Islamic identity and that cannot rely on group-based trust will struggle to build and maintain a following, especially where and when generalized trust is low. In these same places and times, Islamic-based groups will be comparatively advantaged, particularly where Islamic identity is salient and group-based trust is robust.

EXISTING THEORIES OF ISLAMIC POLITICS AND ECONOMICS

In their ability to leverage a group identity and trust to their advantage, Islamic-based groups are hardly unique: a range of identities – from ethnicity and nationality, to class and gender – can be and have been evoked in the same way. In that respect, my trust-based theory is hardly new. But in the context of Islamic-based politics and economics, it represents a significant departure from the existing literature, which has a decidedly different take, both on the obstacles to collective mobilization in the Muslim world and how references to Islam might help to attenuate them. A first set of extant theories suggests that *grievances* can explain Islam's advantage: since secular regimes and movements have failed to usher in the peace and prosperity they promised, Islam offers a clear alternative to the status quo (Ayubi 1991; Zubaida 1989). In this view, the most aggrieved and impoverished under the current system are those most likely to turn to Islam. They are also the most motivated to push for change, explaining the sustained popularity of Islamic-based movements. Further the selective incentives that Islamic-based organizations tend to offer their supporters – from foodstuffs to medical care, micro-financing to job opportunities – only strengthen the relationship between poverty and the Islamic advantage.

A second set of existing theories pushes back against this focus on grievances, motivation, and selective incentives, insisting that the costs and risks of being politically and economically active in most Muslim countries cannot be rationalized with meager club goods. In this view, Islamic-based movements offer their supporters not instrumental benefits but *spiritual* ones, either the promise of salvation in the afterlife (Wiktorowicz and Kaltenhaler 2006) or an alternative way (e.g., "transvaluation") of looking at the costs and benefits of political and economic activity (Wickham 2002, 2004). Here, the advantage of Islamic-based groups is explained by *faith*: pious devotion helps overcome the costs and risks of mobilization that keep non-religious activists from participating.

A third set of extant theories argues that neither instrumental concerns nor faith can explain the success of Islamic-based movements. Instead, these movements succeed by leveraging an *informational* advantage, either because references to Islam signal something clear and credible about what the organizations stand for (Pepinsky, Liddle, and Mujani 2012), how likely they are to follow through on these commitments (Cammett and Luong 2014), or because Islamic-based movements leverage their connections to religious networks to make their case more effectively, speaking directly to potential supporters (Masoud 2014). Within this set of theories, uncertainty about secular groups or the environment as a whole creates a comparative advantage for Islamic-based organizations, whose policy positions are more legible to their support base.

Although the three sets of existing theories have differing views of the obstacles to political and economic mobilization in Muslim-majority contexts – insufficient motivation, astronomical risks, uncertainty – and have different

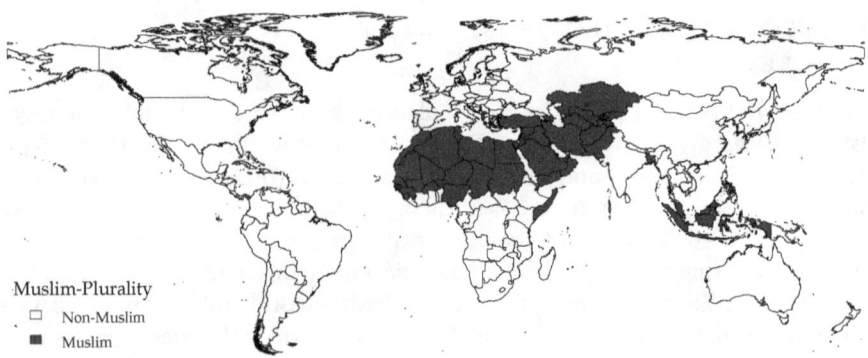

FIGURE 1.1 Map of the Muslim World

explanations for how references to Islam help to attenuate these obstacles – selective incentives, religious beliefs, informational cues – they all tend to see politics and economics in decidedly individualistic terms: what keeps people from participating or, alternatively, supports their activism happens to them *as individuals*. And most have been tested in only a case or two, and few have leveraged variation in the key outcome (i.e., participation in or support of Islamic-based groups) to do so effectively.

Improving upon these methods, I test the empirical implications of each existing theory, alongside those of my own. To do so, I rely on qualitative observations, as well as quantitative evidence gathered over fifteen months of field research in Istanbul in 2011–2012. In each case, to make the results legible for a broad readership, I offer illustrations of empirical patterns in the raw data before introducing more complicated statistical methods. (The majority of these statistical results are available in an Online Appendix.) While most of the data I employ come from the Turkish case, whenever availability permits, I confirm that patterns hold in other Muslim-majority contexts. In these cross-national comparisons, my aim is to use the Turkish case to shed light on these other contexts, to explain why Islamic-based movements have or have not succeeded there. My universe of cases – settings in which Muslims constitute a majority or, at least, a plurality of the population – was chosen because these are the places in which latent, mainstream Islamic-based movements have the potential to succeed. (Elsewhere, the population of possible supporters is simply too small.) Figure 1.1 defines this set of cases, what I will refer to throughout this book as the "Muslim world." As defined by Pew Research Center (2015), there are fifty-one Muslim-plurality countries, spanning four of the world's continents.

Within the Turkish case and across the Muslim world, I leverage variation across a number of different dimensions. Across space, I compare Turkish districts (*ilçeler*) and provinces (*iller*) where Islamic-based political parties are more or less successful. I also contrast the popularity of Islamic politics in Turkey to countries in which Islamic-based political movements have been less successful (e.g., Indonesia) or entirely absent (e.g., Mali). Across time, I trace

Introduction

the rise of the AKP and the growth of firms that are part of MÜSİAD, an Islamic-based Turkish business association, comparing these trends to the rise (and fall) of Islamic-based political and economic movements elsewhere (e.g., Tunisia). And, using the results of nationally representative surveys I designed, I examine patterns of political participation across individual Turks, comparing these to individual-level trends from twenty-four Muslim countries, using existing survey sources.

PREVIEW OF FINDINGS

In my empirical analysis from Turkey and from across the Muslim world, I find little support for the existing theories of Islamic-based political and economic mobilization. In contrast to grievance theory, I find that the most aggrieved and most impoverished are not the most mobilized; and in contrast to the faith-based theory of "transvaluation," I find that those with the strongest religious beliefs are similarly sidelined. Moreover, the popularity and success of Islamic-based movements – whether political or economic – rarely follow patterns of piety in the aggregate, neither across space nor across time. Further, I find inconsistent evidence that references to Islam are informative about the policy positions of Islamic-based parties: there is remarkable variation in what these groups stand for and considerable overlap between them and their secular competitors.

In contrast, I find evidence of a generalized trust problem, in Turkey and across the Muslim world, one that undermines the potential for political and economic mobilization there. Using an extensive survey dataset, I find that generalized, interpersonal trust (in "most people") is significantly lower in Muslim-plurality countries, by nearly six percentage points. Moreover, the absence of generalized trust in the Muslim world creates a number of "trust problems" for the practice of politics and economics there. To begin, generalized distrust lowers rates of participation in everyday politics, in Turkey and across the Muslim world. Interpersonal trust is also key to supporting coordination among strategic voters, so that coordination failure (in the form of wasted votes) is higher in more distrusting electoral districts. Finally, long-term inter-firm cooperation (i.e., "quasi-integration") is also trust dependent and is therefore hindered by uncertainty, in the form of macroeconomic volatility. In identifying each of these trust problems, theoretically and empirically, this book stands to contribute to a broad literature on social capital and its (many) consequences (Benson and Rochon 2004; Inglehart 1999; Putnam 1993; Zak and Knack 2001).

Although generalized trust is low in Muslim-plurality contexts, importantly, I find that the *potential* for cooperation still exists there: levels of honesty and trustworthiness are robust – if anything, they are significantly *higher* than elsewhere – and low generalized trust expectations are able to be updated, as evidenced by migrants from the Muslim world to Europe. I argue that the generalized trust deficit can also be overcome in Islamic-based movements: using references to Islam to prime a shared Islamic identity, they trigger group-based trust expectations, which can effectively substitute for trust in "most people." Those who respond to this priming are not those with the strongest religious beliefs, as the faith-based theory of "transvaluation" would argue, but those with the most salient religious *identity*. I find that those who identify with their religious identity and who take an active role in religious group activities have higher levels of group-based trust and are more likely to join political and economic movements *even when they distrust most people*. Further, I demonstrate how this substitution effect gives Islamic-based parties and economic groups a comparative advantage over similar, secular ones, especially in places and times when generalized interpersonal trust is most limited.

My trust-based theory of Islamic-based political and economic mobilization has a number of non-intuitive implications, which I explore with available data. First, I argue that state repression of Islamic-based political movements is likely to backfire: by raising the costs of collective action, repression makes individual decisions to participate even more interdependent, reinforcing the need for interpersonal trust and increasing Islamic groups' trust-based comparative advantage. Additionally, I show how the trust-based coordination advantage of Islamic voters can help attract strategic support to Islamic-based parties from conservative but secular voters, increasing these parties' support-base beyond their "natural" constituency. I also illustrate how trust-based long-term cooperative relationships between Islamic-oriented businesses, while helping to protect them from economic shocks during periods of economic instability, are inefficient in more stable times. Ironically, in the Turkish case, this implies that these religiously conservative firms are actually worse off during the period of Islamic party rule.

Taken together, the theory and evidence presented in this book speak to an important Turkish phenomenon – the success of Islamic-based politics and economics, in the absence of a religious resurgence among the masses – with implications for other Muslim-plurality contexts. Overall, I seek to bridge a long-standing gap between the discussion of Islam and Islamic politics, on the one hand, and the discussion of collective action, identity politics, and interpersonal trust, on the other. In so doing, I simultaneously highlight the Turkish case, while contributing to broader debates in political science and political economics.

PLAN OF THE BOOK

The book proceeds as follows. Part I offers an empirical and theoretical exploration of the phenomenon of Islamic-based politics and economics, considering the main existing explanations of the Islamic mobilization advantage before introducing my own trust-based theory. In Chapter 2, I assess the landscape of political and economic activity in the Muslim world, providing evidence of a "participation gap" there: levels of collective political and economic activity are significantly lower in Muslim-plurality countries, relative to other parts of the world. I interpret this difference as indication of one or more obstacles to collective action in the region. While most secular forms of political and economic mobilization are depressed in Muslim countries, I provide a number of examples of Islamic-based groups which have been able to flourish under identical conditions, pointing to a comparative advantage of political and economic activities that explicitly refer to Islam. I then introduce the three existing explanations for this comparative advantage – grievances, faith, and information – articulating how each conceives of the obstacles to collective action and how Islamic references help to address them. I conclude Chapter 2 by defining a set of falsifiable hypotheses of the three existing theories that I empirically assess in Chapter 3.

Leveraging variation in Islamic-based mobilization across individuals, space, and time, I test the three theories. I find little evidence to support either grievance or information theory: there is no indication that the lack of motivation or information is keeping individuals from being politically or economically active in the Muslim world; neither are the most aggrieved the people who are being most effectively mobilized; further, there is little evidence that references to Islam, alone, provide a clear signal of what Islamic-based movements stand for, challenging the assumption that they are truly informative. And while I find that the costs associated with political and economic activity are significantly higher in the Muslim world – as presumed by the faith-based theory of "transvaluation" – I see no evidence that personal religious beliefs help to overcome them. If anything, individuals with stronger religious beliefs are *less* likely to participate in collective political and economic activities. Similarly, there is no evidence that the popularity of Islamic-based movements tracks onto piety in the aggregate, across space or time. Instead, I find that many apparently secular voters support Islamic-based movements, a puzzle which I return to in Chapter 7.

In Chapter 4, I make a case for the importance of interpersonal trust in collective political and economic activities, arguing that existing theories of Islamic-based mobilization underestimate the *interdependence* of individual decisions to participate. Further, heterogeneity in individuals' preferences – with a sizable minority willing to free ride off of others' efforts – introduces considerable *uncertainty* into each individual's decision, so that political and economic participation is only possible when those who want to work together – so-called "conditional cooperators" – expect to engage with others like them, trusting them. I argue that large-scale (latent) political and economic activities require trust expectations that are non-particularized and broadly applicable, extending to many people with whom one has no previous direct experience. I show that the broadest form of non-particularized trust – generalized trust, in most people – is largely absent in Turkey and across the Muslim world, and I suggest that this trust deficit could help explain the participation gap in the region, undermining political and economic activity unless an alternative basis of interpersonal trust can be identified.

I explore a potential solution to the generalized trust problem in Chapter 5, arguing that trust among members of the same identity group can serve as an effective substitute for low expectations of "most people." Trust among group members is naturally occurring in humans, especially when they are primed to think of one another in terms of their shared identity, and particularly among those who already feel an attachment to their group. I argue that Islam can be experienced by some as a group identity, in addition to functioning as a personal faith; and I go on to reveal an empirical distinction between the two, finding that Islamic group identity is expressed through active participation in communal religious activities. Using the results of a nationally representative survey from Turkey, I show how those with a salient Islamic identity have higher trust expectations of in-group members. I go on to suggest that this group-based trust can substitute for more generalized trust expectations to support participation in political and economic movements that are Islamic-based.

In the chapters of Part II, I test my main hypotheses: first, that generalized distrust undermines political and economic activity; and, second, that a salient Islamic identity and group-based trust can be used as an effective trust substitute, to the advantage of Islamic-based groups. Each chapter explores the importance of trust for a different collective activity, from participation in politics, to strategic voting, and the quasi-integration of independent businesses; and each examines variation across a different dimension – individuals, electoral districts, and firms. In Chapter 6, I test my trust-based theory in the case of political participation, using survey data from Turkey and across twenty-four countries. I find evidence that generalized distrust indeed lowers individuals' propensity to participate in politics, while a salient Islamic identity supports higher levels of participation through group-based trust. I also test an additional implication of the theory, finding that state repression of political organizations boosts the Islamic advantage by making interpersonal trust even more critical to participation.

In Chapter 7, I apply my trust-based theory to strategic voting (i.e., the selection of a second- or third-choice political party when one's most-preferred party is unlikely to gain representation). I argue that for strategic voting to be successful, voters must have a good sense of what others in their district are likely to do. This, in turn, rests on their ability to trust what they hear about others' vote intentions. Using a panel of Turkish general election results, I reveal how more votes are "wasted" – cast for a party that fails to gain representation – in more distrusting districts. This pattern holds except for districts in which there is a thriving Islamic community, where the trust problem in vote coordination is effectively eliminated. I argue that the superior ability of Islamic voters to consistently coordinate among themselves makes Islamic-based parties an attractive target of strategic support from conservative but secular voters, explaining the broad appeal of the AKP in Turkey.

Finally, in Chapter 8, I extend my theory to the case of economic exchange, using firm-level data to assess the conditions under which members of an Islamic-based business association – the Independent Industrialists' and Businessmen's Association (MÜSİAD) – are most successful. Existing theories of identity-based economic exchange emphasize the role of reputations, but using a first-of-its-kind dataset, I find extensive turnover in MÜSİAD membership, which makes it difficult to maintain a reputation mechanism. Instead, I argue that group-based trust forms the basis of long-term cooperative relationships among member-firms. These "quasi-integrative" relationships mimic the benefits of vertical integration enjoyed by larger non-member firms, protecting the smaller member firms from volatility in the macroeconomy. While profitable for MÜSİAD members during periods of instability, I find that these quasi-integrative relationships are inefficient in more stable times, costing member firms in terms of both sales and profits. Remarkably, this includes the period of growth overseen by the AKP, so that MÜSİAD members have been significantly *worse* off under Islamic party rule. I discuss the implications of all these findings, as well as their external validity, and avenues for future research, in the Conclusion.

PART I

THEORETICAL DEVELOPMENT

2

Understanding the Rise of Islamic-Based Movements in the Muslim World

Across the Muslim world, appeals to Islamic themes and symbols have been used to support a wide array of political and economic activities. These Islamic-based appeals appear to have a comparative advantage relative to similar but secular ones: they have proved successful in motivating individuals to take an active role in a variety of organizations and in sustaining their participation in these organizations over time. Meanwhile, political and economic appeals that are similar but which do *not* invoke Islamic language have struggled to develop or maintain the same level of enthusiasm and commitment.

In the political realm, Islamic references have been used to encourage voters to turn out for elections (Blaydes 2011), or to boycott them (Ibrahim 1998), to support a particular political party in a local or general election (Yavuz 2004), or a particular position in a national referendum (Kalaycıoğlu 2012). Beyond the practice of electoral politics, appeals to Islam have been used to galvanize mass support for grassroots movements, from street demonstrations, to strikes and boycotts (Tuğal 2009; White 2002). Whatever form they take, Islamic-based political movements have become dominant in many Muslim-majority contexts, leading scholars to state emphatically that "Islam has eclipsed secular ideologies as the primary source of political activism in much of the Muslim world" (Wickham 2002, p. 1).

Beyond politics, across urban and rural communities alike, appeals to Islam have supported the collection and redistribution of a range of public goods, including foodstuffs, health services, education, and job-training programs (Clark 2004a; Sullivan 1994). As Muslim states have proven unwilling or unable to provide these types of goods to their citizenries, Islamic-based organizations have stepped in to play a vital role in the provision of social welfare, arguably becoming "the most successful grassroots initiatives helping the poor and the middle classes today" (Clark 2004a, p. 18). Further, in the economic arena, religious references have been used to encourage individuals to come together and invest their resources in informal savings clubs (Singerman 1996) and, more recently, in Islamic "participation" banks (Demirgüç-Kunt, Klapper, and Randall 2013). Appeals to Islam have also been used to build trade relationships between like-minded companies (Buğra 1998) and Muslim countries (Lewer and Van den Berg 2007). Together, these types of economic activities – Islamic-based business and Islamic-based finance – have "formed vibrant subeconomies" (Kuran 1995, p. 155), stimulating economic growth in a number of otherwise underdeveloped Muslim-majority economies.

I have witnessed the remarkable success of mainstream Islamic-based movements first hand in the Turkish context. In the political arena, during the 2010 constitutional referendum, members of the AKP-backed Yes (*Evet*) coalition were able to construct an extensive network of grassroots organizations, effectively connecting independent groups who had no prior history of working together. Similarly, in the lead-up to the 2011 general elections, AKP field organizers made good use of neighborhood leaders to identify the most effective location for canvassing and signage. Even during the protests in and around Istanbul's Gezi Park in 2013, members of the Anti-Capitalist Muslims (Anti-Kapitalist Müslümanlar) used their identity as Muslims to motivate more protesters to join them, organizing community meetings to coincide with daily prayers, which regularly took place in their makeshift camp.

Alongside these political advances, the rise of Islamic-based economics in Turkey has been similarly impressive. Islamic-oriented banks have grown in popularity and prominence over the course of my years living in and visiting Turkey, operating alongside the largest mainstream banks, in both urban and rural contexts. The gleam of the Istanbul headquarters of MÜSİAD, an Islamic-oriented association of small- and medium-sized businesses, speaks to the success of the group, whose members have grown to become some of Turkey's most successful firms. In the provision of public goods, Islamic-based groups, including those organized by Fethullah Gülen, have become go-to providers of afterschool programs preparing students for their university entrance exam, while networks of private Islamic-oriented hospitals offer excellent medical care, especially in underserved communities.

Across these different contexts, the success of "Islamic-based" organizations, which make active use of Islamic language and symbols in their day-to-day activities, has been unparalleled. This begins, first, in their remarkable capacity to mobilize individuals to join them; it then extends to their ability to support cooperation among those who join; and it also includes their success in sustaining this commitment and cooperation over the long-term. Compared to the Yes campaign, the No group in the 2010 referendum inspired little enthusiasm among most of my Turkish interlocutors, including those who had serious doubts about the proposed constitutional amendments. Similarly, many described the main opposition parties in the 2011 general elections as "lifeless" (*cansız*), especially when compared to the catchy slogans and flashy banners put together by the AKP team.[1] Meanwhile, a number of them told me

---

[1] The main exception to this general rule is the enthusiasm that has built around the Kurdish-based political movement, represented over the years by the People's Labor Party (Halkın Emek Partisi, HEP) (1990–1993), the Freedom and Democracy Party (Özgüürlük ve Demokrasi

how advertising campaigns during Ramadan had encouraged them to increase their household savings and deposit these in a local branch of an Islamic participation bank. Before doing so, some had never even had an account at a physical bank, preferring to keep cash savings stored at home. Although they did not draw connections between these different observations, I took them as evidence of a mobilization advantage for political and economic movements that were explicitly Islamic-based.

To specify and then explain this comparative advantage, it is important to move beyond isolated anecdotes to a more systematic study of political and economic activity. This is true for Turkey, where the success of Islamic-based movements is clearest, given data availability, and particularly surprising, given its secularist history; but it also holds for other contexts where Islamic-based groups have the potential to thrive (i.e., the Muslim-plurality countries that comprise the Muslim world). During my fieldwork, I developed a growing sense that something about the explicitly Islamic appeals that these movements used could explain how they were able to galvanize supporters, in the first place, and then sustain their cooperation and coordination, over time. For this reason, to specify the "Islamic advantage" in mainstream politics and economics, I wanted to look beyond the actions of group leaders or the design of organizations and, instead, examine the process of Islamic-based mobilization from the bottom up. Are there obstacles to participation in these types of collective political and economic activities in the Muslim world? And how did existing theories account for why references to Islam were particularly well positioned to help overcome these obstacles?

In the chapter that follows, I tackle both of these questions. I begin by empirically assessing how rates of political and economic mobilization in Muslim-plurality contexts compare to those elsewhere. Next, I discuss three key explanations for the success of Islamic-based politics and economics. The first emphasizes the importance of grievances and selective incentives; another focuses on the role of faith and spiritual incentives; and a third argues for an informational advantage within Islamic-based groups. To the best of my knowledge, the empirical implications of the three have never been explicitly articulated and compared; and rarely have any been systematically tested, leveraging variation in the outcome of interest. As such, I conclude the chapter by defining a set of falsifiable hypotheses implied by each theory, which I test in Chapter 3.

Partisi, ÖZDEP) (1992–1993), the Democracy Party (Demokrasi Partisi, DEP) (1993–1994), the People's Democracy Party (Halkın Demokrasi Partisi, HADEP) (1994–2003), the Democratic People's Party (Demokratik Halk Partisi, DEHAP) (1997–2005), the Democratic Society Party (Demokratik Toplum Partisi, DTP) (2005–2009), the Peace and Democracy Party (Barış ve Demokrasi Partisi, BDP) (2008–2014) and, most recently, the People's Democratic Party (Halkların Demokratik Partisi, HDP) (2012–present). I would argue that the appeal of these movements is similar to that of Islamic-based parties: references to a shared identity trigger group-based trust among Kurds with a salient identity, supporting higher levels of cooperation and coordination among them.

2.1 POLITICAL AND ECONOMIC ACTIVITY IN THE MUSLIM WORLD

While interviewing a diverse group of political organizers and members of different economic organizations in Turkey, I came to two realizations: first, that Islamic-based organizations seemed to be quite successful at getting individuals to join them and keeping those individuals involved over the long-term; and, meanwhile, that other political and economic groups seemed to be struggling to do the same. To confirm that these observations are representative of a broader pattern, I look to examine levels of economic activity and political participation in Turkey and the Muslim world, as compared to elsewhere. My goal here is to assess whether there is evidence of a "participation gap" in Muslim-plurality countries that could explain the difficulties that non-Muslim organizations in Turkey seemed to be having in recruiting individual members and keeping them mobilized. Given my interest in understanding large-scale, "latent" types of movements, I focus my comparison on those political and economic activities that require large numbers of participants to be successful and in which individual members remain largely anonymous.

In democratic and autocratic systems alike, and across the Muslim world, a lot of day-to-day political activity takes place in the streets. Individuals come together to petition, demonstrate, or boycott, in support of the status quo or in the hopes of changing it. (Meanwhile, other political activities, like voting, are restricted to more democratic or semi-democratic settings.) Similarly, in the context of economics, it is helpful to look at participation in a collective activity that is broadly relevant. Towards that end, I explore rates of bank savings – the act of putting one's own assets, anonymously, into a common resource pool – which occurs in developed and underdeveloped economies (Guiso, Sapienza, and Zingales 2004). In both cases, I compare rates of activity in Muslim-plurality countries to those outside of the Muslim world.

2.1.1 Political Participation in Comparative Perspective

In this initial assessment of political activity in the Muslim world, as well as in some of the models in Chapters 3 and 6, I follow a host of others, estimating participation using survey respondents' willingness to take part in three different types of mass political activity – signing a petition, attending a lawful demonstration, and joining a boycott (Inglehart 1977; Kaase and Marsh 1979).[2] In addition to being broadly relevant, these activities play a large role in existing theories of Islamic politics, not only because they impose significant costs on individual participants, but also because Islamic-based groups appear to have a particular advantage when it comes to mobilizing their supporters to petition, boycott, and demonstrate.

---

[2] Self-reported participation in strikes is also available, but coverage is considerably more limited. For that reason, it is excluded from the forthcoming analysis, although results are broadly consistent.

2.1 Political and Economic Activity

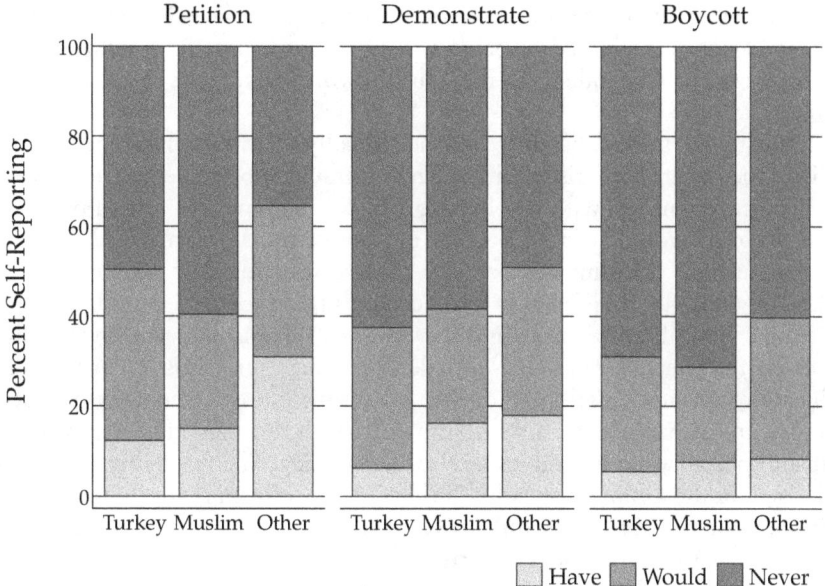

FIGURE 2.1 Participation in Collective Political Activities in the Muslim World
Notes: Participation in three political activities – signing a petition, attending a lawful demonstration, and joining a boycott – having participated, being willing to, or being unwilling. Respondents from Turkey compared to respondents from other parts of the Muslim world and to those from non-Muslim-plurality countries.

Cross-national survey firms have now asked respondents from 147 countries whether they "have actually done, might do or would never, under any circumstances, do" at least one of the three activities.[3] Although this self-reported measure of participation may suffer from some response bias (e.g., an unwillingness to accurately report participation where political activity is heavily regulated and/or perceived as anti-systemic), the fact that respondents have the option to say that they "would consider" participating should help ameliorate some of these concerns (Persson and Solevid 2014).

As an initial test of whether rates of political participation are significantly lower in the Muslim world, I compare responses to the three questions among Turkish respondents, among those in other Muslim-plurality countries, and those in countries outside the Muslim world (Figure 2.1).[4] The results indicate that levels of participation in all three activities are indeed lower in the Muslim world, on average, differences that are statistically significant in a two-group difference-of-means *t*-test (Online Appendix Table OA.2). Across the

---

[3] Cross-national surveys that ask about political participation include the Afrobarometer, AsiaBarometer, East Asian Barometer, European Values Study (EVS), Latinobarómetro, and World Values Survey (WVS).
[4] A table of which countries are included in the different empirical models in this book can be found in the Online Appendix (Table OA.1).

three activities, while 72.6 percent of respondents outside the Muslim world report having participated or being willing to participate in at least one, just 49.6 percent of respondents in the Muslim world have done or would do the same.

Importantly, these substantive and statistically significant differences remain when I focus the comparison within a more similar subset of countries. Among democratic countries, with a Polity score of six or above, the rate of participation (have or would) is 74.9 percent outside of the Muslim world, but only 54.8 percent in Muslim democracies. This distinction also remains when I take individual-level differences into account in a series of hierarchical models (Gelman and Hill 2007; Jusko and Shively 2005). These models allow me, first, to assess the effect of individual-level demographic characteristics (age, gender, education) on participation, and, then, to estimate how these individual-level factors are impacted by those at the country-level, including the country's Muslim-plurality status and its level of democracy. The results of these models, listed in the Online Appendix (Table OA.3), confirm that rates of political participation remain significantly lower in Muslim-plurality countries. Further, they indicate that differences in participation are largest and most consistent in terms of individuals' *willingness* to take part in these latent political activities.

There are reasons to worry that some of these results might be a function of social desirability bias – respondents giving the answers they think they should, rather than reporting their participation honestly. If we consider that, in many Muslim-majority contexts, including in some Muslim democracies, political activities tend to push back against the current regime, there may be some implicit pressure on respondents to under-report their level of activity. For this reason, it is useful to look at self-reported voter turnout, where the bias is likely to go the other way, reflecting pressure to over-report (Selb and Munzert 2013). Comparing levels of turnout in a slightly different set of surveys,[5] I find remarkably similar patterns: while 72.0 percent of respondents living outside the Muslim world self-report having voted in the last election, only 60.0 percent of respondents in Muslim-plurality countries say the same, a difference that holds in democracies as well (72.5 percent and 67.9 percent, respectively). In other words, across a range of political activities, there is evidence of a "participation gap" in the Muslim world.

2.1.2 Economic Activity in Comparative Perspective

Having found that rates of political participation are significantly lower in the Muslim world, I turn to assessing rates of economic activity. To capture differences between Muslim and non-Muslim countries, I compare rates of investment in formal banking institutions in Muslim-plurality countries to rates of investment elsewhere. Bank saving is arguably a collective activity because, in addition to reflecting an investor's willingness to entrust her assets

---

[5] The surveys included in this analysis include the Afrobarometer, Arab Barometer, Caucasus Barometer, East Asian Barometer, Latinobarómetro, and the WVS.

2.1 Political and Economic Activity

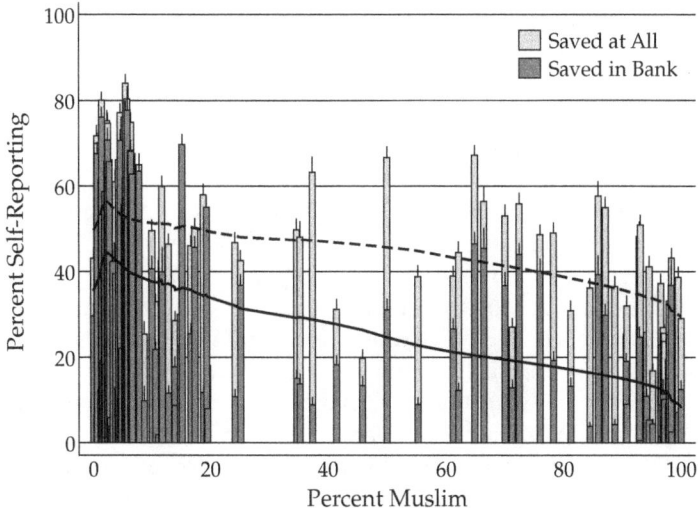

FIGURE 2.2 Saving Activity, In and Outside of the Muslim World
Notes: Average levels of self-reported saving over the previous year and whether savings were deposited in a formal bank, across the percent of the country's inhabitants identified as Muslim. Spikes indicate 95 confidence intervals and lines show the overall LOWESS trends.

to a particular financial institution, it also reflects her willingness to make those assets part of a common resource pool, from which they can be lent out to other community members in the form of credit. Speaking to my interlocutors in Turkey about their own economic decisions, especially those individuals who were just starting to invest their savings in a physical bank, it was clear that the communal aspect of their choices was not lost on them. The notion that their neighborhood bank was one of countless branches across the country was obvious, if a little intimidating, as was the understanding that their own savings would not be kept in their local branch but sent where it was most needed.

To understand how rates of bank savings within the Muslim world compare to those elsewhere, I use data from the Financial Inclusion Database, a set of surveys conducted by Gallup and the World Bank, first in 2011 and then again in 2014, to capture cross-national variation in a number of economic activities. Each survey asks respondents a series of questions about their investment behavior, including whether they have managed to save any money over the previous year, and what they did with those savings. More specifically, it asks them whether they deposited their savings into a physical bank. Using responses to these questions, I calculate average rates of household savings as well as bank-deposited savings in each surveyed country ($N=155$); I then see how these correlate with the percentage of the country's population that is Muslim. Figure 2.2 indicates that while overall saving and bank savings are both negatively correlated with the share of Muslims in a country, the relationship is much stronger in the latter case ($r=-0.268$ and $r=-0.506$, respectively). In other words, while respondents in Muslim-plurality countries are somewhat less likely to save any money at all – 58.5 percent vs. 68.1 percent, on average – they are significantly less likely to deposit their savings into a bank – a mere 15.8 percent, compared to 36.1 percent outside the Muslim world. The obstacle to investment in a shared resource pool, therefore, is not merely financial.

This substantive and significant difference remains when I restrict the comparison to a more similar subset of countries – all those with an explicit deposit insurance scheme, as identified by Demirgüç-Kunt, Karacaovali, and Laeven (2005), and those above the global median income. In the former case, the difference is almost unchanged – 16.0 percent vs. 38.4 percent. And in the latter, the rates of bank savings increase both within and outside the Muslim world, but the difference between the two persists: 28.3 percent compared to 44.9 percent. In additional analysis, I confirm the substantive and statistical significance of these differences, using hierarchical models to assess the impact of individual-level covariates and national characteristics on the likelihood of savings, overall, and bank savings, in particular. The results of these models are available in Online Appendix Table OA.4. They reveal a persistent negative effect of Muslim-plurality-status on bank savings, even after accounting for individual demographics (age, gender, education, income) and other national-level variables (deposit insurance and national income, but also the quality of regulation). Meanwhile, with the addition of these controls, I find that the effect of Muslim-plurality-status on *overall* savings is considerably diluted, if not reversed, in some specifications. As above, there seems to be an obstacle to the use of banks, in particular, in Muslim-plurality countries that goes beyond individual financial constraints. I take this as evidence of an economic "participation gap" in the Muslim world.

2.1.3 The Islamic Advantage in Political and Economic Cooperation

In terms of both political and economic activity, I find a significant participation gap in Muslim countries: in instances where individuals must join together, to cooperate or coordinate for a collective purpose, whether to demonstrate, vote, or invest, those in the Muslim world show less willingness to do. The difference in political and economic participation remains, even when the comparison is restricted to more similar countries, based on income or institutions. These patterns beg for an explanation. What are the obstacles to collective action in this part of the world?

Given this participation gap, the success of Islamic-based political and economic movements in many Muslim countries is even more remarkable. In the wake of the Arab Spring, Islamic-based political parties emerged victorious in elections held in both Egypt and Tunisia. Elsewhere, beyond Turkey's AKP, Islamic-based parties have won decisive victories in Bahrain, Palestine, Morocco, and, earlier, Algeria; and outside of the Middle East, rival Islamic groups dominate political competition in Malaysia. While not a universal phenomenon, the success of Islamic parties in a variety of contexts has garnered the attention of scholars and those within the policy community, who remark on the sustained popularity of these political movements. In the Turkish case, in particular, the popular view is that the AKP has done what was seemingly impossible: it has built a majority support base *and kept it*, a remarkable feat in what has been a historically volatile electoral system (Hazama 2004; Müftüler-Baç and Keyman 2012).

Similarly, while rates of formal bank savings are indeed lower in the Muslim world, there is some evidence that *sharī'ah*-compliant "participation" banks may be helping to boost savings rates there (Demirgüç-Kunt, Klapper, and Randall 2013). And while international trade is significantly lower in the Muslim Middle East (Yousef 2004) and between Muslim and non-Muslim countries (Lewer and Van den Berg 2007), there is some indication that trade levels are more robust *among* Muslim countries (Helble 2007). In both cases, as with Islamic-based politics, obstacles to collective action appear to be overcome whenever Islam is being explicitly referenced. For a theory of Islamic-based movements to help make sense of these patterns, it must first account for the reasons why individuals tend not to get involved in collective political and economic activities, as well as how references to Islam attenuate these obstacles to participation. In the section that follows, I explore the three main existing explanations for the Islamic mobilization advantage, focusing on how each defines the obstacles to participation and the role of Islamic references in overcoming them.

2.2 EXISTING THEORIES OF ISLAMIC-BASED MOBILIZATION

Early interest in Islamic-based organizations was sparked by the emergence of noteworthy groups in the mid-twentieth century, from the Society of the Muslim Brothers in Egypt, in 1928, to the Iraqi Islamic Party, in 1960. But it took the Islamic Revolution in Iran in 1979 for scholars to start investing considerable energy in trying to explain the popularity of political movements founded on Islamic ideals and principles. More recently, with the development of Islamic-based sub-economies in many parts of the Muslim world, there has also been a growing interest in explaining the success of Islamic-based banks and businesses, including the rise of professional associations founded on a shared commitment to Islamic values and practices.

Below, I review three key theories that have been developed to explain the popularity of Islamic-based movements.[6] Most existing explanations for the Islamic advantage are focused on the more political aspects of the phenomenon; but theories of Islamic-based sub-economies, while fewer, strike similar notes. To support the direct comparison of the three sets of theories,

---

[6] Because I am focused on explaining the comparative advantage of Islamic-based groups, this review makes no more than brief mention of the extensive literature on the *moderation* of these movements, since these address a fundamentally different research question (Gurses 2014; Mecham 2004; Schwedler 2006).

I define each in two ways: first, in terms of how it views the *obstacles to collective action* in the Muslim world, to account for the region's participation gap; and, second, in terms of how it sees of the *advantage of Islamic-based groups* in overcoming these obstacles. I do so in order to define a set of observable implications of each theory – falsifiable hypotheses that can be tested empirically.

2.2.1 The Grievance Theory of Selective Incentives

The earliest explanations for the rise Islamic-based movements argued that the popularity of these religious groups is based on frustration with the (secular) status quo and a search for an alternative political and economic system. This "grievance-based" theory of Islamic mobilization developed in the context of the Middle East, where overextended states have failed to attend to the most basic needs of their citizens, especially the most impoverished among them (Anderson 1987). Because many of these failing states are decidedly secular, Islamic-based groups represent a natural counterpoint; and because of Islam's emphasis on charity and good works (*zakat*), Islamic groups are expected to do more (or at least better) for those in greatest need (Dzutsati, Siroky, and Dzutsev 2016; García-Rivero and Kotzé 2007).

Within this grievance theory, two main strands can be identified. The first focuses on frustrations with the economic failures of secular-nationalist regimes (Beinin 2005; Kepel 2003; Roháč 2013).[7] This instrumental failure foments anger among the poor, aimed at the wealthy, Westernized elite. As Nazih Ayubi explains,

When modernization stumbled, failing to achieve the promised economic development and instead deepening the alienation and dependency of society, groups that were previously excluded or were promised what was never given, came forward with their alternative ideational system: "Islam" (1991, p. 163).

As a direct response to the status quo, many Islamic-based movements have tended to be largely anti-capitalist and, to a certain extent, anti-democratic.

Meanwhile, a second line of thinking emphasizes how intervention in domestic politics by outside powers, during the Cold War and after, delegitimized the secular leadership, alienating their constituents. In this view, the secular state's failure is more psychic than instrumental. In his description of the "Arab predicament" in the wake of the 1967 loss to Israel, Fouad Ajami explained the turn (back) to Islam thusly:

In the aftermath of defeat, the turning of the masses to religion for solace and consolation and the continual appeal, couched in religious terms, for faith and patience... served as a reminder that God may be dead elsewhere... but was alive and well in the Arab world (1991, p. 61).

---

[7] For an elegant formalization of this argument, see Binzel and Carvalho (2016).

2.2 Existing Theories of Islamic-Based Mobilization

In response to the failings of the current regime, the masses have gone in search of political leaders who look and sound more like them (i.e., who are more overtly religious (Zubaida 1989)).

In this grievance-based view, Islamic groups are assumed to recruit supporters from among the most deprived and alienated, those who stand the most to gain from changes to the status quo (Davis 1984; Ibrahim 1980; Kepel 2003; Kurzman and Naqvi 2010b). Although their anger makes them inherently motivated to mobilize and demand change, with little to left to lose, the aggrieved can be further motivated to participate via material and psychosocial benefits that many Islamic-based groups distribute. These benefits range from employment opportunities, health services, and foodstuffs (Beinin 2005; Brooke 2017; Clark 2004a; Singerman 1996), to generic feelings of meaning and belonging (Ayubi 1991). Although they do not explicitly refer to Mancur Olson's *Logic of Collective Action*, grievance-based theories of Islamic mobilization suggest that these benefits act as "selective incentives," further motivating the poor and alienated to take part in collective activities.[8]

In summary, per the grievance theory, the comparative advantage of Islamic political and economic groups rests heavily on the anger and frustration of the aggrieved and impoverished, bolstered through the instrumental and psychic benefits that groups offer their members. The empirical implication, therefore, is that political and economic participation should be highest among the most aggrieved – defined in terms of their level of frustration and/or their level of economic need – with the impoverished, in particular, most likely to participate in order to gain access to selective incentives.[9] Although never stated explicitly, in this model, the main obstacle to participation, more generally, would be a general sense of satisfaction with the status quo or, at least, an overarching sense of apathy. This would imply that the political and economic participation gap in the Muslim world would be explained by lower levels of motivation in Muslim-plurality countries.

2.2.2 The Faith-Based Theory of "Transvaluation"

Just as consensus was starting to form around the grievance-based theory, a new generation of scholars emerged with an alternative view of Islamic-based politics and economics. For these scholars, the main critique of grievance theory was its singular focus on the purported benefits of participation for the aggrieved. Instead, it was suggested that that more attention be paid to the significant costs and risks associated with collective action in the Muslim world.

---

[8] Olson defines selective incentives as ones distributed only to those who join the group and work for its interest, noting that they can be either positive (benefits) or negative (costs) (2002, p. 51).

[9] This expectation stands in direct contrast to other theories in political science and sociology, which posit that participation is lower among the poor, because they lack either the time or the resources to participate (Brady, Verba, and Schlozman 1995). The main exception is during periods of acute economic crisis, which have been shown to mobilize the more aggrieved (Kern, Marien, and Hooghe 2015).

These risks, it was noted, tended to be large and could not easily be counterbalanced by selective incentives. Carrie Wickham, in her *Mobilizing Islam*, makes a compelling argument of this nature in the case of political participation:

> In [Muslim-majority] settings, in which the risks associated with participation in an opposition movement are high and the prospects of affecting change are, at best, uncertain, the "rational" response of the self-interested actor would appear to be a retreat into self-preserving silence.... Interest-based appeals thus help account for initial, lower-risk forms of Islamic activism. But they cannot explain... [a] transition from lower-risk to higher-risk and more overtly political forms of activism (2002, p. 14).

In this framework, rather than channeling the frustrations of their aggrieved members, Islamic organizations enjoy a different mobilization advantage, especially when it comes to higher-risk activities. By explicitly referencing Islam, these organizations tap into the faith of their members. When actively primed, these deeply held religious beliefs attenuate the high costs and risks of political and economic activity by transforming them into smaller costs (or even benefits), a process that Wickham calls "transvaluation."[10]

Taking their cues from social movement theory, Wickham and other proponents of the faith-based theory argue that "ideological frames mediate the progression from preferences to behavior by shaping the perceived costs and benefits of different paths of action" (2002, p. 148). Specifically, the risks of political and economic participation become less relevant to an individual once she feels "called" (*da'wa*) to God's service: the costs she might face as a result of her participation are "replaced" by collective benefits, and spiritual concerns come to substitute for material ones (Eligur 2010; Ibrahim 1980; Wickham 2002, 2004; Yavuz 2003). The process of transvaluation is triggered by the heavy use of religious language and symbols in the appeals of Islamic-based organizations; and those most likely to respond to these appeals – to be "called" to take part in the political or economic activity, no matter the costs – are those with the deepest commitment to their faith. In other words, in this model, piety makes it more likely that the costs and risks of activity will be transformed through Islamic-based appeals.

In contrast to the instrumental or psychic selective incentives emphasized by the grievance-based theory, the faith-based theory of Islamic-based mobilization describes a set of *spiritual* selective incentives that the faithful enjoy when taking part in collective activities.[11] Chief among these incentives is the the promise of rewards in the afterlife, gained not from any tangible success but from an honest attempt to do God's work. By this logic, even suffering can be transformed into a benefit, taken as "a divine signal that the activist is on the right path and will achieve salvation as part of the saved sect" (Wiktorowicz and Kaltenhaler 2006, p. 316). In this way, for a true believer, the

---

[10] In moving away from selective incentives targeting the poor – the most aggrieved – faith-based theories tend to focus more on the urban middle class (Clark 2004a, 2004b).

[11] In this way, the faith-based theory of latent groups has some things in common with club models of participation in smaller religious organizations.

cost of participation is entirely ameliorated, making it a rational choice to join in. Meanwhile, non-believers still face the staggering costs of participation and rationally choose to remain sidelined.

Examples of this faith-based logic abound in the existing literature. Beyond Wickham's (2002) description of Islamic-based politics in Egypt and Wiktorowicz and Kaltenhaler's (2006) take on al-Muhajiroun in Britain, Thomas Barfield (2005) highlights similar themes among the Taliban in Afghanistan,[12] as does Kikue Hamayotsu (2011) in the case of the Prosperous Justice Party (Partai Keadilan Sejahtera, PKS) of Indonesia.[13] In many ways, the faith-based theory of Islamic mobilization is similar to theories of religious-based voting developed outside of the Muslim world. For example, in explaining why poor religious voters opt to support right-wing parties across Europe, De La O and Rodden (2008) argue that faith operates as a valence dimension, overwhelming voters' instrumental concerns and driving them to make what is, for them, a surprising yet rational choice.[14] Similarly, some existing theories of religious-based economic activity, including those focused on Islamic sub-economies, posit that a sense of religious duty drowns out traditional economic calculations about profits and margins, supporting investment and trade where it would otherwise be deemed "irrationally" risky (Abou-Youssef et al. 2015; Noussair et al. 2013).

In contrast to the grievance theory, the faith-based theory of Islamic mobilization defines the general obstacle to collective activity in the Muslim world not in terms of apathy or satisfaction, but in terms of the costs and risks associated with these behaviors. In this view, references to Islam made by Islamic-based organizations help to attenuate the obstacles to collective action by priming pious individuals to think of these costs differently, as collective benefits or as incentives to be enjoyed in the afterlife. This implies that those most likely to participate are the "true believers," those committed to their faith and to God, who are able to make the rational choice to take part despite the sizable costs and risks. In the aggregate, this would also imply that the popularity of Islamic-based movements should track onto levels of piety, so that Islamic groups are most successful where and when people are most pious. For example, by this view, the rise of the AKP in Turkey in recent years would indeed be the result of a religious resurgence among Turkish voters, much as has been commonly presumed.

---

[12] Barfield writes that the "advantage of a religious movement for rival Pashtun leaders was that there was no honor or prestige lost in subordinating oneself to the will of God or God's agents" (2005, p. 227).

[13] Hamayotsu argues that the PKS was able to gain the loyalty of young voters through "the party's emphasis on collective interests over personal private interests" (2011, p. 237), an argument also made by Tarek Masoud in the case of the Muslim Brotherhood in Egypt. He explains that "[a]nyone who has witnessed a Muslim Brotherhood rally firsthand cannot help but be struck by the totemic power of religious rhetoric, by the ways in which invocations of the will of Allah and the way of Muhammad can imbue voters with a sense of religious duty" (2014, p. 5).

[14] For an application to the Turkish case, see Esmer and Pettersson (2007).

2.2.3 The Role of Information in the Success of Islamic-Based Groups

In contrast to the grievance and faith-based theories, a third explanation emphasizes the importance of information in the Islamic advantage. By this theory, references to Islam represent a credible signal to potential supporters about what an organization stands for, something that is particularly valuable in an information-low environment. What exactly is being signaled by the use of Islamic language and symbols varies considerably from theory to theory. For example, Pepinsky, Liddle, and Mujani (2012) suggest that it informs voters about the economic priorities of Islamic parties in Indonesia. In the case of Dzutsati, Siroky, and Dzutsev (2016), Islamic language signals change away from the status quo in the North Caucasus region of Russia, attracting the support of religious and non-religious voters who are dissatisfied with the current regime. Meanwhile, both Roháč (2013) and Brooke (2017) argue that Islamic-based organizations use Islamic references to effectively signal their commitment to the provision of public goods, in large part because of their history of doing so effectively. Masoud (2014) supplements all these theories by emphasizing that Islamic-based groups, like the Muslim Brotherhood in Egypt, also have an organizational advantage when it comes to sharing information with potential supporters: a dense network of Islamic-based organizations, spanning the political and economic, and including those offering social services, are used by different groups to speak directly and convincingly to a broad, captive audience. In the case of Islamic-based parties, voters are left with a better sense of what these groups stand for, to their advantage on election day.

In these different ways, references to Islam inform potential supporters about what organizations are likely to do. Alternatively, and according to a recent theory developed by Cammett and Luong (2014), Islamic references may also communicate something about how the organizations are going to go about doing so. Here, references to Islam signal a reputation for good governance (Henderson and Kuncoro 2011), a tactic that, if successful, may help to enlarge the organization's support base beyond its "natural" constituency of pious individuals to include more secular individuals who want to take a stand against corruption. In emphasizing the reputational advantages of Islamic-based groups, this strand of the information theory has a lot in common with theories of Islamic-based economics, which posits that religious groups do well at policing one another and upholding a collective reputation for honesty (Carr and Landa 1983; Iannaccone 1992; Kuran 1995, 2005).

Focusing on how references to Islam might inform would-be supporters, the information-based theory implies that low levels of information limit political and economic participation in the Muslim world. Alternatively, even if individuals have a good sense of what different groups represent, they may doubt their intentions, overwhelmed by a deep distrust of their leaders. In either case, references to Islam help to overcome the obstacles to collective action by offering supporters a clear sense of what to expect from Islamic-based groups. Within the policy space of each country (and possibly even across countries), we might therefore expect Islamic-based groups to occupy a well-defined, distinctive, and consistent position. Or, if the advantage of Islamic-based groups is more about reputation, we would expect low levels of political trust in the Muslim world, especially of non-Muslim organizations.

2.3 A THEORETICAL EVALUATION OF EXISTING EXPLANATIONS

The three existing theories of Islamic-based political and economic participation have substantially different views of the obstacles to collective action in the Muslim world and how references to Islam are able to overcome these obstacles. In reviewing the three theories, I defined observable implications of each – things that we would see in the world if each were true and whose absence would raise questions about a theory's validity. The expectations of the different theories have not been directly compared in this way, and rigorous tests of each have been rare. Existing support has tended to come from ethnographic observation of Islamic activists and has not always leveraged variation in the outcome of interest, making it difficult to draw causal inferences (Geddes 2003; King, Keohane, and Verba 1994). Even where the existing evidence has been more systematic, it has tended to come from a single case, making it difficult to assess validity in other settings. For all these reasons, I believe a more thorough theoretical and empirical investigation is warranted.

In the forthcoming chapter, I devote considerable space to testing the set of hypotheses, leveraging variation in different collective political and economic activities across different dimensions, comparing individuals, places, or periods of time. In each case, I look for evidence of the empirical pattern that a given theory expects to see. Is there a general disinterest in politics in Muslim-plurality countries that can explain the lack of political participation there, as the grievance theory holds? And are the most aggrieved indeed more likely to participate? Are the costs and risks of political and economic activity indeed higher in the Muslim world, as the faith-based theory argues? And are those with the strongest religious beliefs better able to withstand these costs, so that participation rates are highest among the pious? And does the popularity of Islamic-based movements track onto patterns of religiosity across space and time? Or is a lack of information the key obstacle to participation in the region? Do individuals simply know more about what to expect of Islamic-based groups in terms of policy or reputation?

Bringing evidence to bear on the theoretical expectations of the existing theories is critical to establishing their validity. But even before turning to the empirical tests, it is important to consider the *theoretical* merit of the three extant theories. The assumption that motivation and information are necessary for collective action is neither new nor controversial (Hardin 1982; Ostrom 1998). In a rational choice framework, it is also clear that the costs of collective action – whether objectively or subjectively defined – play a critical role in determining who takes part in a political or economic activity (Olson 2002).

But even if individuals are sufficiently motivated and informed, and even if they see the benefits as outweighing the costs, I would argue that they may still rationally opt out of participating. That is because their decision to take part in a collective activity does not just depend on their own level of motivation and information and the extent to which their own risks might be attenuated.

Ultimately, any one individual's decision to participate in a collective political or economic activity – to join a political movement, to contribute to a public good, to vote for a political party, to invest with an institution, to enter into an economic exchange with another individual or firm – is rarely made in isolation. Quite to the contrary, individual decisions are inherently interdependent. Whenever the costs and benefits of a collective endeavor is a function of the number of individuals who take part, the best decision for any one critically depends on the choices of others. Meanwhile, the existing theories of the Islamic advantage take a quite individualized view of political and economic activity, overlooking their more collective dimensions.[15] If the extant theories fail to account for the empirical realities of political and economic participation in the Muslim world, this over-emphasis on the individual may be to blame.

---

[15] For example, the faith-based theory of transvaluation focuses on how an individual's religious beliefs change her expected costs of participation. In game-theoretic terms, this supposes that religious beliefs redefine preferences over outcomes to make participation a dominant strategy for pious individuals.

3

Evaluating Existing Theories of the Islamic Advantage

In Chapter 2, I introduced three existing theories of the Islamic advantage in political and economic mobilization: grievances, faith (or "transvaluation"), and information. I defined each in terms of what it sees as the key obstacle to collective action in the Muslim world, generally, as well as why it believes references to Islam help to overcome this obstacle (see Table 3.1). Each of these theoretical assertions can be restated as a falsifiable hypothesis and tested by leveraging variation in the identified variables. For example, to evaluate whether the costs and risks of political and economic participation explain lower levels of activity in the Muslim world, as suggested by the faith-based theory, the relative costs of participation in Muslim-plurality countries can be compared to those outside the Muslim world. A statistically significant difference would not constitute definitive proof that these costs are the direct cause of the participation gap in the region, but it would lend some support to the hypothesis and the faith-based theory. Meanwhile, the absence of such a difference would constitute important evidence against the theory.

In the chapter that follows, I evaluate the empirical expectations of these theories using a variety of data sources. Existing support for each theory has tended to come from ethnographic accounts of a single case, almost always focusing on members of a given Islamic-based political or economic group. In noting that these individuals tend to be poor or pious, scholars have drawn the conclusion that their poverty or their piety are at the heart of their reasons for joining the movement. But to conclude with any confidence that grievances or faith play such a pivotal role, those who join Islamic-based movements must be compared to those who do not, with the former found to be significantly more aggrieved or pious than the latter. Similar comparisons can be made across countries or regions, or across time, depending on the empirical expectations and data that are available. Repeated comparisons, using different data sources at different levels of analysis, can help to establish that a pattern holds across a wide set of conditions and is not unique to any particular case or moment.

In the sections of the forthcoming chapter, I leverage variation in different outcomes to assess the plausibility of each existing theory. For the grievance

TABLE 3.1 *Comparing Existing Theories of Islamic-Based Mobilization*

	Obstacle to Participation	Source of Islamic Advantage
Grievance Theory	Insufficient motivation	Selective incentives for the impoverished
Faith-Based Theory	Risks too high	Personal piety transforms risks
Information Theory	Insufficient information	Better sense of Islamic groups' position

theory, I explore whether apathy or satisfaction is higher in Muslim countries and whether participation rates are indeed most robust among the most aggrieved. To test the faith-based theory, I assess whether the risks of political and economic participation are indeed higher in the Muslim world and could account for the participation gap. And using a number of indicators of religious faith, I look to see whether personal piety supports participation across individuals and whether the popularity of Islamic-based movements tracks onto faith in the aggregate, across space and across time. Finally, to test the information theory, I look for evidence that individuals are unclear about their political environment, as well as any indication that they have a better sense of what to expect of Islamic-based movements. I also check to see whether Islamic-based groups have a reputational advantage relative to their competitors.

In almost all cases, I struggle to find support for the extant theories. Across a number of indicators, I see no evidence that individuals in the Muslim world are less aggrieved or more apathetic than those outside the region, challenging a key assumption of the grievance theory. Moreover, within the region, as elsewhere, participation rates tend to increase with wealth, contradicting the hypothesis that the poor are most likely to become mobilized. And while there is evidence that the costs of political and economic participation are indeed higher in the Muslim world, as the faith-based theory would suggest, these costs do not seem to explain the participation gap in the region. More importantly, neither individual participation nor the aggregate popularity of Islamic-based movements track onto indicators of faith: if anything, the most devout Muslims are *less* likely to take part in political activities. In terms of information, I find little evidence that citizens of the Muslim world are underinformed or that they have a better sense of what to expect of Islamic groups. The only slight advantage that these groups seem to have is in terms of their reputations.

3.1 EMPIRICAL IMPLICATIONS OF THE GRIEVANCE THEORY

As discussed in Chapter 2, the grievance theory was one of the first developed to explain the rise of Islamic-based social, political, and economic groups, especially in the context of the Muslim Middle East. The two strands of the theory agree that the failings of secular states in the region – whether instrumental

3.1 Empirical Implications of the Grievance Theory

(Ayubi 1991) or psychic (Ajami 1991) – have made them unpopular and that the aggrieved turn to Islam and Islamic-based groups as an alternative to the secular status quo. The link between grievances and Islam is further strengthened by the selective incentives that Islamic groups distribute to their supporters. Between the push of grievances and the pull of selective incentives, the poor are expected to be especially susceptible to mobilization. This stands in contrast to existing theories in political science, which hold that political participation is more likely among the wealthiest, who have more time and resources to devote to collective causes (Brady, Verba, and Schlozman 1995; Gallego 2007).

Although the grievance theory does not directly address the participation gap in the Muslim world, we can extend its basic logic to generate a hypothesis about the obstacles to mobilization, more generally. With its focus on motivation, the theory is likely to identify satisfaction with the status quo or apathy as the source of the participation gap. And then, within the region, those most likely to participate would be the most aggrieved, whether in terms of their self-reported motivation or, more basically, their level of income. Using indicators of political and economic satisfaction from a number of different sources, I can test both of these hypotheses, looking for the expected patterns when comparing Muslim-plurality countries to others and, within the Muslim world, comparing those who participate to those who do not.

3.1.1 Assessing Political and Economic Grievances in the Muslim World

To explore the possibility that the absence of frustration or motivation can explain the political and economic participation gap in the Muslim world, I gather a number of indicators of satisfaction with global coverage. From the set of cross-national surveys first introduced in Chapter 2, I select measures of socio-political and economic satisfaction, motivation, and apathy with the broadest coverage inside and outside the Muslim world. First, self-reported happiness, measured using responses to the question "Taking all things together, would you say you are... ." For ease of analysis, I recode "Very happy" and "Quite happy" as happy (1) and "Not very happy" and "Not at all happy" as unhappy (0).[1] Second, satisfaction with life, measured based on responses to the question "All things considered, how satisfied are you with your life as a whole these days?" Answers ranging from 1 to 5 are recoded as dissatisfied (0) and those ranging from 6 to 10 as satisfied (1).[2] To capture apathy, I use responses to the question "How interested would you

---

[1] This question is included in the EVS, WVS, and some iterations of the Latinobarómetro. Taken together, data are available for nearly 550,000 respondents from 117 countries, including nearly 90,000 from 30 different Muslim-plurality countries (see Online Appendix Table OA.1).

[2] Life satisfaction was included in the EVS and WVS along with some waves of the Caucasus Barometer, covering just over 535,000 respondents from 111 countries, including over 95,000 from 30 Muslim countries.

say you are in politics?," recoding responses "Very interested" and "Somewhat interested' as interested (1) and "Not very interested" and "Not at all interested" as disinterested (0).³ I also captured the importance of politics in respondents' lives, recoding "Very important" and "Rather important" as important (1) and "Not very important" and "Not at all important" as unimportant (0).⁴

In terms of economics, I mix indicators from the cross-national surveys with some from the Global Financial Inclusion (Findex) Database, first introduced in Chapter 2. To assess the "demand" side of economic activity, I look at satisfaction with "the financial situation" in respondents' households, recoding responses ranging from 1 to 5 as dissatisfied (0), while those ranging from 6 to 10 coded as satisfied (1).⁵ From the Findex Database, I examine the reasons that respondents without a bank account give for their decision not to participate in formal banking. Among the possible responses, some respondents report that they simply "have no need for financial services at a formal institution."⁶ On the "supply" side of economic activity, I need an indicator that the system is unable to offer individuals the basics of what they would need to become economically active. This is based on the assumption that the absence of basic services could drive up grievances, on the one hand, or could generate apathy, on the other. Ultimately, I use self-reported "confidence" in "major companies," taking "A great deal" and "Quite a lot" as indicators of having sufficient confidence (1) and "Not very much" and "None at all" as indicators of not having enough (0).⁷ From the Findex Database, I estimate the proportion of respondents without a bank account who reported that they "don't trust financial institutions."⁸

For each of these eight indicators of political and economic grievances, I calculate average levels of satisfaction among respondents from Muslim countries

---

³ Political interest was asked in a larger subset of surveys: the EVS and WVS, but also most waves of the Afrobarometer and Latinobarómetro, and all waves of the East Asian Barometer and Arab Barometer. Taken together, these sources cover nearly a million respondents from 143 countries, including over 175,000 from 35 countries in the Muslim world.

⁴ The importance of politics was included in the EVS and the WVS as well as an iteration of the Eurobarometer (EB) and one Latinobarómetro, covering just over 500,000 respondents from 116 countries (nearly 88,000 from 30 Muslim-plurality countries).

⁵ Responses to this item were available for a smaller sample: just under 400,000 respondents from 106 countries, including 81,480 from 28 Muslim-plurality countries, surveyed by either the EVS or the WVS.

⁶ Over 65,000 respondents from 141 countries answered this question, including nearly 25,000 from 37 Muslim-plurality countries. In addition to not needing banking services, respondents could offer any of the following reasons for not having an account: the bank is too far away; its services are too expensive; the respondent lacks the required documentation; s/he does not trust the bank; religious concerns; a lack of sufficient funds; a family member already has an account; and the respondent is unable to get an account for unspecified reasons.

⁷ This question was also only asked in the EVS and WVS, but responses are available for a slightly larger sample – nearly 450,000 individuals from 110 countries – although fewer from the Muslim world – under 75,000 from 30 countries.

⁸ A larger sample – over 135,000 respondents from 154 countries – answered this question, including a larger sample from the Muslim world: over 50,000 individuals from 43 countries.

3.1 Empirical Implications of the Grievance Theory

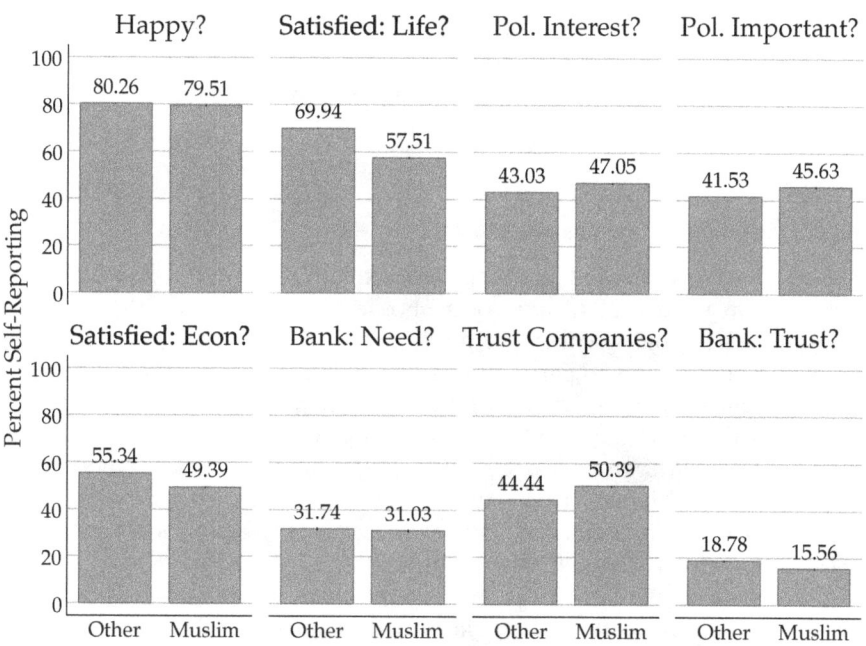

FIGURE 3.1 Political and Economic Grievances in the Muslim World
Notes: Levels of agreement with statements about political and economic satisfaction. Respondents from non-Muslim-plurality countries are compared to those in the Muslim world.

and among those from outside the Muslim world.[9] The results of these calculations are displayed in Figure 3.1. Average levels of political satisfaction and engagement with politics, inside and outside of the Muslim world, are displayed in the top row. In all cases, the patterns contradict the expectations of the grievance theory. On average, individuals in the Muslim world are less happy – not more – and are less satisfied with their lives, overall. Perhaps because of this dissatisfaction, they tend to be more interested in politics and consider politics to be more important in their lives, on average. In each case, the difference is statistically significant in a two-tailed difference-of-means t-test.

Similarly, across the four economic indicators, the patterns challenge the presumptions of the grievance theory. Individuals in the Muslim world are less satisfied with the economy, on average, indicating that there should be sufficient demand for (improved) economic services. Further, they are *less* likely to explain their lower levels of engagement with formal banks in terms of a lack of basic need – the obstacle to this type of activity must be something else. On the "supply" side, I do not find evidence that individuals opt out

---

[9] In these and all of the forthcoming cross-sectional comparisons, I calculate weighted averages, based not only on the sampling weights within each survey, but also on the number of surveys conducted in each country.

of engaging with economic institutions because they believe that they are of poor quality. There is more confidence in companies and in banks in Muslim-plurality countries than outside the region. As above and in all cases, each of these differences is statistically significant.

3.1.2 Participation among the Most Aggrieved

Even if dissatisfaction and apathy cannot explain the political and economic participation gap in the Muslim world, another key hypothesis of the grievance theory may still hold – within Muslim-plurality countries, the most aggrieved may still be most likely to participate. To test this expectation, I return to measures of political participation introduced in Chapter 2. Using these, I assess whether petitioning, boycotting and/or demonstrating covaries with income. Recall that the grievance theory holds that the impoverished are most likely to participate in Islamic-based activities, not just because they are least satisfied with the secular status quo, but also because they are most vulnerable to selective incentives offered by Islamic groups.

To maximize coverage, I opt for a 5-bin measure of household income, recoding 10-bin indicators where they are available.[10] And to streamline the forthcoming analysis, I combine respondents' self-reported participation in the three separate political activities – petitions, boycotts, and demonstrations – into a single index of participation.[11] A composite index tends to be more reliable in cases where multiple survey questions capture the same underlying phenomenon because it reduces bias from measurement or respondent error.[12] In my political participation index, I differentiate those who say that they "have done" at least one of the three activities, from those who "would do" at least one of the three and those who say that they "would never do" any of them.

Rates of self-reported participation in the Muslim world across income levels are illustrated in Figure 3.2. The trend lines indicate that the pattern in Muslim-plurality countries is broadly consistent with those identified elsewhere (Brady, Verba, and Schlozman 1995; Gallego 2007), namely that participation rates are *increasing* with income. This stands counter to the expectations of the grievance theory. The most impoverished individuals are least likely to "have done" a political activity and are most likely to say they "would never" do any of the three. In additional analysis, I run a number

---

[10] This allows me to include responses from earlier waves of the East Asian Barometer that group income data into only five categories.

[11] Note that responses for the three separate activities are quite tightly correlated, ranging from a correlation coefficient of 0.586, in the case of petitioning and boycotting, to 0.433 in the case of petitioning and demonstrating.

[12] As Ansolabehere, Rodden, and Snyder Jr. explain, using "[m]ultiple survey items [to estimate a single phenomenon], combined either as a simple average or as a score using factor analysis, reduce[s] measurement error at the rate of approximately $1/K$, where K is the number of items" used (2008, p. 218).

3.1 Empirical Implications of the Grievance Theory

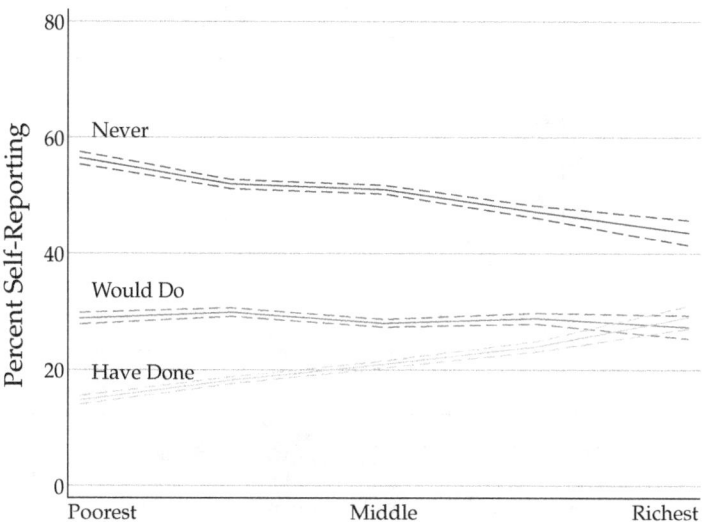

FIGURE 3.2 Income and Political Participation in the Muslim World
Notes: Solid lines indicate the average level of political participation across five income categories, among respondents from Muslim countries. Dashed lines indicate 95 percent confidence intervals.

of robustness checks, confirming that the trends hold for each activity separately, that they reflect differences across individuals within the same country, and that they are not driven by other demographic differences across income groups. I do this by estimating a series of mixed-effects hierarchical models of each activity, controlling for the age, gender, and education of individuals. The results of this analysis are available in Online Appendix Table OA.5. In all cases, I confirm the patterns found in the raw data: as elsewhere, within the Muslim world, the poorest are *least* likely to participate in mass politics.

I also extend the analysis to another indicator of grievances – respondents' self-reported level of happiness. Comparing levels of political participation across the four categories of happiness – "Not at all" (4.9 percent of all respondents), "Not very" (15.5%), "Quite" (52.5%), and "Very" (27.1%) – I find the highest levels of participation not among the most aggrieved, but among those in the second category, who are not very happy. Meanwhile, those who are "not at all" happy are actually the *most* likely to report that they would never participate in any political activity (Online Appendix Figure OA.2).[13] A series of mixed-effects models confirm this patterns holds within countries, after accounting for individual-level demographic differences (Online Appendix Table OA.5).

---

[13] From a certain perspective, this non-linear result could be supportive of the grievance theory: if the most aggrieved lack the resources to participate, those who are relatively unhappy would need to lead the charge. But when I compare rates of actual participation within this group, I find that they are no different from the other "happiness" groups.

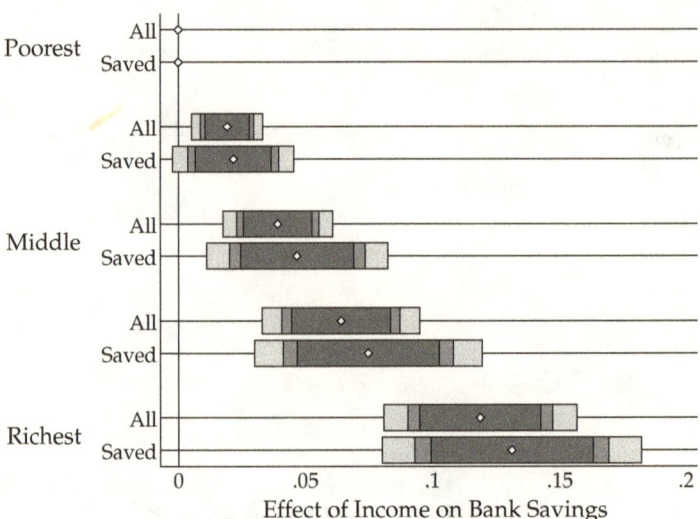

FIGURE 3.3 Income and Bank Savings in the Muslim World
Notes: Marginal effect of income on the likelihood of having saved in a bank in the previous year, from an OLS model of respondents in Muslim countries with country fixed-effects. "All respondents" compared to those who self-report that they "have saved" any money at all in the previous year. All models include demographic controls. 90 percent, 95 percent, and 99 percent confidence intervals indicated.

Assessing levels of economic activity across income groups is difficult because poverty may inhibit individuals from being able to engage in certain collective activities, especially bank savings, the main individual-level indicator I have available. Because the Findex Database does not include a subjective assessment of grievances among those with a bank account, I use poverty as a proxy and examine levels of bank savings across income groups. I do this, first, among all respondents and, then, among the subset of respondents who reported having saved anything over the previous year. The results are illustrated in Figure 3.3. As expected, bank savings is indeed increasing with income; but limiting the sample to only those who have been able to save over the previous year does little to attenuate this pattern. If anything, the poorest respondents who managed to save some money are even *less* likely to invest these savings in a bank. (For full statistical analysis, see Online Appendix Table OA.6.) As above, I take these results as evidence that the most aggrieved are least likely to participate, independent of their level of resources.

Taken together, the evidence therefore stands against the grievance theory. Grievances are not minor in Muslim-plurality countries and so the absence of sufficient motivation cannot account for the political and economic participation gap in the Muslim world. And within the region, there is no indication that the most aggrieved are those most likely to become politically or economically active. Although I have not assessed how grievances track onto support for Islamic-based groups, specifically, that the aggrieved are least likely to participate *overall* indicates that the comparative advantage of Islamic organizations is unlikely to operate through the dissatisfaction of their supporters. The empirical patterns go decidedly against this conclusion.

3.2 ASSESSING THE FAITH-BASED THEORY OF "TRANSVALUATION"

The faith-based "transvaluation" theory of Islamic politics and economics developed, in large part, in response to the grievance theory, which was criticized for not taking the costs and risks of collective action seriously enough. As Carrie Wickham writes, "Once the risks of participation extend to a potential loss of livelihood, psychological intimidation, arrest, imprisonment, torture, and death, an explanation [of mobilization] grounded in the logic of narrow self-interest appears strained" (2002, p. 14). In other words, when individuals face significant risks for taking part in a political or economic activity, no amount of motivation or selective incentives could make participation a rational choice for them. These risks, if larger in the Muslim world, could very well explain the participation gap in the region. But this assumption, though widely held (Hafez and Wiktorowicz 2004; Khalili and Schwedler 2010), has not yet been directly tested.

The faith-based theory's second hypothesis also stands largely untested. It holds that the comparative advantage of Islamic-based groups in mobilization rests on the faith of their supporters, which helps to transform the high costs of participation for them, making it a rational choice. Extensive case studies illustrate that some supporters of Islamic-based organizations are indeed quite pious, with deeply held religious beliefs and a different subjective understanding of the costs and risks of participation (Wickham 2002; Wiktorowicz and Kaltenhaler 2006). But it is not yet clear if these qualities differentiate them, as a group, from non-participants, nor has it been established that this distinction holds across multiple cases.

In the sections that follow, I test the expectations of the faith-based theory, using a variety of data sources and leveraging variation across countries, individuals, and time. To assess the relative costs of political and economic participation, I compare the obstacles to collective action inside and outside of the Muslim world. And to understand whether those with deeply held religious beliefs are indeed more likely to participate, I assess the relationship between participation and faith across individuals. I also see whether the popularity of Islamic-based political and economic movements tracks onto levels of piety in the aggregate, testing the expectation that they should be most successful in the most religious places and times.

3.2.1 The Costs of Collective Action in the Muslim World

To assess whether there are higher risks that could explain the participation gap in the Muslim world, I compare the average cost of participation inside and outside the region, using measures that are widely available and broadly comparable, across democracies and autocracies alike. In my search for good measures, I begin with the observation that barriers to collective mobilization, whether political or economic, are most often erected by the state. So, in both cases, I assess the risks of participation using institutional barriers to collective action.

In the political arena, the Freedom of Assembly and Association index, from the Cingranelli and Richards (CIRI) Human Rights Data Project, encompasses the various ways that the state can block citizens' ability to collectively mobilize. The index is available for nearly 200 countries between 1981 and 2011 and ranges from a value of 0 – "severely restricted or denied completely to all citizens" – and 1 – "limited for all citizens or severely restricted or denied for select groups" – to 2 – "virtually unrestricted and freely enjoyed by practically all citizens." Since I am interested in broad trends in each country, rather than any particular period, I average the index within each country for the entire set of years.

Comparing the average index inside ($N=48$) and outside ($N=146$) the Muslim world, I find a statistically significant difference (99.99%) in a two-tailed difference-of-means t-test. While countries outside the Muslim world average 1.38 on the index – half-way between limited restrictions and total freedom – Muslim-plurality countries average only 0.52, half-way between limited and severe restrictions. In other words, the institutional obstacles to collective political participation in the Muslim world are substantively and significantly higher than elsewhere, creating a potential barrier to collective action, as the faith-based theory hypothesizes.

It is possible that the high costs of political activity in the Muslim world could be driven by the fact that Muslim countries tend to be less democratic than their non-Muslim counterparts. In the index of democratic institutions published by the Polity IV Project (2010), countries in the Muslim world have significantly lower average (1975–2016) scores (–3.60 vs. 3.20) and spend significantly fewer years above the accepted democratic threshold (with a Polity score of six or above) – 4.02 years vs. 19.3 years. But when I repeat the above comparison among democracies and then among autocracies, I still find the same pattern. Figure 3.4 displays how the average Freedom of Assembly and Association index varies across the size of each country's Muslim population, averaging the index across all democratic years and then across non-democratic ones. The comparison indicates that there are indeed more restrictions to assembly and association in the Muslim world, across democracies and autocracies alike.

Turning to the costs of economic activity, I recognize that obstacles to trade and investment are also largely erected by the state. Most often, these obstacles take the form of extensive or inconsistent regulation of markets and industry. Among the Worldwide Governance Indicators (WGI) published by the World Bank is an index of Regulatory Quality which captures "perceptions of the ability of the government to formulate and implement sound

3.2 Assessing the Faith-based Transvaluation

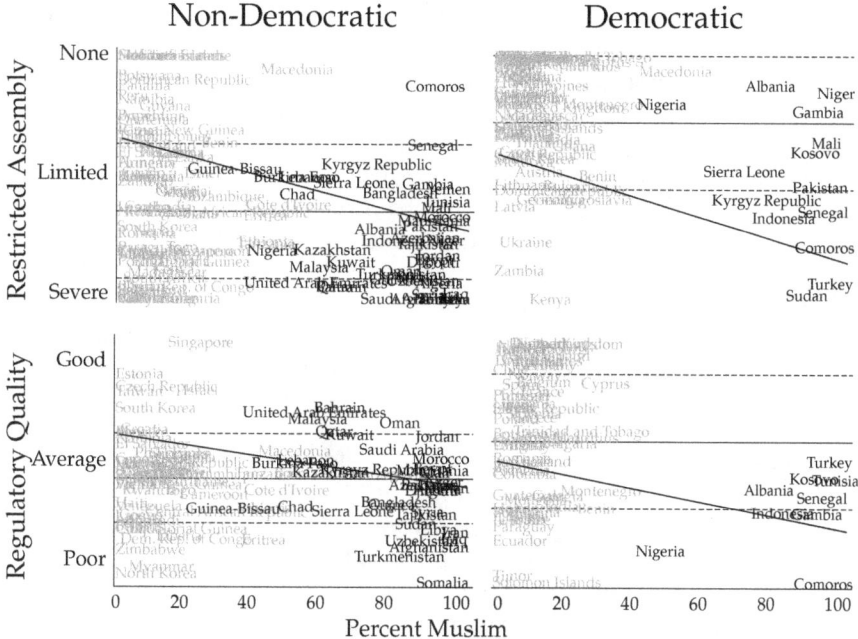

FIGURE 3.4 Obstacles to Political and Economic Participation
Notes: Indices of Freedom of Assembly and Association and of Regulatory Quality, across Muslim population and democratic status, averaging values in all autocratic years and democratic years. Global averages, plus/minus one standard deviation, indicated by the solid and dashed lines, respectively.

policies and regulations that permit and promote private sector development." Based on a large number of indicators, the composite index is constructed to be normally distributed, with a mean of 0 and a standard deviation of 1, with scores ranging from approximately −2.5 (poor quality) to 2.5 (excellent quality).

To assess longer-term trends, I again begin by averaging the index for all available years (1996–2016) and find a statistically significant (99.99%) and substantive difference inside and outside the Muslim world: −0.550 in forty-eight Muslim countries vs. 0.173 in 161 non-Muslim ones. In other words, regulatory quality is much lower in the Muslim world and could very well account for lower levels of economic activity in the region. Assessing the relationship between regulatory quality and the size of the Muslim population across democratic status reveals a surprising pattern: the negative correlation is driven mostly by democracies, while the relationship is more flat in non-democratic settings (Figure 3.4). Still, not a single Muslim economy – whether democratic or autocratic – sits more than one standard-deviation above the global average in regulatory quality, while a large number fall more than a standard-deviation below it.

Although barriers to political and economic participation appear to be significantly higher in the Muslim world, as the faith-based theory hypothesizes, it is not yet clear that these constraints can explain the participation gap in the region. To examine this more directly, I compare rates of activity in Muslim-plurality countries with lower barriers to collective action to participation rates in similar places outside the Muslim world. In the case of political participation, since no Muslim-plurality country averages unrestricted rights to assembly and association through the whole period, I identify years in which ones did and for which I also have survey data on political participation.[14] To understand the role of institutional restrictions on political participation within the Muslim world, I compare average levels of political activity in these unrestricted Muslim country-years ($N=5$) to those in the remaining Muslim country-years ($N=321$), in which assembly and association were more restricted.

I find some evidence that respondents in the unrestricted cases are more willing to participate in politics, although, if anything, they are less likely to have actually done so.[15] In other words, the importance of these state-imposed restrictions on participation rates is not entirely clear. Similarly, when I compare the unrestricted Muslim country-years to non-Muslim unrestricted country-years ($N=178$), I continue to find significantly less participation in the Muslim cases. For example, while 45.9 percent of respondents in unrestricted non-Muslim country-years report having participated in one or more political activity, just 31.1 percent of respondents in the unrestricted Muslim ones report doing the same. In other words, there still appears to be a participation gap in the Muslim world, even holding institutional restrictions constant.

Similarly, in the economic realm, I am able to compare rates of bank savings in Muslim and non-Muslim countries in years in which regulatory quality was above the mean score of 0.[16] Doing so, I continue to find a significant difference in banking activity: while 49.2 percent of respondents in the better-regulated non-Muslim countries report having saved their money in a bank in the previous year, only 38.0 percent of respondents in similar Muslim countries say the same. And while 74.3 percent of the non-Muslim group report having an account at a formal banking institution, only 53.4 percent of the

---

[14] The five country-years that meet these criteria are Albania (1998, 2002, 2008), Burkina Faso (2007), and Mali (2007).

[15] While only 27 percent of respondents in the most restricted Muslim countries said they would consider participating in at least one activity, 32.5 percent of respondents in moderately restricted countries and 44.8 percent of those in the free ones said the same. But at the same time, self-reported participation in one or more activities, while significantly higher in the totally free countries (31.1%) was roughly the same for countries that were fully or partially restricted (16.6%, 17.1%).

[16] There are no country-years in the Findex Database in which a Muslim-plurality country was more than a standard-deviation above from the mean, although some Gulf countries approach an index of 1 in certain years.

3.2 Assessing the Faith-based Transvaluation

Muslim respondents do. As in the case of the political participation gap, while the institutional barriers to economic investment are high, it is not yet clear that they can account for the difference observed in the Muslim world.

3.2.2 Faith and Political Participation among Muslims

The main force of the faith-based theory is less about the obstacles to participation and more about how references to Islam help to attenuate them: by transforming them, in order to make participation a rational choice. Those most likely to respond to these appeals and to have their expected costs thusly transformed are those with the deepest faith, who believe they have a religious obligation to serve God. Across individuals, this implies that participation rates will be highest among the most personally pious, with a relationship between faith and participation that holds independent of the underlying costs of participation.

Although the faith-based theory is primarily concerned with the power of piety, it has not been well-conceptualized by the theory's proponents. Moving forward, I suggest a conceptualization that is derived from the theory itself – namely, deeply held, personal religious beliefs – as opposed to one's nominal religious identity or the regularity of one's religious practice. In my cross-national survey dataset, I identify three measures of personal piety with broad coverage in the Muslim world: the importance of religion in respondents' lives,[17] the importance of God in their lives,[18] and whether they self-identify as a religious person.[19] The three measures are strongly correlated, but not perfectly so: correlation coefficients between the three range from $r=0.252$ to $r=0.439$.

To assess how rates of political activity vary across degrees of faith in Muslim-plurality countries, I average the composite index of participation within each group of respondents: those who attach no importance to religion or God in their lives or who self-identify as non-religious, and those who say religion or God is very important in their lives or who identify themselves as religious. To narrow in on the effect of faith on political activity that could advantage Islamic-based groups, in particular, I restrict the comparison

---

[17] Respondents are asked "*For each of the following aspects, indicate how important it is in your life: Religion,*" with responses ranging from 0 (not at all important) to 3 (very important). Data are available from the EVS and WVS for 67,422 respondents in 24 Muslim-plurality countries.

[18] The EVS, WVS and AsiaBarometer include a question that asks respondents "*How important is God in your life?*," with answers ranging from 1 (not at all important) to 10 (very important). For ease of comparison, I collapsed these into just three groups: those ranging from 0 to 5 ("not very"), 6 to 9 ("somewhat"), and 10 ("very"). Responses are available for 66,593 respondents from 24 Muslim countries.

[19] Respondents surveyed by the EVS and the WVS are asked whether they identify as a "religious person," independent of whether they participate in communal prayer, with responses ranging from 0 (a convinced atheist) to 1 (not a religious person) or 2 (a religious person). In total, 62,298 respondents were surveyed in 23 Muslim countries.

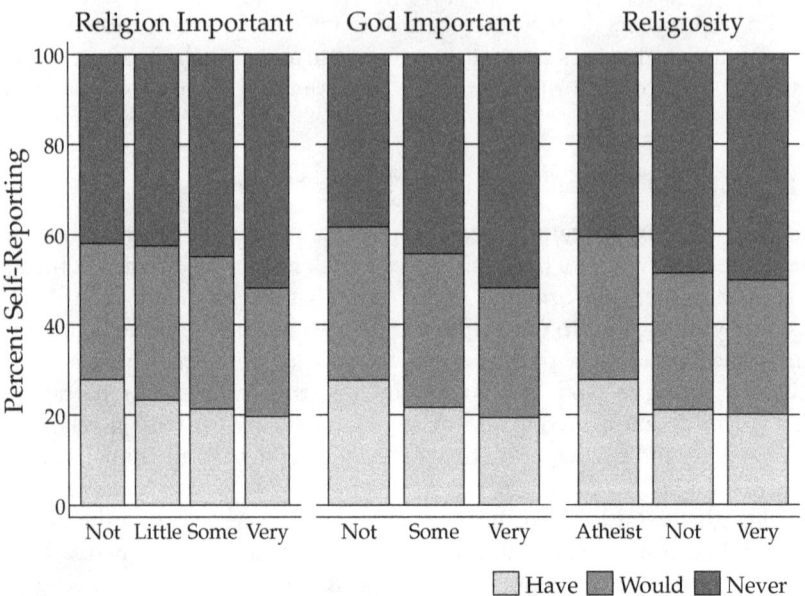

FIGURE 3.5 Political Participation and Religious Faith
Notes: Rates of participation in any one of three political activities, among Muslims in Muslim countries, compared across levels of self-reported religiosity: the importance of religion and God in respondents' lives, and self-identification as a religious person.

to respondents who self-identify as Muslims, removing non-Muslim minorities who reside in Muslim-plurality countries.[20] The results of these comparisons are illustrated in Figure 3.5.

Across the board, I find that rates of political activity are actually *lower* among the most pious Muslims in the Muslim world, a finding consistent with some existing case-based and cross-national studies (Arikan and Bloom 2018; Driskell, Embry, and Lyon 2008). In additional analysis, I find the same pattern using other indicators of faith: the importance of raising a child religiously, and confidence in religious leaders.[21] I confirm that these patterns hold within each

---

[20] I rely on self-identification by respondents with five notable exceptions: religious denomination is not asked in Algeria (2002), Bahrain (2014), Kuwait (2014), and Qatar (2010) and has a very low response rate in Turkey (1990). I looked but could not find clues in the WVS documentation as to why this question received so few responses (N=51) in the Turkish survey in 1990. My best guess is that Turkish citizens are generally averse to answering questions about their religious denomination since these data are not even collected by the national census (Dündar 2000). Rather than lose these data, and given that the populations in these countries are nearly entirely Muslim, I opted to include any respondents who did not explicitly identify themselves as non-Muslim. In other cases in which information on religious denomination was missing – notably, in Egypt (2013) – I did not code all respondents as Muslims given the sizable number of Coptic Christians living there.

[21] Among those who say that "religious faith" is an important quality for a child to have (N=42,112), 19.8 percent have participated in at least one activity and 52.4 percent would

3.2 Assessing the Faith-based Transvaluation

country in the sample, taking individual-level differences and other country-level factors into account via multilevel modeling (Online Appendix Table OA.7). The models indicate that personal religious beliefs are never associated with higher levels of participation and often predict significantly lower levels of activity.

3.2.3 Faith and Banking Practices across the Muslim World

Having tested the implications of the faith-based theory vis-à-vis political participation, I turn to assessing its expectations for economic activity. Since the Findex Database – my preferred individual-level measure of economic activity – lacks any information about respondents' religious beliefs, I consider the theory's expectation across countries. In the aggregate, the faith-based theory expects the popularity of Islamic-based movements to roughly reflect (and never exceed) the proportion of pious individuals in a given community at a given time. This is based on the assumption that only the faithful will respond to Islamic-based appeals and join Islamic-based movements.[22]

In the case of economic investment, the theory would expect the intensity of local religious beliefs to explain low levels of investment in traditional banks, as well as the rising popularity of Islamic banking. In existing studies of bank savings in the Muslim world, it is commonly presumed that the limited use of formal banks in the region stems from Qur'anic prohibitions on interest (Demirgüç-Kunt, Klapper, and Randall 2013; Naser, Ahmad, and Al-Khatib 1999). At the same time, the recent growth of *sharīʿah*-compliant Islamic banks is assumed to reflect their ability to alleviate these same concerns: a religious solution to a religious problem (Abou-Youssef et al. 2015). But neither hypothesis – that religious beliefs restrict conventional banking, nor that they support Islamic-based services – has been effectively tested across the Muslim world.[23]

---

never participate in any activity, while 21.9 percent of those who say that faith is not an important quality (N=24,384) have participated and only 45.2 percent would never take part. Meanwhile, for those who say they have "a great deal" or "quite a lot" of confidence in religious authorities (N=31,028), 20.5 percent have participated in an activity and 50.8 percent would never participate in any, while 21.8 percent of those who have "not very much" confidence in religious authorities or "none at all" (N=32,459) have participated and only 46.2 percent would never do so.

[22] Although I find that the pious are less willing to participate in politics, faith may yet explain the success of Islamic-based movements: so long as the community of the faithful makes up a large enough segment of the population, the share that becomes mobilized could still out number supporters of secular movements. In this version of the faith-based theory, the comparative advantage of Islamic-based groups rests not on the transformative power of beliefs but rather on a numeric advantage, based on the assumption that the faithful, when they participate, will always do so in support of Islamic-based movements.

[23] Some single case studies exist in the extant literature, including Abou-Youssef et al.'s (2015) study of religious-based attitudes towards Islamic banking in Egypt, Kaabachi and Obeid's (2016) study in Tunisia, and Nugroho, Hidayat, and Kusuma's (2017) and Pepinsky's (2013) work on Islamic banking in Indonesia.

Moving away from self-reported bank savings to actual bank holdings, I rely on Bureau van Dijk's BankScope database, available for a larger set of Muslim economies ($N=43$). To support comparison across countries, I aggregate assets from all the banks operating in each country-year, converting these from the local currency to 2010 US dollars, and then averaging across the entire period (1990–2013). I rely on the BankScope typology of banks to compare assets invested in conventional banks to those held in Islamic ones.[24] To account for differences in national income, I normalize these assets using the country's national GDP, also in 2010 US dollars. And because there is considerable skewness in these data, I take their natural logarithm.[25]

To assess whether faith can explain cross-national patterns of conventional banking, I rely on two measures of religious beliefs. The first reflects religious beliefs about banking, specifically. Recall that the Findex Database asks respondents without a bank account a series of yes-or-no questions about their reason(s) for not having one. Among the possible responses are "religious reasons." I calculate the percent of respondents who give this answer in each country-survey and then average these within each country to get a single estimate of religious-based objections to banking. Although responses to this question are able to capture religious-based objections to conventional banking in places where this is the only available option, the availability of *sharī'ah*-compliant Islamic banks in some countries might introduce systematic error into the measure.[26] For this reason, I also use another measure of religious beliefs, more generally: the average importance of religion in respondents' lives, with a simple yes–no response, from Gallup's World Poll (2005–2013). Although there is considerably less variation in these data than there is in the measure of religion's importance used above, with its four-category responses, the Gallup data are available for a larger number of Muslim-majority cases – forty-four compared to just twenty-four in the sample from the EVS and WVS.

In my first comparison, I look to see how conventional bank assets are impacted by religious concerns about formal banking. I find a modest negative

---

[24] Twenty-seven countries have no Islamic bank in operation during the years in question, while twenty-one have some portion of their total bank assets held in Islamic banks: Bahrain, Bangladesh, Egypt, Indonesia, Iraq, Jordan, Kuwait, Malaysia, Maldives, Mauritania, Pakistan, Palestine, Qatar, Saudi Arabia, Sudan, Syria, Tunisia, Turkey, the United Arab Emirates, and Yemen. Finally, in Iran, all bank assets are held in *sharī'ah*-compliant banks, following the Law for Usury-Free Banking passed in 1983.

[25] Skewness decreases from 6.04 to 0.76 after taking the natural log of all bank assets as a percent of GDP, and from 4.11 to −0.34 in the case of Islamic assets.

[26] Individuals with religious-based objections to conventional banks may opt to deposit their savings in an Islamic bank, if one is available. In this case, they will respond that they are actively using bank services and will not be asked the set of questions about why they do not bank. Alternatively, even if the availability of a *sharī'ah*-compliant bank is not sufficient to get them to invest their savings in such a financial institution, it may reduce their religious-based objections to banking since there is an available banking option that complies with religious regulation.

3.2 Assessing the Faith-based Transvaluation

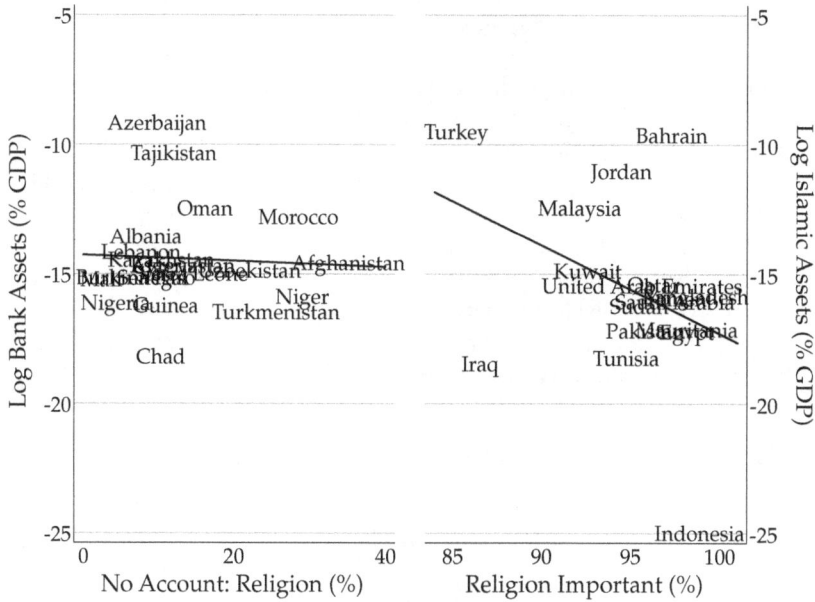

FIGURE 3.6 Faith and Bank Assets across the Muslim World
Notes: Natural logarithm of assets held in all banks (% GDP), across the percent of respondents who report they do not have a bank account because of religion; and of assets held in Islamic banks (% GDP), across the percent of respondents who report that religion is important in their daily lives.

correlation between the two ($r=-0.083$) (Figure 3.6). This means that the monetary holdings in conventional banks are somewhat lower in Muslim countries where many people cite religious reasons for not having a bank account (e.g., Niger and Afghanistan). But the relationship is nowhere near statistically significant, and there are numerous exceptions to the general trend. For example, Chad has the lowest level of conventional bank savings in the entire sample, but very few Chadians respondents cite religious reasons for not investing.

While this weak cross-national pattern lends some support to the presumption that religious beliefs keep the faithful from investing in banks, it is possible that the real relationship is much stronger, but that the comparison I have conducted is being muddied by the availability of *sharīʿah*-compliant banks in some countries. This would be the case if their availability reduces religious obstacles to banking, on the one hand, and increases (overall) bank assets, on the other.[27] Given this, it seems important to ask whether the use of Islamic

---

[27] To test for this possibility directly, I ask whether the availability of Islamic banks significantly reduces religious obstacles to banking. Creating a binary indicator of whether there is at least one *sharīʿah*-compliant bank operating in the country, I look to see whether the proportion of respondents who cite religious reasons for not having a bank account is lower in places with an active Islamic banking sector. But the results indicate no statistically significant difference between the two sets of countries.

banks reflects religious beliefs in countries that have access to them. A comparison of Islamic bank assets (as a percent of GDP) and Gallup's estimate of the importance of religion in each country is also presented in Figure 3.6. Remarkably, it reveals that there is *less* Islamic banking in countries with a higher degree of religiosity. The negative correlation in this case is larger ($r= -0.369$) and approaching statistical significance despite the small sample size. In additional analysis, I confirm that this pattern holds across individuals as well, returning to the Findex survey data on the use of banks. Across all Muslim-plurality countries, as well in the subset without an Islamic bank, I find that average levels of piety tend to be associated with *higher* levels of conventional bank usage, even after accounting for other individual- and national-level covariates (Online Appendix Table OA.8).

3.2.4 Faith and the Success of Islamic-Based Parties

My final test of the faith-based theory of transvaluation examines cross-temporal trends in the Turkish case. In Chapter 1, I described an interesting juxtaposition: on the one hand, there is a common assumption that the rise of the Islamic AKP is based on a religious resurgence in this historically secular country (Roy 2012; Yeşilada and Noordijk 2010); on the other, there is at least some empirical evidence that indicates little change in piety over time (Çarkoğlu and Toprak 2007). But that initial cross-temporal comparison focused on just one measure of piety – women's head-covering – over just two points in time. To really assess the relationship between faith and the popularity of Islamic parties in Turkey, it is helpful to include additional measures and observe them over a longer period, alongside temporal trends in Islamic party vote share.[28]

Islamic-based parties have been competing in Turkey long before the rise of AKP – as far back as 1973 – and have organized under a variety of labels: from the National Salvation Party (Millî Selamet Partisi, MSP) (1973–1977); to the Welfare Party (Refah Partisi, RP) (1987–1995); the Virtue Party (Fazilet Partisi, FP) (1999); and, most recently, the AKP, the Felicity Party (Saadet Partisi, SP), and the People's Voice Party (Halkın Sesi Partisi, HAS). Since 1987 there has been an almost monotonic increase in popular support for these parties, culminating in six consecutive general-election victories for the AKP beginning in 2002.[29] To capture their overall popularity, I calculate the national vote

---

[28] In her book, *The Mobilization of Political Islam in Turkey*, Banu Eligur contends that "[t]here seems to be a correlation between the increased number of Qur'an courses, *imam-hatip* [religious vocational high] schools, and mosques ... and the mobilization of the Islamist movement in Turkey" (2010, p. 26), but provides little evidence to support this assertion. What follows is an empirical test of her argument.

[29] The June, 2015 election is often interpreted as a loss for the AKP, since their vote share declined for the first time since 2002, despite remaining the largest party in the Grand National Assembly (Kemahlıoğlu 2015). Regardless, through some political maneuvering, the party returned to its previous level of support in the elections that followed in November, albeit through some less-than-democratic means (Bardakci 2016; Çarkoğlu and Yıldırım 2015). Meanwhile, the results

3.2 Assessing the Faith-based Transvaluation

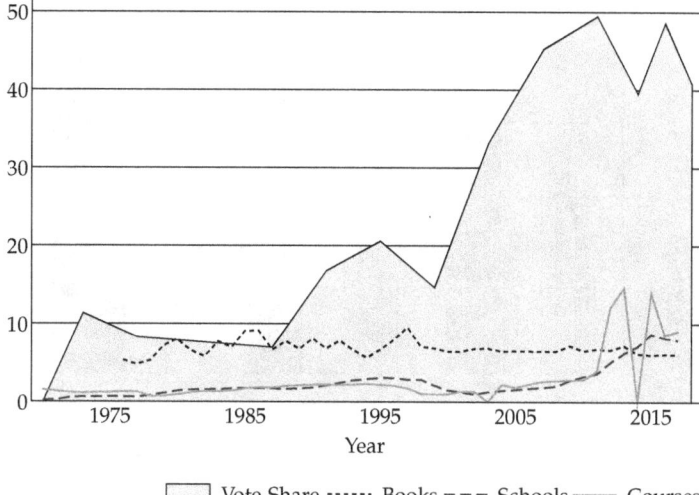

FIGURE 3.7 Faith and Islamic Party Vote Share in Turkey
Notes: National vote share for Turkey's Islamic parties (MSP, RP, FP, AKP, SP, HAS) in general elections and piety: the percent of books and periodicals published on religious subjects, the number of mosques per 10,000 people, the percent of high school students enrolled in religious vocational schools, and enrollment in public Qur'an courses (per 1,000 people).

share for all Islamic-based parties between 1973 and 2018 using official elections results published by the Turkish Institute of Statistics. I then compare these to different cross-temporal measures of religiosity.

Observational measures of faith in Turkey are hard to come by since the Turkish government makes no official record of its citizens' religion, let alone the intensity of their religious beliefs (Dündar 2000). Still, I have been able to identify four measures of religiosity in the aggregate, ones that are more likely to reflect the "demand" for religion among average Turks, as opposed to the "supply" of religious goods by the state or other actors.[30] First, the Ministry of Culture and Tourism (Kültür ve Turizm Bakanlığı) publishes statistics on the number books and periodicals published in Turkey, including those on religious topics, beginning in 1976.[31] Using these, I calculate the share of all materials published on religious subjects. Second, the Ministry of Education produces annual accounts of enrollment, including in public religious vocational schools (*imam hatip liseleri*), for most years since 1968. I normalize

---

of 2018 election may not have been free of manipulation (Cook 2018), although no hard evidence has yet to indicate that the party would not have won a free and fair contest.

[30] This criterion excluded the possibility of using data on the construction of new mosques, which is largely directed by the Office of Religious Affairs (Diyanet İşleri Başkanlığı) and its foundation (Diyanet Vakfı) (Turan 2008).

[31] Since 2012, the data have been published by the General Directorate of Libraries and Publications (Kütüphaneler ve Yayımlar Genel Müdürlüğü) as part of its ISBN statistics.

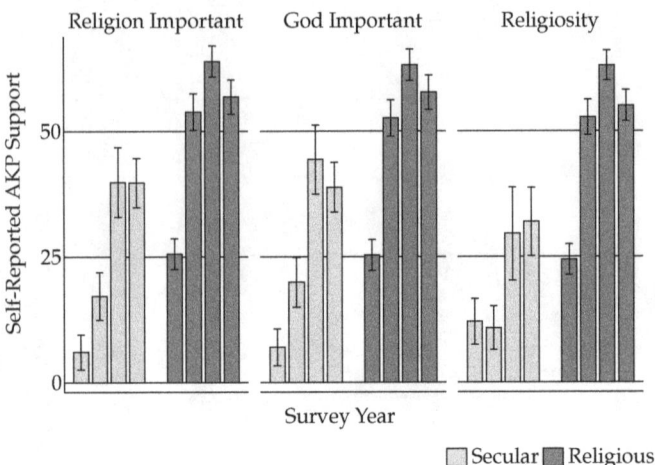

FIGURE 3.8 Faith and Support for the AKP
Notes: Levels of support for the AKP in a hypothetical election across survey years (2001, 2007, 2009, 2011), comparing religious and secular respondents.

these using annual population estimates, published by the Turkish Institute of Statistics. Finally, using statistics on informal education, I trace enrollment in public Qur'anic courses, also normalized per capita.

Figure 3.7 displays the national vote share of Islamic-based parties in each general election in Turkey since 1973, along with the cross-temporal trends in religiosity. While the vote share of Islamic parties has steadily increased since 1987, all three measures of religiosity – the percent of books published on religious topics, the percent of high school students enrolled in religious vocational schools, and enrollment in Qur'anic courses per capita (1,000) – have remained remarkably stable over the same period. If there was any change that preceded the AKP's rise, it was a *decline* in religious high school enrollment after education reforms of the late 1990s (Özdalga 1999; Pak 2004). More recently, there has been a slight increase in *imam hatip* enrollment rates as well as a surge in enrollment in Qur'anic courses, but this has occurred just as Islamic party vote share has stabilized.[32]

The empirical patterns displayed in Figure 3.7 present somewhat of a puzzle: if aggregate piety has remained relatively stable over time, what explains the recent rise in the success of Islamic-based parties in Turkey? Indeed, what has changed in recent years is not the percentage of voters who are religious but the rate of support for Islamic parties among *secular*, conservative voters. Figure 3.8 displays rates of support for the AKP in EVS and WVS surveys conducted

---

[32] The empirical patterns presented here raise the possibility of reverse causality: that the success of Islamic-based parties has created an uptick in religiosity among the Turkish public, a hypothesis raised by Yeşilada and Noordijk (2010), among others.

3.2 Assessing the Faith-based Transvaluation

in 2001, 2007, 2009, and 2011.[33] I compare levels of AKP support among religious voters to those among secular ones, as defined by the three markers of faith introduced above: the importance of religion in respondents' lives, the importance of God, and whether they self-identify as a religious person.[34] The comparison reveals that, while support for the AKP has more than doubled among religious voters between 2001 and 2011, support for the party has increased *more than five-fold* among non-religious voters over the same period. This means that by 2011, over 40 percent of voters for whom religion is not very important were openly stating their support for an Islamic-based party, as were almost 40 percent of voters for whom God is not very important. Meanwhile, support for the party among religious voters even saw a slight decline between 2009 and 2011. Robust support for the AKP among non-religious voters challenges a central assumption of the faith-based explanation for the party's success.

Although the AKP has been cited as an example for other Islamic-based parties in other contexts (Çavdar 2006; Nasr 2005; Torelli 2012; Tuğal 2016), it is possible that these results are anomalous to the Turkish case. The AKP's ability to appeal to secular voters could be a function of its need to moderate when competing for votes in a largely secular, democratic country (Gurses 2014; Mecham 2004; Tezcür 2010). It is important, therefore, to establish that the pattern holds in other, more religious, less democratic cases. Is there evidence that secular voters support Islamic-based parties in other contexts? To address this question, I extend the above analysis to twelve Muslim countries in which Islamic-based parties actively compete and for which there is available survey data: Algeria, Bangladesh, Indonesia, Iraq, Jordan, Libya, Malaysia, Morocco, Pakistan, Palestine, Tunisia, and Yemen. In many of these countries, multiple Islamic-based parties compete for votes, so I calculate the percent of respondents – religious and secular, using the same three measures – that openly support any Islamic-based party, as identified by Kurzman and Naqvi (2010a).[35]

---

[33] Party preferences are elicited from the question *"If there were a national election tomorrow, for which party on this list would you vote?"* with responses coded one (1) for the AKP and zero (0) otherwise.

[34] For ease of comparison, I recode these into binary indicators of faith. The three indicators are defined: one (1) if respondents report that religion is "very important" in their lives and zero (0) otherwise; one (1) if they say that God is "very important"; and one (1) if they define themselves as "a religious person."

[35] Islamic parties in Algeria include the Movement for the Society of Peace (Ḥarakat Mujtamaʿ as-Silm, HMS) and the Islamic Renaissance Movement (Ḥarakat an-Nahḍah al-Islāmiyya, MN). In Bangladesh: Islamic Society Jamaat-e-Islami. In Indonesia: the National Awakening Party (Partai Kengkitan Bangsa, PKB); the United Development Party (Partai Persatuan Pembangunan, PPP); the National Mandate Party (Partai Amanat Nasional, PAN); the Crescent Star Party (Partai Bulan Bintang, PBB); the Prosperous Justice Party (Partai Keadilan Sejahtera, PKS); the Ulema National Awakening Party (Partai Kebangkitan Nasional Ulama, PKNU); and the Reform Star Party (Partai Bintang Reformasi). In Iraq: the Islamic Daʿwa Party (Ḥizb al-Daʿwa al-Islāmiyya); the Iraqi Islamic Party (Ḥizb al-Islāmī al-ʿIraqi, IIP); the Kurdistan Islamic Union (Yekgirtûy Islâmî Kurdistan, KIU); the Sadrist Movement (al-Tayyār al-Sadri),

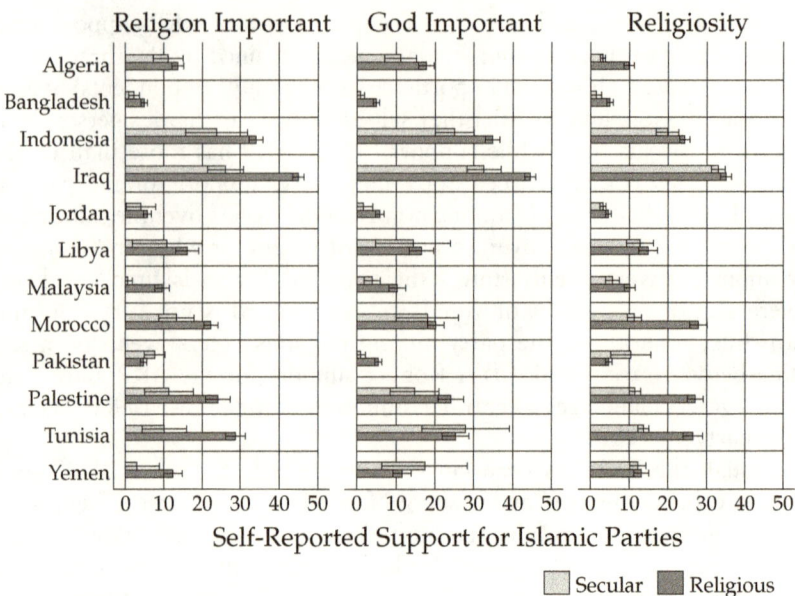

FIGURE 3.9 Faith and Support for Islamic Parties, Cross-Nationally
Notes: Levels of support for Islamic political parties among religious and secular voters. Averages with 95 percent confidence bands.

The results, illustrated in Figure 3.9, indicate that it is not often the case that religious voters support Islamic parties significantly more than secular ones do. In addition, there are important inconsistencies within countries across the three measures. For example, while respondents who emphasize the importance of God and religion in their lives are more likely to support Islamic

also known as the Liberal Bloc (Kotlat al-Ahrar); and the Islamic Virtue Party (Hizb al-Fadhila) In Jordan: the Islamic Action Front (Jabhat al-ʻAmal al-Islami, IAF), also identified as the "Muslim Brotherhood," and the Islamic Centrist Party (Hizb al-Wasat al-Islamiyya, ICP). In Libya: The Justice and Construction Party (Hizb al-ʻAdala wa al-Bina). In Malaysia: the Islamic Party of Malaysia (Parti Islam Se-Malaysia, PAS). In Morocco: the Justice and Development Party (Hizb al-ʻAdalah wal-Tanmiyah, PJD) and the Party of Renaissance and Virtue (Hizb al-Nahda waʼl-Fadila). In Pakistan: the Islamic Party (Jamaat-e-Islami), and the Assembly of Pakistani Clergy (Jamiat Ulema-e-Pakistan, JUP), as well as a catch-all "Religious Groups" category. (Both the Pakistan Muslim League (Nawaz, PML-N) and the Pakistan Movement for Justice (Pakistan Tehreek-e-Insaf), although often considered Islamic parties, are not listed as such by Kurzman and Naqvi (2010b) and are therefore not included.) In Palestine: the Islamic Resistance Movement (Ḥarakat al-Muqāwamah al-ʼIslāmiyyah Hamas), as well as independent Islamic candidates. (Kurzman and Naqvi (2010b) do not include the Islamic Jihad Movement in Palestine (Ḥarakat al-Jihād al-Islāmi fi Filastīn) in their list of Islamic parties in Palestine.) In Tunisia: the Renaissance Party (Hizbu Ḥarakatu n-Nahḍah). (Kurzman and Naqvi (2010b) do not include the Party of Freedom (Hizb al-Tahrir), nor the Supporters of Islamic Law in Tunisia (Ansar al-Sharia in Tunisia).) In Yemen: the Yemeni Association for Reform (at-Tajammuʼu al-Yamanī lil-Iṣlāḥ).

parties in Iraq, those who self-identify as religious are less likely to do so. Indeed, only in Bangladesh, Indonesia, and Malaysia is there a statistically significant difference in the expected direction across all three measures. Outside of these three countries, across twenty-four tests, the faith-based theory is supported in only seven. These findings are in line with a small number of studies which note the rising popularity of Islamic parties among secular voters (Gorman 2018; Hamayotsu 2011; Hicks 2012).

Taken together, the evidence stands quite strongly against the empirical expectations of the faith-based theory. The most pious individuals do not seem to be more willing to bear the costs of political participation. Patterns of bank savings across the Muslim world are not explained by religious beliefs, about savings or otherwise. Finally, there is little evidence that the success of Islamic political parties is a reflection of piety. Instead, a new puzzle has been identified – high levels of support for Islamic parties among *secular* voters – a phenomenon that the faith-based theory struggles to explain.

3.3 THE ROLE OF INFORMATION IN ISLAMIC POLITICS

While the faith-based theory cannot account for the support of Islamic parties among secular voters, the information theory has a straightforward explanation: in a setting where political information about party platforms is limited, voters – religious and secular alike – simply have a better sense of what Islamic-based parties are likely to do. This could be the case either because references to Islam signal a particular policy orientation (Brooke 2017; Pepinsky, Liddle, and Mujani 2012; Roháč 2013) or a commitment to change (Dzutsati, Siroky, and Dzutsev 2016), because party leaders are able to tap into dense Islamic social networks to communicate their positions more effectively (Masoud 2014), or because Islamic politicians have a better reputation for following through on their promises (Cammett and Luong 2014; Henderson and Kuncoro 2011).

These different strands of the information-based theory have a number of empirical implications that can be directly tested: first, that political information is generally low in the Muslim world, so that citizens there have an especially difficult time correctly identifying what different political movements stand for; second, that in this under-informed environment, Islamic-based parties are more identifiable, either because they have a *unique* policy position, compared to their competitors, or because their position is more *precisely* identified by observers; and, lastly, that Islamic-based organizations are seen as more trustworthy than their secular rivals. In the sections that follow, I test of these hypotheses, in turn.

3.3.1 Are Muslim Voters Under-Informed?

I begin by assessing how well-informed citizens of the Muslim world are about all of the different parties competing in national elections. In the absence of questions about political information in my larger cross-national dataset, I turn to a reasonable proxy from another source. The Comparative Study of Electoral Systems (CSES) conducts surveys in the lead-up to elections around the world and often asks voters to place each local party on a single left–right spectrum. Across its four waves, the CSES has surveyed three Muslim countries a total of four times: Albania in 2005, Kyrgyzstan, also in 2005, and Turkey in both 2011 and 2015. Of these, only Turkey has an active Islamic-based political party competing, so I focus on it alone. I assess the quality of political information in Turkey, relative to the other CSES countries, in two ways: first, by calculating the standard deviation of left–right placements for each party across all respondents, to capture domestic disagreement about the parties' positions, a plausible indicator of political uncertainty; and, second, by assessing the proportion of respondents who say that they "don't know" each party's position, a more direct measure of uncertainty. In both cases, I take the average across all parties in each country.[36]

On both metrics, Turkey does not appear to be an especially information-poor environment. On the first – the standard deviation in estimated party positions across respondents – Turkey falls squarely in the middle: twenty-sixth of the fifty-five countries included in the CSES dataset. On the ten-point left–right spectrum, the spread of Turkish responses averages 2.36 across the two surveys, while the average across all fifty-five countries is 2.38.[37] In general, then, Turkish respondents are quite average by international standards when it comes to agreeing on where their political parties fall from left to right. Moreover, very few Turkish respondents opt out of the exercise entirely by saying they "don't know" the placement of parties: across the fifty-five countries in the CSES dataset, Turkey ranks fifth, with only 5.1 percent of respondents, on average, saying they do not know enough about the different parties to give a precise answer.[38] The cross-national average was just over 17.8 percent, ranging from none to 65.6 percent.

3.3.2 The Clarity of Islamic-Based Party Platforms

Even if the political information environment is not poor, overall, Islamic-based parties could still have an advantage if their policy position is especially distinctive, relative to those of their competitors. To assess the relative "uniqueness" of Islamic party platforms, I estimate the various parties' positions in two ways: first, using the distribution of policy preferences of their supporters; and, second, using the range of party positions as identified by a survey of experts.

---

[36] I compare Turkey to the other countries represented in the CSES, most of which have had a longer experience with competitive democratic elections, meaning they are likely to have a better developed information environment. This biases the comparison in favor of the information theory.

[37] The average distribution of responses in each of the two Turkish surveys was roughly equivalent: 2.35 in the 2011 survey and 2.38 in the 2015, ranked eighty-seventh and ninety-second, respectively, across the 164 CSES surveys.

[38] Across all 164 surveys, Turkey ranked sixteenth on this metric in 2011 (1.1%) and forty-sixth in 2015 (9.1%).

3.3 The Role of Information in Islamic Politics

In the latter case, I was fortunate to find an expert survey of party positions that includes a Muslim country with an active Islamic-based party: the main parties that competed in the 2002 Turkish general election – including the AKP – are covered by Benoit and Laver's *Party Policy in Modern Democracies*.[39] Using the 2001 wave of the Turkish EVS, I was also able to identify the supporters of each of these parties.[40] Using both data sources, I compare the parties' positions, as assessed by the experts (N=29) and as defined by their self-identified supporters. I do so along four key dimensions: left–right orientation, economic policy, social policy, and religion.[41]

Figure 3.10 illustrates the distribution of the parties' positions according to their supporters and the experts along the four dimensions, ranging from left/liberal (negative values) to right/conservative (positive values). In terms of uniqueness, the Islamic AKP ranks quite low, overlapping with at least one other party on every dimension, across both measures. Indeed, both measures agree that the party is not statistically distinguishable from the center-right DYP on any issue, including religion. Rather than representing a unique platform, the AKP appears to be in stiff competition with a number right-wing

---

[39] The main parties that competed in the 2002 general elections include the Kurdish-based Democratic People's Party (Demokratik Halk Partisi, DEHAP), the center-left Republican People's Party (Cumhuriyet Halk Partisi, CHP) and Democratic Left Party (Demokratik Sol Parti, DSP), the center-right Motherland Party (Anavatan Partisi, ANAP) and True Path Party (Doğru Yol Partisi, DYP), and the far-right Nationalist Action Party (Milliyetçi Hareket Partisi, MHP), alongside the Islamic-based AKP.

[40] For reasons that are unclear (even after reading through the related methodological report), the AKP was not offered as a response category in the 2001 WVS in Turkey when respondents were asked about their party preferences.

[41] To assess parties' left–right orientation, Benoit and Laver (2006) ask experts to "locate each party on a general left–right dimension, taking all aspects of party policy into account." Survey respondents were told that "[i]n political matters, people talk of 'the left' and 'the right'" and then asked to place themselves on a scale from left (1) to right (10). This survey measure, as well as those that follow, was standardized to have a mean of zero and a standard deviation of one. Meanwhile, responses to the expert survey – ranging from 1 to 20 – were transformed to have the same basic properties. Economic policy in the expert survey contrasted "raising taxes to increase public services" and "promoting maximum state ownership of business and industry" to "cutting public services to cut taxes" and "opposing all state ownership of business and industry." In the survey, I took the first principal component factor of responses to the following statements: "Private ownership should be increased vs. Government ownership of business should be increased"; "People should take more responsibility to provide for themselves vs. The government should take more responsibility to ensure that everyone is provided for"; and "Competition is good – it stimulates people to work hard and develop new ideas vs. Competition is harmful – it brings out the worst in people." In the expert survey, social policy contrasts parties who favor "liberal policies on matters such as abortion, homosexuality, and euthanasia" from those who oppose them. In the survey, I used the first principal component factor of responses to three questions about the "justifiability" of abortion, homosexuality, and euthanasia. Finally, parties were evaluated by experts in terms of whether they support "religious principles in politics" or secular ones. To capture this among voters, I calculated the first principal component factor of responses to two statements: "Politicians who don't believe in God are unfit for public office" and "It would be better if more people with strong religious beliefs held public office."

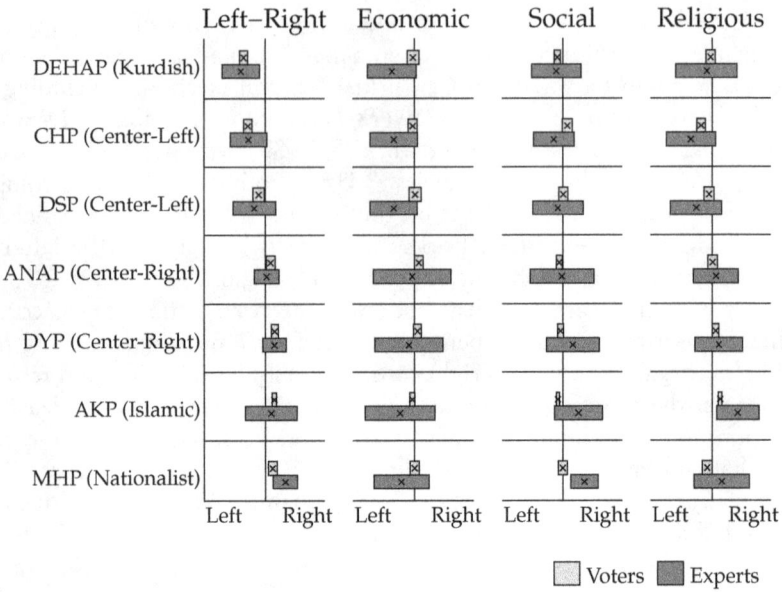

FIGURE 3.10 Policy Positions of Turkish Political Parties
Notes: Policy positions of largest parties competing in 2002 Turkish general election, across four dimensions. As defined by self-identified supporters of each party and a panel of "experts." Bars indicate 95 percent confidence bands around each average.

parties, on social issues, and with some left-of-center parties, on economic ones. This means that voters who support the AKP are choosing it over a number of other parties that could plausibly represent their interests.

Even if the AKP's informational advantage is not in the uniqueness of its policy platform, it could be based on its easy identifiability. Comparing the distribution of the experts' assessments of AKP policy positions relative to that of the other parties, I can gauge the extent to which they can better identify (and agree on) what the party stands for.[42] I find that the experts converge in their evaluations of the AKP only in the case of its position on religious policy, and even there, the spread of their evaluations of ANAP's position is roughly similar ($\sigma = 0.651$ vs. 0.695). When it comes to evaluating the parties' left–right orientation, the experts disagreed about the AKP's position *the most*, and the spread of their assessments of the AKP's economic position was the second highest in the group. In other words, the party's policy platform is not clearly identifiable to the experts, even on issues of religion.

Similarly, among Turkish respondents in the two waves of the CSES, there was not a lot of agreement about the left–right position of the AKP ($\sigma = 2.44$ in

[42] In assessing relative identifiability, the distribution of supporter preferences is less useful. The variation in that metric speaks more to the level of similarity and coordination among the parties' constituents. On this measure, the AKP's constituents stand out for being particularly in sync with one another.

3.3 The Role of Information in Islamic Politics

2011 and 2.03 in 2015, 2.23 on average) compared to other parties. This was just below average ($\mu=2.36$), but hardly the best-defined of the major parties, an honor enjoyed by the CHP. At the same time, plenty of respondents said that they did not know what the party's left–right position was: 4.2 percent across the two surveys. Again, this was below average ($\mu=5.1$ percent), but well above the CHP (2.3 percent).[43]

3.3.3 Reputational Signals from Islamic Politicians

The final information-based theory to consider is one which focuses less on parties' stated positions and more on their likelihood of following through on their promises. If references to Islam are used to signal a reputation for good governance, then Islamic-based parties will have an advantage over their secular rivals vis-à-vis political trust. Assessing the confidence that individuals have in different organizations – from parties to banks to business associations, Islamic-based or otherwise – is not straightforward. Even when surveys ask respondents about their level of trust in different institutions, they tend to refer to umbrella categories – for example, "government," "political parties," "major companies" – rather than specific organizations or movements. So to assess confidence in Islamic-based organizations relative to secular ones, I use respondents' self-reported trust in "government" and leverage variation across two dimensions: whether the respondents support an Islamic-based party versus a secular one; and whether that party is currently part of the governing coalition. In doing so, I assume that if respondents' preferred party is government, their assessment of that party will be reflected in their assessment of the government as a whole.

Across the countries included in the cross-national dataset that have one or more Islamic-based political party, only four – Iraq, Jordan, Palestine, and Turkey – have had both Islamic and secular parties, in and out of government.[44] In each of these four cases, I calculate the percent of respondents in each of four categories – Islamic-in-government, Islamic-out, Non-Islamic-in-government, Non-Islamic-out – who report having no confidence in the government. In general, the highest level of distrust is among supporters of Islamic-based parties that are out of government (43.7 percent across all four countries), followed by supporters of other parties that are not part of the governing coalition (33.2%). But among those whose preferred party is represented in government, the pattern is reversed, although the difference is smaller – 20.4 percent of those who support non-Islamic parties and only 15.2 percent of those who support Islamic-based ones.[45] In other words, there is at least

---

[43] Indeed, in the 2011 survey, the AKP's "don't know" rate was below the CHP, while in 2015, nearly 7 percent of respondents could not identify the party's position, more than any other party except the HDP.

[44] Data on political trust and party preferences is available from the Arab Barometer in addition to the EVS and WVS.

[45] I see the same pattern in three of the four countries: supporters of governing Islamic-based parties are less distrusting than supporters of other governing parties in Iraq (18.1% vs. 26.8%),

some evidence of a reputational advantage for Islamic-based organizations in this small subset of cases. Moving forward, the role of political trust will need to be carefully considered, alongside other explanations for the Islamic advantage.

3.4 THE PUZZLE OF THE ISLAMIC ADVANTAGE

This second chapter has tested empirical implications of three existing explanations for the Islamic advantage: grievances, faith, and information. Across a number of tests, evidence in support of the theories has been slim. Overall, citizens in the Muslim world do not appear to be under-motivated or misinformed, and although the costs of political and economic activity are indeed higher in the region, there is little evidence that personal religious beliefs help to attenuate them to support participation.

Taken together, the empirical findings of the chapter are unable to address the puzzle of the participation gap in the Muslim world. There are considerable obstacles to political and economic mobilization in the region; but faith alone is unable to sufficiently address them. And yet, Islamic-based movements – both political and economic – are clearly succeeding: I have presented evidence of the growth of both Islamic-based political parties and Islamic-compliant banking. But rather than being buoyed by a religious resurgence, these Islamic-based activities and organizations appear to be supported by many secular individuals. It would seem, therefore, that Islam is ameliorating the obstacles to mobilization for them too, even though they are not deeply faithful.

The questions that remain at the end of this chapter concern the obstacles to political and economic participation in Muslim-majority countries: What is keeping individuals in this part of the world from joining together to affect change, to make their voices heard, and to help better themselves economically? And how are references to Islam able to address these obstacles, among the faithful and the secular alike? In the next two chapters, I present an alternative theory of the Islamic advantage, one that puts greater emphasis on the collective dimensions of both mobilization and Islam. In Chapter 4, I begin by explaining why individuals in the Muslim world tend to avoid taking part in collective political and economic activities; then in Chapter 5, I explain how references to Islam help to overcome these obstacles, to the advantage of Islamic-based movements. Both dynamics, I argue, can be explained in terms of trust.

Jordan (7.1%, 17.7%), and Turkey (12.0%, 18.1%), though there is no statistically significant difference in Palestine (18.4%, 17.8%). An illustration of all of these trends is displayed in Online Appendix Figure OA.3

4

Generalized Distrust and the Participation Gap in the Muslim World

> I am a Turk, honest and hardworking. My principle is to protect the younger, to respect the elder, to love my homeland and my nation more than myself.
>
> Turkish Student Oath (*Öğrenci Andı*)

Over the first two chapters of this book, the puzzle of Islamic-based movements in Turkey and the Muslim world has come into sharper focus. In Chapter 2.1, I presented evidence of a "participation gap" in Muslim-plurality states, where individuals are less willing to take part in collective political and economic activities. Despite this general deficit in collective action in the region, there is a sense that political and economic movements that made regular reference to Islam – from Islamic-based political parties, to banks and business associations – have an advantage when it comes to mobilizing individual supporters to join them. In Chapter 2.2, I introduced the three existing explanations for this apparent Islamic advantage – grievances, faith, and information – defining each in terms of how it sees the main obstacle to collective action and why it believes Islamic-based groups are able to overcome it. After dedicating a section of Chapter 3 to testing each theory, I found that neither information nor motivation are lacking in the Muslim world. Further, personal religious beliefs do not seem able to attenuate the sizable costs and risks of being politically and economically active in the region.

As such, I am left with the same two critical questions to address: what are the obstacles to political and economic activity in the Muslim world? And how do references to Islam help Islamic-based groups address these obstacles? In developing my own theory of the Islamic advantage, my initial point of departure from the three existing explanations is the observation that any one individual's decision to become politically or economically active – to join a political movement, to contribute to a public good, to vote for a political party, to invest in a bank, to trade with a particular company – is rarely made in isolation. Instead, individual decisions to participate in collective activities are inherently interdependent to a degree that has not been appreciated in the existing literature.

Consider the following tweet sent during the protest events that erupted in and around Istanbul's Gezi Park in the summer of 2013. Looking not simply to recruit other protesters but to express his intentions and expectations, Rob (@robi) wrote, "Does anyone want to go to Ankara to support [the movement]? We are going today by car. Get in touch, we are expecting your support. (RTplz) #direngeziparki."[1] His request that his call for participation be retweeted speaks to the value he places on this information being spread beyond his immediate social circle, and in a manner that he can track. While it is clear that he is personally motivated to participate, his tweet recognizes the inherently collective dimensions of his individual decision to join the mass protest. Despite having gathered some friends to join – intimated by the repeated use of the word "we" (*biz*) – he looks out to a broader circle to join too, so that he (and his friends) will not go it alone.

In his efforts to share information about his intentions and to monitor how that information is disseminated, this individual actor seeks to create "common knowledge" about his intention to participate. He is not merely telling others about what he plans to do, but also tracking that they have understood his message through retweets and responses.[2] The need for this type of reciprocal information – that is, that you know what I know, and I know that you know this, *ad infinitum* and vice versa – is clearly important when trying to identify just how many people are likely to show up for a mass protest, but it is also relevant for other types of collective political and economic activities, including the coordination of individual votes within a large electoral district (Myatt and Fisher 2002) and investments in a collective enterprise, such as a formal bank or savings club (Besley, Coate, and Loury 1993).

The need for common knowledge in these individual decisions could well explain the role that social media played during the Arab Spring and the Gezi Park protests in Turkey (Eltantawy and Wiest 2011; Tufekci and Wilson 2012). But merely tweeting one's support is insufficient, as it seems to have been during the Green Movement in Iran (Esfandiari 2010; Tusa 2013), as well as in the Egyptian Arab Spring (Lynch 2011; Tufekci and Wilson 2012). In my own experience observing mobilization efforts in Istanbul during the Gezi Park events, there were countless instances in which promises to attend or support were tweeted or posted on Facebook but never actually materialized. This reversal can be explained by the incentives that individuals have to play it safe and easy. Broken promises of this kind result from an uncomfortable truth:

---

[1] Posted on June 13, 2013. Original tweet, in Turkish: "*Anakaraya destek için gitmek isteyenler var mı? Bugün araba kaldıracağız. Ulaşım destekleriniz beliyoruz.* (RTplz) #direngeziparki (#resistegezipark)."

[2] Michael Suk-Young Chwe defines common knowledge thusly: "We [can] say that an event or fact is common knowledge among a group of people if everyone knows it, everyone knows that everyone knows it, everyone knows that everyone knows that everyone knows it, and so on" (2003, pp. 9–10).

many are interested in the movement succeeding, but not all have an incentive to put in the work needed to make that happen.

The incentive to stay home is at the heart of the "free-rider problem," an obstacle to collective action that is especially acute when the benefits of success would naturally extend to everyone, regardless of whether they helped make it happen (Olson 2002). This dynamic of unfulfilled promises was first been developed in the context of large-scale political organizations, but it is just as relevant for other types of collective activities, such as commitments to support small parties on election day, to boycott a certain establishment, or to continue making pre-committed investments as economic conditions change. In all of these cases, what is required is not just common knowledge of others' intentions, but an expectation about whether they are actually likely to follow through on the promises they make. Are they the type of person to succumb to the incentives to free ride? Or can they be counted on to do the right thing?

The expectation that others will follow through on their promises is a common definition of trust. In the case described here, the expectation of follow-through is not between an individual citizen and her government (i.e., "political trust") but among individual citizens themselves, what is often referred to as "interpersonal" or "social trust." In the Muslim world, this conceptualization of trust is similar to the Turkish word *güven*, *amān* in Arabic, or *etemad* in Persian (Rosen 2000). According to Zand (1972), a need for interpersonal trust arises in all cases in which individual decisions are interdependent and where there is some uncertainty surrounding whether others will do as they say.

In the pages that follow, I describe just how prevalent both interdependence and uncertainty are in citizens' everyday political and economic decision making. Based on this, I make the case that trust plays a critical role in the types of political and economic activities being considered in this book. I explore different kinds of interpersonal trust and the types of activities that each can support. Ultimately, I argue that broad forms of "non-particularized trust" – not based on direct previous experience with the entrusted – are often needed to support most latent activities. I then explore levels of trust and trustworthiness in the Muslim world, uncovering a deficit in the broadest form of non-particularized trust – so-called "generalized trust," an expectation of trustworthiness from "most people." Remarkably, I find this trust deficit in the Muslim world despite the healthy levels of honesty in the region. I suggest that this implies a potential for collective action, but only if trust expectations can be improved. Otherwise, generalized distrust is hypothesized as a key reason for the participation gap in the Muslim world. (Islam's solution to this trust problem is the topic of the Chapter 5.)

4.1 THE VALUE OF INTERPERSONAL TRUST

Interpersonal trust has been called an "important lubricant of the social system" (Arrow 1972, p. 23), supporting cooperation and coordination in a number of settings. It can be defined as an expectation of honesty or reciprocity from another person when they have incentives to be dishonest or to defect. As Zand defines it, trust is any action

> that (a) increase[s] one's vulnerability, (b) to another whose behavior is not under one's control, (c) in a situation in which the penalty (disutility) one suffers if the other abuses that vulnerability is greater than the benefit (utility) one gains if the other does not abuse that vulnerability (1972, p. 230).

In other words, trust is required in the face of (a) interdependence, (b) uncertainty, and (c) rationality. Assuming the latter is a basic requirement for most decision making, two basic trust conditions remain: interdependence and uncertainty.

In the sections that follow, I describe each of these conditions in turn, emphasizing that both are common in most political and economic activities involving more than one person. Based on this, I argue that interpersonal trust is a necessary condition for political and economic participation. Different forms of interpersonal trust address interdependence and uncertainty in different ways, supporting different types of cooperation; but I contend that the broadest form – generalized, non-particularized trust – is needed under most conditions.

4.1.1 Interdependence of Individual Decisions to Participate

The "vulnerability" that creates interdependence according to Zand (1972) is not just a function of the fact that Person A, she who trusts, asks the entrusted (Person B) to do something of inherent value to her. It is also a reflection of the fact that her (A's) best course of action depends almost entirely on what he (B) is likely to do. She cannot decide what to do (i.e., whether or not to trust him) without considering what he might do. And she is unlikely to get what she wants without his cooperation. In other words, the success of their exchange hinges on both of them: she must trust him, and he must follow through and behave in an honest way that is worthy of her trust.

This interdependence is perhaps most clear in an interpersonal exchange between two individuals. But there are similar dynamics at play in groups, particularly in large, anonymous latent ones.[3] In these group interactions, interdependence stems from the same two principles. First, the outcome is still of value to each participant. As Brian Barry notes,

> whatever the reason why a person may attach himself to a cause, more enthusiasm for its pursuit is likely to be elicited if it looks as if it has a chance of succeeding than if it appears to be a forlorn hope. Nobody likes to feel that he is wasting his time, and that feeling may be induced by contributing to a campaign which never looks as if it has a chance (1978, p. 30).

---

[3] Indeed, Russell Hardin (1971) famously argues that the collective action problem is essentially a series of interpersonal decisions made between each pair of would-be participants.

4.1 The Value of Interpersonal Trust

No matter how positively an individual evaluates a given objective – the overthrow of a government, the election of a party, the success of an economic exchange – she is unlikely to contribute to that effort unless she feels it is likely to be achieved. At the same time, she knows that it cannot be achieved without others' help. This is the second principle: success in these interactions is a collective endeavor.

On the morning of January 25, 2012, when a large-scale demonstration had been called for in Cairo, early risers looked out their windows and tweeted their concerns: "streets r empty. Police r everywhere. #jan25."[4] As the day progressed, those who took to the streets tweeted to let others know that they were being allowed to march and that their numbers were swelling: "This is great, we r in nayha street, ppl r walking by our side #jan25."[5] They tweeted to encourage others to join them, to help build a critical mass: "our strength is in our collective action. Egyptians, believe in yourselves. BELIEVE IN US. #25jan #egypt."[6]

It is hard to imagine that anyone posting or marching early that day could have foreseen what was about to happen in Tahrir Square. But regardless of the expected outcome, their hopes for any kind of change depended on large numbers of individuals taking to the street, together. In those early tweets, there was a real awareness that no one individual or small group could go it alone, that there was strength in numbers, and that knowledge of those numbers could change the cost–benefit calculations for others. As Dennis Chong notes in the case of the American Civil Rights movement, the success of any large-scale movement critically depends on the total number of supporters. Therefore, before deciding to join in, each would-be participant must ask "whether the movement can attract enough support to stand a reasonable chance of succeeding" (1993, p. 129). In this way, the primary concern about success becomes a concern about adequate numbers. Many of the tweets sent out on that January morning in Cairo aimed to ask, and answer, that precise question.

For a range of political and economic activities, numbers matter for at least two reasons. First, in order to be successful (i.e., to put sufficient pressure on a government and achieve reform, to vote an incumbent out of office, to raise the funds necessary to take advantage of an economic opportunity), a critical mass of participants is required. At the same time, beyond that critical threshold being met and surpassed, the total number of participants will define the expected costs and benefits for each individual who takes part: the chances of success increase as that number grows; meanwhile, the potential costs of participation for each individual decline as the risks involved spread over a larger group.

This dynamic is perhaps clearest in the case of large-scale demonstrations – more protesters equals more pressure and a better chance of reform, as well

---

[4] Hossam's (@3arabawy) tweet came in just before 9:30 AM on January 25 (Idle and Nunns 2011, p. 33).
[5] Tweeted by monashosh (@monashosh) at 1:56 PM on January 25 (p. 35).
[6] Mo-ha-med (@TravellerW) at 2:57 PM on January 25 (p. 36).

as a larger crowd in which to hide if arrests are made or violence is used. But consider the challenge entailed in voting when the party system is so saturated that not every party will win sufficient support to gain representation. Here, where "success" is defined as casting a vote for a party that wins at least one seat, each individual must coordinate with others in their district in order to achieve his objective (Cox 1997; Myatt 2007). A critical number of individual voters will need to vote similarly in order for their joint effort to be successful, and their success (i.e., the number of seats gained) will increase with the total number of supporters. Indeed, even in economic exchanges between as few as two people, there are obvious interdependencies between customer and supplier. Here, the "success" of the exchange depends on goods being delivered and purchased, as promised, once they have been manufactured (Smith 1986; Williamson 1985). Both buyer and seller have to do their part for either to succeed.

Because interdependence is almost always reciprocal (i.e., what Person A should do depends on what Person B is likely to do, and what he should do depends on what he expects her to do) the solution to this thorny issue is information that is *common*: at a minimum, Person A needs to know what Person B is likely to do, but he must also know that she knows this, and she must know that he knows that she knows, and on and on, and vice versa. Developing (and maintaining) this kind common knowledge is difficult (Chwe 2003), and it could well explain the increasingly important role of social media in contemporary political and economic organization around the world.

Facebook posts and tweets can offer individuals the kind of social information they need to formulate an expectation of what others are likely to do. Whether they use that information to inform their expectations, however, hinges on whether they deem those posts and tweets to be *credible*. There is evidence that the Green Movement in Iran failed to some extent because many simply tweeted words of encouragement rather than actually taking to the streets (Esfandiari 2010; Tusa 2013). As game theory would predict, the collective action problem prevailed in this case: cooperation unraveled due to individuals' self-interest in saving their energy and staying home, even when working together could have secured mutually beneficial gains for them all (Hardin 1971). Social media and other forms of communication cannot always address the incentives that each individual has to promise to attend, but ultimately to stay home. In other words, there is another issue to address: that of uncertainty.[7]

4.1.2 The Free-Rider Problem and Uncertainty over Type

The problem with taking Facebook posts, tweets, and other declarations at face value is the fact that people have real incentives to say they will do

---

[7] Promises made but ultimately reversed are not necessarily signs of malice. Those who promise to participate may very well hope that the effort succeeds. In fact, they may hope that their promise will encourage others to take part, even if they have no intention of doing the same.

something, but ultimately to not follow through on this promise. These incentives are at the heart of the so-called "free-rider problem." The problem stems from the fact that most political and economic goals can be classified as public goods: they are non-excludable and not susceptible to crowding. This means that the benefits of a successful effort are shared by everyone, irrespective of whether they actually contributed to its success. At the same time, each individual's own contribution to the activity's success is relatively small, so that if any one individual does not do her part, no other member will be significantly affected by her defection.

A public good combined with the anonymity of most latent groups means that there are few reasons for any one to actually make the effort to join in. Rather than putting in the effort to participate, and running the risks involved with doing so, it is far easier (and safer) to stay home and simply benefit from everyone else's efforts. Indeed, this is what self-interest or "rational egoism" would prescribe. The logic of the free-rider problem is perhaps clearest in the case in which it was first developed – public goods, protests – but it is also at work in the other political and economic activities. For example, when attempting to coordinate one's vote with others in one's district, if there are more parties running than can win representation, there may be a need to vote strategically (i.e., for a second- or third-best party), especially if one's most-preferred one seems unlikely to gain a seat (Cox 1994; Myatt 2007). Here, small deceptions about one's own vote intentions may be enough to switch the target of the collective vote towards one's more-preferred party, or away from a less-preferred one (Brams and Zagare 1977). Similarly, in the context of economic exchange, where most decisions are made sequentially, there is a need for trust: because underlying conditions often change over time, there are incentives for one party to take advantage of short-term opportunities at the expense of another, breaking whatever promises he made earlier.

When doing field work for this book, my interlocutors told me that the question of who will actually show up was a constant concern in their previous efforts to mobilize people around a common cause. Among student organizers, most efforts to create clubs on their campus had largely failed because of limited attendance: scores would sign up and say they would attend, but few ever did. A student's time is precious, the organizers would say, so each needs to think carefully about where to invest his. These sorts of cost considerations are even more acute when the time demands and risks involved are larger, as in the case of large-scale protests. Indeed, Wael Ghonim, in his memoir about the Arab Spring, notes how the Mubarak regime understood the free-rider problem all too well, using pointed crackdowns to encourage would-be protestors to stay home:

Why do they attack us? ... The objective is not to scare people who attended the demonstration in order to keep them from participating again; police officers know well that demonstrators who were attacked once will come back again and again. The objective is to scare the people at home so they never engage in political activity in the first place (2012, p. 105).

TABLE 4.1 *Heterogeneous Preferences in a Public Goods Game*

	Possible Outcomes			
	Both Cooperate	I Cooperate, You Defect	I Defect, You Cooperate	Both Defect
Free Rider	1	b	a	0
Altruist	$1 + w$	$b + w$	a	0
Conditional Cooperator	$1 + w$	b	a	0

Notes: Payoffs in a one-shot Prisoner's Dilemma game. $a > 1, b < 0, a + b < 2$.

By increasing the costs of participation, the Egyptian police made free riding even more attractive, undermining the potential for a larger turnout.

The incentives that others have to free ride must be taken seriously by any participant, who cannot naïvely assume that others will join him in demonstrating, voting, or investing, even when they say that they will. That said, it is not entirely clear that he needs to be as pessimistic about others as the assumption of rational egoism would dictate. Decades of lab-based public goods experiments indicate that there is considerable heterogeneity in individuals' preferences when it comes to collective decision making (Ostrom 2000). Specifically, when comparing individual preferences in a situation where cooperation is mutually preferred but unstable (e.g., the Prisoner's Dilemma), three "types" of people can be distinguished – free riders, altruists, and conditional cooperators (see Table 4.1).[8]

Although estimated to make up only 20 percent of the human population (Ahn, Ostrom, and Walker 2003), free riders (or rational egoists) have what are considered to be "standard" preferences: their payoff from defection is always larger than that from cooperation, regardless of what others do ($a < 1$; $b < 0$). In other words, they strictly prefer to defect and are best off if they do so when others cooperate. As a result, double defection is the predicted outcome whenever two free riders meet, making their individual decisions no longer interdependent (Kreps et al. 1982). In stark contrast are the altruists, estimated to make up less than 2 percent of the human population. These individuals are defined by the "warm glow" (w) they get from doing the right thing and cooperating (Andreoni 1990). When this bonus is large enough, altruists will opt to cooperate regardless of what the other player decides to do.[9] As with the free riders, this implies the altruists' decisions are no longer interdependent.

---

[8] Although the distinction between these three "types" of individuals is based on differences in their preferences in a particular type of interaction, evidence collected by Carlsson, Johansson-Stenman, and Nam (2014) indicates that these preferences are stable over time and across contexts.

[9] This is the case when the "warm glow" term (w) is larger than the incentives to defect ($w > a - 1$; $w > |b|$).

4.1 The Value of Interpersonal Trust

But this covers less than a quarter of the population. The vast majority of those who remain are the so-called conditional cooperators.[10] These individuals also enjoy a warm glow, but only when cooperation is reciprocated (Fischbacher, Gächter, and Fehr 2001). Given this, as long as w is larger than the incentive to free ride *and they believe the other person will cooperate*, conditional cooperators will cooperate. Otherwise, they prefer to defect rather than be taken advantage of. This implies that, for a conditional cooperator, her best strategy depends critically on her opponent and her perception of his "type," making her decision inherently dependent on his.[11] In line with the experimental evidence, my observations from the field indicate that conditional cooperators make up the largest proportion of would-be participants in Turkey, across a variety of political and economic groups. They generally like the idea of working with others to achieve collective ends. In this way, they are fundamentally honest people, worthy of being trusted. But they are not willing to do this at all costs. (They are not altruists, after all.) They feel quite strongly that their willingness to work together should be met with a similar willingness by others.

The best way to understand the existence of these different "types" of people in the world is to recognize that the incentives to free ride are ever present, but not everyone is equally swayed by them. As a result, the ultimate outcome when two or more people meet and interact is at least initially unclear, stemming from uncertainty about what type each person is. Existing theories of the Islamic advantage, with their more individualistic view, see Islamic activists as altruists: motivated to participate no matter what others are doing.[12] But altruists comprise such a small segment of the population that it seems unlikely they could populate a large-scale political or economic movement. Instead, it

---

[10] Conditional cooperators are estimated to comprise between 40 and 60 percent of the human population, according to studies conducted by Ahn, Ostrom, and Walker (2003). But even these numbers may be an under-estimation of the true proportion of conditional cooperators. In their cross-national study, Kocher et al. (2008) find that over 80 percent of American subjects behave like conditional cooperators, while the proportion of Austrian and Japanese subjects was closer to the numbers reported elsewhere: 45 percent and 42 percent, respectively. The number of free riders also varies considerably across contexts, ranging from just 8 percent in the United States to 22 percent in Austria and 36 percent in Japan. In a diverse online sample, Cherry, McEvoy, and Sælen (2017) find conditional cooperators to make up nearly 75 percent of all subjects, while free riders constitute just over 15 percent.

[11] Of course, if he too is a conditional cooperator, then his best strategy will depend on his perception of her type, as well as his perception of her perception of his type, and so on, *ad infinitum*, so that reciprocal cooperation depends on their types *and* common knowledge of this information.

[12] Altruists are usually thought to avoid conditioning their behavior on others' actions, but Jon Elster argues that even the purest altruists will become conditional cooperators under certain circumstances. He explains, "Altruism may be pure and disinterested, in the sense that you derive positive utility from the well-being of another, regardless of his character or conduct, but more frequently you act altruistically towards someone as a function of his character, a minimum condition being that he is not trying to cash in on your altruism" (1985, p. 144). If an altruist feels he is being taken advantage of because of his altruism, he may also choose to make his cooperation conditional.

seems more likely that these activists are conditional cooperators – willing to take part, but only under certain conditions. To sustain their joint participation, not only must these individuals be sufficiently informed and motivated to participate, they must also expect that there are other informed, motivated, conditional cooperators willing to work with them, who will not free ride off of their efforts. This expectation – that others will follow through on their promises to support you, rather than free riding if given the opportunity – is what is commonly referred to as trust (Hardin 2002).

4.1.3 A Typology of Trust and Collective Action

Thus far, I have argued that when two conditions are met – interdependence of individual decisions, and uncertainty about others' expected behavior – trust becomes a necessary condition for individual participation in group activities. Uncertainty stems mostly from heterogeneity among people: while some (altruists, conditional cooperators) can be expected to cooperate under certain conditions, others (free riders) are less likely to. For conditional cooperators, whose best response depends critically on what they expect others are likely to do, there is an important choice to make: cooperate if they believe they are working with someone honest like them, who can be trusted to cooperate, and defect otherwise. In the latter case, despite the warm glow that they would earn from joint cooperation, they behave just like a rational egoist. Without the right expectations, therefore, the potential for reciprocal cooperation among conditional cooperators quickly unravels.

Trust is usually defined as the expectation of honest, trustworthy behavior in the face of incentives to do otherwise. In the framework developed here, trust can be restated as the expectation of encountering a conditional cooperator.[13] In this view, conditional cooperators become "honest" or "trustworthy" types: although not willing to cooperate under all conditions, they prefer to do the right thing as long as they expect others will do the same. This interpretation of conditional cooperators as trustworthy fits with a number of competing definitions of trust, including the "encapsulated-interest" view, which requires trust expectations to be linked to a particular context or activity (Hardin 2002), and the social-intelligent one, where individuals search for public clues about who is worthy of their trust (Aghion et al. 2010b; Uslaner 2002).[14]

Interpersonal trust comes in a variety of forms, with the majority of the extant literature focusing on two types: particularized (or relational) trust, based on specific information about others' past behavior; and generalized trust, a non-particularized (or depersonalized) form extended to generic strangers or to "most people." Particularized trust is perhaps the strongest

---

[13] This definition could also be expanded to include the expectation of meeting an altruist, since they can also be expected to cooperate (i.e., be trustworthy). But since altruists comprise such a small segment of the population, and for the sake of brevity, I will focus on conditional cooperators from this point forward.

[14] For a discussion of these different definitions, see an excellent review by Nannestad (2008).

4.1 The Value of Interpersonal Trust

form of trust, but its scope is narrow, by definition. Paul Stirling (1998), in his ethnographic account of Turkish village life, described villagers' strong preference for multi-stranded relationships in which someone who has already been proven trustworthy in one capacity (e.g., as a shopkeeper) is entrusted with another task (e.g., money-lending). In Stirling's description, while this type of trust promotes cooperation among villagers, it also closes them off to new opportunities when these would involve someone from outside the community, with whom they have no personal history. In other words, while particularized trust "chains" are remarkably strong – with one trustworthy experience informing positive trust expectations in the next encounter – they almost always require a non-particularized form of trust to start in the first place.

A common way of extending personal experiences and particularized trust expectations within a larger group is through a reputation mechanism, in which information about each individual's past behavior is shared among all group members (Greif 1989; Rousseau et al. 1998). Because of the heavy demands that come with information sharing among group members – creating a second-order collective action problem – reputation mechanisms tend to work best in smaller groups that share a common language and culture, the latter of which creates a shared understanding of what constitutes honesty and dishonesty (Greif 1996; Weber 1976). In larger groups or those that do not have a single understanding of right and wrong, reputation mechanisms struggle to function effectively.

Therefore, while particularized trust and reputation mechanisms can support cooperation and mobilization in some cases, they have difficulty doing so on a large scale, including in the types of latent groups considered here. Generally speaking, in a modern society, where interactions are unpredictable, infrequent, and one-shot, trust based on direct (or even indirect) experience is bound to be insufficient (Greif 1996). Among non-particularized forms of trust, the broadest form is so-called generalized trust. Generalized trust expectations extend to most people, including those whom one does not know personally and whom one may never have the opportunity to meet again, but who, nonetheless, one can expect to behave honestly.

Generalized trust is especially valuable in establishing cooperation among strangers in one-shot transactions. Many political and economic interactions are of this type: unlikely to be repeated, taking place among strangers. For example, to succeed, most political movements need to amass support from a group far larger than any one person's social circle. In addition, voter coordination takes place across vast districts, among individuals who might live in reasonable proximity to one another but who are unlikely to have ever met before. Non-particularized trust can also be valuable in establishing the first link in a particularized trust "chain" that develops between a pair or small group of people, those who will one day become partners or even friends, but who initially begin as strangers. For instance, what eventually become well-established business relationships will require an initial basis of non-particularized trust in order to start.

Given all this, it is not surprising that generalized trust has been found to support a number of social, political, and economic outcomes, boosting everything from democracy to health, and development.[15] But while this broad type of non-particularized trust is extremely valuable, my observations from the field indicate that it may be scarce in Turkey. Anecdotal evidence supports this observation and indicates that it might extend to other parts of the Muslim world. For example, Turkish journalist Mustafa Akyol notes the following in an op-ed article:

> In this country, you don't smile at strangers. You simply look the other way, and, if you come eye to eye, you try to look tough ... . I have been wondering why this is the case. Gradually, I have become convinced that that this no-smile attitude tells us a lot about the nature of Turkish society ... . Turks are very good to people that they know well, such as their family and kin. Yet, for the people with whom they are less familiar, their attitude dramatically changes. In other words, if they see a familiar face on the street, they go out of their way to show affection. For unfamiliar faces, however, they have nothing but suspicion.

Translating Akyol's observation into the terms of this discussion, Turkish society may have plenty of particularized trust, but little generalized trust, a juxtaposition that may reinforce itself over time.[16]

Meanwhile, there are those who even question the robustness of particularized trust in Turkey. Surveying new migrants living in Istanbul's shantytowns as part of his study, *The Gecekondu*, Kemal Karpat uncovered the absence of interpersonal trust of all types:

> The questionnaire had the following two questions: "Who do you rely upon and trust most in the city?" and "Who do you rely upon and trust most while you lived in the village?" ... The squatters replied that they relied more on their own judgment than on the advice of elders and relatives. Expressions such as these abounded: "I trust and believe only in myself." "Outside of God, I rely on and trust nobody in Istanbul." "I have traveled enough not to trust anybody." "Who else is better to trust than myself?" (2009, pp. 114–15).

Similarly, Turkish novelist Orhan Pamuk, in his memoir *Istanbul*, questions the authenticity of particularized trust displays he witnessed among adults as a child.

---

[15] In social interactions, generalized trust is associated with higher public goods provision (Anderson, Mellor, and Milyo 2004; Habyarimana et al. 2007), improved health outcomes (Kawachi, Subramanian, and Kim 2008; Poortinga 2006) and general well-being (Helliwell 2003; Helliwell and Putnam 2004). Politically, trust boosts the performance of democracies (Inglehart 1999; Jamal and Nooruddin 2010; Putnam 1993) through its impact on political participation (Benson and Rochon 2004; Kaase 1999; Knack 2001). Economically, generalized trust is associated with higher levels of investment (Bottazzi, Rin, and Hellman 2016; Guiso, Sapienza, and Zingales 2004), trade (Guiso, Sapienza, and Zingales 2009), productivity (Bjørnskov and Méon 2010), and growth (Knack and Keefer 1997; Zak and Knack 2001).

[16] In a survey conducted in Turkey by USAID in the late 1960s, Hopper and Levin note that an "unrealistic fear of being taken advantage of ... reinforced the tendency ... to rely on relatives and friends" (1968, p. 141).

4.1 The Value of Interpersonal Trust

From the way they asked after one another's health to the way they treated us students, from their shopping habits to their political pronouncements, it seemed to me that their every expression in life was two-faced, and that "experience in life" – the thing they were forever telling me I didn't have – meant the ability, after a certain age, to be hypocritical and manipulative without trying and then to be able to sit back and pretend innocence (2004, p. 307).

Descriptions of a low-trust environment extend well beyond Turkey (see also Delaney 1993; Shehata 2009; Tuğal 2009) to other parts of the Muslim world. From Bosnia (Bringa 1995) to Egypt (Clark 2006; Wickham 2002), scholars note the trust barriers that impede their research in Muslim-plurality societies. In Uzbekistan, Maria Louw describes her interlocutors'

... feelings of estrangement from and distrust towards [their] immediate surroundings; the unraveling of and unpredictability in [their] social relations; envy and evil eyes hiding behind seemingly friendly faces (2007, p. 167).

More systematically, in their survey of post-Soviet Central Asia, Sapsford and Abbott describe "an atomized society, one in which trust is confined to small local pockets of interaction" (2006, p. 62). In describing market exchanges in Morocco, Geertz, Geertz, and Rosen highlight a "personalist" type of trust in which one is expected to be "honest (or not honest or not quite honest) with someone, about something, in a given instance, not as such" (1979, p. 204). This translates into view of truth or credibility (*shīh*) that

is more a skeptical question expecting a negative answer than an expression of confidence or an affirmation of belief. One searches for what may be wrong – a juggled measure, a product switch, a disguised cost – and for the false signals – an evasive response, an over-ready agreement, an excessive promise – that reveal its presence. In the message-saturated world of the bazaar... [the] credulous do not thrive (Geertz, Geertz, and Rosen 1979, p. 208).

If these descriptions are correct, low trust of strangers and of "most people" in these Muslim contexts would make it difficult for conditional cooperators to identify one another and work together. In other words, a generalized trust deficit could plausibly explain the political and economic participation gap in the region.

If trust expectations are indeed low in the Muslim world, why might that be? Most theories of trust assume it to be rationally based (i.e., a reflection of how trustworthy "most people" actually are). If Russell Hardin is right that generalized trust "is the stance of, for example, the child who has grown up in a benign environment in which virtually everyone has always been trustworthy," (2002, p. 61) distrust in the Muslim world could reflect the absence of trustworthiness there. As Nannestad explains, almost all conceptualizations of trust suggest that "trust and trustworthiness should be linked" (2008, p. 415), at least at the aggregate level, an expectation supported by some existing empirical work on the subject (Aghion et al. 2010b; Delhey,

Newton, and Welzel 2011).[17] But recall that conditional cooperators will act a lot like free riders when their expectations of others are low. In that case, an observer, like Pamuk, above, would think that most people cannot be trusted, *even though they can*. As such, both empirical questions remain open: Are "most people" in the Muslim world really distrusted? And, regardless of whether they are, should they be?

4.2 TRUST AND TRUSTWORTHINESS IN THE MUSLIM WORLD

In Chapter 3, I concluded that individuals in the Muslim world are sufficiently motivated and informed to be politically and economically active; and yet participation rates remain significantly low. I have argued that motivation and information are necessary but insufficient conditions to support collective action, and that trust and honesty are also needed. Could it be that the Muslim world is teeming with free riders? If so, the absence of honest, trustworthy conditional cooperators could account for the participation gap in the region. On the other hand, even if the region does not have a problem with trustworthiness, cooperation could be similarly stymied by a *trust* problem: despite the actual number of conditional cooperators, as long as they are not able to correctly identify one another, they will behave exactly like free riders, with participation rates suffering, as a result. Existing assessments of trust and trustworthiness in the Muslim world have been mixed, with results based on a much smaller dataset than the one I have assembled here. Therefore, both deserve to be examined again.

4.2.1 Should Most Muslims Be Trusted?

To capture trustworthiness, I prefer having honest individuals self-identify rather than relying on external assessments of honesty, which is remarkably similar to trust itself.[18] The existing literature suggests a reasonable measure: a set of survey questions about the justifiability of behaviors that serve the individual at the expense of others. These behaviors include claiming government benefits for which one is not legally entitled, avoiding paying fares on public transportation, and cheating on one's taxes. Although no existing study has used these questions to assess something called "honesty" or "trustworthiness" – rather "civic cooperation" (Balliet and van Lange 2013; Herrmann, Thöni, and Gächter 2008; Knack and Keefer 1997), "other-regarding values" (Hall 1999), "civic morality" (Letki 2006), or just plain "civicness" (Aghion

---

[17] In his meta-analysis, Bjørnskov (2006) finds that these aggregate patterns vary depending on the size of the sample and methodologies used.

[18] This precludes the use of Transparency International's Corruption Perception Index as a measure of (dis)honesty.

4.2 Trust and Trustworthiness in the Muslim World

et al. 2010b; Algan, Cahuc, and Sangnier 2011; Guiso, Sapienza, and Zingales 2011) – the crux of these traits is clearly the same, even if the names differ.[19]

In line with these existing studies, I estimate trustworthiness using the justifiability questions. While, Aghion et al. (2010b) use just one of the series – claiming unentitled benefits, with the broadest coverage – I begin by looking at all three.[20] Data are available from the EVS, WVS, and some iterations of the Caucasus Barometer and Latinobarómetro.[21] I recode each measure to equal one (1) if respondents say that the action is "never justifiable" and zero (0) otherwise. To capture the latent element that the three questions have in common, I also extract the first principal component factor of the three indicators (Thompson 2004).[22] Principal component factor analysis is a method which "reduces the dimensionality of a data set in which there are a large number of interrelated variables, while retaining as much as possible of the variation present in the data set" (Jolliffe 2002, p. ix).[23] This is especially useful when multiple indicators ostensibly capture the same underlying concept – in this case, trustworthiness.

Calculating the average level of trustworthiness in each country, I assess how the Muslim world compares to non-Muslim countries. Remarkably, across all three individual indicators and their principal component, I find *higher* levels of honesty and trustworthiness in Muslim-plurality countries (see Online Appendix Figure OA.4).[24] In additional analysis, I confirm that these patterns are not driven by demographic factors, estimating mixed-effects hierarchical models that control for demographic differences across individuals. The indicator of Muslim-plurality countries in these models is positive in all specifications and statistically significant, except in the case of claiming unentitled benefits (see Online Appendix Table OA.9).

There is always the possibility that this pattern – higher levels of self-reported honesty in the Musim world – could be the result of social desirability bias: rather than reflecting *true* honesty in the region, it could be based on a

---

[19] Knack and Keefer assert that "civic cooperation reflects respondents' own stated willingness to cooperate when faced with a collective action problem; it thus can be thought of as trustworthiness" (1997, p. 1258). Further, Natalia Letki suggests that "civic morality represents honesty in the context of the public good ... deterring [citizens] from engaging in corruption and free-riding" (2006, p. 306).
[20] Like Letki (2006), I drop an additional question referring to buying stolen goods because of extremely limited data coverage.
[21] I have responses to at least one of the three questions for just over 700,000 respondents from 118 countries, including nearly 80,000 from 30 Musim-plurality countries.
[22] The composite factor is available for just under 450,000 respondents across 108 countries, including just over 70,000 from 27 countries in the Muslim world. The first principal component has an Eigenvalue (λ) of 2.01, and the three indicators load onto the factor quite evenly: 0.567 for unentitled benefits, 0.578 for evaded taxes, and 0.587 for transportation fare.
[23] The multi-dimensionality of a dataset is "achieved by transforming [it] to a new set of variables, the principal components, which are uncorrelated, and which are ordered so that the first *few* retain most of the variation present in *all* of the original variables" (p. ix).
[24] This difference is statistically significant in a two-tailed *t*-test for evaded taxes, transportation fares, and the principal component of all three individual indicators.

particular pressure to say that one is so in response to a direct question (Fisher 1993). This type of bias is difficult to disentangle within the survey data itself. But I can look for additional evidence in a common behavioral measure of honesty: the amount "returned" in a standard trust game (Berg, Dickhaut, and McCabe 1995).[25] In their meta-analysis, Johnson and Mislin (2011) list the average amount sent and returned in trust games conducted in thirty-four countries, including four sets of games played in a single Muslim country – Bangladesh.

As I did with the survey-based measure, I compare the average amount returned in the Bangladeshi games to those in the 130 sets of games conducted in non-Muslim countries. And as in the survey data, I find evidence of more honesty in Bangladesh: the average return rate is 133.8 percent, compared to 102.8 percent elsewhere, a difference that is statistically significant (95%) in a two-tailed test. When I control for the experimental design features that Johnson and Mislin find explain variation in trustworthiness – the rate of return, whether the experiment was conducted among students, even the percent of the money originally sent – I continue to see a positive boost in Bangladesh, even if the difference is no longer statistically significant. Across the two measures, therefore, I conclude that there is little evidence of a trustworthiness deficit in the Muslim world. Quite the contrary.

4.2.2 *Are* Most Muslims Trusted?

Given that trustworthiness is robust in the Muslim world, and given the presumption that generalized trust expectations track onto aggregate levels of honesty, we might expect healthy levels of trust in the region. Of course, this would challenge the anecdotal evidence discussed earlier, all of which points to *lower* levels of interpersonal trust in Turkey and across some parts of the Muslim world. While these anecdotes paint a coherent picture of the region as a place of little trust, they could represent a non-random sample of observations, leading us to draw a false conclusion about the region as a whole (Seawright and Gerring 2008; Geddes 1990). A more valid conclusion can be drawn from a more representative sample. In this regard, the set of cross-national surveys I have gathered should prove useful.

Since it was introduced by Almond and Verba (1963), scholars have used the same survey question to assess generalized interpersonal trust: "Generally speaking, would you say that most people can be trusted, or that you can't be

---

[25] In a trust game, one player (the "sender") is given a sum of money and must decide what portion of it (if any) to send to an anonymous partner (the "receiver"). Whatever amount of money is sent by the sender is then doubled (or tripled) before the receiver decides how much of it to return. The amount sent by the sender to the receiver is commonly interpreted as the sender's level of trust, while the amount returned by the receiver is interpreted as her level of trustworthiness. Across the twenty-eighty countries for which I have both survey and experimental data, I find a positive correlation ($r=0.30$) between the honesty factor and the average amount returned in a trust game, although it just fails to achieve statistical significance at conventional levels.

4.2 Trust and Trustworthiness in the Muslim World

too careful in dealing with people?" with a binary response: "Most people can be trusted" (1) or "You can't be too careful" (0). Given the impressive growth in cross-national surveys (Heath, Fisher, and Smith 2005; Lupu and Michelitch 2018), responses to this same question are now available for over 1.2 million respondents across 936 surveys from 144 countries between 1981 and 2016.[26] Although self-reported trust may not be an ideal measure given its susceptibility to response biases, the validity of the survey question has been confirmed at the individual level by Fehr et al. (2003), as well as cross-nationally by Johnson and Mislin (2012) in their meta-analysis of trust games.[27] Further, Bjørnskov finds remarkable stability in reported levels of trust over time in sixty-four countries, concluding that the survey measure of generalized trust "can indeed be treated as a time-invariant feature of national cultures" (2007, p. 5).[28]

Using these survey data, as an initial assessment of generalized trust in the Muslim world, I calculate average trust levels for each country, using all available responses. I find tremendous variation in trust across countries, ranging from 69.2 percent in Norway to less than 3.5 percent in Trinidad and Tobago, with an average trust level of 25.1 percent and a standard deviation of 12.8 percent. In Muslim-majority countries ($N=36$), trust averages just 23.2 percent, while it averages 26.3 percent in non-Muslim-majority countries ($N=108$).

---

[26] The trust question has been asked most often by the WVS, in a total of 243 surveys in one hundred countries (1981–2015). Additionally, the EVS has included the question in all 121 of its surveys in forty-seven European countries (1981–2009). The question has also been asked in most of the regional Barometers including: (i) Afrobarometer: sixty-three surveys in thirty-five African countries between 1999–2013; (ii) Arab Barometer: thirty-six surveys in thirteen Arab-majority countries (2006–2016); (iii) AsiaBarometer: thirty-six surveys in eighteen East Asian countries (2003–2007); (iv) East Asian Barometer: fifty surveys in fourteen Asian countries (2001–2015); (v) Eurobarometer: two surveys across twenty-seven European countries (1986, 2004); and (vi) Latinobarómetro: 348 surveys in nineteen Latin American countries (including Spain) between (1996–2017). Because of numerous problems with the 2005 round of the AsiaBarometer, it was excluded from the dataset. Still, the full sample includes responses from 168,906 individuals from thirty-six Muslim countries.

[27] According to Johnson and Mislin, behavior in a trust game is strictly preferable to survey responses because, "in contrast to attitudinal measures, experimental measures of trust between anonymous individuals and with monetary incentives offer a concrete exchange setting which can capture generalized trust behavior more effectively" (2012, p. 210). Still, when comparing the two measures across 152 experiments conducted in thirty-five countries, they find that they are positively correlated, concluding that the "Trust Question measures the same thing as experimenters call 'trust' in the lab" (p. 212). This stands in contrast to an earlier study which indicated that the trust question may pick up trustworthiness more than trust (Glaeser et al. 2000). Critics of this particular study noted its subjects had the opportunity to get to know one another, challenging the interpretation of their trust as non-particularized (Wilson 2018), although others have since found similar patterns in other contexts (Johansson-Stenman, Mahmud, and Martinsson 2013).

[28] More specifically, he finds that the cross-temporal data show a "strong regression-to-mean effect, indicating that the national generalized trust scores seem to fluctuate around stable levels" (Bjørnskov 2007, p. 4). Similarly, in my larger dataset, where there are multiple surveys per country ($N=123$), I find that average trust levels cluster within each country case ($\sigma=0.031$). While this time-invariance may make it difficult to use these survey data in panel analysis, it does bode well for the cross-sectional comparison I conduct here.

Although this difference just fails to attain statistical significance at conventional levels in a two-tailed difference-of-means test, it remains remarkable nonetheless, especially considering the number of war-torn, impoverished (and therefore distrusting) countries outside the Muslim world. When making an arguably more appropriate comparison – between Muslim and non-Muslim countries within the same geographic region – the difference is both statistically and substantively significant.[29] Within the Muslim world, Turkey stands out as being especially distrusting, with only 10.1 percent of respondents reporting that "most people can be trusted," the twelfth least-trusting country in the entire sample.

Even when comparing Muslim countries to non-Muslim ones in the same region, there are a number of factors that differ systematically between the two sets of countries that could plausibly drive the difference in trust levels, leading us to draw the false conclusion that there is a relationship between trust and Muslim-plurality status where, in fact, there is none. As such, it is important to consider what country-level characteristics, aside from having a predominantly Muslim population, could drive differences in generalized trust. Once we have a sense of what these other differentiating factors might be, we can introduce them into the analysis and assess how they compare to (and impact) the Muslim effect.

The existing literature discussing cross-national variation in generalized trust is extensive. Ever since Robert Putnam (1993) argued that trust and other forms of social capital could boost the performance of democratic governments, social scientists have sought to track and explain which countries qualify as high trust and which as low trust. Further, Knack and Keefer's (1997) finding that high-trust societies tend to enjoy robust economic growth has prompted even more interest in this question. The result is a long list of possible trust covariates – ranging from social distance, social contact, economic development, and political institutions – all of which have been included in existing models of cross-national trust.[30] To narrow down this extensive

---

[29] Steven Fish (2002), in his "Islam and Authoritarianism," finds no significant difference between Muslim-majority and non-Muslim-majority countries in terms of generalized trust. But this null result is likely a function of his much smaller sample, thirty-six countries compared with my set of 133.

[30] Social distance is usually thought to affect trust through the polarization of tastes and preferences, and has been defined either in economic or cultural terms – as income inequality (Uslaner 2002; Zak and Knack 2001) or ethno-linguistic diversity (Alesina and La Ferrara 2002; Delhey and Newton 2005; Knack and Keefer 1997), respectively. In addition, and following Durkheim's (1973) theory of social order and anomie, Delhey and Newton (2005) have posited that internal armed conflicts should lower trust, while foreign wars are likely to boost patriotism, solidarity, and trust. Meanwhile, an alternative set of trust theories focuses less on the distance between individuals and more on the ways in which these distances can be bridged: interpersonally, via education (Bjørnskov 2009; Knack and Zak 2003; Uslaner 2002), as well as physically, through infrastructure (Fisman and Khanna 1999; Labonne and Chase 2010). In addition to the social barriers to trust, the existing literature considers economic factors that could create opportunities for trust building – income (Knack and Keefer 1997; Zak and Knack 2001) and growth (Algan and Cahuc 2010; Bjørnskov 2012) – as well as those that

4.2 Trust and Trustworthiness in the Muslim World

list, I follow the careful work of Bjørnskov (2007) in identifying trust's only cross-national covariates: social distance (in the form of income inequality and ethno-linguistic diversity), economic development, and political institutions (i.e., historical experience with either monarchy or Communism).[31]

By introducing each of these country-level indicators into a multi-level mixed effects model of generalized trust, I am able to compare how they – and the country's Muslim-plurality status – impact trust levels across over 1.1 million individuals in 144 countries.[32] I measure household income inequality by taking the 1975–2010 average as calculated by United Nations University (2010); ethno-linguistic diversity is the Herfindahl index taken from Alesina et al. (2003); and development is measured using the natural log of GDP per capita in each survey year, as calculated by the World Bank (2014). To capture variation in political institutions, I create a binary indicator of whether the country has ever had a monarch, using data from Norris (2009), and whether it has Socialist legal origins, as defined by La Porta et al. (1999). The full results are available in the Online Appendix (Table OA.10), but Figure 4.1 plots the standardized coefficients of the six country-level indicators from the fully specified model.

Although income inequality has the largest impact on trust levels in terms of magnitude (–0.086), Muslim-plurality status continues to exhibit a significant, negative effect on generalized trust (–0.015). Moreover, this effect is larger in magnitude than that of ethno-linguistic diversity (–0.010) and Communism (–0.005), and statistically indistinguishable from the effects of income (0.017) and monarchy (0.015).[33] In other words, there is compelling evidence of a generalized trust problem in the Muslim world, one that is separate from (and indeed, in many cases, larger than) existing explanations for cross-national variation in trust. Unless these low-trust expectations can be improved, they stand to pose a significant obstacle to political and economic cooperation in the region.

---

might inhibit the formation of trust, e.g., non-productive economic factors like resource rents (Leite and Weidmann 1999). Finally, there are theories about the kind or quality of institutions that could support trust by reducing risk (Levi 1996) or instilling the kind of predictability that helps trusting dispositions to form (Rothstein and Stolle 2008), especially if the institutions themselves are seen as trustworthy (Knight 2001; Levi and Stoker 2000; Sztompka 1998). On the other hand, some argue that too many institutions can "crowd out" intrinsic motivations for individuals to behave honestly, thereby lowering trust (Berggren and Jordahl 2006; Frey 1994).

[31] In addition to these, and in line with my findings here, Bjørnskov (2007) includes a number of indicators of religious composition in his final model: not just the percent of the population that is Muslim, but also the proportion of Protestants, Catholics, and those who profess an Eastern religion.

[32] These country-level effects can also be compared to the impact of individual-level demographic factors: age, gender, and education.

[33] The direction of these effects is in line with those published by Bjørnskov (2007), although his comparison is strictly cross-national rather than hierarchical.

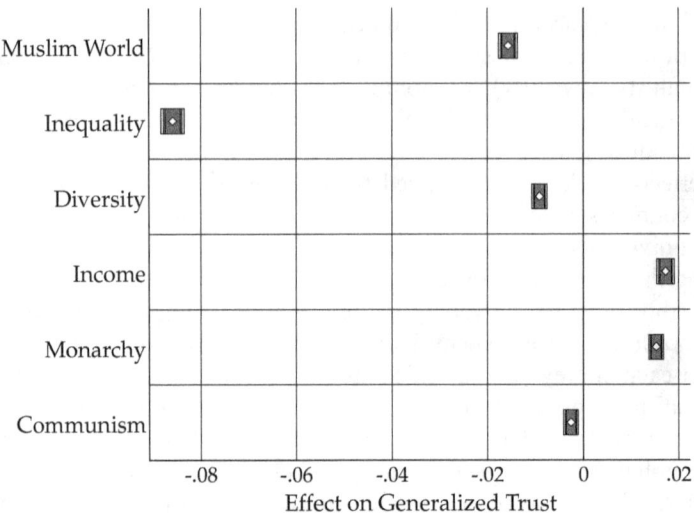

FIGURE 4.1 Determinants of Generalized Trust
Notes: Standardized coefficients from multi-level mixed effects model of generalized trust. Indicators include whether a plurality of citizens identify as Muslim, income inequality, ethno-linguistic fractionalization, log GDP per capita in the survey year, and binary indicators of whether the country has ever had a monarch or has Socialist legal origins. Shaded bars indicate confidence intervals at 99, 95, and 90 percent levels.

4.3 CAN TRUST EXPECTATIONS BE IMPROVED?

Thus far, I have unearthed a strange pattern: the Muslim world is distinguished for its high levels of trustworthiness and low levels of generalized trust. In the Conclusion, I briefly consider the source(s) of these seemingly irrationally low trust expectations, but for now, I focus on a more pressing question: can the common expectation that "you can't be too careful" when dealing with people in the Muslim world be changed? If it can, then – despite the considerable participation gap in Muslim countries – there should yet be an underlying potential for collective action in the region, given the healthy levels of honesty there. Alternatively, if generalized distrust in the region reflects a culture of skepticism or risk aversion, it may be "sticky" and less likely to change, making the trust problem and the participation gap considerably more difficult to overcome.

In the social sciences, culture is defined as "those customary beliefs and values that ethnic, religious, and social groups transmit fairly unchanged from generation to generation" (Guiso, Sapienza, and Zingales 2006, p. 23). As such, cultural values are thought to be inherited from one's parents (Bisin and Verdier 2001) and carried with individuals as they migrate (Algan and Cahuc 2010; Luttmer and Singhal 2011). Already, the extant literature has suggested a cultural foundation for generalized trust expectations in different settings (Bohnet et al. 2008; Buchan, Johnson, and Croson 2006; Croson and Buchan

1999).³⁴ Moreover, some specific arguments of this type have been made in the case of the Muslim world: either that a distrusting "tribal" mentality dominates the region (Gellner 2000), or that Islam is an inherently distrusting religion (Uslaner 2002). If either is true, the region's low trust expectations would be difficult to update, so that the potential for cooperation and collective action there would remain unrealized.

To address this possibility, I turn to testing each of the two hypotheses, in turn. First, I assess whether Islam is a distrusting faith by examining the relationship between Islam and trust, across individuals, both inside and outside of the Muslim world. Next, I ask whether distrust in the Muslim world is indeed a cultural trait by tracing whether migrants from the region are able to update their low trust expectations after settling elsewhere.

4.3.1 A Faith-Based Theory of Trust?

Beginning with Weber's *The Sociology of Religion*, scholars have taken a great interest in the social consequences of different faiths. In particular, many have focused on how the structure of authority differs across faiths and how these differences impact believers' preferences and behaviors. For his part, Weber speaks highly of "congregational religions," which, he argues, support more egalitarianism, especially between the laity and the leadership.³⁵ Daniel Levine (1986) applies this same logic to relationships within congregations, arguing that non-hierarchical religions are distinguished by strong bonds of solidarity between adherents. Putnam (1993) too latches on to this idea, suggesting that Catholicism, with its emphasis on hierarchy and obedience, impeded the development of trust and democracy in Italy.

Despite the contention of some that Islam is an egalitarian faith,³⁶ most scholars assessing the relationship between religion and generalized trust have grouped Islam together with Catholicism and Orthodoxy, labeling them all as hierarchical faiths. These have been contrasted with Protestantism, Confucianism, and Buddhism, which tend to be more trusting, on average, at the national level (Bjørnskov 2007; Inglehart 1999; La Porta et al. 1997; Zak and Knack 2001). Meanwhile, Eric Uslaner contends that Islam is a distrusting faith despite being "more collectivist. Many Muslims" he argues "find Western

---

34 Peter Nannestad has offered culture as a "hypothetical explanation for the within-country stability of levels of generalized trust... as well as for the existence of relatively stable cross-country patterns... [It] could be that respondents apply largely the same mental frame when selecting their response [to the survey question], and that this mental frame... could be part of a common historical and cultural background" (2008, p. 419).
35 Weber defined congregational religions as non-hierarchical ones "where the laity has been organized into a continuous pattern of communal behavior, in which it actively participates in some manner" (1922, p. 64).
36 An argument can and has been made that Islam – at least its largest Sunni branch – has much more in common with congregational faiths than hierarchical ones (Marlow 1997). If there is hierarchy within Islam, it is to be found in some of its smaller Shi'a sub-sects and Sufi offshoots (Black 2011).

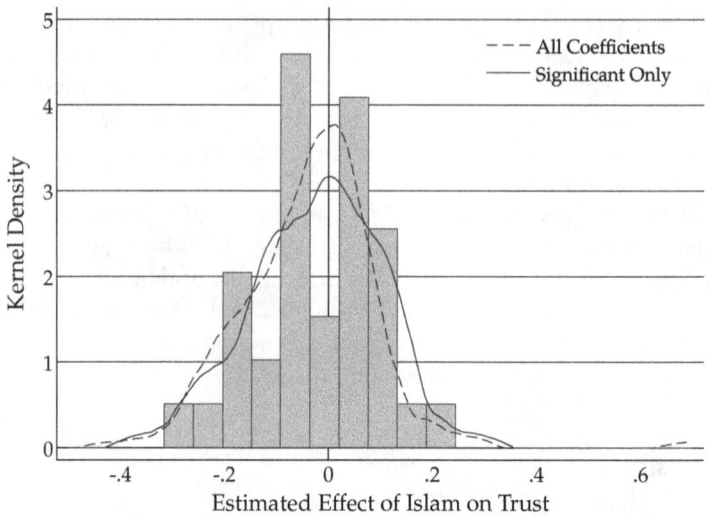

FIGURE 4.2 The Effect of Islam on Trust across Individuals
Notes: Estimated effects of Islam on trust across OLS regressions in each of 122 countries. All models control for age, gender, and educational attainment, as well as a binary indicator of Muslim religion. Dashed line indicates the density of all estimated effects; solid line and histogram indicate statistically significant effects.

culture threatening and are thus less likely to trust people unlike themselves." Moreover, "Muslims... see themselves as a community apart: non-Muslims, according to Islamic law, belong to a 'second class' of citizens" (2002, p. 232). As with those who classify Islam as hierarchical, Uslaner finds a negative association between Islam and generalized trust at the country level.

And yet, these aggregate patterns could very well be driven by low levels of trust in Muslim countries, and therefore may not indicative of Islam's distrusting impact on individual adherents. For example, the cross-national correlation between Islam and distrust could reflect the types of institutions found in Muslim-plurality countries or a historical antecedent many share, and not the distrusting nature of Islam as a faith. If we are to conclude that Islam, itself, impedes the development of trust, then the relationship between Islam and trust should hold at the individual-level, in Muslim and non-Muslim countries alike. To assess this, I return to my cross-national survey dataset, identifying all those that include a measure of respondents' religion.[37] In each

---

[37] This criterion excludes just the Eurobarometer surveys. Both the EVS and WVS ask "Do you belong to a religious denomination? In case you do, answer which one," while Afrobarometer asks "What is your religion, if any?" The Arab Barometer simply lists respondents' religion; AsiaBarometer asks "Do you regard yourself as belonging to any particular religion? If yes, which?"; while the East Asian Barometer and Latinobarómetro ask respondents "What is your religion?" Using these responses and following Fish's (2011) coding scheme, I create a binary indicator of Islam, coded one (1) if respondents self-identify as "Muslim," "Al-Hadis," "Shi'a," "Sunni," or "Druze" and zero (0) otherwise.

4.3 Can Trust Expectations Be Improved?

of 122 countries in which there were both Muslim and non-Muslim respondents, I estimate an OLS regression of Islam on generalized trust, controlling for individuals' age, gender, and education.

The distribution of the estimated coefficients in these 122 separate regressions are displayed in Figure 4.2. In the vast majority of cases ($N=87$), Islam has no statistically significant impact on individuals' level of trust in "most people." Only in twenty cases does Islam significantly lower trust, while in an additional fifteen, Islam is associated with significantly higher trust expectations. As the figure indicates, the distribution of all coefficients (as well as the statistically significant ones) average to roughly zero (–0.035 and –0.022, respectively). The appropriate conclusion to draw, therefore, is that Islam has no effect on individual trust within a given country.

In additional analysis (Online Appendix Table OA.11), I confirm this result in the full dataset using a multi-level mixed effects model which includes the same individual-level covariates (age, gender, education) and a binary indicator of Islamic faith, as well a country-level indicator of each country's Muslim-plurality status. I find that Islam indeed has a negative impact on individuals' level of trust *until the country's status is accounted for*. When interacting Islam on the individual- and country-level and when estimating two separate models – one among non-Muslim countries only, another strictly within the Muslim world – I find the same result: Muslims in the non-Muslim world are indeed less trusting than their compatriots of other faiths; but, within the Muslim world, if anything, they are *more* trusting than their non-Muslim neighbors.[38] If we put all of the respondents into four categories along two dimensions – individual Islamic faith and country's Muslim-majority status – the result is as follows: most trusting are non-Muslims, and then Muslims, outside of the Muslim world, followed by Muslims, and then non-Muslims, within the region, the least trusting group. In other words, it appears that there is something about living in a Muslim country, *rather than being Muslim*, that produces lower trust expectations.

4.3.2 Trust among Emigrants from the Muslim World

In finding that trust levels are lowest among non-Muslims in the Muslim world, I was able to push back against the presumption that Islam is a distrusting faith. Instead, evidence indicates that there may be something about living in a Muslim country that limits the development of trust, regardless of one's religion. Further, there are indications that this "Muslim world" effect may

---

[38] The interaction model takes the following form: $Trust_{ij} = \beta_0 + \beta_1 Muslim_{ij} + \beta_2 MusPlur_j + \beta_3 Muslim_{ij} \times MusMaj_j + X_i + \mu_j + \epsilon_i$ where $Trust_{ij}$ is a measure of respondent i's trust in "most people," $Muslim_{ij}$ is a binary indicator of whether she self-identifies as Muslim, $MusPlur_j$ is a binary indicator of whether her home country j qualifies as Muslim-plurality, $Muslim_{ij} \times MusMaj_j$ is the interaction between the two, X_i is a vector of her individual-level characteristics, μ_j is a fixed-effect term for her home-country, and ϵ_i is the error term.

linger: Muslims living outside the region also tend to be less trusting than their average compatriot; and, assuming that many of them emigrated from the region or descended from Muslim migrants, their lower trust expectations may stem from cultural norms carried with them from their native countries to their new homes and passed down from generation to generation. In this view, low levels of trust among Muslim migrants would be a cultural vestige, first developed in the Muslim world – migrants' home country – but maintained in their new country of-residence. This low-trust culture also could help explain the distrust among both Muslims and non-Muslims still living in the Muslim world, where the same culture still dominates.

Among some scholars, generalized distrust in Muslim societies has been linked to a so-called "tribal mentality," which emphasizes particularized forms of trust, based on a shared history, over non-particularized expectations that most people can be trusted (Gellner 2000; Rosen 2000). Bohnet, Herrmann, and Zeckhauser (2010) translate this mentality into game-theoretic terms and suggest that members of tribal societies have higher reference points for trustworthiness, requiring more information and reassurance before they are willing to trust. This worldview arguably developed when the majority of the inhabitants of Northern Africa, the Middle East, and Central Asia were nomadic. As such, it is decidedly less relevant today, in what is an increasingly urbanized Muslim world. But this cultural understanding, like others, will have been passed down from generation to generation, like a sort of normative inheritance, lasting far longer than the circumstances in which it first developed (Bisin and Verdier 2001; Greif 1996).[39]

The argument that the Muslim world's trust problem is a cultural vestige is yet untested, but it fits nicely within an existing literature in political economics that presumes the inheritability of trust expectations. Indeed, a growing set of studies measure migrants' trust expectations in terms the level of trust in their country of origin (Algan and Cahuc 2010; Guiso, Sapienza, and Zingales 2006; Uslaner 2008).[40] Still, most of this extant empirical work has focused on emigrants from Western Europe and is untested among Muslim migrants. Does a migrant from the Muslim world maintain her low trust expectations after settling elsewhere, indicating that her generalized distrust is culturally determined? Or are her expectations updated to reflect her new surroundings, in contrast to the cultural theory of trust?

I assess the "stickiness" of migrants' trust expectations using a different survey dataset: the European Social Survey (ESS). The ESS has been conducted biannually in thirty European countries since 2002 and, unlike other surveys discussed above, it includes questions about respondents' migration history,

---

[39] In this way, culture – as an "informal institution" (North 1991), operates like other, more formal institutions in over-staying its welcome.
[40] This is in line with similar studies of the inheritability of other norms, including preferences for redistribution (Luttmer and Singhal 2011) and social insurance (Eugster et al. 2011).

4.3 Can Trust Expectations Be Improved?

as well as a version of the standard trust question.[41] In addition to asking respondents where they were born, the ESS asks them about their parents' birthplaces. Over 36,000 (9.3%) self-report having been born abroad, with nearly 7,000 (1.8%) immigrating to Europe from a Muslim country. An even larger number – 67,639 (17.6%) – report that one or both of their parents immigrated to Europe, with 17,629 (4.6%) having at least one parent born in a Muslim country.[42]

Combining these individual migration histories with the country-level estimates of trust from my larger survey dataset, I am able to calculate the level of trust in most (84.1%) immigrants' country of birth. I then compare the self-reported trust of three groups of respondents – native-born Europeans, emigrants from non-Muslim countries, and emigrants from Muslim-plurality countries – to the average level of trust in their country of birth (Figure 4.3).[43] Overall, I find that all individuals' trust expectations reflect the level of trust in their country of birth, but this relationship is far weaker for immigrants than native-born Europeans. And it is weaker still for migrants from the Muslim world.[44] In other words, Muslim migrants trust expectations are significantly influenced by their present environments – where trust levels tend to be considerably higher than in their birth countries – and are less affected by the trust expectations of their country of origin. Their apparent ability to shed their distrust upon migration speaks decidedly against the cultural theory of the region's trust problem.

In additional analysis, I confirm this pattern in a mixed-effects hierarchical model (Online Appendix Table OA.12). I find that Muslim migrants are the lone group to not be impacted by their birth-country trust in a statistically significant way.[45] I also estimate the effect of trust from *parents'* country

---

[41] Unlike the other surveys, the ESS allows for generalized trust to range from one (1) "You can't be too careful" to ten (10) "Most people can be trusted." But after recoding responses to range from (0, 1), I find that country averages are remarkably similar to the binary responses in the larger dataset, with a correlation coefficient of 0.887.

[42] Note that the population of interest in this study is migrants from Muslim countries, rather than self-identified Muslims or Muslims from the Muslim world. This is because the comparison is intended to assess whether the low levels of trust in Muslim countries, common to Muslims and non-Muslims alike, is a cultural vestige, that both groups would be expected to carry with them upon migration.

[43] Because there is one Muslim-plurality country in the ESS dataset – Turkey – I exclude it from this analysis. It is reintroduced in an additional set of tests below.

[44] Although migrants from the Muslim world have slightly lower trust compared to native-born Europeans and non-Muslim migrants (48.6 percent compared to 49.5 percent and 51.1 percent, respectively), their trust expectations remain significantly less impacted by the level of trust in their country of birth, which are considerably lower than the other two groups (22.4 percent compared to 35.1 percent and 28.8 percent, respectively.)

[45] To assess heterogeneity in the effect of birth-country trust on current trust expectations, I estimate an interaction model of the following form $Trust_{ijb} = \beta_0 + \beta_1 \bar{Trust}_b + \beta_2 Muslim_b + \beta_3 \bar{Trust}_b \times Muslim_b + X_i + \mu_j + \epsilon_i$, where $Trust_{ijb}$ is trust of respondent i who currently resides in country j and born in country b, $\bar{Trust}_b$ is the average trust level in i's country of birth b, $Muslim_b$ is a binary indicator of the Muslim-majority status of i's country of birth b, and $\bar{Trust}_b \times Muslim_b$ is an interaction between it and the average level of trust in that country, X_i is

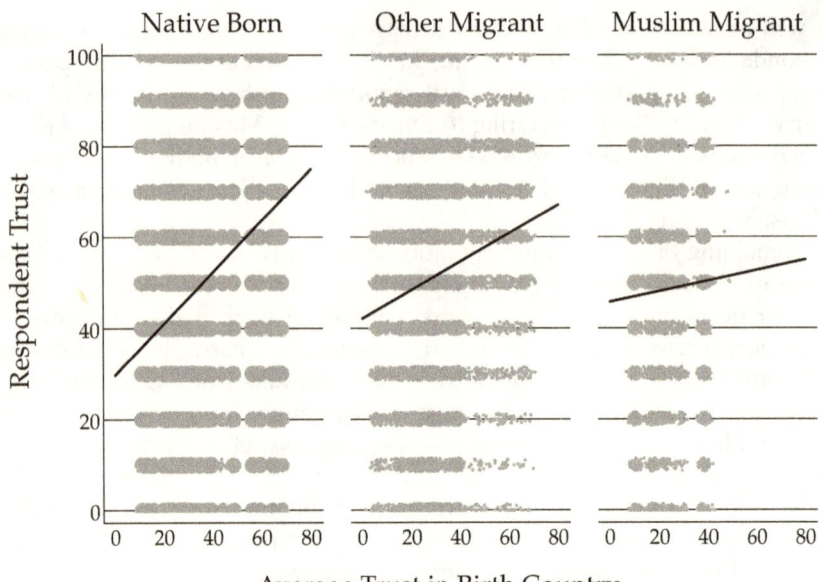

FIGURE 4.3 Trust among Migrants
Notes: Correlation between respondent trust and the average level of trust in their country of birth. Two percent random noise added to distinguish between observations. Linear association across respondents indicated by black lines. Comparing three populations: native-born residents; migrants from non-Muslim countries; and those from Muslim countries.

of origin among second-generation native-born respondents, finding a similar pattern (Online Appendix Table OA.13).[46]

It would seem, therefore, that any distrust developed in the Muslim world is not particularly sticky, far less so than trust "inherited" by other migrants and developed among native-born Europeans, and quite unlike what one would expect of a cultural trait. Still, it is reasonable to question my interpretation of the patterns on a number of grounds. First, I am relying on a different data source to measure birth-country trust than what I use to assess respondents' own level of trust. The two could diverge in particular a subset of countries or regions, driving the results I see. Similarly, if there is more noise in estimates of trust in Muslim countries, this difference could explain why birth-place trust

---

a vector of individual-level characteristics, μ_j is a fixed-effect for i's country of residence, and ϵ_i is the error term. In the estimated model, the effect of birth-country trust (β_1) is statistically significant and positive, while the coefficient on the interaction term (β_3) is significant, negative, and of a magnitude that makes the marginal effect of birth-country trust indistinguishable from zero for Muslim migrants. Meanwhile, the direct effect of emigrating from a Muslim country (β_2) is large, positive, and significant, indicating that Muslim migrants have more positive trust expectations than their country of birth and other demographic characteristics would predict. I see neither of these effects when estimating the same model of non-Muslim migrants.

[46] Interestingly, the direct effect of parents' country of birth on second generation migrants' trust expectations (β_1) operates primarily through their mothers' country of birth.

has a smaller impact on trust among respondents from the region. Ideally, I would want to assess the inheritability of trust among Muslim-majority migrants within the ESS dataset itself. Luckily, the inclusion of one Muslim country in the sample – Turkey – allows me to do just that: comparing the trust of those born *and currently residing in Turkey*, to those born in Turkey but residing elsewhere, and to native-born Europeans with Turkish parents. And since Turkey is the least trusting country in the ESS sample, the direction in which migrants should "update" their trust expectations is the same, no matter where they now reside.

Making this comparison, I find a remarkably consistent pattern. Trust levels are lowest among Turks who still reside in Turkey: 25.6 percent on average, with a 95 percent confidence interval of 24.7 percent to 26.5 percent. Meanwhile, trust expectations are significantly higher, both among first-generation migrants to Europe – averaging 46.7 percent (45.1, 48.2) – and second-generation immigrants, who were born in Europe to one Turkish parent or more – 44.6 percent (43.1, 46.2). In regression models, I confirm that these differences are not driven by demographic factors: Turks who no longer reside in Turkey appear to be simply more trusting than their co-ethnics still living in Turkey (Online Appendix Table OA.14). Again, I take this as evidence that their low trust expectations have been positively updated.

As further evidence that trust levels are likely changing upon migration, I confirm that Muslim migrants are not simply more trusting to begin with, even before migration. In the second round of the Arab Barometer 2012, respondents were asked "Do you think about emigrating from your country?" Comparing those who answer in the affirmative (31.7%) to those who say they have no plans to move elsewhere, I find that, if anything, potential migrants are significantly *less* trusting – 17.8 percent compared to 32.4 percent among non-migrants – a pattern I also see in regression analysis, taking demographic factors into account. Although these survey responses do not indicate which of those considering emigration will actually end up moving, they are still illustrative of a basic pattern: there does not appear to be a trust advantage among would-be migrants. It seems more likely that trust among immigrants from the Muslim world, as seen in the ESS data, emerged upon resettlement rather than before migration.

4.4 THE TRUST PROBLEM IN THE MUSLIM WORLD

In the preceding chapter, I explored the importance of generalized, interpersonal trust for collective activities of all sorts and then identified a curious pattern in the Muslim world: despite high levels of honesty and trustworthiness in the region, generalized trust expectations remain significantly lower than elsewhere, a difference that is not easily explained by established cross-national trust-covariates. Further empirical investigations reveal that this trust deficit is neither faith-based nor a cultural vestige; instead, the generalized distrust in the Muslim world seems to be context dependent, even despite the fact that most people in the region *should* be trusted. In other words, the mismatch between high honesty and low trust appears to reflect something about life in the Muslim world, an inefficient equilibrium that could be driven by formal or informal institutions that make it difficult for citizens to identify who can be trusted.

Although a full explanation for this curious pattern is beyond the scope of this book, it is still important to note that most people in the Muslim world are conditional cooperators and should be trusted, and that low trust expectations in the region can be updated. Together, these two patterns speak to the potential for cooperation, coordination, and collective action in Muslim-plurality countries. In addition to being sufficiently motivated and informed, individuals living in the Muslim world appear to be trustworthy, conditional cooperators who would like to work with others, as long as they believe they will not be taken advantage of. In other words, collective action can be sustained in the region if individuals can update their trust expectations of one another and realize that most people really can be trusted. But, until that happens – as long as their expectations of their compatriots remain low – individuals in the Muslim world will struggle to work well together, and this trust deficit will present an obstacle to political and economic participation.

This expectation – that generalized distrust will undermine political and economic activity – is the first hypothesis of this book, one that I test in the empirical chapters of Part II. While the results presented thus far indicate that there is generalized trust deficit in the Muslim world, it is not yet clear that this deficit accounts for the participation gap in the region. There is a small extant literature linking generalized trust, on the one hand, to some political and economic activities, on the other. For example, in the case of political participation, Benson and Rochon (2004) identify a strong correlation between trust and participation across thirty-three, mostly OECD countries. Meanwhile, Knack (2002) applies a similar logic to voter turnout, a more institutionalized form of participation, across US states. But while these empirical patterns are compelling, it is not yet clear whether they would extend to developing countries, including to the Muslim world.

Similarly, in the economic realm, it has been argued that interpersonal trust can support investment, savings, and trade. It does so, primarily, because it "can reduce transaction costs, enforce contracts, and facilitate credit at the level of individual investors" (Knack 2001, p. 1). In the case of bank savings, trust is expected to play a particularly large role (Guiso, Sapienza, and Zingales 2004). For similar reasons, trust impacts any economic transaction that involves a temporal lag (Zak and Knack 2001). As a result, economic activity should be more limited in low-trust societies. And yet, the empirical relationship between trust, on the one hand, and economic activity, on the other, has never been explored specifically within the Muslim world.[47]

---

[47] Importantly, a theoretical connection between the two in this context has been made previously, both by Greif (1989, 1996) and even more explicitly by Kuran (1995, 2005).

4.4 The Trust Problem in the Muslim World

My expectation is that both of these patterns will extend into Muslim-plurality countries, with the trust deficit going a long way towards accounting for the participation gap in the region. Further, I hypothesize that the importance of trust in supporting political and economic cooperation helps to explain some counter-intuitive patterns, including why targeted repression of Islamic-based groups can actually bolster their comparative advantage and why Islamic-based business associations are actually less successful under Islamic party rule in Turkey. Moreover, in addition to confirming the validity of these existing theories in the Muslim world, I identify new trust problems in the practice of politics and economics. Specifically, in Chapter 7, I emphasize the importance of interpersonal trust for voter coordination in fractionalized electoral systems. In addition, in Chapter 8, I highlight the role of generalized trust expectations in the beginning of longer-term economic partnerships.

But before elaborating on the nature of the trust problem in Turkey and the Muslim world, I first turn to exploring trust's role in the comparative advantage of Islamic-based groups. If low generalized trust expectations are indeed the main obstacle to political and economic participation in Muslim-plurality countries, how might references to Islam help groups overcome this trust problem and successfully mobilize their individual supporters? And why has the existing literature under-estimated the importance of trust in Islamic-based mobilization?

5

Muslim Identity and Group-Based Trust

> The idea of a solitary westernized individual whose faith in God is private is very threatening to you. An atheist who belongs to a community is far easier for you to trust than a solitary man who believes in God. For you, a solitary man is far more wretched and sinful than a non-believer.
>
> O. Pamuk (2005)

> Get to know each other: This is the first pillar of the system. Get to know and love each other in the spirit of God, and feel the true meaning of complete Brotherhood in what is between you, and strive to ensure that nothing clouds the purity of your relationship...
>
> H. al-Banna (n.d.)

In the preceding chapter, I made the argument that interpersonal trust is necessary for most collective activities. Moreover, I argued that a non-particularized form of trust – one not based on prior experience with the entrusted – is particularly valuable in sustaining cooperation in large, anonymous, latent political and economic groups, as well as in the beginning of smaller-scale, longer-term cooperative relationships, the first link in a particularized trust chain. Although I find that most individuals in the Muslim world are trustworthy and should be trusted, there remains a generalized trust deficit in the region. Linking this pattern to earlier assessments of political and economic activity in the region, I hypothesized that the generalized trust deficit could well explain the participation gap in the Muslim world. Although conditional cooperators clearly out number free riders, they appear to be struggling to locate each other, making it difficult to begin and sustain cooperation and coordination among them. In the forthcoming chapter, I will expand upon this point, arguing that trust can explain both the participation gap in many Muslim countries, as well as the comparative advantage of Islamic-based groups operating there.

To understand the role that trust plays in the Islamic advantage, it is important to recall that, while generalized distrust may undermine participation in collective activities, trustworthiness in the Muslim world indicates the potential for political and economic cooperation, if only trust-expectations can be updated. My earlier investigations reveal that generalized distrust in the region is not culturally determined and can, indeed, be improved; but this seems to occur only upon out-migration. Given how slow-moving generalized trust expectations are within countries, it seems unlikely that generalized trust will improve overnight. Therefore, if the potential for collective action is to be realized in the shorter term, an alternative type of trust becomes critical. And since trust based on firsthand experience is so narrow in scope, an alternative source of non-particularized trust is what is required.

In the pages that follow, I introduce the concept of group-based trust – a non-particularized form of trust, conditioned on a shared group identity. I make the argument that group-based trust and a salient Islamic identity are the key foundations of the Islamic advantage, in Turkey and in much of the Muslim world. Lengthy existing literatures in social psychology and behavioral economics indicate that individuals who belong to the same identity group naturally cooperate with one another (Brewer and Kramer 1986; Habyarimana et al. 2009; Tajfel 1974). This group-based cooperation is based on a mutual expectation among group members that they will do right by one another, even when given the opportunity to do otherwise (Jin and Yamagishi 1997; Yamagishi and Kiyonari 2000). This trust, intrinsically shared among group members, may well be the result of an evolutionary process (Boyd et al. 2003) and appears to operate across a wide range of contexts (Goette, Huffman, and Meier 2006; Wit and Wilke 1992).

In the framework introduced in Chapter 4, we can say that a shared group identity helps make conditional cooperators out of rational egoists. Further, group boundaries help these cooperators successfully identify one another: in-group members are to be trusted and cooperated with, while out-group members may still be distrusted. So long as shared group membership is recognized and salient among those involved, trust and cooperation can be sustained. Remarkably, that means that, simply by framing an interpersonal interaction in terms of a shared identity, trust and cooperation can emerge where otherwise there was none. Two distrusting individuals, who share an identity but do not know it, or who are not primed to think of one another in those terms, will not have their group-based trust expectations activated, and will be unlikely to cooperate; but once they mutually recognize one another as coming from the same group, reciprocal trust and cooperation are the likely outcome. This happens even when their expectations of most people are low, so that group-based trust becomes an effective replacement for generalized trust.

Building off of this basic logic, I argue that references to Islam, made by leaders of Islamic organizations, effectively prime individuals to think of themselves and others as sharing a single group identity. In this way, the use of Islamic language and symbols triggers reciprocal expectations of trust and trustworthiness, encouraging individuals to participate in collective activities and making cooperation and coordination among them more likely. In an otherwise low-trust environment, this in-group trust becomes immensely valuable, supporting collective action where it would otherwise falter, to the considerable advantage of Islamic-based organizations. In this way, Islamic references pay considerable dividends.

The existing literature on Islamic-based politics and economics has largely overlooked the important role played by trust because it tends to endorse a conceptualization of religion as something decidedly personal. In this view, religion defines an individual's beliefs about herself and her place in the world, articulates a set of personal obligations for her, and creates a one-on-one relationship between her and her God. But I would argue that many religions, especially those that are more egalitarian, like Islam, can also function as a social identity. Here, religion is decidedly more collective, developing relationships among individual adherents as they build a sense of commitment to one another. Although these two dimensions of religion – personal piety and religious group identity – are oftentimes related, they remain distinct. So in contrast to my earlier findings, which showed a negative effect of Islamic faith on political and economic activity, I expect to see Islamic *identity* supporting higher levels of cooperation and coordination, in a variety of contexts.

In the pages that follow, I review the existing literatures in social psychology and behavioral economics on group-based identity, cooperation, and trust (Section 5.1). I then develop a conceptualization of Islam as a group identity, contrasting it with personal piety and faith (Section 5.2). I explore the distinction between these two dimensions of religion, both theoretically and empirically, finding that participation in communal religious activities is a strong indicator of a salient Islamic identity. I discuss how these communal activities operate both as a marker of identity and a mechanism for strengthening its salience, as well as a method for developing common knowledge of a shared identity among group members. For all these reasons, I suggest that individuals with a strong Islamic identity, who regularly participate in their local religious communities, are the ones most likely to be affected by references to Islam. These references prime them to think of themselves and others in terms of a shared group identity, making them more willing to work together towards a political or economic end.

5.1 TRUST WITHIN IDENTITY GROUPS

As I have argued previously, interpersonal trust is a necessary foundation for cooperation and coordination in a number of contexts: from participation in mass political activities, including boycotting, demonstrating, and voting; to social activities, such as contributions to a local public good or investments in community projects; and even economic behaviors, like saving in a formal banking institution or establishing a new business relationship. Because of the scale of most of these activities – large, anonymous, latent – and because of their basic nature – infrequent, one-shot, with strangers – they require a non-particularized form of trust, such as generalized trust, which expects honesty and cooperation from "most people." But where generalized trust expectations are low, as they are in many Muslim-plurality countries, an

5.1 Trust within Identity Groups

alternative source of non-particularized trust is needed to support cooperation and coordination.

Decades of research in social psychology and behavioral economics point to a consistent pattern: individuals who belong to a common group – even one that is entirely fictitious – have an advantage when it comes to collective action. They are significantly more likely to cooperate with one another, even in one-shot, anonymous interactions. The source of this advantage is none other than trust: members of the same group cooperate with one another in large part because they expect that same sort of cooperation in return. These reciprocal expectations, common even to strangers assigned to their groups in an artificial lab setting, are not based on any direct first hand experience and are therefore not particularized, that is, what Marilynn Brewer (2008) describes as "depersonalized." I call this form of non-particularized trust "group-based trust" because it is naturally extended to any member of one's group. Further, I argue that this type of trust can function as a near-perfect substitute for generalized trust, supporting cooperation and coordination in large-scale, latent organizations, provided they can effectively leverage a shared, salient group identity.

In the section that follows, I review the existing literature on group-based cooperation and argue that similar feelings of in-group trust can be found across the Muslim world, including within religious communities. I then bring together disparate observations from social psychology, behavioral economics, and anthropology to define the conditions under which group identities and group-based trust are most likely to be activated. Finally, I consider how trust within groups can substitute for more generalized trust expectations, to support cooperation and coordination. This will then lead into a discussion of personal faith and religious group identity in Section 5.2.

5.1.1 Cooperation within Groups

In-group cooperation is now a well-established phenomenon: decades of lab- and field-based experimental research find that a shared group identity supports more generosity, cooperation, and coordination among group members (Brewer and Kramer 1986; Chen and Chen 2011; Goette, Huffman, and Meier 2006; Jensen et al. 2015; Kramer and Brewer 1984; Wit and Wilke 1992). The earliest experimental work, led by Henri Tajfel, identified this pattern in entirely fictitious (so-called minimal) groups. Simply calling a subset of individuals a "group" was enough to support cooperation among them.[1] Extrapolating from this, scholars have largely agreed that the tendency for groups to cooperate is almost automatic within humans. Human preference for in-group members has been identified in artificial laboratory settings (Charness, Rigotti, and Rustichini 2007; Jin, Yamagishi, and Kiyonari 1996; Platow

---

[1] As Tajfel and his coauthors concluded, "the very act of social categorization... isolated from other variables [can] lead – under certain conditions – to intergroup behavior which discriminates against the out-group and favors the in-group" (1971, p. 151).

et al. 2012) as well as in field-based experiments that rely on real-world (mostly ethnic) groups (Charnysh, Lucas, and Singh 2015; Chuah et al. 2014; Goette, Huffman, and Meier 2006). The cooperative advantage of groups uncovered by these studies is often cited to explain why (ethnolinguistic) homogeneity is correlated with greater public goods provision (Alesina, Baqir, and Easterly 1999) and higher rates of economic growth (Easterly and Levine 1997) across communities.

To explain the consistency of this in-group favoritism, many rely on an evolutionary logic. In this view, group-based cooperation originates within smaller, well-defined groups capable of monitoring members' reputations and sanctioning transgressions; later, it expands to become part of all human social interaction (Boyd et al. 2003; Fehr and Fischbacher 2003). Social psychology suggests that the tendency to work well as part of a group hinges on one's social identity, something integrated with but distinct from one's identity as an individual (Ellemers, Spears, and Doosje 2002; Tajfel 1974). In general, social identities mark individuals as members of a "social category, defined by membership rules and allegedly characteristic attributes or expected behaviors" (Fearon 1999, p. 36). By definition, these identities link individuals to other members of the same category. And a large part of this common group membership is an almost instinctive tendency to cooperate with one another.

A number of lab- and field-based experimental studies have identified the phenomenon of group-based cooperation in Muslim-plurality settings, from Whitt and Wilson's (2007) study in Bosnia using real-world ethnic identities; to Chuah et al.'s (2014) work on cooperation within religious communities in Malaysia, and Hewstone, Islam, and Judd's (1993) similar study in Bangladesh; to the work of Binzel and Fehr (2013) on generosity within social circles in Cairo. Beyond the experimental research, there are countless additional examples of this type of group-based cooperation cited by ethnographers in the Muslim world. Both Carol Delaney (1993) and Jenny White (2002) make mention of the Turkish practice of *imece* (community projects) within neighborhoods in rural and urban contexts, respectively. These are collaborative efforts, aimed at building a communal resource or helping a community member in need, based on a sense of mutual obligation, and they are described as having the potential to support cooperation in other contexts. As White explains in her study of the Ümraniye neighborhood in Istanbul,

> ... [m]utual obligation wove a web of support where everyone put into the family and the community, and could rely on the resources of the family and community when they needed them.... [*İmece*] provided economic support for community members and also a basis for political and civic mobilization (2002, p. 71).

A similar phenomenon is the practice of *gotong royong* (mutual assistance) in Indonesia (Mujani 2003). John Bowen clarifies that "[t]he term corresponds to genuinely indigenous notions of moral obligation and generalized reciprocity, [and] it has been reworked by the state to become a cultural-ideological instrument for the mobilization of village labor" (1986, p. 546). Other examples of this type of collective collaboration in the Muslim world

5.1 Trust within Identity Groups

include the practice of *vartan bhanji* (an institutionalized custom of service exchange) among the urban and rural poor in Pakistan (Beall 1995; Saher, Khan, and Khan 2012), *moba* (joint work in the field) in Central Bosnia (Bringa 1995), and feelings of *semangat gotong royong* (unity in community), identified by Hassan (1997) in suburban communities of Malaysia.

In each of these cases, the basis of cooperation is a group identity that is more about proximity than common kinship or affinity, but there are similar reports of collaboration among ethnic and, increasingly, religious communities in the region. In fact, while geographic-based forms of cooperation still operate in the Muslim world, there is some evidence of their diminished significance as migration and urbanization break down traditional patterns of association. For example, in Kemal Karpat's (2009) *The Gecekondu*, he notes how young migrants initially brought village- and kinship-based bonds with them to Istanbul before soon discarding them. Though some of the traditional constructs remain, they are increasingly being redefined within an explicitly religious context.[2] As once-isolated groups interact and intermix via migration, trade, and even social media, Islam has tended to become a key unifying thread, supporting even larger circles of cooperation than what were previously possible. As Asef Bayat explains in the Egyptian case:

> A modern city like Cairo tends, on the one hand, to differentiate, fragment, and break down the traditional face-to-face ethnic or religious-based communities by facilitating the experience of sharing with other cultural-religious groupings. At the same time, however, religious-ethnic identities may persist or get reinvented not necessarily through face-to-face interactions, but through the construction of imaginary or "distanciated" communities (2010, p. 188).

A similar trend is noted in Turkey by M. Hakan Yavuz: "The only social capital that facilitates cross-family or hometown-identity-based association has been the religious networks. Most of Turkey's provincial foundations and associations are [increasingly] formed around a religion or institution" (2009, p. 115). The notion of Islam as a unifying factor is hardly new – indeed, Ibn Khaldûn mentions it in his *Muqaddimah* – but it has found renewed attention as local, national, and international movements increasingly rely on it (Deeb 2006; White 2012). In other words, as we bring the extant literature on group-based cooperation to bear on the Muslim world, the "group" at play is increasingly religious – Islamic – in nature.

5.1.2 Group-Based Trust

Having identified a widespread cooperative advantage within groups – whether "minimal" or substantial, ethnic or religious – social psychologists and behavioral economists have sought to identify the cause(s) of this striking pattern.

---

[2] White (2002) offers a compelling discussion of the enduring significance of "vernacular politics," borrowed from village-based constructs, within Turkish urban communities, including the aforementioned practice of *imece*.

In their ground-breaking study, *Coethnicity*, James Habyarimana, Macartan Humphreys, Daniel Posner and Jeremy Weinstein specify three potential mechanisms that could plausibly underlie cooperation within groups: group-based *preferences* – that group members either intrinsically care about one another, tend to care about the same things, or enjoy a warm glow from cooperating with one another; group-based *technology* – that group members are better at working together, are better able to understand one another, have more frequent contact with one another, or are better able to track one another down; and group-based *strategy selection* – that "people play the same game differently depending on the identity of their partners" (2009, p. 11). To evaluate these alternatives, the team carefully designed a series of experiments to isolate and assess each in the context of Kampala, Uganda.

In contrast to other preference-based explanations (Alesina, Baqir, and Easterly 1999), the authors find little evidence of intrinsic biases against out-group members.[3] Instead, they find consistent support for the strategy selection mechanism: group members cooperate with one another because they expect (i.e., trust) that other group members will cooperate with them. While there is some evidence that a technological advantage within groups may rationalize this feeling of trust,[4] the instinct to expect more of group members is almost automatic whenever individuals know that they are interacting with members of their own group.[5] And because these in-group trust expectations are symmetric, they end up being self-fulfilling: because Person A expects her group-mate B to be honest, she trusts and cooperates, and vice versa, so that both A and B's trust is met with trustworthy behavior, further strengthening their overall expectations that group members are to be trusted.

A few additional details are important here. Critically, group-based trust is a non-particularized (or depersonalized) form of trust. Although it is conditioned on shared group membership, that is the only piece of information needed to activate it. Members of the same group will tend to trust one another even when they know nothing else about one another, when they are essentially strangers except for the identity they share. Most likely, this is because they use their group identity as a heuristic – an informational shortcut – that simplifies the complex process of identifying who should be trusted (Brewer 2007, 2008; Foddy and Dawes 2008). Remarkably, the instinct to trust other members of one's own group (and behave in a trustworthy manner towards them) appears to affect even free riders (Habyarimana et al. 2009). Moreover, as I will explore in more detail below, it seems that the instinct to trust in-group members extends even to those who generally distrust most people.

---

[3] For a similar result in a different context, see Yamagishi and Kiyonari (2000).
[4] Habyarimana et al. suppose that these technological strengths might support in-group trust by allowing in-group members to better monitor and sanction one another, as argued elsewhere by Miguel and Gugerty (2005).
[5] Further evidence of this intrinsic group-based trust has been identified in studies conducted by Jin and Yamagishi (1997), Yamagishi, Jin, and Kiyonari (1999), and Yamagishi and Kiyonari (2000), to name but a few.

5.1 Trust within Identity Groups

Although the tendency to trust in-group members is automatic, it is still somewhat context-dependent. First and foremost, each group member must know that she shares a common identity with her partner(s) and, beyond that, she must know that they know this as well, and vice versa. In other words, shared group membership must be common knowledge (Chuah et al. 2014; Jin and Yamagishi 1997; Platow et al. 2012). Moreover, there is evidence that group-based trust expectations are strengthened when either of two additional conditions are met: communication and identity salience. The first holds that when group members are able to talk among themselves prior to interacting, they are even more likely to trust one another and cooperate (Billig 1973; Dawes, McTavish, and Shaklee 1977; Kerr and Kaufman-Gilliland 1994); the second holds that group-based trust is strengthened whenever the shared identity is more salient, whether attachment to the identity is naturally occurring (Falk, Heine, and Takemura 2014; Robinson 2016) or manipulated through priming (Charness, Rigotti, and Rustichini 2007; Kramer and Brewer 1984).[6]

As with group-based cooperation, examples of group-based trust abound in the Muslim world, although rarely are they linked to the social scientific literature cited here. In her rich description of interpersonal interactions in Cairo, Salwa Ismail makes numerous mentions of trust and how it is used to support cooperation within different sub-communities, from networks extending informal credit (2006a, p. 30) to youth fraternities (p. 99). In the latter case, she explains how "bonds, ties, and exchanges between [fraternal members] are constructed around norms of trust, loyalty, and obligation" (p. 101). Meanwhile, Clifford Geertz and coauthors highlight the importance of identifying trustworthy individuals (*umanā*) when doing business in the Moroccan *souk*. They also emphasize the conditionality of these trust expectations, explaining how occupation and religious denomination are often differentiated, so that trustworthy "Jewish cloth sellers and shoe repairmen are distinguished from [trustworthy] Muslim cloth sellers and shoe repairmen" (1979, p. 192).

This emphasis on conditionality is also noted by Alan Dubetsky in his study of factory workers in a shantytown (*gecekondu*) outside of Istanbul. He writes that "what is considered *dürüst* (honest) toward one's kinsman or *hemşeri* is not necessarily so toward impersonal organizations, strangers or society at large" (1976, p. 13). Similarly, based on an interview with a Saudi interlocutor, Pascal Menoret explains how group boundaries are used to limit the trust developed in Qur'anic reading circles to in-group members only. While students were taught to "care about... [n]ot only our society; [but]... about Muslim society as a whole," this expanded circle of care did not extend beyond the *ummah*. The interlocutor states bluntly that he "could not trust a non-Muslim," explaining that they "were brought up this way" (2011, p. 48). Similarly, Toprak et al. (2009) note that religion has become an important

---

[6] There is some evidence that the effect of communication on trust and cooperation may operate via salience, as conversation deepens the importance that individuals place on their shared social identity (Orbell, Kragt, and Dawes 1988).

factor in Turkey when it comes to developing trust and identifying trustworthy friends and trading partners. While dividing society in this way – into us and them, Muslim and non-Muslim – limits the circle of trust that can support cooperation, in an otherwise distrusting environment, higher trust expectations of in-group members can bolster collective action where there would otherwise be none.

5.1.3 Activating Trust within Groups

Given the real value of group-based trust for supporting cooperation within groups, it is important to consider what might help to activate these elevated trust expectations. This will help to identify the conditions under which group-based movements – including Islamic-based ones – are able to leverage group identity and group-based trust to their comparative advantage. When specifying what devices might prove most useful, I return to the three elements introduced above: first, common knowledge of shared identity, which appears to be a necessary condition for triggering group-based trust expectations; second, prior communication or interaction among group members; and third, the salience of the group identity, which is both naturally occurring in some group members and, for others, can be manipulated through conscious and subconscious priming of the shared identity. I now expand upon each of these, in turn, focusing on actions that political and economic entrepreneurs can take to help bolster in-group cooperation via trust.

For knowledge of the shared identity to be common, not only must each individual be aware that they share an identity, but each individual must know that the others know this as well. Outside of an artificial, lab-based setting, the best opportunities for creating common knowledge in the real world involve large-scale ceremonies and rituals. Michael Suk-Young Chwe notes that rituals are defined by their repetition and formalization: the first helps to ensure that the message is heard, the second, that it is understood, two key ingredients in the process of knowledge production (2003, p. 29). But for the knowledge thusly produced to be common, Chwe also emphasizes how information is conveyed, highlighting the role of eye contact between attendees via inward-facing circles or lines (p. 30).

It is for these reasons that the leaders of group-based political and economic organizations – including Islamic-based ones – focus on making regular, repeated reference to their shared group-identity, doing so using similar language or common symbols, in a setting in which the audience is large and likely to interact, even if that interaction is mostly silent. Recall that my definition of Islamic-based political and economic movements rests entirely on their (explicit and consistent) use of Islamic tropes and symbols. In other words, a key element of knowledge production is hard-baked into the definition of the phenomenon I seek to explain. In addition, many Islamic-based groups facilitate the creation of common knowledge through public speeches and rallies, held in stadiums, convention centers, or other open areas. Like other identity-based movements, they use televised events and advertisements

5.1 Trust within Identity Groups

to create common knowledge, especially at moments when it is well known that the audience is large and captive (e.g., during the Super Bowl in the United States (Chwe 2003, pp. 45–49), or during Ramadan in the Muslim world (Armbrust 2006)).

Large-scale events of these types also support group-based trust, beyond creating common knowledge of shared group membership, when they allow for interaction among attendees. Recall that communication among group members, prior to their attempts at cooperation and coordination, tends to improve both outcomes (Billig 1973; Kerr and Kaufman-Gilliland 1994). For this reason, many political rallies and associational meetings include gaps between programming (to allow for informal mingling among participants), or scheduled networking events (for more formalized interaction). Similar exchanges can occur outside of events organized by community leaders: any repeated interactions among group members, even if they are informal, will help to create a common sense that they share a common identity (Patel 2007).

When the leaders of identity-based groups seek to activate group-based trust among their members, besides thinking about how to trigger those trust expectations, they must also consider who best to target. Studies show that trust, cooperation, and coordination within groups are most common among those for whom the shared identity is particularly salient (Charnysh, Lucas, and Singh 2015; Robinson 2016). The salience of identity is often context-dependent, based on whether individuals have recently been primed to actively think about their identity; but salience also varies across individuals, with some coming into the same situation with a deeper pre-existing attachment to their group identity.[7] Those individuals for whom the group identity is already salient, who actively identify with it, may respond more strongly to primes triggering them to think of themselves in those terms. Alternatively, they may not need any prime at all in order to think in this way. In either case, the salience of an individual's group identity – whether pre-existing or primed – will encourage individuals to think of a given situation and those involved in it as members of a single group, elevating trust in them.

The importance of common knowledge and priming in the activation of group-based trust can help explain an apparent contradiction: the coexistence of generalized distrust in Muslim countries and the tendency for members of the same group (e.g., Muslims) to trust one another. To put the juxtaposition more succinctly: how can Muslims who instinctively trust other Muslims distrust most people in a context that is majority Muslim? Recall that the key distinction between generalized and group-based trust is that the latter is conditioned on a shared group identity – one that is commonly known and salient – whereas the former has no such condition. While a plurality of citizens in

---

[7] The higher salience of a group identity for these individuals may reflect the fact that their social identity has become part of their personal identity – one or more "socially distinguishing feature[s] that [they take] a special pride in" (Fearon 1999, p. 36). Evidence suggests that the intertwining of an individual's personal identity and her social one is common, although not universal (Greenaway et al. 2016).

the Muslim world are, indeed, nominally Muslim, not all of them actively identify as such; and even among those that do, not every situation primes them to think of themselves and each other in those terms. Therefore, when an average Muslim citizen is asked whether "most people can be trusted," he is unlikely to answer with his Muslim identity (and that of his compatriots) in mind. Only when primed to think of himself and others in those terms – as sharing a common Muslim identity – may he deem them worthy of his trust. This helps explain why Islamic-based appeals are so critical to the success of Islamic political and economic movements and why they represent a defining characteristic of the phenomenon: by priming Muslim group identity, the use of Islamic language and symbols activate mutual expectations of trust among those who identify as Muslims.

5.1.4 Can Group-Based Trust Compensate for Generalized Distrust?

Given the importance of non-particularized trust for collective action, the coexistence of group-based trust among those who identify as Muslims, on the one hand, and the generalized trust deficit in the Muslim world, on the other, begs the question of whether the former can be an effective substitute for the latter. Indeed, I argue that the basis of the Islamic advantage in spurring collective action rests precisely on this substitution effect: whereas generalized distrust normally prevents individuals from participating in most collective activities, references to Islam made by Islamic-based groups prime their shared Islamic identity, activating group-based trust expectations that support cooperation and coordination.

To the best of my knowledge, the substitutability of these two types of trust has not yet been suggested nor empirically established. In the chapters of Part II, I test this hypothesis using data from Turkey and from across the Muslim world; but here, I offer two sets of existing experimental results that suggest that substitutability may be possible. First, research conducted by James Fowler and Cindy Kam (2007) assesses two norms – generalized cooperative ones (what they call "altruism") and group-based ones (what they term "social identification") – and the effect of each on political participation across subjects.[8] Ultimately, they find that both generalized and group-based cooperative norms support political mobilization and that the magnitude of each effect is essentially identical. This would suggest that the two types of norms have the potential to be near-perfect substitutes.

Moreover, returning to the experimental results presented by Habyarimana et al. (2009), there is evidence that shared (ethnic) group membership boosts trust, cooperation, and altruism especially among rational egoists (i.e., free

---

[8] Although Fowler and Kam do not focus specifically on trust expectations, rather on altruism (measured using the results of a dictator game), the link between these concepts is now relatively well established. In their cross-national study, Ashraf, Bohnet, and Piankov find that "trust decisions are related to both expectations of return *and unconditional kindness* [emphasis added]" (2006, p. 201). The latter they also measure using contributions in a dictator game.

riders). These are individuals who lack a generalized norm of cooperation: they neither trust most people, nor behave in a trustworthy manner towards them.[9] And yet, once group-based norms are made salient (in this case via common knowledge of a shared group identity), these egoists become conditional cooperators, willing to trust and behave honestly towards their in-group members. Here, group-based norms appear able to support cooperation even in the absence of more generalized ones, further evidence that one may be a reasonable substitute for the other.

Beyond these lab-based results, there are plenty of ethnographic observations from the Muslim world that describe the importance of communal (i.e., group-based) solidarity in the face of generalized distrust or disfavor. For example, White describes how in "a context of mutual suspicion [in Turkey]... other communities of belonging take on heightened importance" (2012, p. 106), while Armando Salvatore and Dale Eickelman emphasize the importance of "warm circles [that] offer mutual trust and familiarity" in different Muslim societies that are usually filled with "cold" ones (2004, p. 18). And yet, to the best of my knowledge, the substitutability of group-based trust for generalized trust has not yet been discussed in the context of Islamic-based politics and economics, in particular. That is precisely what I do here.

Specifically, I look for evidence that group-based trust and/or a salient Islamic group identity within Islamic communities can mitigate the negative effect of generalized distrust on political and economic participation, to the advantage of Islamic-based political and economic movements. I do this, first, by establishing that generalized distrust undermines a variety of political and economic activities, from participation in mass politics, to voter coordination, and cooperation among independent business owners. Next, I look for evidence that group-based trust or a salient Islamic identity boosts participation in these same activities. Combining these, I aim to identify the substitutability of one for the other by seeing how the two effects interact. In particular, I am interested in identifying how generalized distrust impacts participation among those individuals or communities with healthy levels of group-based trust or a strong attachment to an Islamic group identity. My expectation is that the trust problem will be effectively solved for these people, in these settings. These are the empirical tasks that await me in the chapters of Part II.

5.2 ISLAM AS A GROUP IDENTITY

A careful reader will note that I have suggested that group-based trust and salient group identity might be interchangeable. Although the social psychology literature indicates that this is plausible, in a broad sense, it has not yet

---

[9] Similar to my definition of free riders, Habyarimana et al. define egoists as "individuals who, absent the reciprocity norms made salient by shared [group] identities, show a stronger tendency to look out for their own interests at the expense of others" (2009, p. 23).

been established in the specific case of the Muslim world and Islam. Further, and perhaps more importantly, it is not yet clear what exactly is meant by an "Islamic group identity." The concept of an Islamic identity has been largely overlooked in existing theories of Islamic-based politics and economics, which tend to focus more on the power of personal faith than the importance of group-ness. I attempt a response to both of these questions in the section that follows.

First, I make the theoretical distinction between personal religious beliefs – the more individualized dimension of religiosity – and a religious identity – its more collective aspects. Particularly in the case of Islam, I argue that the two are related but nonetheless distinct. To make this distinction, I rely on a definition of group identity as a social category to which individuals belong and upon which they condition their behavior, including their behavior towards one another. I suggest that an Islamic group identity is primarily about an attachment to other members of one's religious community (*ümmet* in Turkish, *ummah* in Arabic), rather than a sense of individualized attachment to a set of beliefs or a duty to God.

Based on this conceptualization, and relying on an extant literature that links the salience of one's social identity to regular interaction with other group members, I suggest that an Islamic group-identity is indicated by frequent participation in religious group activities (e.g., regular attendance at mosque, enrollment in religious schools, membership in religious associations). In contrast, the more personal dimensions of religion are reflected in the intensity of personal religious beliefs, similar to the measures of faith used in earlier tests of the faith-based theory.

Using novel data from Turkey, as well as cross-national surveys, I demonstrate the distinction between personal piety and an Islamic identity. I find that indicators of the two concepts are relatively weakly correlated with one another; and the results of principal component factor analysis reveal that they are statistically distinguishable. Moreover, and in contrast to some existing theories of religious group activities, I show that what distinguishes those who take an active role in their religious communities is neither prosociality nor efficacy. Instead, they stand out for having more in-group trust, an indicator of their salient group identity, one that is independent of their personal religious beliefs.

5.2.1 Conceptualizing Personal Religiosity and Religious Group Identity

For an individual who considers herself to be religious, her faith may be decidedly personal, reflecting the depth of her religious convictions and her individual relationship to God.[10] But for another, religiosity might (also) be about being part of a religious community, about the relationships he has with

---

[10] In her study of prayer in the Egyptian context, Saba Mahmood notes that her interlocutors described piety as "the quality of 'being close to God'" (2001, p. 830).

other believers. Consider the difference between those Muslims who pray regularly at mosque and those who prefer to carry out the same religious obligation in the privacy of their own homes. Both can be said to be devout, but only the former behaves in a way that indicates a desire to perform his religious duty in the company of others. The extent of an individual's attachment to and involvement in his religious community is what I call collective religiosity or a religious group identity. I contrast this with personal religiosity or piety – the strength of devotion to God and the intensity of beliefs. Among Muslims, I expect that these two types of religiosity are related for some, but not for all. Moreover, the two should have different implications for the practice of politics and economics. Importantly, I expect that only Islamic group identity will be associated with higher levels of group-based trust.

The distinction between personal piety and religious group identity is not exactly new, but it remains relatively understudied in the existing literature on religion, including the sociology of religion (Durkheim 1973; Weber 1922) and the economics of it (Iannaccone 1998; Iyer 2016).[11] The difference between the two is somewhat related to that between "intrinsic" and "extrinsic" religiosity (Allport and Ross 1967), but the overlap in conceptualization is not perfect.[12] Rather, as Jesse Grahm and Jonathan Haidt put it, a "social-functionalist perspective on religious practice [i.e., religious group identity] complements the more widespread belief-centric approach [i.e., personal religiosity], increasing our understanding of what religion is, and why it makes people do the things they do" (2010, p. 147). For them, a "group-focused approach to religion treats God as a maypole – it is indeed the center of the action, but the action itself is the creation, enacting, and maintaining of an emergent community by the collective behaviors taking place all around it" (p. 142). Or, as Ismail describes it in the specific case of Islam: "Religion as a set of rules involving reference to the divine/transcendental cannot be understood outside of the social context of practices" (2004, p. 618).

To better understand the theoretical distinction between personal religiosity and religious group identity, I begin with a closer look at the concept of identity itself, something from which one might derive one's sense of pride or honor. In the context of cooperation or coordination with others, the *social* dimensions of one's identity are clearly most salient. As discussed above, in its social role, identity is essentially a label one is given or, more likely, with which one chooses to identify (Ashmore, Deaux, and McLaughlin-Volpe 2004). More specifically, it is a label that is "invoked often enough or in sufficiently important situations that people condition their behavior or thinking on it"

---

[11] An excellent first step in the development of the concept of religious identity in political science can be found in the work of Wilcox, Wald, and Jelen (2008), but the mantle has yet to be taken up by others, in this field or beyond.

[12] Cohen et al. offer a nice summary of these two concepts: "intrinsic religiousness [involves] normative motivations and practice, in which religion [is] the master motive in one's life. Conversely, extrinsic religiousness [captures] the use of religion for instrumental purposes, such as to gain comfort, protection, social connectedness, and so on" (2005, p. 49).

(Fearon 1999, p. 13). That is, identity is a group marker that has meaning through its impact on behavior; and not just the behavior of any one member of that group, but any and all individuals who identify as part of it.

Bringing this view of social identity to bear on religion, a religious group identity becomes a label (e.g., Catholic, Hindu, Sunni Muslim) that individuals may identify with, one that inherently connects them to others who identify with that same label. Their collective connection to this label comes with some prescriptions that impact how they behave in their day-to-day lives, including how they behave towards one another, especially when compared to an outgroup member. Using Vassilis Saroglou's (2011) conceptual scheme, a religious group identity is primarily about "bonding" and "belonging," although it also has considerable impact on "behaving," as well as "believing," insofar as it intersects with members' personal religiosity. Meanwhile, personal religiosity is primarily about "believing" and to a certain extent also about "behaving." If there is a sense of "bonding" that occurs as a result of personal piety, it occurs between the individual believer and her God.

As previously discussed, one of the key ways that a group identity conditions the behavior of its members is in the way they approach other group members. Specifically, those who share the same group identity cooperate more frequently with, and expect more cooperation from, one another. Emerging research indicates that the phenomena of in-group cooperation and trust also extend to religious identities: in a pair of studies Chuah, Fahoum, and Hoffmann find an in-group trust advantage among Hindus and Muslims in India, as well as similar effects across religious groups in Malaysia. As with all group identities, in order for religious group identity to condition behavior thusly – supporting group-based trust, cooperation, and coordination – it must be commonly known among group members. To help individual members correctly and easily identify one another, many religious groups, like others, are associated with clear rules of membership and/or a set of ascriptive characteristics, including particular norms of dress or demeanor (Chandra 2006; Carr and Landa 1983).

In the case of religious group identity, these defining characteristics and symbolic acts are not always as informative as they are for other groups. This is because many of the same characteristics and symbols are used to signify both personal religiosity and religious group identity. For example, the wearing of religious headwear could plausibly indicate that one identifies strongly with one's religious group; alternatively, it could simply indicate that one takes the personal religious obligation to do so seriously. Indeed, in the Turkish case, Çarkoğlu and Toprak find that women who cover tend to do so for decidedly personal reasons.[13] The question therefore remains: how are we to assess the strength of an individual's religious group identity, in a way that differentiates it from the intensity of her personal faith?

---

[13] They find that "94.1 percent of covered women stated that they would not uncover even if most women in their family or close environment" did so (2007, p. 69.)

5.2.2 Participation in Religious-Group Activities

To capture the strength and salience of religious group identity, I suggest a focus on religious group activities, such as attendance at religious service, enrollment in religious schools, and membership in religious associations. Regular participation in these types of collective activities – especially in cases where it is not considered a religious obligation – may reflect an individual's personal faith, but it is more likely to reflect her sense of attachment to her religious community. Many of these activities involve more significant time commitments with considerably less flexibility than private religious experiences.[14] And depending on how the religious group is perceived socially, these activities can even come with steep reputation costs. As such, the decision to take part in collective religious events and activities indicates something of real importance to an individual.

In the particular case of Islam, participation in certain collective activities may be particularly indicative of a salient religious identity. While Muslims are obligated to pray five times daily, they are free to fulfill this obligation wherever they see fit. The decision to go pray at mosque, therefore, is not primarily about fulfilling a religious obligation. Rather, it speaks to a desire to fulfill this obligation in the company of others, as part of a religious community (*ummah* or *ümmet*). In contrast, religious beliefs and practices that do not involve the religious community (e.g., private acts of prayer, reading of religious texts) speak more to personal piety than to a religious group identity.

In my interactions with interlocutors in Turkey, the distinction between these two types of religiosity – and the role of communal gatherings in differentiating them – was a recurring theme. Originally, I was surprised to see that many happily engaged in seemingly contradictory behavior. Many university-aged women, for example, made a conscious choice not to don a headscarf, what they saw as a symbol of religious obedience (to God) they did not personally support. Yet, at the same time, they were regular participants in Qur'anic reading circles and even made a point of attending mosque at least once a week, huddling in the crowded women-only sections in the back.[15] The latter they did *not* out of an obligation to God or because of their commitment to their faith – they often joked that they were not totally sold on the traditional view of Allah and submission to him. Instead, as they explained it to me, these types of activities brought them into harmony with a community of like-minded individuals. They valued the time that they shared together and the bonds that they created through regular and repeated interactions. And

---

[14] Indeed, applications of club-goods models to religious groups focuses on the costs of participation in activities organized by the club. Here, the fact that taking part in these group activities is costly is hardly a coincidence: a willingness to pay these costs plays an important role in helping the clubs separate out the "true believers" (or, alternatively, true "identifiers") from free riders (Iannaccone 1992).

[15] I met a young student for tea just after Friday prayers and vividly remember the image as she removed her headscarf, without hesitation, just as she exited the mosque.

by virtue of the fact that they made the same choices about how to spend their time and how to express their relationship to their religion, they felt a real attachment to one another, including to each newcomer who joined their circle. They did not often call this feeling "identity," but they made regular mention of "community" (*cemaat*) and were clear about how much it meant to them.

From these conversations, I came to understand that the decision to take part in collective events and activities is indicative of a salient religious group identity. Further, I began to understand that participation in these activities also works to strengthen participants' attachment to that identity. As Cohen et al. explain, regular "ritual and social connection between members of a religion would presumably increase the social embeddedness and behavioral involvement dimensions of collective identity" (2005, p. 55). Indeed, in separate studies, both Páez et al. (2015) and Khan et al. (2016) find a significant, positive effect of participation in collective rituals on subsequent religious group identity.[16] Ostensibly, this effect operates through interactions among group members during the activities, in line with research in social psychology indicating that "groupness" and group-based trust are both increasing in the level of intra-group communication (Dawes, Kragt, and Orbell 1988; Kerr and Kaufman-Gilliland 1994). Therefore, not only does the decision to participate in religious group activities indicate that individuals already value their religious communities, their religious group identity is also strengthened by these activities, in a feedback loop that deepens the link between participation, on the one hand, and identity, on the other.

From my interlocutors, I also came to understand that individuals learned a lot about one another simply through participation in these activities. It signaled that they had the same values and preferences – to be together, as a community – which meant that even newcomers were quickly welcomed into the fold. To me, this meant that joint participation helped them to recognize one another as members of a single community (or group). And because Muslims pray at the most proximate mosque whenever they hear the call to prayer, it is not as though these feelings of communal solidarity were confined to small circles within neighborhoods. Instead, as a fish-monger in Kadıköy explained to me, when he joined with others to pray, he understood his connection to the *ümmet* – the community of believers – not just those particular people praying around him. I see this process as a part of the "belonging" and "bonding" aspects of religious group identity, as a necessary condition for group-based trust to form. Collective religious rituals have already been recognized for their ability to produce common knowledge among individual participants (Aslam 2017; Chwe 2003; Patel 2007). I extend this logic to suggest that one of the key pieces of information learned by attendants in

---

[16] Similarly, in a cross-sectional comparison, Hoffman and Nugent (2017) find that communal religious practice (e.g., mosque attendance) in Lebanon is associated with an increasingly salient group identity, as captured in sect-based party identification.

5.2 Islam as a Group Identity

collective religious events is the basic fact of their group-ness, which in turn, primes expectations of group-based trust.[17]

Looking beyond my interlocutors' personal experiences, I discovered many examples of Islamic religious-group activities and their significance for Islamic group identity and group-based trust. Consider the following description of life in the suburban community of Sungai Pencala, Malaysia:

> The Islamic network of mosques, *surau* [small prayer houses], Qur'anic classes and *yassin* groups [women's Qur'an reading circles] in Sungai Pencala was perceived as an essential context in which Muslims from diverse ethnic backgrounds could interact and forge a sense of brotherhood. In the local parlance, it helped reinforce *semangat gotong royong* [unity in community], which as the hallmark of village life in Sungai Pencala. People imbued with this spirit of togetherness and co-operativeness were the ones who understood Islam well. (Hassan 1997, p. 35)

Similarly, Kikue Hamayotsu quotes a member of the PKS in Indonesia as saying that "it is through religious service and dedication that we develop *espirit de corps* among us" (2011, p. 9). Hassan al-Banna, founder of the Egyptian Muslim Brotherhood, saw mosque-prayer (and other religious activities) as "the place for the fraternization of believers" (Lia and Banna 1998, p. 33). More broadly, Gregory Starrett finds this same sentiment printed in Egyptian textbooks: "Prayer accustoms us to order ... and the binding together of Muslims with cooperative ties and love and harmony" (1995, p. 962). And, in their description of "public Islam" across the Muslim world, Armando Salvatore and Dale Eickelman note how these "practices and the resulting social spaces involve both emotional and intellectual engagement among participants ... and the building of bonds of identity and trust" (2004, p. xiii).

Within Turkey, I also find scholars noting the "social" significance of different religious group activities, from mosque services (Özaloğlu and Gürel 2011), to religious schools (Kaplan 2006), and Islamic organizations (Shively 2008). When using participation in these types of activities as an indicator of religious group identity, it will be important to differentiate participants' attachment to their religious communities, in particular, from a tendency to be more social, in general. The latter trait is often called "prosociality" in the social scientific literature, and while this overall social-ness may have some of the same features of a salient religious group identity – including a tendency towards increased cooperation and generosity – these will not be confined to in-group members, but will instead be extended to all others. In the framework developed here, the difference is between group-based trust expectations, which are conditioned on shared group membership, and more generalized ones, extended to most people.

Beyond prosociality, it will also be important to evaluate whether religious group activities might signal other individual traits. In particular, there is a lengthy extant literature in the study of American politics that considers the

---

[17] Note that since attending these types of events may not always indicate an elevated level of personal piety, what is being communicated is a shared identity, not religiosity.

political significance of religious services. Originally interested in examining why church attendance might impact the politicization of attendants (Jones-Correa and Leal 2001; Kwak, Shah, and Holbert 2004; Singerman 2004), this framework has now also been applied to mosque attendance among American Muslims (Jamal 2005). Here, the mosque (like the church) is seen as a site where individuals gain the resources and information needed to become politically active (Brady, Verba, and Schlozman 1995; Harris 1994) or, alternatively, where they become increasingly motivated to become politicized via ideologically charged sermons (Wald, Owen, and Hill Jr. 1988).[18]

In this way, the existing view of religious service attendance is similar to most existing theories of the Islamic advantage: both focus, almost exclusively, on individualized processes and resources, whether motivation, skills, or information. But in coming together to study and worship, participants do not just accrue resources as individuals; they also form relationships with one another – a collective resource – that can help to support their cooperation in other contexts. Moreover, American churches and mosques differ in important ways from those in the Muslim world. For example, mosques in Turkey are tightly regulated by Office of Religious Affairs (Diyanet İşleri Başkanlığı), which determines the content of each Friday's sermon.[19] Regulation of mosque activity has also been noted in the Jordanian case (Wiktorowicz 1999) as well as in the Malaysian one (Samuri and Hopkins 2017), among others. This implies that it will be considerably more difficult for participants to be politicized by the content of religious services. At the very least, it would mean that any politicization that does occur in mosques in these cases will not be anti-systemic, by design. But it still remains an open question whether mosque attendance (and other religious group activities) are noteworthy as indicators of identity, prosociality, motivation, or resources.

5.2.3 Contrasting Faith and Identity

I have suggested a conceptual distinction between personal religiosity, on the one hand, and a religious group identity on the other. While the former reflects the depth of an individual's religious beliefs and her connection to God, the latter reflects the extent to which she identifies with her Islamic community. And while the former is best measured in terms of an individual's religious convictions and beliefs, as well as her private religious acts, the latter is better captured in terms of participation in religious-group activities, such as regular

---

[18] Note some exceptions to this claim, including Norris and Inglehart (2004), who challenge the presumed relationship between church attendance and political participation across a large sample of countries and Lussier (2019), who compares the political effects of mosque and church attendance in Indonesia and finds that the latter (but not the former) imparts the types of civic skills described above.

[19] This does not mean that sermons are devoid of all political content, rather that the political messages tend to be more implicit than explicit and, prior to the start of AKP rule, unlikely to be used to incite Islamic-based political mobilization (Gürpinar and Kenar 2016; Yılmaz and Barry 2018).

5.2 Islam as a Group Identity

attendance at mosque, membership in a religious organization, or the decision to take part in religious education programs.

While the theoretical distinction between the two concepts might be clear, and while there are *a priori* reasons to accept the connection between religious group activities and religious group identity, neither of these propositions has been established empirically. To see whether there is such a dimensionality to religiosity, differentiating personal piety from a religious group identity, I look at the bivariate correlations between different markers of religion, before conducting principal component factor analysis of these same measures. Recall that factor analysis aims to reduce the dimensionality of data by transforming variation across indicators into the data's principal components, each of which is uncorrelated by design. It can be useful for identifying commonalities among multiple indicators of the same concept, as well as for identifying multiple, distinct concepts, where more than one exists.

In conjunction with KONDA Research and Consultancy, I was able to field two nationally representative, face-to-face surveys in Turkey in support of this book, the first in September 2012, the second in September 2015.[20] In both, I included four questions on religion. Three of these are standard in KONDA's monthly Barometer survey and capture respondents' personal religious beliefs or behaviors: the first asks about respondents' self-reported "lifestyle" (*hayat tarzı*) – whether modern (*modern*), traditional conservative (*geleneksel muhafazakâr*), or religious conservative (*dindar muhafazakâr*); the second asks about their level of "religiosity" (*dindarlık*) – varying from non-believer and non-practicing believer, to a somewhat-practicing believer or a devout one;[21] and the third asks whether they (or their wives, for married male respondents) wear a head-covering.[22] The fourth question was one I added,

---

[20] The 2012 survey covers 2,528 respondents from ninety-one districts (*ilçeler*) across twenty-nine provinces (*iller*, NUTS-3), at least one in each of Turkey's twelve statistical regions (*istatistiki bölgeler*, NUTS-1). The 2015 survey reached 3,491 respondents from 134 districts across thirty provinces in all twelve regions. Across the two, the following provinces were surveyed: Adana, Ankara, Antalya, Balıkesir, Bursa, Denizli, Diyarbakır, Erzurum, Eskişehir, Gaziantep, Giresun, Hatay, Istanbul, Izmir, Kars, Kayseri, Kocaeli, Konya, Kutahya, Malatya, Mersin, Niğde, Ordu, Samsun, Şanlıurfa, Sivas, Tekirdağ, Trabzon, Van, and Zonguldak. Both surveys followed KONDA's sampling protocol which involves stratification on population and education, based on the Address-Based Population Registration System (Adrese Dayalı Nüfus Kayıt Sistemi, ADKS), as well as the results of the most recent general election. Age and gender quotas were then applied in every sampled unit, across rural and urban locales. Reflective of the Turkish population, the final sample was 51.5 percent urban, with 28.1 percent coming from towns, and 20.3 percent from villages.

[21] The precise categories are as follows: "someone who does not believe in the necessity of religion" (*dinin gereklerine pek inanmayan biri*); "someone who has faith but does not fulfill religious obligations" (*inançlı ama dinin gereklerini pek yerine getiremeyen biri*); "a pious person who tries to fulfill religious obligations" (*dinin gereklerini yerine getirmeye çalışan dindar biri*); and "a religious person who fulfills all religious obligations" (*dinin tüm gereklerini tam yerine getiren dindar biri*).

[22] Respondents are asked "do you/your wife cover your head when you go/she goes out?" They are then asked to describe "how do you/does she cover?" (In Turkish: "*Eşiniz veya siz, sokağa çıkarken başınızı örtüyor musunuz? Nasıl örtüyorsunuz?*") Head-covering options include

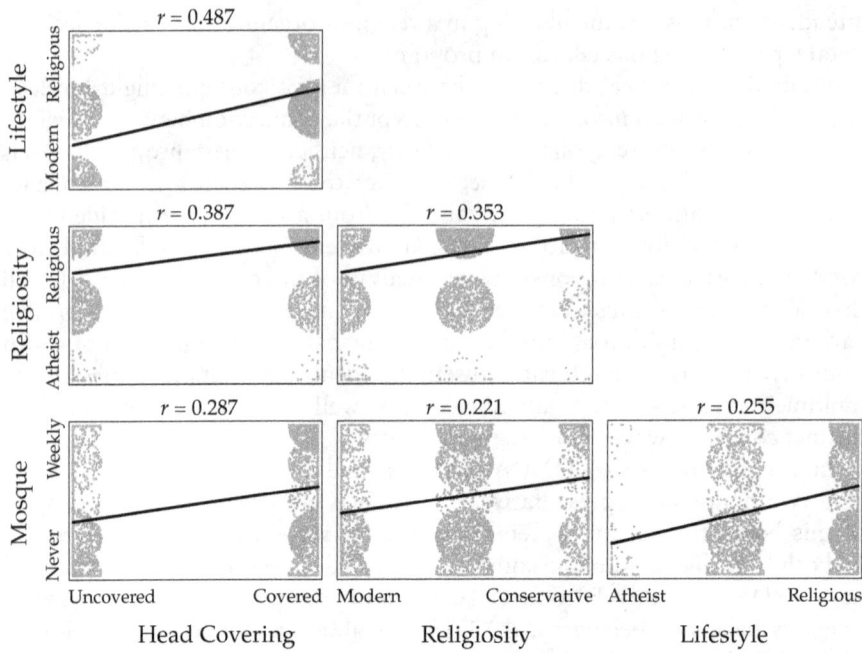

FIGURE 5.1 Relationships between Markers of Religion in Turkey

Notes: Bivariate scatterplots with fitted lines between four markers of religiosity, with correlation coefficients reported, across 4,894 Turkish Muslims. Thirty percent random noise added to jitter each observation and minimize overlap.

about mosque attendance, a quintessential religious group activity. Its phrasing is based on a similar question posed by the WVS in Turkey, with responses ranging from "every day" to "never."[23]

Bivariate correlations between each pair of measures are displayed in Figure 5.1. For each pair, scatter plots with fitted lines are presented along with the correlation coefficient (r), printed above each figure. Overall, I find that the three measures of personal religiosity are more interrelated than any one of them is with my proposed indicator of religious group identity. Among the pairs, the strongest relationship is that between a religious "lifestyle" and women's head-covering ($r=0.487$), followed by the correlations between "religiosity" and head-covering ($r=0.387$) and between "religiosity" and "lifestyle"

---

başörtüsü – described by Ali Çarkoğlu as fabric "used to cover only the head, leaving some hair visible" – *türban* – one that "leaves the face bare but covers all the head including the neck and shoulders with no hair seen" – and *çarşaf, peçe* – which Çarkoğlu describes as covering "the entire body from head to toe except for the eyes" (2009, p. 455).

[23] The question asks respondents, "outside of funerals etc., how often do go to house of worship?" (In Turkish: "*Cenazeler vs. dışında bugüunlerde ibadethaneye ne sıklıkta gidiyorsunuz?*") Respondents can say they go every day (*her gün*), a couple times per week (*haftada bir, iki*), once a week (*haftada bir*), a couple times per month (*ayda bir, iki*), on special days and holidays (*özel günlerde, bayramlarda*), once a year (*yılda bir*), or never (*hiç gitmem*).

5.2 Islam as a Group Identity

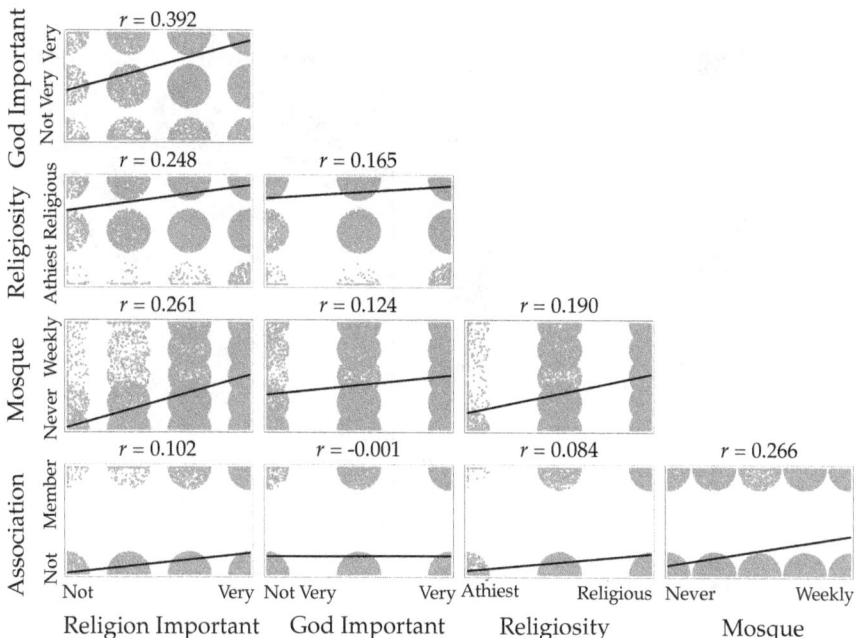

FIGURE 5.2 Relationships between Markers of Religion, Cross-Nationally
Notes: Bivariate scatterplots with fitted lines between five markers of religiosity, with correlation coefficients reported, across 125,588 Muslims in thirty-six Muslim-plurality countries. Thirty percent jitter added to each observation to minimize overlap.

($r=0.353$). Considerably weaker are the relationships between each of these three indicators of personal religiosity and the marker of religious group identity, mosque attendance, with correlation coefficients that range from 0.221 to 0.287.

I am able to repeat this same exercise, beyond the Turkish case, by looking at the relationship between similar markers of personal religiosity and religious group identity from more than 125,000 respondents across thirty-six Muslim-plurality countries.[24] Markers of personal religiosity are the same ones used to test the faith-based theory – the importance of religion and of God in respondents' lives, as well as how religious they say they are. I contrast these with participation in two types of religious-group activities, as markers of religious group identity: the frequency of mosque attendance, as above, but also self-reported membership in a religious association.[25]

---

[24] Data are available from the Afrobarometer, AsiaBarometer, Caucasus Barometer, East Asian Barometer, the EVS, and WVS.
[25] Associational membership is assessed using either of two survey questions: "Please look carefully at the following list of voluntary organizations and activities and say which, if any, do you belong to: religious organization," included in the East Asian Barometer, the EVS, and some waves (2, 4) of the WVS; and "I am going to read out a list of voluntary organizations; for each one, could you tell me whether you are an active member, an inactive member, or not a

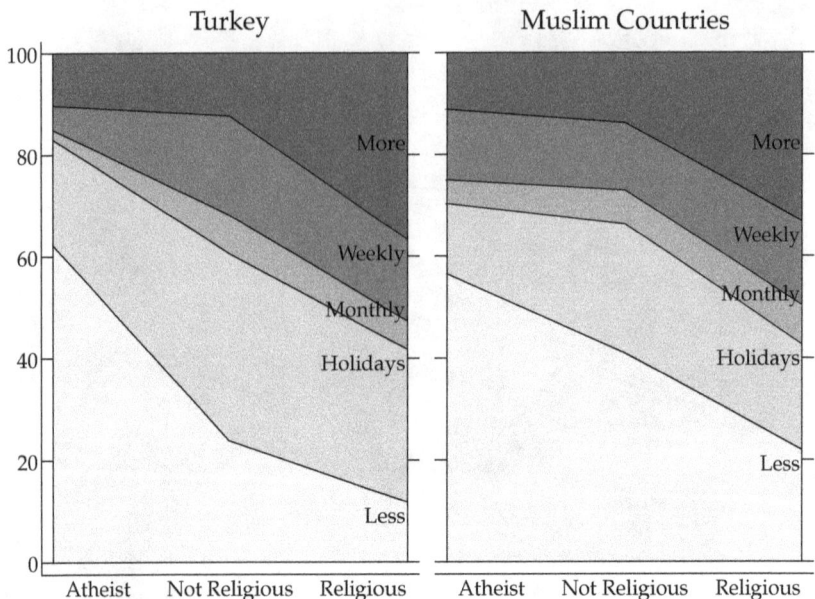

FIGURE 5.3 Self-Reported Religiosity and Mosque Attendance
Notes: Self-reported frequency of mosque attendance across levels of religiosity. Turkish analysis based on two nationally representative surveys; cross-national analysis reflects 64,471 Muslim respondents across twenty-seven Muslim countries.

The results of the bivariate correlations between the five indicators are presented in Figure 5.2. As above, the strongest correlations are between different markers of personal religiosity and then between the two markers of religious group identity. With the exception of the importance of religion and mosque attendance, the bivariate correlation between each marker and the other(s) of its "type" – whether intended to pick up personal religiosity or religious group identity – is stronger than its correlation with markers of the other type. For example, the importance of God in respondents' lives is more strongly correlated with the other two indicators of personal religiosity – the importance of religion ($r=0.392$) and self-reported religiosity ($r=0.165$) – than it is with either marker of religious group identity – mosque attendance ($r=0.124$) or membership in a religious association ($r=-0.001$). Similarly, associational membership is most strongly correlated with mosque attendance ($r=0.266$), compared to the importance of religion ($r=0.102$) or God ($r=-0.001$), or self-reported religiosity ($r=0.084$).

Both within Turkey, as well as cross-nationally, the same pattern emerges: indicators of religiosity that are more personal – that define an individual's beliefs or her relationship with the divine – are distinct from those that are

member of that type of organization: religious organization," included in the Afrobarometer and the remaining WVS waves (3, 5, 6). The indicator is coded 0 if the respondent mentions belonging to a religious organization in the first question or reports that she is either an "active member" or "inactive member" in the second.

5.2 Islam as a Group Identity

TABLE 5.1 *Personal Religiosity and Islamic Identity Factor Loadings*

	Personal Religiosity	Religious Identity	Difference (ψ)
Religion Important	0.752	−0.249	0.372
God Important	0.608	−0.523	0.357
Religiosity	0.586	−0.014	0.656
Mosque Attendance	0.624	0.391	0.458
Religious Association	0.350	0.769	0.285
Eigenvalues (λ)	1.791	1.080	

Notes: Principal component factoring over 45,057 observations from self-identified Muslims in Muslim-plurality countries. Varimax rotation.

more about her relationship to her religious community. To see how the two diverge, consider the relationship between self-reported religiosity, on the one hand, and mosque attendance on the other. Figure 5.3 displays the frequency with which respondents in each "religiosity" category attend mosque services, in Turkey and elsewhere.[26] While it may not be surprising that 62.3 percent of Turkish atheists (57.3 percent, cross-nationally) report never attending mosque, the fact that over 10 percent, in both samples, say they attend more than once a week challenges the traditional view of religious belief and practice as unidimensional. Similarly, while nearly 37 percent of religious Turks (30.7 percent elsewhere) attend mosque more than once a week, nearly 12 percent (23.2 percent cross-nationally) say they never do.

As further confirmation of the distinction between personal religiosity, on the one hand, and religious group identity, on the other, I conduct principal component factor analysis on the five indicators for the 45,047 respondents in the cross-national sample for which all markers are available.[27] My aim is to identify the dimensionality of the data by defining its principal components, which are uncorrelated by design (Jolliffe 2002). Applying the method here, I find two distinct dimensions within the five markers (see Table 5.1): while all five load positively onto the first factor, only mosque attendance and religious associational membership load onto the second. That is, while all the markers of religiosity are part of a single dimension – what I have called "personal religiosity" – only participation in religious group activities are related to the second dimension – what I call "religious identity."

5.2.4 Islamic Identity and Group-Based Trust

That participation in religious group activities is theoretically and empirically distinct from personal piety and religious beliefs does not necessarily imply that the former is a good indicator of a salient religious group identity. Recall

---

[26] To achieve comparability between the measure of religiosity from the Turkish surveys and the one in the cross-national surveys, the two more religious responses in the former (a "pious person" and a "religious person") were collapsed into a single "religious" category.

[27] For a similar application of factor analysis to markers of religiosity from the Indonesian case, see Pepinsky (2016), later published as Pepinsky, Liddle, and Mujani (2018).

the extensive literature in American politics which posits an entirely different role for these types of religious activities: not as a marker of identity but rather as a site for gathering important skills, resources, and motivation that can be applied to political ends. In contrast to this existing hypothesis, which holds that participation in religious group activities is associated with feelings of efficacy or motivation when it comes to political engagement, I argue that taking part in these collective religious events should bolster something else entirely – namely, group-based trust.

In the existing literature, religious group activities are politically important for one of two reasons: either because of the resources they disseminate, in the form of civil skills (Brady, Verba, and Schlozman 1995; Djupe and Gilbert 2006); or alternatively (or additionally), because they inform and motivate individual participants through politically charged rhetoric (Wald, Owen, and Hill Jr. 1988).[28] Both of these presumed effects plausibly fit under the rubric of political efficacy "the sense of being capable of acting effectively in the political realm" (Finkel 1985, p. 892). Political efficacy is considered to have two distinct but interrelated dimensions: internal efficacy or "beliefs about one's own competence to understand, and to participate effectively in, politics" (Niemi, Craig, and Mattei 1991, p. 1407) and external efficacy, "beliefs about the responsiveness of governmental authorities and institutions to citizens demands" (p. 1408).[29] The civil skills that religious group activities are thought to impart should bolster internal efficacy, while any impact these activities have on motivation may boost external efficacy, if the government's response is a function of citizen fervor.

In contrast to most of the extant literature, I expect participation in these religious group activities to bolster not efficacy, but group-based trust through its role as indicator and strengthener of religious group identity. In making this argument, I am joined by a smaller subset of existing research, including Lussier's (2019) work on Indonesian mosques and churches, as well as Hoffman and Nugent's (2017) study of mosque attendance in Lebanon. My hypothesis is also supported by lab- and field-based experiments that find a specific religious group-based trust advantage (Chuah, Fahoum, and Hoffmann 2013; Tan and Vogel 2008).

A closely related but alternative theory holds that religious identity and personal piety bolsters not group-based trust, but prosociality, a general

---

[28] On the one hand, participation in one's religious community, much like other forms of social capital, can help individuals "learn, maintain, or improve civic skills" (Brady, Verba, and Schlozman 1995, p. 273). On the other, community leaders can use religious services as a way of communicating political messages directly to participants, promoting "a common political outlook among" them (Wald, Owen, and Hill Jr. 1988, p. 545).

[29] External efficacy, itself, has two dimensions: beliefs about whether government institutions are able to be held accountable – a concept that is remarkably close to political trust; but also a sense of "the ability of citizens, in general, to influence what the government does" (Craig, Niemi, and Silver 1990, p. 298). It is this latter aspect of external efficacy that is most closely related to theories of church attendance, since how one perceives one's ability to affect change is closely related to one's commitment to trying to do so.

5.2 Islam as a Group Identity

preference for being among and cooperating with others (Atkinson and Bourrat 2011; Norenzayan and Shariff 2008; Shariff et al. 2016). In the framework developed here, this expectation can be restated thusly: religious group identity, including participation in religious group activities, should support more *generalized* trust expectations. Despite some existing evidence against this hypothesis – including experimental results that indicate no religion-based effect on prosociality (Anderson, Mellor, and Milyo 2004; Condra, Isaqzadeh, and Linardi 2017) nor cooperation beyond the confines of the religious group (Akay, Karabulut, and Martinsson 2015; Orbell et al. 1992), as well as a pointed critique of Shariff et al.'s (2016) meta-analysis on the subject (van Elk et al. 2015) – it deserves to be considered, alongside my own.

To test these divergent expectations – whether religious group activities heighten group-based trust, more generalized trust expectations, or internal or external efficacy – I return to the representative surveys I conducted in Turkey in 2012 and 2015. As above, I measure religious group activities using self-reported frequency of mosque attendance. Group-based trust was estimated using responses to a direct question – "I'd like to ask you how much you trust people from various groups: People of your same religion."[30] – while generalized trust was measured using the standard binary question.[31] Respondents who said that they trusted members of their own religious group completely or somewhat were coded as having group-based trust (1) while those who said that they did not trust them very much or did not trust them at all were coded as having none (0). Unlike generalized trust, which is almost entirely absent among survey respondents (a mere 6.3 percent), group-based trust is less rare: 46.3 percent of all respondents self-report trusting members of their religious in-group.

To measure internal efficacy, I used a relatively standard survey protocol that asks respondents whether they agree with the statement "Sometimes politics and government seem so complicated that a person like me can't really understand what's going on" (Niemi, Craig, and Mattei 1991).[32] Respondents who disagreed or disagreed strongly with the statement were coded as feeling internally efficacious (16.0%). For its part, external efficacy was measured as agreement with a different statement, "If an unjust law were passed by government, the people could work together to change it."[33] Respondents who

---

[30] In Turkish, the question reads, "*Size çeşitli gruplardan insanlara ve kurumlara ne kadar güvendiğinizi soracağım: Sizinle aynı dinden insanlara.*" Each respondent was asked about their trust a number of different groups and institutions, including members of their own religious group and members of a different group.

[31] The translation of the generalized trust question was identical to that used in the Turkish iterations of the EVS and WVS: "*Sizce genelde insanların çoğunluğuna güvenilebilir mi? Yoksa başkalarıyla bir ilişki kurarken veya iş yaparken çok dikkatli olmak mı gerekir?*"

[32] The Turkish version used in the survey: "*Bazen siyaset meseleleri o kadar karmaşık gözüküyor ki ne olup bittiğini anlamam bile mümkün olmuyor.*"

[33] The Turkish translation: "*Hükümetin adil olmayan bir kanun çıkarması karşısında insanlar bir araya gelip onu değiştirmeye çalışabilirler.*"

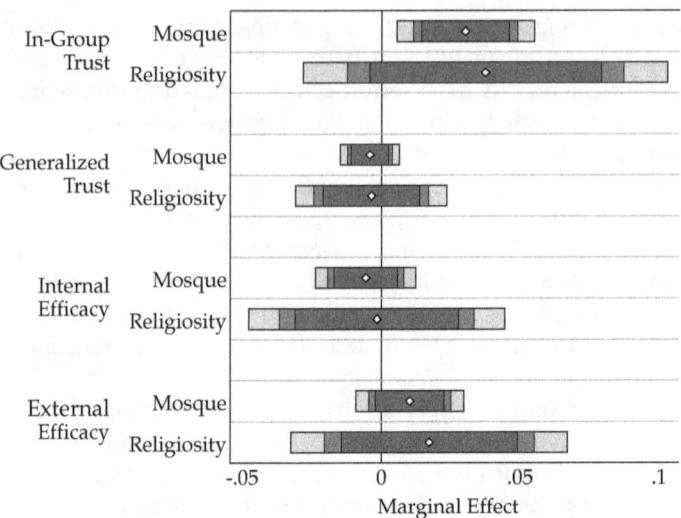

FIGURE 5.4 Religious Identity, Efficacy, and Trust
Notes: Coefficients from four OLS regression models of mosque attendance and religiosity on group-based trust, generalized trust, and internal and external efficacy, all with demographic controls. Shaded bars indicate statistical significance at the 90%, 95% and 99% level.

agreed or agreed strongly with the statement were coded as feeling externally efficacious (67.4%).[34]

To compare the four hypotheses, I estimate the effect of mosque attendance on each variable: group-based trust, generalized trust, and internal and external efficacy. To minimize bias from omitted correlates of both mosque attendance and the different explanatory variables, I also include basic demographic controls (age, gender, and education). And to confirm that the significance of religious group activities is an indicator of religious group identity, in particular, I also include a measure of personal religiosity: self-reported religiosity, as described above. An illustration of the results of these four different models is presented in Figure 5.4. (The full results are available in Online Appendix Table OA.15.)

Reviewing the results, two patterns immediately become clear. First, the only variable that mosque attendance significantly affects is the level of respondents' group-based trust. It has a small, but ultimately insignificant effect on external efficacy; and, if anything, it *lowers* both generalized trust and internal efficacy. In other words, if religious group activities, like mosque attendance, have an impact on collective action, the effect is unlikely to operate through these other mechanisms, but it may very well operate through group-based trust. The second main result is a null one: personal religiosity has no effect on any variable, including group-based trust. Along with the evidence presented earlier, this

---

[34] Interestingly, internal and external efficacy were found to be negatively correlated ($r=-0.053$) across individuals.

should increase our confidence that personal religiosity and religious identity are distinct concepts, with distinct consequences. Importantly, only the latter is related to trust of co-religionists.

5.3 CONCLUSION

In Chapter 4, I provided evidence of a trust deficit in the Muslim world. Generalized trust-expectations are significantly lower in Muslim-plurality countries and this distrust stands to pose a real challenge to political and economic cooperation and coordination in the region. This is especially true for large-scale latent activities, but should also undermine initial exchanges that could develop into longer-term relationships, built on particularized trust. In other words, the trust deficit could help explain the region's political and economic participation gap.

The goal of this chapter has been to explain how references to Islam, made by Islamic political and economic groups, might address this trust problem. I have argued that a shared, salient Islamic identity can compensate for generalized trust to support collective action. It does so through feelings of group-based trust, a form of non-particularized trust extended to other group members, whenever there is common knowledge of a shared identity and that identity is made salient. When Islamic-based groups reference religious language and symbols, they create common knowledge and prime individuals to frame mobilization in terms of their Muslim identity, triggering heightened trust expectations of other group members. Cooperation and coordination can then be sustained within the group, even when generalized trust expectations are low. Without this group-based trust, non-Islamic political and economic groups struggle to overcome the generalized trust problem and have difficulty competing effectively, to the comparative advantage of Islamic-based groups.

The remainder of the chapter developed a theoretical and then empirical distinction between personal religiosity, on the one hand, and a religious group identity, on the other. I suggested that participation in religious-group activities can be used as an indicator of a salient religious group identity and then demonstrated how these activities are related to group-based, but not generalized trust. In the empirical chapters that follow in Part II, I rely on this operationalization strategy to capture variation in religious identity across space and time, using a diverse set of religious-group activities, including mosque attendance, enrollment in religious schools, and membership in religious associations.

Using these indicators of religious identity, along with estimates of generalized and group-based trust, I test my central hypotheses: first, that generalized distrust undermines the potential for collective action of various forms; second, that collective action is bolstered by a salient Islamic identity; and third, that the positive effect of Islamic identity on participation, cooperation, and coordination operates through a substitution effect, whereby identity and group-based trust compensate for the absence of more generalized trust expectations. In the three empirical chapters of Part II, I examine these expectations in different cases – participation in mass politics, strategic voting, and economic cooperation – leveraging variation across different dimensions – individuals, space, and time.

PART II

APPLICATIONS AND EMPIRICS

6

Explaining the Islamic Advantage in Political Participation

> When you know there are thousands upon thousands upon thousands behind you, you don't stop. And essentially, your heart takes over your body. It takes over your mind. We're fighting for bigger than this.
>
> K. Abdalla (2011)

In democracies and autocracies alike, across the Muslim world, individuals regularly join together in the hopes of affecting political change. Increasingly, large-scale political movements in the region have relied on Islamic language to motivate and mobilize individuals to join them. And those movements that are Islamic-based appear to be outpacing their secular rivals. Jenny White makes note of this differential in the Turkish case:

> [O]ne finds that secularist, Kemalist, and feminist... associational activities and party platforms do not inspire sustained followings and loyalty in neighborhoods like Ümraniye [in Istanbul], even if the activists are local, not outsiders, and even if their modus operandum... was similar in some respects to that of the Islamists, who [tend] to be more successful in this regard (2002, p. 259).

White explains the difference in terms of what she calls "vernacular politics" – "local networks of people united within a complex set of norms of mutual obligation... [in which people] assist one another in open-ended relations of reciprocity, without calculating immediate return" (pp. 20–21). My trust-based explanation is similarly focused on reciprocity, but one that is less localized, based on expectations that all those with a shared Islamic identity will honor their commitments to one another.

Whether they involve gathering signatures, organizing boycotts, or taking to the streets, political movements require significant numbers and broad-based cooperation if they are to be successful. Based on my theory, this implies a need for broad trust expectations among would-be participants. A small existing literature has identified an association between generalized interpersonal trust and mass political participation, but the evidence has come almost exclusively from Western democracies, and the mechanism linking trust to participation remains underdeveloped. So, in the pages that follow, I specify a more explicit trust-based theory of mass political participation. I do so by focusing on the interdependence and uncertainty inherent in latent political movements, arguing that this implies a need for non-particularized trust, both for initial and for sustained cooperation. I then go on to demonstrate empirically that low levels of generalized trust impact individuals' willingness to take part in a number of political activities beyond Western democracies, across the Muslim world. Finally, I show how a salient Islamic identity is able to address this trust problem via a substitution effect.

The chapter begins with a discussion of the role of interdependence and uncertainty in mass political participation. I then discuss the need for non-particularized trust in these types of activities, arguing that either generalized or group-based trust can be used to support participation and cooperation. After reviewing the theoretical expectations, I turn to the empirical results, describing the cross-national survey data I use, before reviewing the patterns I find: the generalized trust "problem" in the practice of mass politics across the Muslim world, and the role of Islamic identity in supporting participation, by effectively substituting for generalized trust where it is lacking.

In a final section, I explore an additional (if unexpected) implication of my trust-based theory: that regulation of political movements by the state, including targeted repression of Islamic-based groups, will often backfire. Because repression increases the risks associated with political participation, it deepens the twin challenges of interdependence and uncertainty, making non-particularized trust even more critical for supporting cooperation. I demonstrate how increases in repression in a set of Muslim countries made the trust problem (and the Islamic advantage) even larger, challenging an existing strand of the literature that presumes state action will effectively sideline Islamic-based groups.

6.1 THE TRUST PROBLEM IN MASS POLITICAL MOVEMENTS

Before delving into my trust-based theory of political participation, it is important to again clarify the scope of my argument: the relevant political activities and movements I intend to explain are those best defined as "latent" per Mancur Olson: "if [any] one member does or does not [participate], no other members will be significantly affected and therefore none has the reason to react to it" (2002, p. 50). This does not imply that numbers do not matter, but it does mean that each individual participant is essentially anonymous and that the success or failure of the broader movement does not rest on any one person's shoulders. Latent activities tend to be organized activities rather than spontaneous ones. They are the kinds of activities that require groups of individuals to coordinate and cooperate in order to achieve their desired objective, but where each individual plays a more-or-less anonymous role. And yet

6.1 The Trust Problem in Mass Political Movements

similar themes are common to more spontaneous events like the Arab Spring and Turkey's Gezi Park protests.[1]

By focusing on large, anonymous, latent movements, whether they are organized or spontaneous, I firmly anchor my theory around more mainstream, mostly legal and peaceful types of political organizations.[2] Narrowing down my focus thusly also clarifies the puzzles I intend to address: What explains why an individual would opt to participate in a political movement when her participation is costly, her contribution is unlikely to make a real impact, and she will enjoy a share of its success even if she remains, safely, on the sidelines? And what role might references to Islam play in her decision to take part? In line with the theory I developed in Part I of this book, my answer to both of these questions is trust.

The link between interpersonal trust, on the one hand, and mass political participation, on the other, has been suggested by other scholars, although never in the specific case of the Muslim world, with the majority of the existing evidence coming from Western democracies (Bäck and Christensen 2016; Benson and Rochon 2004; Kaase 1999; Knack 1992). But there is plenty of anecdotal evidence pointing to the importance of trust for mass politics in the region. For example, Beinin and Vairel discuss the need for "mutual trust to overcome decades of fear" so that post-Arab-Spring political movements in Tunisia and Egypt might succeed (2011, p. 126). There is good reason, therefore, to believe that the association between trust and participation, though first identified elsewhere, will extend to the Muslim world.

While identifying an important empirical pattern, the existing literature has not yet offered a clear explanation for why interpersonal distrust should lower an individual's propensity to become politically active. In his theoretical contribution, Max Kaase mentions the need for effective organization – "[e]ven if people are angry ... [t]hey have to be organized to be politically effective" (1999, p. 16) – while Michelle Benson and Thomas Rochon describe the need for optimism – "a high level of trust should make individuals more likely to anticipate low expected costs of participation while leading to optimistic estimates of the potential benefits of protest" (2004, p. 437). But in neither case is the link between trust, on the one hand, and organization or optimism, on the other, made explicit. As an extension of these extant studies, I aim to specify the role of interpersonal trust in mass political movements, focusing on the twin conditions of interdependence and uncertainty.

---

[1] The themes I discuss below are also central to explaining the success of large, spontaneous movements; but by the very nature of their spontaneity, these types of events face some additional challenges to garnering mass support, which are better explained through tipping models (Kuran 1991; Lohmann 1994).

[2] Illegal, fringe, violent movements are almost always small – what Olson (2002) would call a "privileged" type of group or, possibly, an "intermediate" one.

6.1.1 Interdependent Decisions to Participate

In the case of latent political movements – boycotts, demonstrations, strikes – the interdependence of individuals derives from two basic premises. First, potential participants have no interest in taking part in a political movement that stands little chance of success. Or as Michael Schmidmayr explains in the cases of Kuwait and Bahrain, "using the street... [is only] effective when it draws the necessary attention from the authorities and the public" (2010, p. 171). This is based on the assumption that individuals derive few benefits from futile acts (i.e., small, symbolic gatherings or paltry attempts at policy change) (Barry 1978; Chong 1991, 1993). This should hold whether the benefits individuals stand to receive from their collective efforts are instrumental or expressive. Dennis Chong suggests that even moral obligations do not extend to hopeless causes and that normative commitments do not hold "when the act of adhering to the norm will probably inflict grievous harm on oneself or others without improving the well-being of anyone" (1991, p. 94). The clear imbalance between cost (high) and reward (low) negates any moral imperative to act. Even those who are selflessly committed to a cause and claim to disregard the potential costs are unlikely to be motivated to participate in an activity that is expected to have little positive impact.

Once we accept that participants care about a movement's success, interdependence naturally follows from the fact that success depends critically on the total number of participants. Mass political movements, by definition, require mass participation. Higher numbers of participants better the chances of publicity as well as the chances of outright success, increasing the expressive and instrumental benefits each supporter stands to receive. When participation is particularly costly due to risk of arrest or injury, more participants also reduce the potential costs for each individual crowd member, as the total risk is expected to be spread evenly across the larger group. Indeed, and for this reason, Montserrat Badimon identifies sufficient numbers as a key condition for organizing demonstrations among unemployed youths in Morocco: in order to proceed, they must feel confident that they will be able to "assembl[e] a sufficient number of activists to minimize the effects of eventual repression" (2011, p. 233).

Taken together, these two elements – the importance of success and the need for numbers to achieve it – imply the following:

> ... for a given individual the receipt of such benefits [associated with collective action] is contingent upon the actions of other potential activists. Each individual is thus forced to make certain prospective calculations before he can ascertain the benefits he will derive from his own participation. Will enough others participate so that collective action stands a good chance of being successful? This calculation must be made carefully. (Chong 1991, p. 95)

Before making her own decision about whether or not to join a political movement, each would-be participant must therefore begin by asking herself about

6.1 The Trust Problem in Mass Political Movements

the likely behavior of others, forming a reasonable expectation about what they are likely to do. Her fate is ultimately intertwined with theirs.

6.1.2 Uncertainty about Other Participants

Interdependence requires each individual participant to form an expectation about how many others are likely to join her. Uncertainty implies that she will struggle to form this expectation. Here, her uncertainty stems not from cognitive difficulty or limited information; instead it can be traced back to a lack of clarity about others' motivation. This uncertainty is due to there being real incentives for each potential participant to free ride off of others' efforts. And yet, if everyone were equally inclined to free ride, there would be no uncertainty: the expected outcome is exactly zero participation (Hardin 1971; Olson 2002). Instead, heterogeneity in what different "types" of people prefer creates a variety of motives, expected behaviors, and, therefore, uncertainty.

In every community, there are some rational egoists, with traditionally selfish preferences, who prefer to free ride off of others if given the opportunity. However, an even larger segment of the population are conditional cooperators, who get a "warm glow" from reciprocal cooperation and so prefer to participate if they believe others will do the same (Ahn, Ostrom, and Walker 2003; Fischbacher, Gächter, and Fehr 2001; Ostrom 2000). They are not altruists: they do not enjoy others' taking advantage of their generosity for the sake of kindness. But if they expect that others will show up for a good cause, they would prefer to do the same.

Large-scale political movements are possible if these conditional cooperators can successfully locate one another and join together. For these "honest" types, the traditional collective action problem – modeled as a public goods game or Prisoner's Dilemma – becomes a matter of coordination,

> with two pure strategy equilibria. If both subjects are [conditional cooperators] and if A believes that B will cooperate..., A *prefers* to cooperate. The same holds true for B if B believes that A will cooperate .... Likewise, if both believe that the other person will defect..., they prefer to defect too (Fehr and Fischbacher 2002, p. C14).

In other words, if conditional cooperators are confident that they are working alongside others who are going to show up, they prefer to show up as well. But if they expect less of others, they will act exactly like rational egoists and the potential for collective political mobilization will unravel.

The main challenge for conditional cooperators in locating one another is not just the presence of rational egoists among them but the incentives that these free riders have to mislead. Because free riders ultimately want the movement to succeed (even if they refuse to contribute to its success), they seek to induce participation among cooperators by falsely promising that they too will participate.[3] This creates another layer of uncertainty for

---

[3] For a great example in the context of the Muslim world, see the unfulfilled tweets in support of Iran's Green Movement in 2009, as noted by Tusa (2013).

a would-be participant: not just about what "type" of people she is dealing with, but whether she can believe what she hears from them. As Chong concludes, "each activist might remain nervous about the dependability of others to uphold their end of the agreement" (1991, p. 115). This nervousness, in addition to interdependence, creates a compelling need for trust among participants.

6.1.3 Trust, Islamic Identity, and Political Participation

Many existing accounts of political participation in the Muslim world insist that recruitment into larger movements operates through small, particularized trust networks, in which individuals have direct previous experience with one another (Clark 2004a; Singerman 1996; Turam 2007; White 2002). But in latent movements, it seems implausible that even interlinking social circles will amass sufficient support to have a real impact. Therefore, for a "trustworthy" conditional cooperator to decide to join a mass political movement, she must have a good sense that she can count on many others, far more than the people she knows herself or those who are connected to her through one or two degrees of separation. In other words, she needs an expectation of trust that is non-particularized.

As explained in Chapter 4, the broadest form of non-particularized trust is so-called generalized trust, extended to an average stranger or, in the aggregate, to "most people." Because it is almost universally applicable, it can be used to support collective action of the broadest scope, cutting across internal cleavages and even international borders. In the framework developed above, generalized trust becomes the belief that a given population is teeming with conditional cooperators.[4] In the absence of such an expectation, even honest cooperators – including those who are sufficiently informed and motivated to be politically active – will be unwilling to join in a collective political activity. In other words, those individuals who distrust "most others" are expected to participate less, on average, across a variety of latent political activities.

By the same logic, and following the theory developed in Chapter 5, individuals with a salient Islamic identity are expected to participate in higher numbers. This is because, within identity groups, including in religious communities, another form of non-particularized trust is common – namely, group-based trust, extended to members of one's group. Like generalized trust, these feelings of group-based trust are not specific to a particular place or person, neither are they based on specific knowledge of past behavior; instead, they are conditioned on shared membership in an identity group, extending well beyond any one's personal network to encompass an "imagined community" (Anderson 2006). Because group-based trust is stronger whenever a common group-identity is salient, the expectation is that individuals who

---

[4] It also implies that this expectation about the number of conditional cooperators is shared, since common knowledge is required to support trust and honesty, even among cooperators.

6.1 The Trust Problem in Mass Political Movements

signal and strengthen their religious group identity through participation in religious group activities are most likely to have the group-based trust needed to support cooperation.

This expectation – that those with a salient religious group identity, who take an active role in their religious communities, are more likely to participate in mass politics – appears to contradict the empirical patterns uncovered in Chapter 3: that individuals in the Muslim world with strong religious beliefs are significantly *less* likely to join a latent political movement. But recalling the theoretical and empirical distinction between personal religiosity and religious identity discussed in Chapter 5, it is possible that there is no real contradiction. Only group identity (and not beliefs) comes with the group-based trust to support collective action, a difference that can explain the divergent patterns expected here and identified elsewhere (Bloom, Arikan, and Courtemanche 2015; Driskell, Embry, and Lyon 2008; Westfall et al. 2017).

The role of trust in Islamic-based politics becomes even more apparent if we focus on the substitution effect: the positive impact of Islamic group identity on participation is expected to operate by counteracting the negative impact of generalized distrust. In the aggregate, this should give Islamic-based political groups a comparative advantage over their secular rivals, who lack an effective non-particularized trust substitute. As Robert Springborg describes in the Egyptian case, "secular organizations are particularly vulnerable to ... fissuring because they lack the abstract appeal of membership in the community of the faithful" (1989, p. 185).[5] Since the Islamic advantage rests on the underlying trust deficit, the magnitude of the two should be correlated, with Islamic-based movements better off in times and places with less generalized trust or with heightened levels of interdependence or uncertainty.

In the section that follows, I use survey responses from twenty-four Muslim countries to test my hypotheses: first, that generalized distrust undermines political participation in the Muslim world; second, that a salient Islamic identity, indicated by regular attendance at religious group activities, bolsters political participation; and third, that the latter (positive) effect operates by negating the former (negative) effect, with identity and group-based trust substituting for more generalized trust expectations, to support participation. In Section 6.3, I leverage cross-temporal variation in the repression of political movements to reveal an unexpected pattern: by making interpersonal trust even more important for collective action, heightened repression bolsters the Islamic advantage.

---

[5] Similarly, in the Turkish case, Ali Çarkoğlu and Ersin Kalaycıoğlu blame the secular groups themselves: "The relatively modernized minority in Turkey seems to have severed their ties with the rural society and culture, yet they have not been able to create a new social context rich in social capital that in turn would enable them to construct a countervailing political force to those of [conservative Islamic] patronage groups. Instead, [they] seem to be leading a highly individualistic lifestyle" (2009, p. 119).

6.2 THE TRUST-BASED ISLAMIC ADVANTAGE IN MASS POLITICS

In an ideal test of my hypotheses, I would be able to randomly assign a subset of individuals to generally distrust most people and an additional, cross-cutting subset to have a salient Islamic identity. I would then compare how these two "treatments" impact participation in mass political activities. On the one hand, this test would improve my ability to identify a causal effect of distrust and Islam on participation, that is, that the relationship goes in the direction I have posited, and not vice versa, and that participation is impacted by trust and Islam, rather than factors that are related to both in the real world. At the same time, moving away from survey data to behavioral outcomes would help address concerns about bias in self-reports. When asked whether "most people can be trusted" or whether they "have, would, or would never participate" in political activities, respondents may not always reveal their true disposition. This may be because they misunderstand the question (Krosnick 1991), misunderstand themselves (Krosnick et al. 2002), or are being intentionally misleading, providing the answer that they think they should rather than the one that best reflects reality (Fisher 1993).

But actively generating distrust of "most people," even in the context of a lab, is difficult if not impossible; and while the salience of an identity can be heightened via priming, an Islamic identity cannot be created out of thin air and randomly assigned. For these reasons, I return to observational data, noting which individuals are already less trusting or more attached to their Islamic identity, recognizing the challenge this poses for causal inference. First, the direction of causality will be more difficult to ascertain. Second, there will be concerns about omitted variable bias, those factors that impact both the inputs (distrust, Islam) and outputs (participation) in my model, but which I am unable to identify or capture empirically. Throughout my discussion of the empirical results, I pay careful attention to both of these issues, while continuing to assess whether there is cause for concern about sampling and/or response bias in the survey data I use.

To design an effective test of my hypotheses within the survey dataset, I need to be able to leverage variation in political participation, trust, and Islamic identity. To ensure that the conclusions I draw are broadly applicable, observations from across the Muslim world are useful. But to control for differences within the region, I want to focus in on comparing individuals within each country, across the full sample. Towards that end, I return to the cross-national surveys used in Part I, analyzing responses using multi-level mixed effects models that include both individual- and country-level variables. Given the potential for measurement error in the survey data, I employ come correctives, including calculating indices and principal components across multiple indicators of the same underlying concept. I also consider possible confounding variables and enter proxy measures into my models wherever they are available. Finally, where alternative explanations exist for the same statistical relationship – including reverse causality or causal antecedents – I investigate their empirical implications.

6.2 The Trust-Based Islamic Advantage

6.2.1 Generalized Distrust as an Obstacle to Political Participation

In Chapter 2, I presented evidence that political participation rates are significantly lower in the Muslim world, while the analysis in Chapter 4 revealed that the region suffers from lower levels of generalized trust. But it is not yet clear whether these two patterns are related. To assess the relationship between generalized distrust and political participation, I estimate hierarchical models to assess how respondents' willingness to participate in different mass political activities depends on their level of generalized trust. As earlier, I restrict my analysis to Muslim-plurality countries and self-identified Muslim respondents. This results in just over 62,750 respondents from twenty-four countries.

To capture variation in mass political participation, I return to questions about realized ("have") and hypothetical ("would") participation in three latent political activities – signing a petition, attending a lawful demonstration, and joining a boycott. As in Chapter 2, I collapse the three indicators into a single index, not just to streamline the empirical results, but also to counter potential measurement error. I find that 51.0 percent of respondents would not participate in any of the three activities, while a mere 19.3 percent self-report having participated in at least one, with the remaining 29.7 percent saying they would consider participating in at least one.[6] The three indicators and the composite index all operate as the existing literature would expect: younger respondents and women are significantly less likely participate, while actual and intended participation are increasing with education (Quintelier and Blais 2016; Verba, Schlozman, and Brady 1995; Verba, Burns, and Schlozman 1997).[7]

To measure generalized distrust, I continue to use responses to the standard binary survey question, introduced in Chapter 4: "Generally speaking, would you say that most people can be trusted, or that you can't be too careful in dealing with people?" As discussed, this survey-based measure is considered a reasonably valid one in that it tracks behavior in lab-based trust games, both at the individual level, as well as cross-nationally. In my sample, across individuals within countries, bivariate patterns follow theoretical expectations: older respondents are more trusting, while women trust less, and trust increases with the level of education (Croson and Buchan 1999; Gächter, Herrmann, and Thöni 2004; Sutter and Kocher 2007).

To assess the effect of distrust on participation, I estimate a series of multinomial logit models, predicting actual and intended participation in each political activity, separately, as well in the composite index. The multinomial model captures differences across the three response categories: have done,

---

[6] Of those who self-report having participated in at least one activity (N=11,269), 65.6 percent report participating in only one activity, while 22.8 percent have participated in two and the remaining 11.7 percent report doing all three. Similarly, among those who would participate in at least one (N=16.926), roughly a third (37.0%) would only participate in one activity, while similar numbers would consider participating in two activities (23.0%) or all three (39.1%).

[7] Further, as expected, interest in politics and political trust are both positively associated with all the measures participation (Brady, Verba, and Schlozman 1995).

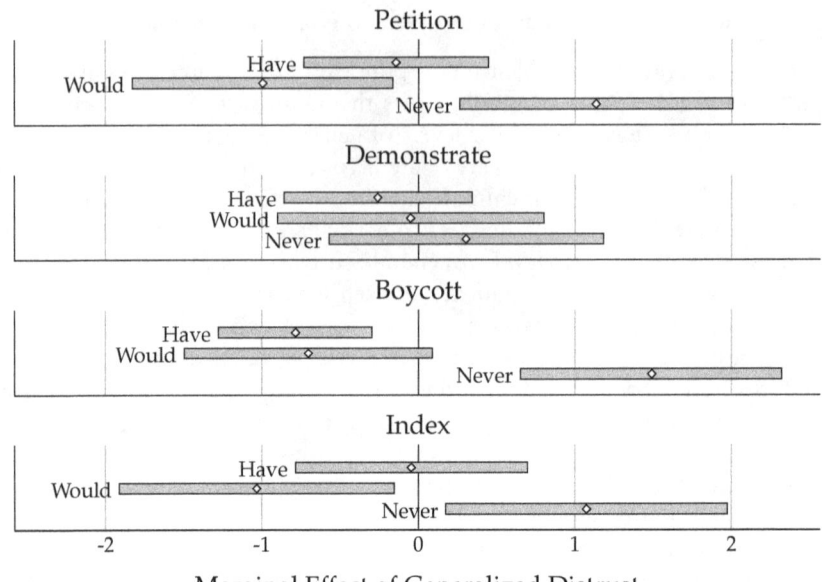

FIGURE 6.1 Political Participation and Generalized Distrust

Notes: Coefficients (with 95% confidence bands) from four multinomial logit models assessing actual participation and willingness to participate in each of three political activities, as well as a composite index capturing actual and intended participation across all three. All models include respondents' age, gender, and educational attainment.

would do, and would never do. In addition to the binary measure of generalized distrust and country fixed effects, I include respondents' age, gender, and level of educational attainment, that is, all variables that could plausibly confound the relationship between trust and participation, known to correlate with both.[8] While the full results are available in Online Appendix Table OA.16, the key coefficients are displayed in Figure 6.1.

Although trust has no distinguishing effect on the most low-cost latent activity – signing a petition – it exerts a statistically significant negative effect on individuals' willingness to attend a lawful demonstration and join a boycott, resulting in a negative effect on the composite index. In other words, distrusting individuals across the Muslim world are significantly less likely to take part in these different latent activities. Both for the index and for demonstrations – arguably the most relevant type of political activity in the region – distrust's main impact is on stated *willingness* to take part, although for boycotts the effect is slightly stronger on having actually participated. Based on this, and to streamline the analysis even further, I recode the indicators of participation into binary measures: coded one (1) if respondents say they have

---

[8] For clarity, I limit the controls to just these most basic demographic variables (Achen 2002), although other indicators are included as robustness checks.

6.2 The Trust-Based Islamic Advantage

or would participate and zero (0) if they say they would never consider doing so. In additional analysis, I confirm that this has no impact on my main results (see Online Appendix Table OA.17).

Using this binary measure of participation, I conduct a number of robustness checks to confirm the validity of my initial results.[9] First, I consider different potential confounders at the individual level. Given the importance of motivation and information to political activity, I include measures of both in two additional models.[10] In terms of motivation, if anything, the negative effect of distrust on participation is strengthened by the inclusion of respondents' self-reported happiness and a binary indicator of their employment status.[11] To capture variation in information, beyond educational attainment, cross-national indicators are difficult to find; but, focusing less on supply of information than the demand for it, I use respondents' interest in politics and the frequency of political discussion as plausible proxy measures. Including both of these in the models drastically reduces the number of observations, and while the coefficient on distrust remains similar in magnitude, it is less well-specified and is no longer statistically significant at conventional levels.

Beyond motivation and information, I consider another potential confounder: political distrust. On the one hand, distrust of politicians or of the current regime could spur political participation (Fennema and Tillie 1999; Kaase 1999; Levi and Stoker 2000); on the other, work by Amaney Jamal (2007) indicates that generalized and political trust are negatively correlated in many non-democratic or underdeveloped contexts.[12] Including the first principal component factor of the available measures of political trust – respondents' confidence in government, parliament, political parties, and the justice system – I estimate yet another model of trust and participation. While political distrust boosts participation, generalized distrust continues to exert a negative effect on political engagement. But with a much smaller sample size, the latter coefficient is somewhat smaller and no longer statistically significant.

---

[9] For full results, see Online Appendix Table OA.18.
[10] The argument for how motivation and information could drive the negative relationship between distrust and participation is not totally straightforward. For motivation, grievances likely spur political participation, a positive relationship; at the same time, they would plausibly boost interpersonal distrust, which would produce a positive but spurious association between distrust and participation, rather than the negative one I find. Similarly, information is expected to promote participation, but the extant literature does not have a clear expectation for how it should impact trust. Knack and Zak (2003) and Bjørnskov (2009) both show that increases in education are associated with lower levels of distrust, implying that information could bolster trust. If true, this could drive the negative association between distrust and participation I have identified.
[11] Respondent income, while arguably a better measure of economic grievances and the motivation to participate, is unavailable for most of the sample. I therefore use employment status as another (if imperfect) proxy.
[12] Here, the potential to confound is more clear: political distrust both increases participation and decreases generalized distrust, plausibly producing a spurious negative correlation if both assumptions are true.

Finally, I move beyond individual-level variation to consider how political context could impact the relationship between distrust and participation: with some suggesting that generalized trust is bolstered by personal freedoms (Berggren and Jordahl 2006) and democracy (Putnam 1993), and given significantly lower levels of both in the Muslim world, these legal restrictions could depress both trust and political participation. I investigate this possibility by including two variables at the country-level, both the CIRI Freedom of Assembly and Association index and the Polity score in the survey year. If anything, their inclusion reinforces the negative effect of distrust on participation. Taken together, these robustness checks serve to strengthen my conclusion that generalized distrust does indeed undermine the potential for political participation in the Muslim world, much as it appears to do elsewhere.

Yet, even if concerns about confounding variables have been addressed, questions surrounding the direction of causality might yet remain: it is possible that I am misinterpreting the association between distrust and participation, so that, rather than distrust undermining participation, participation bolsters trust.[13] If participation does indeed improve trust expectations, then we might expect the association I have found to be strongest among those who have *actually* participated. But as we see above, the association is actually strongest among those who consider taking part, but who have not actually done so. These individuals have not been exposed to the activity that is supposed to impact their trust of others. Rather than supporting an argument of reverse causality, the evidence confirms my view that distrust undermines individuals' mere willingness to participate.

6.2.2 Islamic Identity as a Boost to Participation

Having found evidence of a trust problem in political participation in the Muslim world, I turn to testing my second hypothesis: that a salient Islamic identity bolsters participation rates. I have argued that the relationship between a religious identity and participation is not due to motivation or information, efficacy or prosociality; but rather, because of feelings of group-based trust, shared among members of the religious identity group, which can be used to support cooperation and collective action.

To capture variation in the salience of Islamic identity across individuals in the Muslim world, I return to the operationalization strategy developed in Chapter 5 – the frequency and intensity of religious group activities. As earlier, I use two indicators of collective religious activities. First, the frequency of attendance at communal prayers, with responses ranging from "Practically never" to "More than once a week." And, second, membership in a religious organization. The two measures are positively correlated ($r=0.266$), but the

---

[13] Kaase, in his study of interpersonal trust and political participation in Western Europe, voices this exact concern, suggesting that "it could be argued that through involvement in past action (which usually takes place in a group context) the level of interpersonal trust is pushed up" (1999, p. 17). This possibility is also raised by Putnam (1993), among others.

6.2 The Trust-Based Islamic Advantage

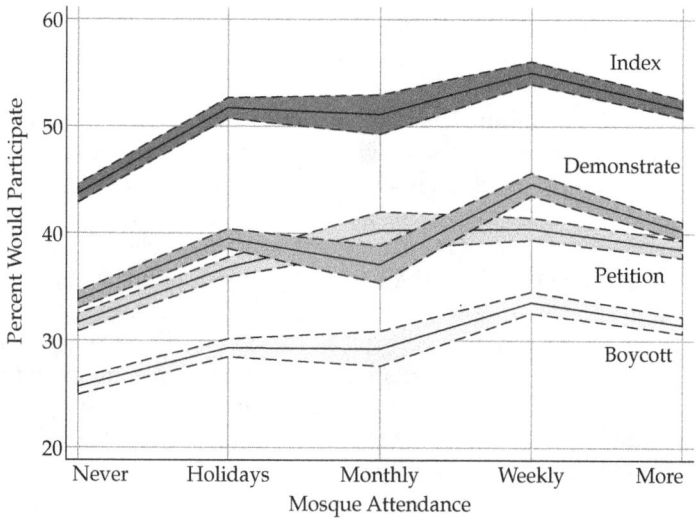

FIGURE 6.2 Political Participation and Mosque Attendance
Notes: Average willingness to participate in three separate political activities and in any of the three. Across frequency of mosque attendance among 63,924 respondents across thirty Muslim countries.

sample size for the former is considerably larger (N=91,130, compared to N=64,219). In some specifications, I also use the "religious identity" component factor extracted from the five indicators of personal piety and religious identity (see Chapter 5.2.3), and compare this directly to the effect of the "personal religiosity" factor.

To begin, I compare the willingness of individuals to participate across levels of Islamic identity, as measured by frequency of mosque attendance (Figure 6.2). I find that willingness to participate is almost monotonically increasing in the frequency of attendance across each individual activity and the composite index. If there is an exception to the linear trend, it is a small spike in participation among those who attend once weekly, followed by a modest decline among those who attend more often (although participation is higher than for those who attend less than once a week).

Of course, there are many factors that could explain both mosque attendance and political activity and that might produce a spurious relationship between the two. Beyond prosociality, information, and resources, there is also the matter of gender: women tend to participate in politics less and are also less likely to attend mosque.[14] I therefore want to conduct more rigorous tests of the relationship between Islamic identity and political participation

---

[14] Indeed, in some cases, their attendance at mosque is heavily restricted by religious authorities. In my dataset, I find a smaller differential than might be expected: although women are significantly more likely to "never" attend mosque (29.5 percent compared to 18.3 percent of men), 41.6 percent self-report attending at least once a week (vs. 58.2 percent of male respondents).

that include different statistical controls: gender, but also age and education. I also want to be able to directly compare the impact of religious identity on participation to the effect of personal piety.

For each activity and in the composite index, I find that respondent willingness to participate is increasing with the frequency of mosque attendance and with membership in religious associations. The main results are available in Online Appendix Table OA.19, and an illustration of these is displayed in Online Appendix Figure OA.5. (A set of robustness checks are also available in Online Appendix Table OA.20.) Self-reported political participation is also significantly increasing in the "religious identity" component factor, but decreasing in the "personal religiosity" factor. This last finding is in line with my earlier results as well as extant studies that differentiate between the political importance of religious activities and beliefs (Arikan and Bloom 2018; Westfall et al. 2017).

I have argued that Islamic identity promotes a willingness to engage in mass politics because of group-based trust, shared by those with a salient religious identity. Without a measure of group-based trust in the cross-national dataset, I am unable to test this hypothesis directly; but I am able to examine a clear empirical implication: that Islamic identity can function as an effective substitute for generalized distrust, to support political participation. I test for this substitution effect using an interaction model, estimating the effect of distrust on participation across the frequency or intensity of religious group activity.[15]

The results of the fully specified model are available in Online Appendix Table OA.21, but an illustration of the key result is displayed in Figure 6.3.[16] I find a statistically significant and negative effect of distrust on political participation among those who self-report attending mosque "practically never" or only on major holidays. But as the frequency of attendance increases, the magnitude of the effect declines and the confidence intervals begin to cross the zero-line, indicating that the coefficient is no longer statistically distinguishable from the null hypothesis of no effect. Indeed, by the time respondents are attending at least weekly, there is no discernible effect of distrust on their level of political participation. I take this as evidence of the substitutability of Islamic identity (and group-based trust) for generalized trust in the case of mass politics.

---

[15] The interaction model takes the form $PolParticipation_{ij} = \beta_0 + \beta_1 Distrust_{ij} + \beta_2 Mosque_{ij} + \beta_3 Distrust_{ij} \times Mosque_{ij} + X_i + \mu_j + \epsilon_i$, where $PolParticipation_{ij}$ is a measure of respondent i's willingness to participate in political activities, $Distrust_{ij}$ is her distrust of most people, $Mosque_{ij}$ is how frequently she attends mosque services, $Distrust_{ij} \times Mosque_{ij}$ is the interaction between the two, X_i is a vector of her individual-level characteristics, μ_j is a fixed-effect term for her home country, and ϵ_i is the error term. I have hypothesized that the effect of distrust on political participation will be significantly negative ($\beta_1 < 0$) but that this effect will decrease across the frequency of mosque attendance ($\beta_3 > 0$) so that the magnitude of the marginal effect of distrust on participation ($\beta_1 + \beta_3 * Mosque$) will decrease as the frequency of mosque attendance increases.

[16] I calculate the marginal effect of distrust on participation at each level of mosque attendance, using a categorical indicator of the latter, following Brambor, Clark, and Golder (2006).

6.2 The Trust-Based Islamic Advantage

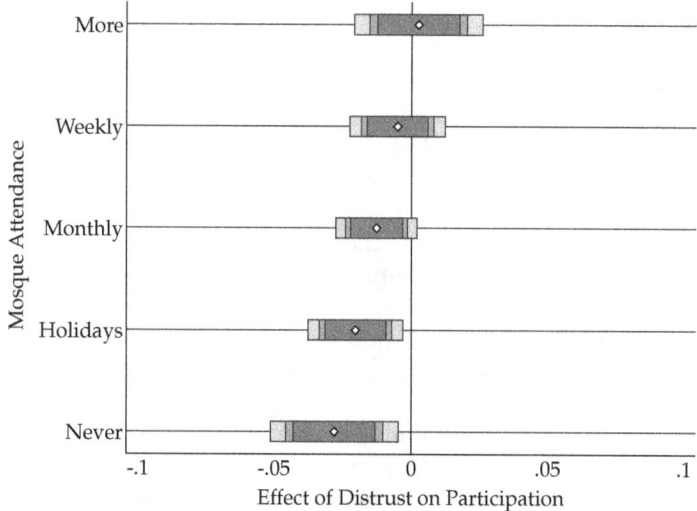

FIGURE 6.3 Distrust and Political Participation, across Mosque Attendance
Notes: Predicted marginal effects of generalized distrust on willingness to participate in any political activity. Across frequency of mosque attendance among 44,251 Muslim respondents from twenty-four Muslim countries.

6.2.3 Testing the Robustness of the Substitution Effect

As above, I conduct a series of additional tests to confirm the validity of this result and my interpretation of it. First, I consider a major potential confounding variable in prosociality. Careful readers may already have noted that "participation" – in religious group activities, on the one hand, and in latent political movements, on the other – is on both sides of the equations I estimate. Could it be that there is a subset of the population that has a higher level of public-spiritedness (i.e., prosociality), which leads them to join together in religious activities, as well as in political ones? To test this hypothesis, I evaluate two of its empirical implications. First, I look to see whether those who regularly attend mosque tend to trust most people generally, as indication of their prosociality. In a simple cross-section across the whole sample, I find the opposite: the most distrustful (79.2%) group are those who attend mosque more than once a week.[17] Next, I reconsider the coefficient on Islamic identity in the interaction model above, which captures the direct effect of religious group activities on political participation, independent of the substitution. Contrary to the expectation of prosociality, I find that this coefficient is negative. This implies that mosque attendance does not have an unconditionally positive effect on political participation. Indeed, religious-group activities only bolster political activity among those who distrust most people, i.e., those who are the least prosocial.

---

[17] In a regression model with country fixed effects, I find no statistically significant relationship between the frequency of mosque attendance and generalized distrust.

Having considered (and dismissed) prosociality as a confounder, I turn to alternative interpretations of the substitution effect. Although I considered (and dismissed) them earlier, there are other explanations for why participation in religious group activities might spur political activism: resources, in the form of information and civic skills, or heightened motivation and efficacy. I can test for the importance of each in the substitution effect by including them in a fully specified model. Unfortunately, the cross-national survey dataset is missing measures of skills and efficacy with broad coverage; so instead, I turn to available proxies: motivation in the form of grievances, measured using respondents' self-reported happiness and employment status; and the "demand" for information about politics, using interest in politics and the frequency with which respondents report discussing politics with family and friends.

Adding in these measures, I find that they do little to diminish the direct effect of mosque attendance on participation. Moreover, their inclusion does not impact the interaction model in a meaningful way, bolstering my interpretation that the substitution effect is primarily about group-based trust. As a final test, I confirm the reliability of my key result by assessing its consistency. I find a statistically significant substitution effect in two of the three political activities (petitions and demonstrations), although the coefficients are in the "right" direction in the case of boycotts as well. I also find that the substitution effect operates in an additional large-scale political activity: participation in national elections. While generalized distrust undermines self-reported voter turnout, the negative effect is eliminated for those who attend mosque at least weekly.[18]

6.3 STATE REPRESSION AND THE ISLAMIC ADVANTAGE

I have offered consistent evidence in support of my three hypotheses: that generalized distrust undermines participation in mass political activities in the Muslim world; that a salient Islamic identity, signaled through frequent religious group activity, supports participation; and that it does so by effectively substituting for generalized trust, ostensibly because of the group-based trust fostered through those religious communal gatherings. Although I have been unable to test this last supposition directly, I have carefully considered and dismissed alternative interpretations for the substitution effect I find.

From these results, I conclude that the Islamic advantage in political mobilization is largely based on the ability of Islamic-based groups to solve the generalized trust problem in the practice of mass politics. This implies that the magnitude of their comparative advantage reflects the size of the underlying trust problem, to their benefit in particularly distrusting times and places. It also implies that the Islamic advantage is likely to be exaggerated when conditions serve to make trust even more critical for collective action. Recall that

---

[18] See Online Appendix Table OA.22 for full results.

6.3 State Repression and the Islamic Advantage

interpersonal trust is needed to support participation in latent political movements because of interdependence and uncertainty. In the case of mass politics, it is important to consider what state policies might impact interdependence and uncertainty. In the section that follows, I ask how state repression of political movements might impact the trust problem and, as a result, the Islamic advantage.

As discussed in Chapter 3, barriers to political activity in the Muslim world tend to be higher, on average. But this has not stopped some state authorities from further deepening their control over their citizens, with many interventions aimed specifically at regulating Islamic-based groups. In Algeria, after the Islamic Salvation Front (Front Islamique du Salut, FIS) won the first round of parliamentary elections in 1991, the military declared a state of emergency and curtailed citizens' participatory rights, hoping to avoid another FIS victory in the second round of elections. Similarly, in Turkey, after an uptick in support for Islamic-based parties in the 1996 general election, the military intervened to remove the Welfare Party (RP) and its representatives from office, shortly before the Constitutional Court effectively shut the party down. Most recently, in July 2013, the Egyptian military intervened to remove President Mohamed Mursi and the Freedom and Justice Party (Hizb al-Hurriya wal-'Adala) from office before suspending the constitution and declaring a state of emergency.

At least one of the existing theories of Islamic politics – the faith-based theory of "transvaluation" – expects increases in state repression to be effective in sidelining Islamic-based movements: when repression increases the costs of participation, every individual, religious or otherwise, is less likely to become politically active. But my trust-based theory has a different expectation: by increasing the risk of going it alone, repression strengthens the interdependence of individual decisions, making trust even more important for political mobilization. As such, it should only magnify the relative advantage of Islamic-based groups in mass politics. In the sections that follow, I explain the logic of this argument before testing some of its empirical implications.

6.3.1 Repression, Trust, and the Islamic Advantage

The existing literature on Islamic-based politics is fairly unified in seeing state repression as an obstacle to Islamic-based political mobilization. So significant is state intervention that the success and failure of Islamic politics is assumed to rise and fall with the extent of repression (Alexander 2000; Mufti 1999; Schwedler 2006). Islamic movements update their goals and tactics due to

> new structural conditions that either shrink or expand opportunity spaces, which in turn shape the goals and strategies of Islamic movements as "withdrawal," "confrontation," or "participation" in politics and the market (Yavuz 2003, p. 27).

Based on this logic, Islamic groups enter the political market as state repression recedes and are effectively sidelined when state pressure increases. In the latter case, the typical response is either to shift attention to non-political activities (Singerman 1996; Tuğal 2009), or to radicalize (Hafez 2003), with all but the most extreme opting for "self-preserving silence" (Wickham 2002, p. 204). Regardless, the potential for latent Islamic-based politics narrows considerably.

In stark contrast, my trust-based theory of Islamic-based political participation implies that repression should bolster Islamic politics. This is because state interference increases the costs and risks of political participation for each individual, making it even more important that she not go it alone. In other words, repression serves to strengthen the interdependence of individual decisions, thereby deepening the need for trust among would-be participants. Additionally, by increasing the costs to participation, state repression may also heighten uncertainty by increasing the incentives to free ride, plausibly converting some honest "conditional cooperators" into untrustworthy rational egoists.

This need for trust among participants may serve to suppress some latent political activity or to limit political engagement to "small personalistic groups based on informal ties and loyalty" (Clark 2004a, p. 28). But large-scale political activity is not impossible, even under conditions of intense state repression (Lawrence 2016; Önver and Taraktaş 2017; Shadmehr and Bernhardt 2011). And so where latent political mobilization does occur, I contend that it is more likely to be Islamic-based, as feelings of group-based trust become an even more important foundation for cooperation and collective action.

6.3.2 Evidence of Islam's Repression Advantage

Panel analysis of the Islamic advantage across space and time, in response to increased state repression, is impossible given data constraints. But a couple of empirical implications of my argument are relatively easy to test using available data sources: first, that increased repression strengthens the association between generalized distrust and political participation; second, that repression similarly deepens the relationship between mosque attendance and participation; and third, that the so-called substitution effect is also strengthened as repression increases.

To assess these, I first identify all those places that saw a change in state repression during the time period covered by the cross-national dataset. Of the seventeen Muslim countries covered by my survey data and which appear in the Cingranelli and Richards dataset, twelve experienced a change in repression within the relevant time frame. When it comes to the CIRI Freedom of Assembly and Association index, the vast majority of these – Bangladesh, Indonesia, Iraq, Jordan, Malaysia, Morocco, Nigeria, Pakistan, Turkey, Uzbekistan – moved between "limited restrictions" and "severe restrictions," although Mali transitioned between "limited restrictions" and unrestricted freedom, while Yemen ran the full gamut. In most of the forthcoming analysis, I restrict the models to individuals in these twelve countries only, including country fixed effects that focus the comparison on cross-temporal differences within each country across periods with more or less repression.

To assess how differences in state policy impact the trust problem and the Islamic advantage, I estimate a series of interaction models. But before

6.3 State Repression and the Islamic Advantage

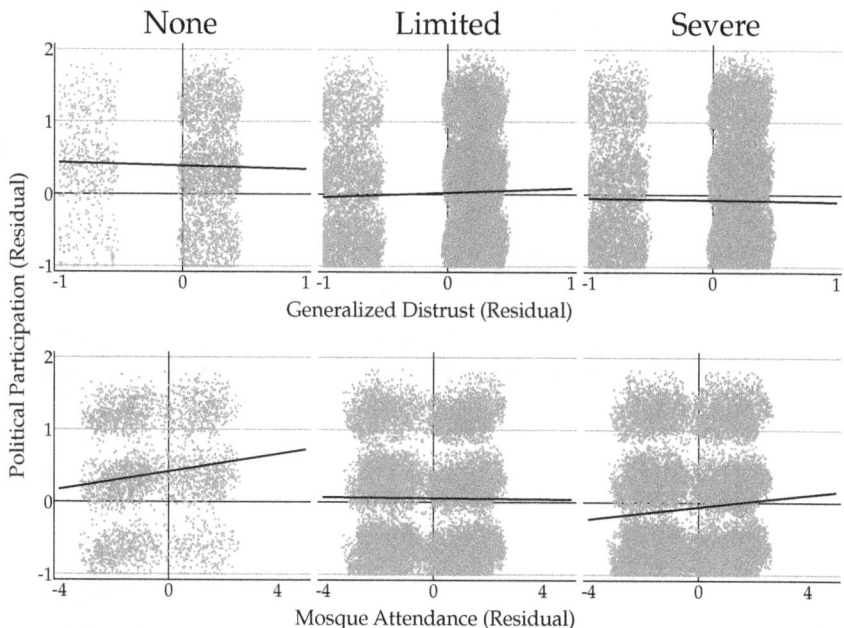

FIGURE 6.4 Distrust, Identity, and Participation, across Levels of Repression
Notes: Partial correlation plots between generalized trust and political participation, and between mosque attendance and participation. Residuals after controlling for demographics. Across levels of Freedom of Assembly and Association, restricted to countries that experience a change in scores. Ten percent noise to jitter observations and avoid overlap.

discussing the statistical results, a basic visualization of the empirical patterns is useful. Figure 6.4 illustrates how the bivariate relationship between generalized distrust and political participation, and that between mosque attendance and participation, differ across levels of repression. To help control for demographic confounders, these are partial correlation plots: in each case, I estimate an OLS model of the key variable – distrust, mosque attendance, political participation – based on respondents' age, gender, and education; only the residuals, that is, the variation that is left unexplained by the demographic variables, are plotted here.

In both sets of figures, I find considerable variation in how distrust and religious group activities impact political participation, depending on the underlying level of repression. Observations in the "no restrictions" category are limited, so I focus most of my attention on the second two panels. The plots reveal that, if anything, distrust tends to *bolster* participation when there are limited restrictions, only undermining the potential for participation when restrictions are severe. Similarly, political participation is negatively correlated with mosque attendance under more limited restrictions; the positive correlation between the two only appears when political activity is severely restricted.

I confirm these patterns in a set of statistical tests: interaction models of distrust and repression, and of mosque attendance and repression, on participation.[19] In both cases, I include country fixed effects and individual-level demographic controls. Across all the models, whether I include all seventeen countries or only those that saw a change in their level of repression, I find the same result: the effects of both distrust and mosque attendance on political participation are strengthened by severe state restrictions (see Online Appendix Table OA.23). In other words, repression seems to deepen both the trust problem and the source of the Islamic advantage.

An even more precise test of my theory would include a triple interaction – between generalized distrust, mosque participation, and state restrictions. This would allow me to gauge the ability of Islamic identity to effectively substitute for generalized trust across different degrees of repression. Because triple interactions are difficult to disentangle and interpret correctly, I instead estimate two separate models: one using respondents in country-years with less than severely restricted Freedom of Assembly and Association; the other among respondents living in severely restricted times and places. Here again, I restrict the analysis to countries that experienced a change in their level of repression, so that the results are not driven by fundamental differences between the types of places that are always restricted and those that are always unrestricted.

The full results of this analysis are available in Online Appendix Table OA.24, but an illustration of the main results is displayed in Figure 6.5. It reveals a set of mostly null effects in the unrestricted cases: no statistically significant effect of distrust or mosque attendance on political participation; neither is there evidence of a substitution effect. But in the restricted cases, a different, more familiar pattern emerges: the coefficient on distrust is negative, though not statistically significant at conventional levels. More importantly, the interaction is now statistically significant and positive, indicating that for those respondents who attend mosque regularly, generalized distrust is no longer an obstacle to their political participation. In other words, this is further evidence that state repression can actually bolster the Islamic advantage, rather than diminishing it.

Before concluding it is important to consider an alternative explanation for these results. If increased state repression directly impacts trust levels and mosque attendance, the interaction effects I have identified could be entirely driven by these changes. But after assessing how generalized trust and mosque attendance covary with levels of repression in the cases in which there is

---

[19] The first of these models takes the form $PolParticipation_{ijt} = \beta_0 + \beta_1 Distrust_{ij} + \beta_2 Restrictions_{jt} + \beta_3 Distrust_{ijt} \times Restrictions_{jt} + X_i + \mu_j + \epsilon_i$, where $PolParticipation_{ijt}$ is a measure of respondent i's willingness to participate in political activities, $Distrust_{ijt}$ is her distrust of most people, $Restrictions_{jt}$ is a binary indicator of whether her country is currently (in year t) experiencing severe restrictions on assembly and association, $Distrust_{ijt} \times Restrictions_{jt}$ is the interaction between the two, X_i is a vector of her individual-level characteristics, μ_j is a fixed-effect term for her home country, and ϵ_i is the error term. The second model is identical, except frequency of mosque attendance takes the place of generalized distrust.

6.4 Conclusion

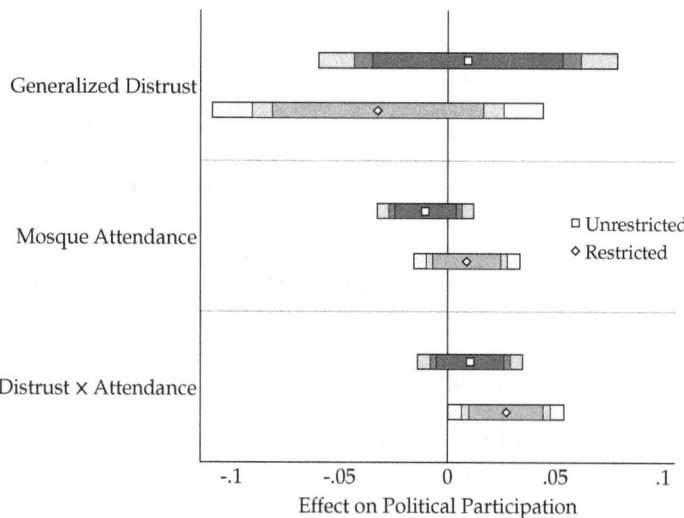

FIGURE 6.5 The Substitution Effect under Repression

Notes: Estimated effects of distrust, mosque attendance, and their interaction, on willingness to participate in any political activity. Self-identified Muslims in Muslim countries that experienced a change in repression during the sample period. Survey years with severe restrictions on assembly and association compared to survey years with fewer restrictions. All models include country fixed effects. Shaded bars indicate statistical significance at the 90%, 95% and 99% level, respectively.

cross-temporal variation, I feel confident that there is little cause for concern. I find no statistically significant relationship between distrust and repression across the full set of cases and, if anything, repression serves to reduce the frequency of mosque attendance. In addition, when I look at the cross-temporal trends within each country, I find that repression rarely boosts distrust and mosque attendance: it does the former only in Iraq, Jordan, Malaysia, and Nigeria (while significantly decreasing it in Indonesia, Mali, and Pakistan), and the latter occurs only in Indonesia, Malaysia, and Uzbekistan (while having the opposite effect in Bangladesh, Mali, Morocco, and Nigeria).

6.4 CONCLUSION

In this first application of my trust-based theory of Islamic-based political and economic activity, I have presented theoretical and empirical evidence to support it in the case of individual participation in latent politics. Across twenty-four Muslim-plurality contexts, those who generally distrust others are less willing to take part in a range of large-scale political activities, from signing petitions, to attending lawful demonstrations and joining boycotts. But a key indicator of a salient Islamic identity – religious group activities – bolsters their willingness to be involved in mass politics. More specifically, these religious group activities and the group-based trust they foster effectively substitute for generalized trust to support political involvement even among those who distrust most people.

Additional analysis confirmed that the effect of religious group activities on political participation was not the result of prosociality: those who attend mosque frequently, for example, tend to be less trusting of most people; and, ultimately, mosque attendance was found to have no direct impact on political participation – it only supported participation through its countervailing effect on generalized distrust. I also confirmed that the substitution effect is unlikely to be based on the resources or motivations that religious group activities might impart. The addition of these variables to my statistical models did little to weaken the association between mosque attendance and political participation and, if anything, they strengthened the substitution effect in an interaction model.

In the final section of the chapter, I explored an additional (and counter-intuitive) implication of my trust-based theory. Based on the assumption that increased state repression would deepen the interdependence between individuals' decisions to join in a collective political movement, I argued that restrictions on political activity would serve to make interpersonal trust even more important to collective political activity, increasing the size of Islam's comparative advantage. And, indeed, I find that trust and Islamic identity are even more valuable for supporting political participation among those living in countries with more severe restrictions on political activity. This last set of results has important implications for recent dynamics in Egypt, where the military sidelined the Muslim Brotherhood and its supporters, and in Turkey, where President Recep Tayyip Erdoğan is doing the same with NGOs associated with Fethullah Gülen.

Beyond these specific cases, the evidence presented in this chapter has important implications for other identity-based movements, in the Muslim world and beyond. Although I have focused here on the ways that an Islamic group identity can foster feelings of group-based trust, other identities (e.g., ethnic, regional, sectarian) can easily do the same. In other words, feelings of trust based on a shared Kurdish, Alevi, Berber, or Coptic identity could substitute for more generalized trust expectations to support political movements representing these other groups. And these movements, much like Islamic-based ones, are unlikely to be easily suppressed by state authorities, as their comparative advantage should also increase with the size of the underlying trust problem. This could explain why Kurdish-based political activism in Turkey has survived recent, violent efforts by Erdoğan's government to sideline it.

Beyond the Muslim world, my discussion of the role of religious group activities in supporting mass political participation serves as a useful amendment to the existing literature on religious-based politics. First and foremost, the positive association I find between regular mosque attendance and political participation shows that the relationship between religious service attendance and participation extends beyond the American case and the Western world. Further, my finding that group-based trust is a key benefit of mosque attendance in the Muslim world adds to a growing critique of those theories of

6.4 Conclusion

church attendance that focus only on personal political resources (Brewer, Kersh, and Petersen 2003; Djupe and Grant 2002). And yet, at the end of this theoretical and empirical investigation, a critical question yet remains: do the benefits of religious group activities and group-based trust in the Muslim world extend beyond the particular case of mass politics? I now turn to answering that question, bringing my trust-based theory to bear on a different political phenomenon: the act of voting.

7

Islam, Trust, and Strategic Voting in Turkey

> [O]ne must not scatter (*tashtit*) the vote and let it be spent uselessly (*ta 'ridua li-al-daya'*).
>
> Ayatollah Ali al-Sistani (2005)

In a number of Muslim countries, Islamic-based political parties have enjoyed a recent spate of success. Nowhere is the rising popularity of Islamic party politics more apparent than in Turkey, the Muslim world's oldest electoral democracy. Beginning in the early 1990s, after forty years of competitive multiparty elections, popular support for Islamic-based parties in Turkey began to steadily increase, a trend that has now culminated in six consecutive victories for the Justice and Development Party (AKP). The consistency of the AKP's performance is new for Turkish electoral politics, where parties have long struggled to build and maintain a solid base of support (Akarca and Başlevent 2010a; Çarkoğlu 1998; Hazama 2007). The rise of Islamic-based politics in Turkey is also surprising given its long history of secularism (Berkes 1998; Kuru 2009; Navaro-Yashin 2002; Özyürek 2006).

Many observers have wondered aloud whether the popularity of Islamic parties should be taken as a sign of a religious resurgence, in Turkey and elsewhere in the Muslim world (Howe 2005; García-Rivero and Kotzé 2007; Tepe 2005). But as I showed in Chapter 3, cross-temporal data from the Turkish case reveal no change in religiosity that could explain the rise of Islamic-based parties there. Quite to the contrary, it seems that the increase in the AKP's vote share is attributable not to a larger number of religious voters, but to more support for the party among *secular* voters. These empirical patterns prompt a reframing of the question of Islamic-based voting, focusing not on a religious resurgence, but on the ability of Islamic parties to win and keep the support of voters – including secular ones – in Turkey and elsewhere.

In addressing this puzzle, I return to a my bottom-up approach, asking how individuals in electoral systems such as Turkey's come to make their vote choices. The Turkish system poses a number of challenges for individual vote decisions. On the one hand, it is incredibly fractionalized, supporting more parties than optimal given the voting rules, most with largely overlapping (and shifting) policy positions. At the same time, it is quite volatile, with wild swings in party vote shares from election to election, as multiple parties enter and exit the field each year, and as those that remain gain and lose supporters quickly. Both fractionalization and volatility make it difficult for voters to make their votes count, selecting a party that both represents their interests and is likely to win representation.

The challenge of voting was especially daunting during the height of Turkey's fractionalization and volatility, beginning in the mid-1970s and lasting through the early 2000s. During this period, voters had multiple proximate parties to choose between and their most-preferred party was liable to change over time, because the party changed its platform, opted to disband, or was forcibly dismantled by the Constitutional Court. With so many parties competing, many did not secure sufficient support in a given district to win a seat there; and even those that were popular enough in a district or two often failed to cross Turkey's steep, 10 percent national electoral threshold. If voters believed that their most preferred party might not clear either one of these hurdles, they tended to vote strategically – for a second- or third-best party, still close to their policy preferences, even if it was not their most proximate one.

When they need to consider voting strategically, each voter's best decision becomes inherently intertwined with what others are doing. This sets up a large-scale coordination problem that must be solved within electoral districts, as well as at the national level. When voters fail to coordinate successfully, the result is large numbers of wasted votes – cast for parties that fail to win seats – which leads to systemic under-representation. In fractionalized electoral systems, and especially where party loyalty is weak, a useful focal point for voters to coordinate around is the result of the previous election (Cox 1997; Rashkova 2010). But when fractionalization is combined with frequent party entry and exit, as well as vote volatility, the past is less indicative of the future. Under these conditions, a vicious cycle can ensue: coordination failure among voters in one election begets vote switching and volatility in the following election, which, in turn, begets even more coordination failure in the future, *ad infinitum*.

To get themselves out of this cycle and successfully coordinate their individual choices, voters require a good deal of information. Much of the extant literature has focused on the need for political information, that is, which parties are competing and what each stands for (Conroy-Krutz, Moehler, and Aguilar 2016; Rozenas and Sadanandan 2018). But the interdependence of individual vote decisions also implies a need for *social* information: each voter needs to know what others are likely to do, in their district and nationwide. Without the ability to use the past as a useful heuristic for the future, voters must develop an intuition on their own, either through informal conversations with other voters or, increasingly, using internet sources or polling data. Given real or imagined concerns that the information voters gather may be inaccurate, its ultimate utility to them will depend on whether it – and the person who has offered it – can be trusted. For this reason, I expect interpersonal distrust to undermine the potential for voter coordination, particularly in fractionalized, volatile electoral systems.

Bringing this argument to bear on the Turkish case, I argue that generalized distrust can explain a long history of voter coordination failure and vote volatility there. Further, I suggest that the trust problem in voter coordination can be successfully addressed within religious communities, where voters share a salient Islamic identity and have reciprocal group-based trust expectations. In analysis of panel data from decades of Turkish elections, I find empirical support for both hypotheses: distrust is indeed associated with more wasted votes and larger inter-election vote swings; and the link between distrust and both outcomes is effectively severed in electoral districts with a larger, more active religious community. In addition, I show how the coordination of votes within religious communities has worked to the advantage of Islamic parties: their consistency over time, especially through a series of political upheavals in the mid-to-late 1990s, allowed their vote behavior to become a credible focal point for other distrusting voters. This served to make the AKP a more reliable target for strategic votes from conservative *yet secular* voters.

In the chapter that follows, I begin by describing the Turkish electoral system – its history of volatility and coordination failure, as well as the remarkable rise of its Islamic-based political parties – making a case for its comparability with other Muslim-plurality countries in the developing world. I then develop my trust-based theory of strategic voting, explaining how coordination is further complicated when voters distrust one another, implying a trust-based coordination advantage within (religious) groups. I follow this with my empirical analysis: first, testing the main hypotheses of my trust-based theory; and then, identifying how consistent coordination among Islamic voters served to attract support from distrusting, secular voters to the AKP, beginning in 2002.

7.1 THE COMPLEXITIES OF THE TURKISH ELECTORAL SYSTEM

For the first time in this book, I will focus my attention almost exclusively on the Turkish case. The choice of Turkey is not based on convenience or personal preference, although it is a place I both know and love. Rather, I would argue that the Turkish case is an ideal one for examining the phenomenon of Islamic-based political parties. With nearly seventy years of competitive elections, and Islamic parties competing in forty-five of these, there is tremendous cross-temporal variation to leverage. And as a large, diverse country, there is also considerable cross-sectional variation within Turkey to exploit.

At the same time, the Turkish case is not wholly unlike other developing democracies in the Muslim world. As I illustrate below, with its high levels of party-system fractionalization and vote volatility, until recently, Turkey looked a lot like a young democracy. Party loyalty has also tended to be low – as in a

7.1 The Complexities of the Turkish Electoral System

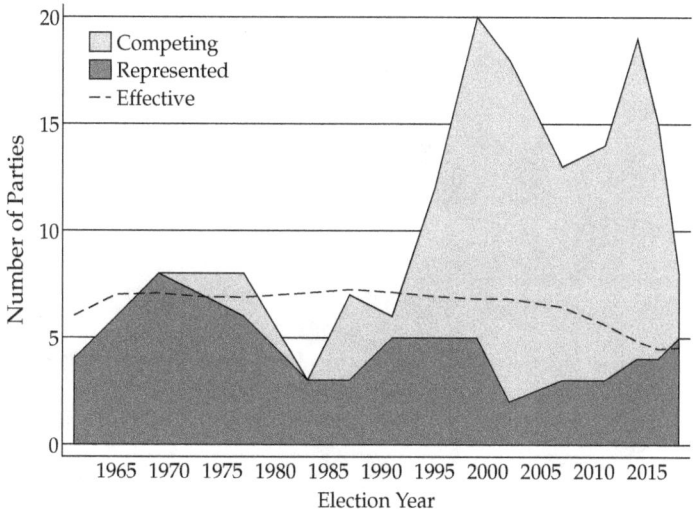

FIGURE 7.1 Party-System Fractionalization in Turkey (1961–2018)
Notes: The total number of competing parties in each general election, the number that won seats, and the effective number of parties, calculated using national vote shares.

new democracy – as political groups have regularly disbanded, been dismantled by the courts, or substantially changed their policy platforms. As such, the theoretical and empirical evidence I bring to bear on the Turkish case is broadly relevant to other developing democracies, inside and outside of the Muslim world.

7.1.1 The Turkish System in Cross-Temporal Comparison

Political parties have been operating in Turkey since the founding of the modern Republic. Early elections (1923–1943) were dominated by a single party – Atatürk's own Republican People's Party (CHP) – with multiparty competition beginning in 1946. A change in the electoral law after the 1957 elections, from multiple non-transferable votes to a proportional representation system, makes it difficult to compare the earliest competitive elections with more recent ones, but a cross-temporal comparison can be drawn from 1961 until the present day.

A cursory look at the Turkish party system over the past fifty-plus years reveals a number of patterns. First, since the mid-1980s the system has been saturated with parties, many more than its electoral rules are able to accommodate (Figure 7.1). While the number of parties garnering sufficient votes to win seats in the National Assembly since 1961 has been relatively consistent – varying between three and six – the number of parties vying for representation skyrocketed after 1983, once the 1980 military regime banned all pre-existing parties from competing. The number of parties increased even further in 1995, when these once-banned parties were allowed to compete again. Only recently

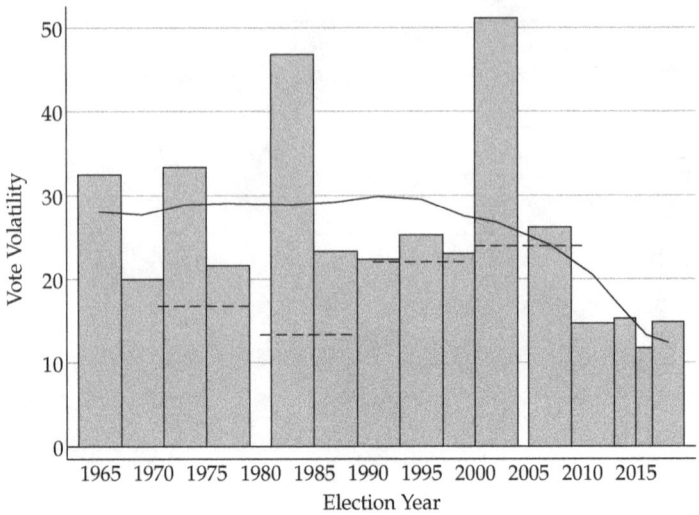

FIGURE 7.2 Vote Volatility in Turkey (1965–2018)
Notes: Vote volatility in each general election since 1965. LOWESS trend line indicated by the solid black line; global averages in each decade indicated by the dashed black lines.

has the number of parties receded, reflecting changes to the electoral law following the 2017 national referendum. Meanwhile, the "effective" number of parties – an index that takes the parties' relative size into account (Laakso and Taagepera 1979) – has historically been high, in comparison to other established and developing democracies, tapering off only since 2007.[1]

The second notable feature of the Turkish system is its extraordinary degree of vote volatility (i.e., wild swings in the popularity of parties from election to election). Mogens Pedersen popularized an index of "electoral volatility," which he defined as "the net change within the electoral party system resulting from individual vote transfers" (1979, p. 3).[2] By this index, the Turkish party system (1965–2018) appears extremely unstable (Figure 7.2). The high degree of inter-election volatility is particularly remarkable because the indices I calculate are based on an understanding of continuities in the Turkish party system, transcending name changes and disbandings.[3] Volatility in the Turkish system

---

[1] While the effective number of parties in Western Europe hovered between 3.5 and 4.5 in Laakso and Taagepera's (1979) sample (1945–1976), the Turkish figures only stayed in that range in 1983, when the military regime tightly controlled which parties were allowed to compete. Otherwise, the number was closer to six in the 1960s, and closer to nine in the 1990s.

[2] Pedersen's index takes half of the sum of the absolute value of all vote differences between a given election and the one that immediately preceded it, across all parties, like Ascher and Tarrow's (1975) index and the measure of "deinstitutionalization" defined by Przeworski (1975).

[3] In the Turkish party system, name changes are frequent as the Constitutional Court regularly intervenes and forcibly disbands parties it deems to have violated constitutional prohibitions on the politicization of religion and ethnicity. Having combed through the history of these disbandings and name changes, I identify the following continuities: a center-right movement – Justice

7.1 The Complexities of the Turkish Electoral System

was particularly high in 1983 – in the wake of the 1980 coup, when a newly formed ANAP won – and in 2002, when another outsider party – the AKP – rose to victory in its first election. Moreover, and unlike most democracies that stabilize over time (Rashkova 2010; Tavits 2005; Tavits and Annus 2006), Turkey's volatility actually grew through the 1980s and 1990s (Çarkoğlu 1998; Hazama 2007). Indeed, compared to international averages in volatility in each decade – indicated by the dashed black lines in Figure 7.2 – Turkey's instability during this period looks even more extreme.[4] The overall trend has only recently reversed, beginning with the rise and continued success of the AKP, since 2002.

Since I do not treat successor parties as new entrants into the party system, a good deal of the volatility identified above is the result of entirely

---

Party (Adalet Partisi, AP) (1961–1977), Nationalist Democracy Party (Milliyetçi Demokrasi Partisi, MDP) (1983), True Path Party (Doğru Yol Partisi, DYP) (1987–2002), and Democratic Party (Demokrat Parti), DP) (2007–present); a center-left thread – Republican People's Party (Cumhuriyet Halk Partisi, CHP) (1961–1977; 1995–present), Populist Party (Halkçı Parti, HP) (1983), and Social Democrat Populist Party (Sosyal Demokrat Halkçı Parti, SHP) (1987–1991); a Turkish nationalist movement – Republican Villagers Nation Party (Cumhuriyetçi Köylü Millet Partisi, CKMP) (1961–1965), Nationalist Action Party (Milliyetçi Hareket Partisi, MHP) (1969–1977; 1995–present), and Nationalist Task Party (Milliyetçi Çalışma Partisi, MCP) (1987); a Kurdish nationalist movement – People's Democracy Party (Halkın Demokrasi Partisi, HADEP) (1995–1999), Democratic People's Party (Demokratik Halk Partisi, DEHAP) (2002), Democratic Society Party (Demokratik Toplum Partisi, DTP) (2007), Peace and Democracy Party (Barış ve Demokrasi Partisi, BDP) (2011), and Peoples' Democratic Party (Halkların Demokratik Partisi, HDP) (2015–present); and an Islamic movement – National Salvation Party (Millî Selâmat Partisi, MSP) (1973–1977), Welfare Party (Refah Partisi, RP) (1987–1995), Virtue Party (Fazilet Partisi, FP) (1999), and Felicity Party (Saadet Partisi, SP) (2002–present); I also identify name-changes in smaller political movements: the Socialist Power Party (Sosyalist İktidar Partisi, SİP) (1999), Communist Party of Turkey (Türkiye Komünist Partisi, TKP) (2002–2011), and Communist Party (Komünist Parti, KP) (2015); the Socialist Party (Sosyalist Parti, SP) (1991), Workers' Party (İşçi Partisi, İP) (1995–2007), and Patriotic Party (Vatan Partisi, VATAN) (2015–present); the Unity Party (Birlik Partisi, BP) (1969) and Turkey Unity Party (Türkiye Birlik Partisi, TBP) (1973–1977); the Reliance Party (Güven Partisi, GP) (1969) and Republican Reliance Party (Cumhuriyetçi Güven Partisi, CGP) (1973–1977); and the Reformist Democracy Party (Islahatçı Demokrasi Partisi, IDP) (1987) and Nation Party (Millet Partisi) (1995–2015). In some cases when a single party divides itself into multiple successor parties – for example, the AKP and SP that emerged from the dissolution of the FP, or the KP and People's Communist Party of Turkey (Halkın Türkiye Komünist Partisi, HTKP) from the TKP – I identify the successor party that maintained the majority of the same leadership as the previous party (as was the case with the SP, as the main successor of the FP) or was the largest representative of the movement in the next election (as was the case in the KP as the successor to the TKP's electoral legacy). If I ignore these continuities, the volatility index is significantly higher, as each newly named party is treated like a new entrant into the electoral system, and the entirety of its vote share enters into the statistic as a vote change.

[4] Among the thirty-nine countries that democratized by the 1980s, only Guatemala (38.9%) and Bolivia (37.6) – countries with far shorter experiences with democracy – surpassed Turkey (29.3) in terms of average vote volatility (1975–2010). Compare this to an average volatility of 13.0 percent in Europe or 15.8 percent in Asia during the same period. These statistics are based on the authors' own calculations, described in greater detail in the Conclusion.

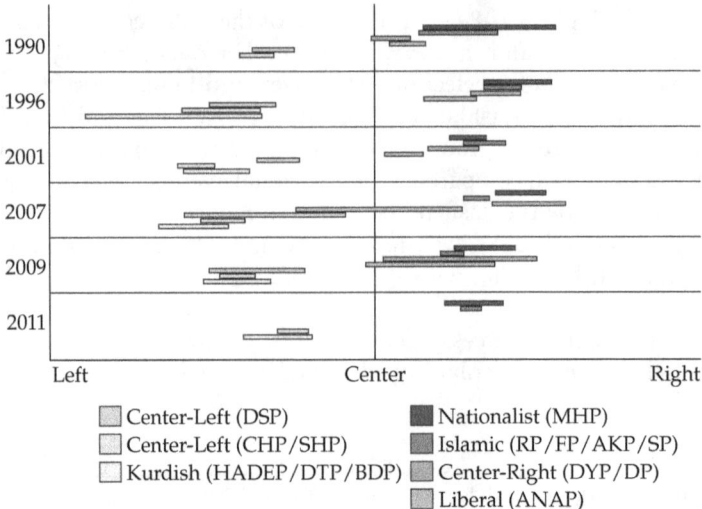

FIGURE 7.3 Turkish Parties' Left–Right Orientation, over Time

Notes: Left–right orientation of Turkey's largest parties, estimated using supporters' positioning on a standardized spectrum. Bars indicate 95 percent confidence intervals around each mean.

nascent parties, as well as the demise (and eventual exit) of once-popular ones.[5] Turkey is notorious for its incumbency disadvantage: since 1961, and prior to the AKP's incumbency, only once – in 1977 – did a winning party (the CHP) increase its vote share in the following election. In every other case during this period, even when an incumbent emerged as the largest vote-getter, its share of the national vote decreased significantly from its previous showing. (For an illustration of this phenomenon, see Online Appendix Figure OA.6.)

The existing literature tends to interpret the rejection of incumbents as a sign of dissatisfaction among Turkish voters, who are presumed to be especially unhappy with the party's economic performance while in office (Akarca and Tansel 2006; Başlevent, Kirmanoğlu, and Şenatalar 2005). But vote swings impact large and small parties alike, affecting those who have the power to shape economic policy as well as those who do not.[6] It is therefore more likely that volatility reflects not party quality as much as the weakness of voter loyalty. And the latter can be explained not just by the frequent disbanding and renaming of existing parties, but also by the sheer number of available options. Figure 7.3 shows the policy positions of Turkey's larger parties between 1990

---

[5] The average lifespan of a Turkish party in the 1961–2018 period (N=46) is remarkably short: fewer than four elections (μ=3.94). Over 40 percent (N=19) of parties during this period competed in only one election, while an additional 13 percent (N=6), competed in just two.

[6] Party disloyalty extends beyond the system's largest parties to its smaller ones as well: in transition matrices calculated at the district (*ilçe*) level, I find that the average level of party loyalty between elections from 1983 to 2018 was 41.3 percent – 55.1 percent for "major" parties that won at least 10 percent in any election and 12.5 percent for smaller ones.

7.1 The Complexities of the Turkish Electoral System

and 2011, as defined by the preferences of their self-identified supporters.[7] It reveals considerable overlap between parties in each year, on the left, but especially on the right, as well as multiple options just to the left and right of center.[8] This implies that voters – unless they sit at either extreme of the left–right spectrum – have multiple parties that could plausibly represent their interests, giving them the opportunity to switch their allegiances from year to year (Akarca 2008; Hazama 2009). Combined with the fact that the system is over-saturated with parties, many of which are unlikely to win representation, this significantly complicates each voter's decision on election day.

The main result of this complex party system – with too many parties and instability in voter preferences from year to year – is a large number of votes in each general election that are "wasted" (i.e., cast for parties that ultimately fail to gain representation). This can happen whenever a party is unable to garner 10 percent of the national vote and cross Turkey's steep electoral threshold.[9] But it is most likely to occur when a party does not win sufficient support in an electoral district to earn a seat. The cross-temporal trend in the rate of wasted votes tracks closely on to variation in vote volatility, indicating that the two might well be linked (see Online Appendix Figure OA.7 for an illustration). And yet, there is still a tremendous amount of variability in the rate of wasted votes across Turkey. Figure 7.4 displays the pattern in wasted votes across Turkish districts (*ilçeler*), nested within provinces (*iller*), the level at which parliamentary seats are allocated.[10] Looking at the average across all elections in the most "wasteful" period – 1961–2002 – some remarkable patterns emerge. While voters across some provinces (e.g., Konya, Manisa) avoid wasting many of their votes, voters in certain districts (sometimes across entire

---

[7] As in Chapter 3, I estimate the policy position of each party in terms of the distribution of their supporters' preferences, lacking any alternative that produces more than a point estimate. Because of this measurement strategy, the cross-temporal comparison here covers survey years, rather than elections. To support comparison across all surveys, I use left–right orientation, the only metric of voter preferences available across all surveys. I standardize the raw scale across the full sample, and calculate the average within each party, along with 95 percent confidence intervals. The comparison is limited to parties with more than a small handful of supporters.

[8] It is very rare for a party to occupy a completely unique position within the policy space. This is the case only for the center-left DSP and liberal ANAP, both in 2001. This clustering in the policy space stands out in comparative perspective as well. Turkish parties, on average, tend to be more tightly clustered than their counterparts in Western Europe. Using the estimated left–right orientation of each party from the Manifesto Project, I find that the standard deviation across all Turkish parties ($\sigma=17.9$ across election years) resembles that in the Czech Republic (16.3) and Portugal (16.6), more than parties in more established democracies, for example, Finland (26.1) and Switzerland (23.3).

[9] The 10 percent threshold was put into place after the 1980 coup, ostensibly to end the fragmentation of the Turkish party system. But most recognize it as an attempt to keep Kurdish-based political parties out of parliament (Ergil: 2000a).

[10] Until the 1991 election, Turkey's electoral districts aligned with its provinces (*iller*). After that, the largest provinces – first Istanbul and Izmir, and then Ankara and Bursa – were divided into two or three districts. To support cross-temporal comparison and because most sub-national statistics are reported at the province level, I aggregate vote results in the post-2002 period within provincial boundaries, for a consistent set of eighty-one electoral districts.

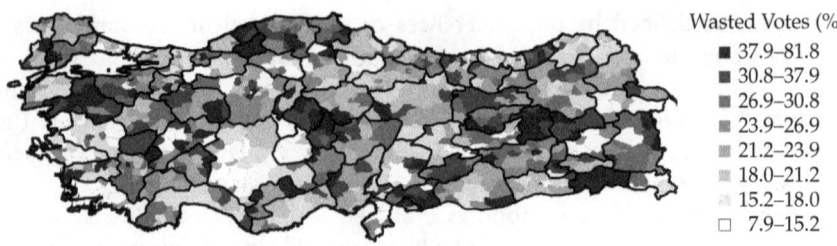

FIGURE 7.4 Wasted Votes, across Electoral Districts (1961–2002)
Notes: The percent of votes cast for parties that failed to win a seat, averaged across all general elections between 1961 and 2002. Provincial boundaries indicated in black.

provinces) waste upwards of 30 percent of their votes.[11] In these places, after each election, a third of the population, on average, ends up unrepresented in parliament.

7.1.2 The Rise of Turkey's Islamic-Based Parties

It is within this complex party system that Turkey's Islamic-based political parties have risen to prominence. The Turkish Islamic party movement dates back several decades, with the first explicitly religious party founded by Necmettin Erbakan in 1970 as part of his National Outlook (Millî Görüş) movement. The National Order Party (Millî Nizam Partisi, MNP) was shut down by the state for violating constitutional prohibitions on politicizing religion. But Erbakan quickly regrouped and formed a successor party, the National Salvation Party (Millî Selâmat Partisi, MSP), which was recognized in time to compete in the 1973 general elections.

Represented by the MSP, the Islamic party movement made a modest showing in 1973, winning just under 12 percent of the national vote. Over time, support for Erbakan and his Islamic party grew slowly but steadily: support for the MSP and its successor party – the Welfare Party (RP), established after the banning of pre-coup parties – hovered around the 10 percent mark, before climbing just past 15 percent in 1991. The RP garnered just over twenty percent of the national vote in 1995, enough to eke out a meager victory and attempt to form a coalition government. After a protracted set of negotiations, Erbakan was elected prime minister in June 1996; but he enjoyed less than eight months in office before the military intervened (by memorandum) to have him removed, in what has been called the country's "post-modern coup." Less than a year later, the Constitutional Court disbanded the RP under accusations that it too had violated the secularist principles of the Turkish constitution. In response, Erbakan quickly formed yet another successor party, the Virtue

---

[11] To put this into comparative perspective, Tavits and Annus (2006) find that an average of 17.8 percent of votes were wasted across elections in Eastern Europe and former Soviet Republics between 1990 and 2004.

7.1 The Complexities of the Turkish Electoral System

Party (FP), to contest the 1999 general elections. This time, he moderated the party's platform slightly in the hopes of avoiding yet another intervention by the courts.[12] While support for the FP fell sharply in some districts between 1995 and 1999, in others, voters continued their consistent support for the Islamic-based movement.

As had now become routine, the courts intervened to disband the FP for anti-secularist activities in June, 2001. Following intense disagreement within the former FP about the future direction of the Islamic political movement in Turkey, a split occurred. In the end, two Islamic-based parties were formed: Erbakan established the Felicity Party (SP) as the immediate successor to the FP; in parallel, a group of young MPs, including Recep Tayyip Erdoğan and Abdullah Gül, who called themselves the Reformists (*Yenilikçiler*), formed the Justice and Development Party (AKP). In terms of its party platform, the AKP looked remarkably similar to the FP and SP, sitting just to the right of center.[13] As such, it reasonably rivaled the SP as the future representative of the Islamic political movement.

With two viable Islamic parties competing against one another in the 2002 election, it was initially unclear which one voters would choose, and there were some concerns that the bloc would split (Mecham 2004). But come election day, the movements' supporters proved just how well-coordinated they were, with an overwhelming majority turning out to support the AKP. These religious voters were joined by a surprisingly large number of secular voters, most of whom had never before supported an Islamic-based party. Together, they lent enough support to the AKP (34.3%) that it was able to form a single-party government. This initial success was repeated in 2007, when the party won 46.7 percent of the national vote, then again in 2011, when it won 49.8 percent. Its vote share dipped slightly in the general elections held in June, 2015 (40.9%), but quickly rebounded in the follow-up election in November (49.5%), and held relatively steady in 2018 (42.5%).

As alluded to earlier, with the rise of the AKP came a number of significant changes to the Turkish party system: although the number of parties remained irrationally high – increasing from an average of 9.1 before the AKP incumbency, to 13.8 after – the number of effective parties subsided – averaging 7.4 through the 2002 election, but only 4.8 from 2007 onwards. Similarly, vote

---

[12] The shift towards the center can be seen in two different data sources. First, looking at the distribution of each party's supporters in Figure 7.3, some moderation between the RP in 1996 and the FP in 2001 is apparent. Further, looking at Manifesto Project estimations of each party's position based on their published platforms, the RP in 1995 ranked as considerably more right-wing (33.5) than the FP in 1999 (7.4), the latter situated clearly to the left of the nationalist MHP (28.1).

[13] The placement of the AKP relative to the other Islamic parties is clearest in Appendix Figure A6.1, where it is differentiated from the SP in the 2007 graph. If anything, the average AKP supporter in 2007 is to the right of the average SP supporter, bringing it closer to the average FP supporter in 2001 and average RP supporter in 1996. Similarly, in an analysis of the parties' manifestos, the AKP is estimated to occupy a moderate position (5.2), quite comparable to the FP's in 1999 (7.4) (Volkens et al. 2018).

volatility at the national level declined considerably, from 25.6 percent in the pre-AKP period to just 14 percent in the post-period, well below the international average. The rate of wasted votes also fell dramatically, from a national average of 23.8 percent through 2002 to 17.7 percent after, similar to the rate in Eastern Europe (Tavits and Annus 2006). In other words, along with the rise of the AKP, the Turkish electoral system has become more stable and more predictable, with a significant increase in the number of voters able to make their votes count. Seeing this parallel trend, a natural question follows: what, if anything, is the relationship between them?

7.2 THE TRUST PROBLEM IN VOTER COORDINATION

The single thread that connects the historical instability of the Turkish electoral system and the rise of the AKP is none other than trust; not trust in Islamic politicians, who could plausibly be expected to be less corrupt (Henderson and Kuncoro 2011) or more redistributionist (Pepinsky, Liddle, and Mujani 2012), but rather trust *in other voters*. Where interpersonal trust is absent, I argue, voters will struggle to coordinate their individual decisions into meaningful outcomes. When this happens, the electoral outcomes are less representative and less stable, complicating voters' ability to coordinate in the future. This is especially likely to happen in over-saturated, fractionalized party systems, such as Turkey's, where voters are likely to have to vote strategically in order to make their votes count.

In developing my trust-based theory of voter coordination, I build off some existing models of strategic voting, but I make the role of interpersonal trust more explicit by discussing how interdependence and uncertainty enter into individual vote decisions. In addition to identifying a trust problem in voter coordination, I argue that voters who live within vibrant religious communities – and who share a salient religious identity – are better able to coordinate their individual votes into meaningful outcomes. I contend that their ability to coordinate is based on the feelings of group-based trust that they share.

7.2.1 Interdependence of Vote Choices

A simplistic model of vote choice assumes that a voter selects her most preferred party by comparing her policy preferences to the estimated positions of all of the competing parties, ultimately voting for the one most proximate to her. But a more accurate model conceives of a voter who is trying to balance two things: both the proximity of a party to her ideal policy position and the party's likelihood of winning. As Downs explains,

A rational voter first decides what party he believes will benefit him most; then he tries to estimate whether this party has any chance of winning. He does this because his vote should be expended as part of a selection process, not as an expression of preference. Hence even if he prefers party A, he is "wasting" his vote on A if it has no chance of winning, because very few other voters prefer it to B or C. The relevant choice in

7.2 The Trust Problem in Voter Coordination

this case is between B and C. Since a vote for A is not useful in the actual process of selection, casting it is irrational (1957, p. 48).

The result of this type of calculation, in which a voter abandons her most-preferred party (A) for one more likely to win (B or C) is known as a strategic vote (Fisher 2004; McKelvey and Ordeshook 1972). What is meant by "winning" will vary by electoral system, depending on how votes are cast and tallied: in first past the post plurality systems, where there is a single winner, voters reap certain benefits for voting for *the* winning party; in a proportional representation system, like Turkey's, where there are multiple winners, benefits can accrue by voting for *any* winning party (Cox 1997).[14] But whatever the rules in a given system, voters care about not senselessly wasting their votes.

For decades, the extant literature took as given that there were obvious benefits to voting for a winning party, whether these were more psychic or instrumental (Duverger 1963; Riker 1982). More recently, empirical studies have been able to estimate and confirm the value of supporting a winner, across a variety of contexts (Blaydes 2011; Chandra 2004; Magaloni 2006). Anecdotal evidence confirms that this type of strategic voting occurs regularly in the Turkish case, spurred by mandatory voting (since 1983), an over-abundance of political parties, and an extremely high national electoral threshold (Schofield et al. 2011). Çarkoğlu and Kalaycioğlu describe a bandwagoning effect that took place in the lead-up to the 2002 elections:

> Weeks before the election it became clear amongst opinion leaders and the elite that the AKP was going to be the largest vote gainer and that the [center-left] CHP would be the second largest party. Their vote shares were obviously uncertain, but for the constituencies of these parties there was no uncertainty as to whether their votes [would] be wasted .... However, for all the other parties this was a major concern. Faced with the difficult task of [choosing] a party, which might not be able to actually represent one's preferences, voters [were] likely to resort to last minute changes in their votes. Such switches [were most] likely to originate within the ranks of the smaller parties towards larger parties who [were] more likely to get into the Parliament. (2007, p. 182)[15]

Similarly, in my conversations with voters in the lead-up to the 2011 general elections, many described feeling conflicted between voting with their conscience (i.e., supporting a small party that stood little chance of success) and having an impact on the overall result. When I followed up with them after election day, all but one (sheepishly) admitted to casting a strategic vote for one of the major parties.

---

[14] Even in a PR system, there are likely to be more benefits to voting for the overall winner, but any party that is represented in government can be expected to distribute some goods to its supporters. Meanwhile, a party left out of government has little way of rewarding its constituents.

[15] Yael Navaro-Yashin also cites a case of strategic voting in the 1995 Turkish election, but here, instead of switching her vote from her most-preferred but less popular party (the center-right ANAP) to one that was still proximate but more likely to win, a woman named Saniye explains that she and her family voted for the center-left CHP in order to undermine the chances of the Islamic-based RP, their least-preferred choice (2002, p. 169).

I find systematic evidence of this type of strategic voting in nationally representative survey data collected by KONDA Research and Consultancy between 2010 and 2015. In each of their monthly surveys, KONDA asks respondents to name the party they would support in a hypothetical election, as well as which party they actually supported in the previous election. In about half of the surveys ($N=25$), KONDA also includes a follow-up question, asking respondents why they chose the party they did. Nearly 20 percent of all respondents ($N=70,147$) admit that their choice of party in the most recent election was made at the last minute.[16] And across all fifty-five surveys, more than 40 percent admit to switching their party allegiances between the last election and an upcoming hypothetical one.[17] I take this to indicate either that they did not actually vote for their most-preferred party (i.e., that they voted strategically), or that their party loyalty is so flimsy as to break down in a matter of months.

In additional analysis, I am also able to confirm that these strategic voters are likely behaving in their self-interest. Following similar studies quantifying the instrumental benefit to strategic voting, I assess panel variation in Turkish municipal budgets – specifically, the share of national tax revenues that are allocated to each municipality by the central government.[18] These allocations from the central government comprise a majority of each municipality's budget, and the government has considerable discretion in how much it allocates (Ersoy 1992; Yılmaz and Güner 2013). Across elections from 1983 to 1999 – the only ones for which disaggregated data are available – I confirm that government allocations are significantly lower to municipalities located in provinces with higher rates of wasted votes, a result that is robust to the inclusion of a lagged dependent variable, election-year fixed-effects, GDP per capita in the province-year, and the vote share for the prime minister's party in the previous election (see Online Appendix Table OA.25). In other words, a failure to coordinate and vote strategically results in a significant cost to the district.

Once we recognize that voters have an interest in voting for a winning party, it becomes clear that their individual vote choices cannot be made independently. Each voter's optimal choice – her best way to balance her twin desires to vote for a proximate party and to vote for one that is likely to win – depends on knowing which party other voters are likely to support come election day (Bendor et al. 2011; Myatt and Fisher 2002). So, in determining their best option, voters must educate themselves: not just about what the different parties stand for – so-called "political" information, which has been the focus

---

[16] Respondents were slightly more likely to cite ideological proximity (27.7%) and leadership qualities (27.7%) than to admit making a last-minute decision (19.3%); but this response was more popular than party loyalty (17.7%) and the party's perceived independence (7.6%).

[17] Further, a significantly larger share of these "switchers" admitted to making a last-minute decision at the last election (27.3 percent, compared to 13.8 percent among party "loyalists").

[18] By focusing on municipalities, I limit the analysis to urban areas only; but according to Yılmaz and Güner, this covers 83.5 percent of the population (2013, p. 127).

7.2 The Trust Problem in Voter Coordination

of most theories of strategic voting (Alvarez and Nagler 2000; Rozenas and Sadanandan 2018) – but also gathering *social* information, about how others are likely to vote (Irwin and Holsteyn 2008; Myatt and Fisher 2002).

7.2.2 Uncertainty in Vote Choice

Early theories of strategic voting assumed that the probable outcome of the election was common knowledge, which would easily support strategic voting among individuals and successful coordination in the aggregate (Cox 1994; Myerson and Weber 1993). But in David Myatt's (2007) updated model, the likely outcome must be inferred from a mixture of private information and imprecise or non-credible public signals. In this more realistic model, coordination failure becomes a real possibility, not only because voters are likely to hold different private beliefs about the state of the world, but also because they are unsure whether they can believe the public signals they receive from others. Their inability to successfully "read the room" results in a higher percentage of wasted votes (Duch and Palmer 2002; Tavits and Annus 2006). Although failure to vote strategically occurs at the individual level, coordination failure occurs within electoral districts, where individual decisions are aggregated into more or less meaningful outcomes.[19]

According to Myatt, coordination failure becomes more likely when voters privilege their own private information and discount the public signals they receive. In other words, coordination failure results from uncertainty about what other voters are likely to do. Although Myatt's model is clear that uncertainty undermines coordination, it does not specify the conditions that might elevate this uncertainty. When it comes to public signals about likely electoral outcomes, I would suggest at least two sources of this social information: what voters have observed in the past, and what they hear others saying about what they are likely to do in the future.

Under what conditions might a voter discount what he has seen in the past? Critically, the credibility of past vote behavior for the future is significantly compromised when vote volatility is high. For this reason, vote volatility in previous elections should beget coordination failure in the current electoral cycle. And when votes are wasted in a given election, this should encourage switching in the next election, generating more volatility. In this way, volatility

---

[19] In Turkish general elections, there is a case to be made for an additional coordination problem at the national level, because of the high national electoral threshold. But looking at rates of wasted votes within districts, they are rarely due to the national threshold alone. In the majority of cases, wasted votes are cast for parties that fail to win sufficient votes at both the district and national level. In most of the remaining cases, the votes are cast for a party that crosses the national threshold but fails to secure sufficient support in the district to win a seat. Only in a small minority of cases, concentrated in southeastern districts in the mid-1990s, were there large numbers of votes cast for Kurdish parties that were wasted due only to the national threshold. For this reason, I focus my analysis solely on district-level dynamics, controlling for the size of the local Kurdish population, in some specifications, to account for these exceptions to the general pattern.

begets wasted votes, and wasted votes produce volatility, in a vicious cycle of voter frustration, electoral instability, and underrepresentation. Examining voting patterns across Turkish provinces over time (1969–2018), I find this precise pattern: vote volatility in the previous election predicts the rate of wasted votes in the following one, a result that holds when including year and province fixed effects, the amount of volatility in the current election, as well as other factors that could explain both volatility and wasted votes, including voter sophistication, proxied by literacy rates, and the scope of the coordination problem, measured by district magnitude and population (see Online Appendix Table OA.26 for full results).[20] Meanwhile, wasted votes lead to more vote volatility, under many, but not all circumstances.[21]

When the past is not a strong predictor of the future, as it is in Turkey and in many other developing democracies, the only source of social information available to voters is what they hear about others' intentions, and this could come from a number of different sources. First, private conversations about vote intentions in the lead-up to elections are not uncommon, and I had open discussions with Turkish voters in the weeks before the 2010 referendum and before the 2011 and June 2015 general elections. In addition, in this increasingly digital age, interpersonal conversations are moving beyond voters' immediate social circles, bringing them into contact with others from across the country. At the same time, polling data are becoming ubiquitous, in Turkey and elsewhere. Altogether given these three distinct sources, I would argue that uncertainty surrounding future vote intentions is unlikely to reflect a basic lack of information. More likely, if any of these sources are being discounted, it is because voters do not believe they can trust them.

Skepticism about what people tell pollsters or other voters about their likely vote choice may be well-founded: there are some real incentives for voters to be dishonest when self-reporting what they are likely to do come election day (Brams and Zagare 1977). More specifically, they could lie about which party or parties they are considering supporting, in the hopes of making one the target of strategic voting. For example, even if a voter is considering abandoning her most-preferred party (Party A) to vote strategically for a second- or third-best option (Party B or C), she may hesitate to say so openly, in the hopes that others will over-estimate the level of support for A and abandon their own parties to strategically vote for it. Similarly, she may misreport the target of her strategic vote, hoping to start a bandwagoning effect towards that party, drawing votes away from a less-preferred one (Party D). At the end of the day,

---

[20] Similarly, in a lab-based voting game conducted at the TOBB University of Economics and Technology in Ankara, Blais, Erisen, and Rheault find a similar pattern: "in the absence of electoral history, voters cannot coordinate their efforts successfully" (2014, p. 386).

[21] The effect of wasted votes on vote volatility is found in a bivariate model with year fixed effects and in a fully specified model with province fixed effects. But when year fixed effects are combined with the control variables – literacy, district population, and district magnitude – the cross-sectional variation is dominated by differences in literacy rates, in particular, and no other variable is statistically significant.

7.2 The Trust Problem in Voter Coordination

she may still end up voting sincerely for her most-preferred party, if she expects it to win; but her deception may have helped her second-most-preferred party (B) win second place, pushing her less-preferred one (D) out of government.

For these reasons, the credibility of stated vote intentions, whether sincere or strategic, can be called into question. But even if voters are not incentivized to deceive one another, they may yet believe that deception is likely. When assessing the value of private political discussion among citizens, Gerber et al. uncovered a remarkable pattern: "most people (almost two-thirds) believe that [discussions of their vote choices] can be informative; [but] many people fear that divulging one's choices may expose them to social pressures, unwelcome influence, or potential conflict" (2013, p. 482). In other words, while many think highly of political conversations, in theory, they are less convinced of their value, in practice. Similarly, while pre-election polling has been found to support voter coordination in some cases (Forsythe et al. 1993; Kunce 2001), it fails to do so if the information is deemed non-credible (Andonie and Kuzmics 2012; Tsfati 2001). Perhaps unsurprisingly, the perceived credibility of these different sources of social information depends on how citizens view one another. In other words, voters' degree of uncertainty hinges on their degree of interpersonal trust.

7.2.3 Trust, Islamic Identity, and Voter Coordination

When examining the value of political discussion, Gerber et al. note, but do not explain, an interesting correlation: "people who are more trusting of others are more likely to see discussion as likely to yield useful, rather than misleading, information about political matters" (2013, p. 490). They also note that the magnitude of trust's effect on the perceived utility of discussion is comparable to that of political resources, a key variable in their theory, along with network agreement.[22] In examining their results a bit more closely, a remarkable pattern emerges: both political resources and networks correlate with all three outcomes – the normative value of discussion, its ability to inform, and concerns about peer pressure; but interpersonal trust impacts only one – namely, discussion's ability to inform. In other words, individuals who distrust others still believe in the value of discussion, but they doubt its actual ability to tell them about what others are likely to do (and what they should do, as a result).

The relationship between interpersonal trust and the credibility of social information implies that, without trust, voters are more likely to discount what they hear in face-to-face conversations about politics. And to the extent that they second guess what they hear directly from others, distrusting individuals are also likely to discount the results of pre-election polling, out of a concern that those polled are not being truthful when stating their most-preferred party. I find some evidence of this in the nationally representative survey I ran in Turkey in September 2012. To capture the perceived credibility of available social information, I asked respondents whether they tended to agree or

---

[22] For Gerber et al., "political resources" is a bundle of goods that includes internal efficacy, political knowledge, and interest in politics (2013, p. 478).

disagree with the following statement: "When people are asked their opinion about politics, most of them usually say what they really think."[23] Across 2,067 respondents, I find that less than half (42.6%) agree that they can believe what others say in political discussions, although the rate is significantly higher (46.3%) for those who generally trust "most people."

This result is also in line with what I heard from my interlocutors in the lead-up to the 2011 general elections. Although pre-election polls were regularly released, especially in March and April of that year, and most pointed in the same direction – another win for the AKP – most voters told me they were not sure what to make of them. Perhaps, they wondered aloud, respondents felt pressured to give a definitive answer even though they had not yet made up their minds, or felt they should say they were supporting a smaller party, hoping that doing so would raise its chances of success. The latter concern was particularly voiced vis-à-vis the Islamic SP, which seemed unlikely to cross the 10 percent threshold, but which some polls had winning 5 percent (or more) of the national vote.

If interpersonal distrust really does threaten the credibility of social information for voters, this implies a generalized trust problem for voter coordination whenever strategic voting is necessary, especially when vote volatility undermines the past as a credible heuristic for future behavior. The type of trust needed to support coordination should be non-particularized given the scope of the coordination problem, encompassing an entire electoral district, and because of the anonymity of the act of voting. Based on this, I expect to find higher rates of wasted votes in electoral districts with less generalized trust. And given the cyclical relationship between wasted votes and vote volatility, this implies a potential correlation between distrust, on the one hand, and volatility, on the other. This should hold above and beyond other factors that could undermine successful coordination, including political sophistication and district size. The role of trust in supporting voter coordination and stabilizing vote behavior, over time, should also be distinct from the main existing explanation for vote behavior and volatility – namely, economic voting, based on grievances (Akarca and Tansel 2006; Başlevent, Kirmanoğlu, and Şenatalar 2005; Lewis-Beck 1999; Roberts and Wibbels 1999).

The main exception to this general pattern should be within communities where religious identity is especially salient, where group-based trust can offer an alternative basis for the sharing of social information and the coordination of votes. This expectation – that group-based trust substitutes for generalized trust to support voter coordination – is a bit different from extant studies that link identity to vote behavior via information (Birnir 2007; Chandra 2004). Rather than hypothesizing that religious identity will impact electoral outcomes where voters are least informed or where Islamic voters stand to dominate the field, I anticipate that coordination will be improved in

---

[23] In Turkish, the statement reads "*İnsanlara siyaset hakkında ne düşündükleri sorulduğunda çoğu genelde gerçek düşüncelerini söylerler.*" This statement was part of a bloc that included other questions about political information, internal and external efficacy, similar to Gerber et al.'s (2013) conceptualization of "political resources."

7.2 The Trust Problem in Voter Coordination

religious communities because the negative effect of generalized distrust will be ameliorated.

Already, I see some evidence of this substitution effect in my Turkish survey data. Among those without group-based trust ($N=544$), generalized distrust undermines how they view political discussions with others: those that distrust "most people," as well as members of their own religious group, are less likely to say that people are honest in their political discussions: 39.9 percent, compared to 47.6 percent among those who distrust their own group, but trust most people. But among those who trust their religious in-group members ($N=956$), there is barely a difference: 45.3 percent among those who generally distrust, and 46.7 percent among those who do not. In other words, regardless of their view of "most people," respondents with in-group trust believe what others tell them in political discussions at the same rate. Moreover, they look remarkably similar to those who trust, generally, but who do not trust their in-group members.

Evidence of this substitution effect across electoral districts and over time will lend further support to my trust-based theory of voter coordination, but there are additional implications of my theory that can be tested. First, recalling the importance of priming in heightening the salience of religious group identity and group-based trust, I expect that coordination among religious voters will depend on there being an active Islamic-based party. If this conditionality holds, it will also help to demonstrate that the superior coordination of religious voters is not based on a basic similarity in their policy preferences, something that should be unaffected by the presence of an Islamic party. For similar reasons, I would not expect the presence of multiple Islamic parties since 2002 to diminish their coordination advantage.

Further, I anticipate that the coordination of religious voters will support the success of Islamic parties. To begin with, I expect that these parties will have a comparative advantage in distrusting, volatile districts, where supporters of other parties regularly waste votes. And to explain the recent rise of the AKP, particularly their growing popularity among non-religious voters, I extend the logic of my theory a bit further. Because vote volatility undermines the credibility of past behavior as a focal point for strategic voters, coordination is less likely, generating further volatility, in an endless cycle. Given the superior ability of religious voters to coordinate, their vote decisions tend to be more stable from election to election, making their past behavior more indicative of what they are likely to do in the future. This piece of social information is especially useful for distrusting voters from the center-right, who otherwise struggle to figure out which of the many available parties deserves their strategic votes.[24]

More specifically, I expect that the consistency of religious voter support for Islamic-based parties through the upheavals of the mid-1990s – through the

---

[24] This implies that Islamic-based parties will succeed where they are in direct competition with other center-right parties with largely overlapping policy platforms. This expectation challenges existing assumptions that they will succeed when they are the only game in town (Esposito and Voll 1996).

"post-modern coup" of 1997, the disbanding of the RP (the movement's first successful representative) in 1998, and the entry of its successor (the FP) in the 1999 elections – would have been especially informative. Those that coordinated effectively and consistently through the 1999 elections proved to other center-right voters that Islamic parties would be a safer target for a strategic vote. This would have translated into a huge benefit for the AKP, beginning in 2002, earning them additional support in distrusting districts where Islamic vote share had been particularly consistent in previous elections. I test this hypothesis, along with all of the others, in the next section.

7.3 TRUST AND THE SUCCESS OF TURKEY'S ISLAMIC PARTIES

Looking at cross-temporal trends in the Turkish electoral system, I have identified a relationship between voter coordination, on the one hand, and the success of Islamic-based parties, on the other. Until 2002 and the rise of the AKP, Turkey had a reputation for ill-coordinated, inconsistent elections, with large numbers of wasted votes. But the AKP, unlike any party before it, has enjoyed consistent success from election to election, stabilizing the party system as a whole.

I have suggested that the link between these two phenomena – the difficulties of voter coordination and the comparative advantage of Islamic-based parties – is interpersonal trust. Generalized distrust undermines the ability of voters to vote strategically and coordinate successfully, especially when inter-election volatility is high. Meanwhile, group-based trust among those with a shared, salient religious group identity effectively substitutes for generalized trust to support consistent, well-coordinated vote outcomes within religious communities. Islamic-based parties benefit from this superior coordination, attracting strategic votes from conservative *but secular*, distrusting voters.

In the sections that follow, I test these expectations using a panel dataset from Turkey – exploiting variation across electoral districts and over time, examining trust, Islam, and vote behavior since 1961. Overall, I find strong support for my trust-based theory of voter coordination. Distrust is a better predictor of instability and wasted votes than political sophistication and economic voting. Further, the generalized trust problem in voter coordination is effectively solved in districts with larger religious communities, where religious group identity and group-based trust are more salient, to the benefit of Islamic-based parties.

7.3.1 Generalized Distrust and Voter Coordination Failure

To estimate the effect of generalized interpersonal distrust on voter coordination, I require measures of both. Assessing variation in voter coordination failure is relatively straightforward: following others (Crisp, Olivella, and Potter 2011; Tavits and Annus 2006), I use the percentage of votes in each

7.3 Trust and the Success of Turkey's Islamic Parties

electoral district that are wasted (i.e., cast for a party that fails to gain representation). Because of Turkey's high electoral threshold, a party can fail to gain representation either by not securing enough votes within a given district to win a seat or, rarely, since 1983, by not garnering 10 percent of the national vote. For this reason, across district-years, the share of wasted votes varies considerably, ranging from none to 73.8 percent, averaging 21.3 percent across all observations, with a standard deviation of 16.9 percent. Recall that the rate of wasted votes in a given election year is strongly impacted by the level of vote volatility in the previous election, so including past volatility as a statistical control in most models seems warranted. Alternatively, inter-election volatility may indicate coordination failure over time and may therefore be directly affected by trust.

Capturing variation in non-particularized interpersonal trust, across space and time, is slightly more complicated. Although responses to the standard survey question are a good option when conducting cross-sectional comparisons, their stability over time presents an obstacle to using them in panel analysis (Algan and Cahuc 2010; Bjørnskov 2007). Moreover, survey coverage across Turkish electoral districts is limited to a few time periods, with only a subset of districts covered in each instance: sixteen represented in the 1990 and 2001 waves of the WVS, seven in the 1996 wave, twenty-nine in my 2012 survey, and thirty in 2015.[25] So, to assess panel variation in trust, I turn to a behavioral proxy that has rarely been applied beyond the case in which it was originally developed.

In their study of social capital and financial development in Italy, Luigi Guiso, Paola Sapienza, and Luigi Zingales (2004) suggest a close link between non-particularized interpersonal trust and a particular financial decision: the use of formal banking services. Earlier, I emphasized how banking reflects an individual's willingness to make her own assets available to members of her community, in the form of credit. Guiso, Sapienza, and Zingales are clear that interpersonal trust between the financier and the financee is a prerequisite for this type of investment:

Financing is nothing but an exchange of a sum of money today for a promise to return more money in the future. Whether such an exchange can take place depends not only on the legal enforceability of contracts, but also on the extent to which the financier trusts the financee (2004, p. 527).

Following this logic, I propose to use formal banking practices as a behavioral proxy for interpersonal trust.[26]

---

[25] The three waves of the EVS in Turkey aggregate results up to the NUTS-1 level (*İstatistiki Bölge Birimleri Sınıflandırması 1. Düzey*), providing variation across only twelve geographic units. Some of the 1996 WVS data is also aggregated up to the regional (*bölge*) level (N=6).

[26] Like survey-based measures of generalized trust, individual-level panel estimates of banking in Turkey are extremely limited. So, going forward, I rely on province-level measures of actual bank deposits. Using aggregate data to say something about the behavior and preferences of

Although Guiso, Sapienza, and Zingales's paper is widely cited, the validity of banking as a correlate of trust beyond the Italian case has not yet been empirically confirmed. To establish that banking is a reasonable trust proxy, I conduct a number of assessments. I begin with a cross-national comparison, using the Findex Database to capture variation in banking behavior. And to capture variation in trust, I use two measures: responses to the standard survey question ($N=135$) and the average amount sent in a trust game ($N=35$) (Johnson and Mislin 2011). In both cases, I find a positive, statistically significant correlation: $r=0.432$ and $r=0.250$ respectively (for an illustration, see Appendix Figure A6.2 and Online Appendix Figure OA.8). In other words, banking appears to be a reasonable stand-in for interpersonal trust across countries.

Perhaps even more importantly, I also confirm the validity of the measure in a Turkish panel. Across Turkish provinces and over time (1981–2018), data on bank deposits are available from the Banks Association of Turkey (Türkiye Bankalar Birliği, TBB). I estimate trust using private savings deposits in each province-year, normalized by total savings, including public and commercial deposits, as a proxy for district wealth ($\mu = 44.9, \sigma = 11.9$).[27] The inverse of this measure captures variation in distrust, my key independent variable. I assess the relationship between banking and distrust by comparing these normalized savings deposits to survey-based estimates of distrust across the ninety-six province-years covered by the WVS and my own surveys. I find a statistically significant correlation in the panel data ($r=0.172$) and when using province-level averages in the forty provinces covered by the surveys ($r=0.342$) (for an illustration, see Online Appendix Figure OA.8). I also confirm that savings behavior is not a proxy for political trust, with the correlation reversed when using survey-based measures of trust in government (see Online Appendix Table OA.27). Based on these results, I move forward with some confidence about the validity of my trust proxy.

In addition to measuring coordination failure and distrust, I need a way of accounting for factors that could plausibly impact both coordination and trust, which might confound my results. For example, one could imagine that some factors which determine the scope of the coordination problem (e.g., district size) could also impact interpersonal trust, if it is more difficult to form positive opinions of "most people" when there are so many of them around. To account for this possibility, many of my forthcoming models include the

---

individuals raises some concerns about ecological inference (King, Rosen, and Tanner 2004). But recall that the outcome of interest – voter coordination failure – is visible in the aggregate only: although an individual ultimately casts each vote, its definition as a wasted one depends on how others in the district voted and how those votes translated into seats.

[27] Because GDP per capita is available for a subset of years only, estimating income within the banking data is preferable. Across the 2,424 province-years for which I have both measures, I find that the two are positively and significantly correlated. Meanwhile, *personal* deposits are not significantly correlated with GDP per capita, alleviating concerns that my measure of trust is a proxy for local wealth.

7.3 Trust and the Success of Turkey's Islamic Parties

population of each province and the district magnitude, in each election.[28] In addition, distrust of the political system, as a whole, could be another plausible source of wasted votes, if these are cast in protest; meanwhile, political trust correlates with interpersonal trust in many contexts (Inglehart 1999; Jamal and Nooruddin 2010). In my panel dataset, with limited survey coverage, I rely on a behavioral measure of political distrust: the percentage of invalid votes cast in each election. While in some contexts, the number of spoiled ballots might indicate voter error, with mandatory voting in place in Turkey since 1983, the majority of invalid ballots are blank, "white" ones, which are used to express displeasure with all of the competing parties.[29]

I also take voter sophistication and grievances into account.[30] The former is captured using illiteracy rates, the only available proxy in the panel, calculated from censuses between 1960 and 2000, and then annual population counts (ADKS) since 2008, interpolating data for missing years. Given data availability, I estimate variation in grievances using unemployment rates, measured in censuses between 1980 and 2000 and in the ADKS since 2007, interpolating in the intervening years. Estimates of GDP per capita at the subnational level are available only between 1987 and 2017, so I use them only in robustness checks and in analysis focused on later elections.

To see whether distrust produces coordination failure, I look for the expected pattern in the raw data. Looking at all district-election years before the rise of the AKP and the stabilization of the Turkish party system (1983–2002), I rank each observation by its level of distrust and assess its rate of wasted votes. Figure 7.5 displays the results, revealing a positive correlation between distrust and coordination failure, as expected. I confirm this result using more sophisticated statistical analysis: OLS regressions of wasted votes over the entire period (1983–2018) with province-fixed effects, focusing the comparison on cross-temporal variation within each electoral district, a harder test of my theory (see Online Appendix Table OA.28).[31] Including my savings-based estimate of distrust into the model, I find a statistically significant and substantive positive effect: distrust in an electoral district in a given year increases the proportion of wasted votes there. This pattern is robust to the inclusion of a host of controls, from the level of volatility in the previous

---

[28] Province-level population estimates are calculated from censuses between 1960 and 2000 and from annual population registries since 2008, interpolating data for the intervening years. District magnitude is taken directly from the results of each general election.

[29] As indication of this, in *ilçe*-level voter transition matrices, I find consistency in the share of the voting population casting invalid votes from year to year – 31.3 percent, on average, between 1983 and 2018 – more than one would expect if the ballots were cast in error.

[30] For its part, sophistication is considered a requisite for solving any complex coordination problem, and generalized trust is generally found to be increasing in the level of education. Meanwhile, economic grievances are predicted to generate vote volatility and, hence, wasted votes. At the same time, there is a well-established relationship between trust and economic growth, at least at the national level.

[31] The inclusion of the province fixed effects helps to control for any time-invariant characteristics of each province that might serve to produce both distrust and coordination failure.

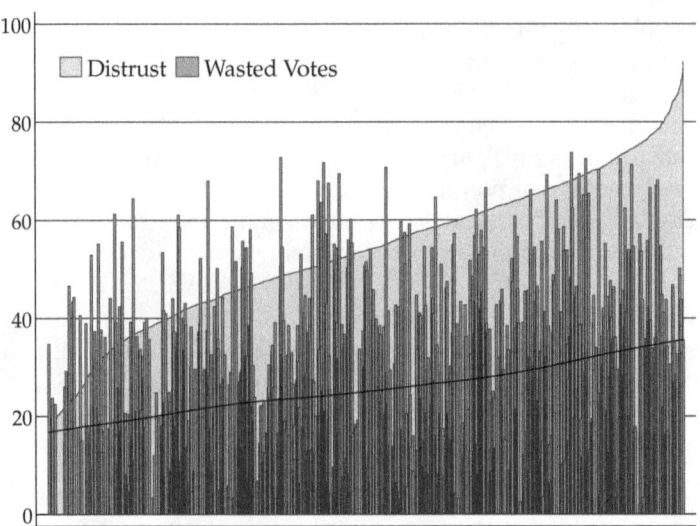

FIGURE 7.5 Distrust and Wasted Votes, across Turkish Provinces over Time
Notes: Wasted votes and distrust, measured as the inverse of private savings deposits, in each province election year (1983–2002). Observations ranked by the degree of distrust, and the LOWESS trend line is indicated by the black line.

election, to district population and magnitude, the share of invalid ballots, illiteracy and unemployment. In addition to being statistically significant, the effect of distrust on voter coordination is also substantively important: one standard-deviation reduction in trust produces more than half a standard-deviation increase in the rate of wasted votes. Further, the effect of distrust on coordination failure is the largest of all the variables in the model.[32] In other words, the trust problem in voter coordination eclipses a number of other explanations for vote behavior across Turkish districts, including electoral institutions and economic voting.

I also confirm the cross-sectional correlation between generalized distrust and wasted votes using the survey-based measure of trust. Even with only forty observations, the correlation between the two is positive and statistically significant. Meanwhile, there is no correlation between coordination failure and political distrust. If anything, the correlation between the two is negative. (For an illustration of both, see Online Appendix Figure OA.9.) I also find that the panel results are robust to the inclusion of two more potential confounders: migration rates and the share of the local Kurdish population.[33]

---

[32] As a comparison, the fully standardized coefficient of distrust on wasted votes in the fully specified model is $\beta=0.560$; the next closest is the effect of population ($\beta=0.491$), followed by district magnitude ($\beta=-0.420$) and illiteracy ($\beta=0.360$).

[33] Turks who migrate from one province to another tend to continue voting as they had in their home region, which could lead to less coordination in their new districts of residence (Akarca and Başlevent 2010b); at the same time, studies show that new arrivals to a community are

7.3 Trust and the Success of Turkey's Islamic Parties

The inclusion of both variables does little to change the main effect of distrust on coordination failure (see Online Appendix Table OA.29). Indeed, time-varying estimates of migration and ethnic composition are not statistically significant, and a time-invariant measure of the Kurdish population actually *decreases* the proportion of wasted votes, after taking all of the other variables into account, an indication that Kurdish voters might be better coordinated than previously thought.

In addition, I am able to confirm that my savings-based measure of trust is not operating as a stand-in for district wealth: not only are personal savings uncorrelated with GDP per capita across district-years, but the effect of distrust on coordination is robust to the inclusion of wealth as an additional control, despite the shortened time frame. The only way I am able to minimize the trust problem for voter coordination in my models is by severely restricting the time period under investigation. Indeed, I find that the effect of distrust on wasted votes operates entirely during the pre-AKP period. After 2002, the relationship between distrust and coordination failure, if anything, becomes negative. In other words, there is some indication that the trust problem in voter coordination in Turkey has been largely ameliorated with the rise of the AKP. But to understand why the two are related, further investigation into the role of Islamic identity in coordination is warranted.

7.3.2 Voter Coordination in Religious Communities

Because voter coordination in fractionalized electoral systems relies heavily on interpersonal trust, I expect to find superior coordination among voters who share a salient group identity. In addition to my earlier finding that the rate of wasted votes is decreasing in the size of the local Kurdish population, I expect to see superior coordination among voters with a salient religious group identity. As earlier, I propose to estimate the salience of Islamic identity using participation in religious group activities.

At the province level, over time, I have access to a handful of measures of religious group activities. As above, survey data is too sparse to use across the entire panel; but province-level data exist on the number of mosques for the periods 1986–1988 and 1992–2018; net enrollment in religious vocational (*imam hatip*) schools are available for the periods 1961–1973, 1975–2005,

---

less trusting of others (Chavez, Wampler, and Burkhart 2006). Meanwhile, Kurdish voters in Turkey face a seemingly insurmountable coordination challenge, with some of the hightest rates of wasted votes cast for Kurdish parties that failed to garner 10 percent of the national vote (Başlevent, Kirmanoğlu, and Şenatalar 2009). And ethnic minorities – particularly those who have experienced discrimination – tend to have lower levels of interpersonal trust (Alesina and La Ferrara 2002). To account for panel variation in migration, I calculate net migration rates from censuses (1980–2000) and from population registries (since 2008), interpolating missing data. To estimate the local Kurdish population, I use raw, adjusted, and projected census results (Mutlu 1996), in addition to the prevalence of Kurdish as a "mother tongue" from the Turkish Demographic and Health Survey and Kurdish "ethnic roots" from KONDA's monthly Barometer series, calculating two measures: the first, time-varying, interpolating missing years; and an average across all available estimates.

and 2015–2018; and enrollment in public Qur'an courses can be calculated between 1961 and 2017, with the sole exception 2003 and 2014.[34] For their part, *imam hatip* schools have been operating in Turkey since 1951 and were originally established to train future employees of the Office of Religious Affairs (Diyanet); but since the number of graduates has long exceeded the number of jobs, most go on to attend university and work in the private sector. The schools are now seen as a place for young people (including women) to be educated in a more religiously minded environment, with religious topics comprising 40 percent of the curriculum (Pak 2004).[35] Meanwhile, Qur'an courses meet mostly during the evening hours and over weekends, catering to a largely adult population (Özdalga 1999; Shively 2008).

I normalize each of the three available measures using province-level population estimates from censuses and population registries, calculating the number of mosques per 1000 people and per capita enrollment rates in both types of religious education. To assess the validity of each measure, I compare them to average levels of mosque attendance from surveys in ninety-four province-years. I find that the correlation between each of the observational measures and average mosque attendance is positive and statistically significant, but especially so in the case of *imam hatip* and Qur'an course enrollment ($r=0.643$ and 0.605, respectively, compared to $r=0.368$ vis-á-vis mosques per capita). I suspect this is the case because enrollment rates, like mosque attendance, speak more to local "demand" for religious group activities than their "supply." For similar reasons, across the full panel, I find that the two measures of enrollment are much more strongly inter-correlated ($r=0.775$ across 3733 province-years) than either is with mosques per capita. (An illustration of the various bivariate correlations is available in Online Appendix Figure OA.10.)

Because they are available for the full time-series, and because they better capture local "demand" for group activities, I rely mostly on the enrollment measures going forward. As an initial assessment of the relationship between Islamic group identity and successful voter coordination, I create a simple bivariate scatterplot across units between 1961 and 2018. Doing so, I find that the rate of wasted votes is decreasing in the extent of both *imam hatip* enrollment and Qur'an course enrollment (Online Appendix Figure OA.11). In regression analysis with province fixed effects, I confirm that effect of Islamic group identity on voter coordination is not driven by time-invariant characteristics of certain provinces. Neither is it driven by differences in information, proxied by illiteracy, or grievances, measured as unemployment, as some extant theories would expect (see Online Appendix Table OA.30).

Further, and in line with my expectation that voter coordination in religious communities is based on a shared, salient Islamic identity, I find that the

---

[34] The majority of these data are publicly available, but the number of mosques in each province between 1992 and 1999 were provided to the author by the Diyanet in response to a direct request.
[35] In contrast to private religious schools in other contexts, these public schools are not attended by non-religious students seeking a better educational environment.

7.3 Trust and the Success of Turkey's Islamic Parties

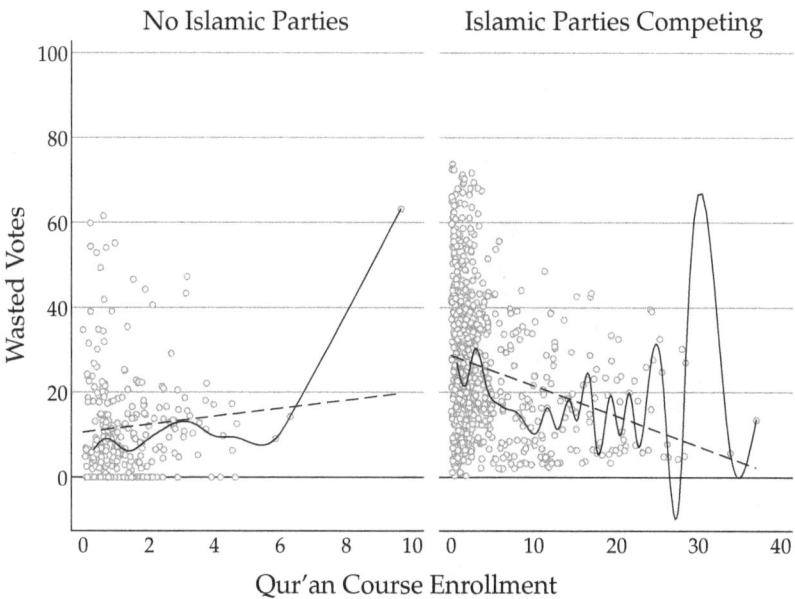

FIGURE 7.6 Islamic Identity and Wasted Votes
Notes: Wasted votes and enrollment in Qur'an courses (per capita) in province election years (1961–2018). In elections in which no Islamic party competed (1961, 1965, 1969, 1983) and all other election years. Trend lines for both are cubic splines, calculated based on cross medians.

relationship between enrollment and wasted votes breaks down in election years in which no Islamic party actively competed (prior to 1973, and in 1983). The stark difference is visible in the raw data (Figure 7.6, illustrating Qur'an course enrollment, and Online Appendix Figure OA.12, for *imam hatip* enrollment), as well as in the results of regression analysis (Online Appendix Table OA.30). Recall that, with the tight regulation of religious based politics in Turkey, in the absence of an Islamic party, there is little to prime individuals to think of political engagement in terms of their Islamic identity. Religious rhetoric in Turkish mosques and schools is strictly prohibited.

There is similarly stark evidence of the substitution effect I have hypothesized, wherein a salient Islamic identity ameliorates the coordination problem in distrusting districts. In the raw data, I find that the correlation between distrust and wasted votes wanes significantly across Qur'an-course-enrollment quintiles (Figure 7.7). The correlation is similar in magnitude and statistical significance across the first three quintiles (r=0.330, 0.391, and 0.390, respectively), but begins to weaken by the fourth group, with enrollment rates ranging between roughly 2 percent and just over 4 percent (r=0.256). By the time enrollment rates hit 4.27 percent and above (the top quintile, N=217 province-years), the correlation is a mere 0.079 and is no longer statistically significant. I find an identical pattern across *imam hatip* enrollment quintiles (Online Appendix Figure OA.13), even though the two measures of Islamic identity are far from perfectly correlated.

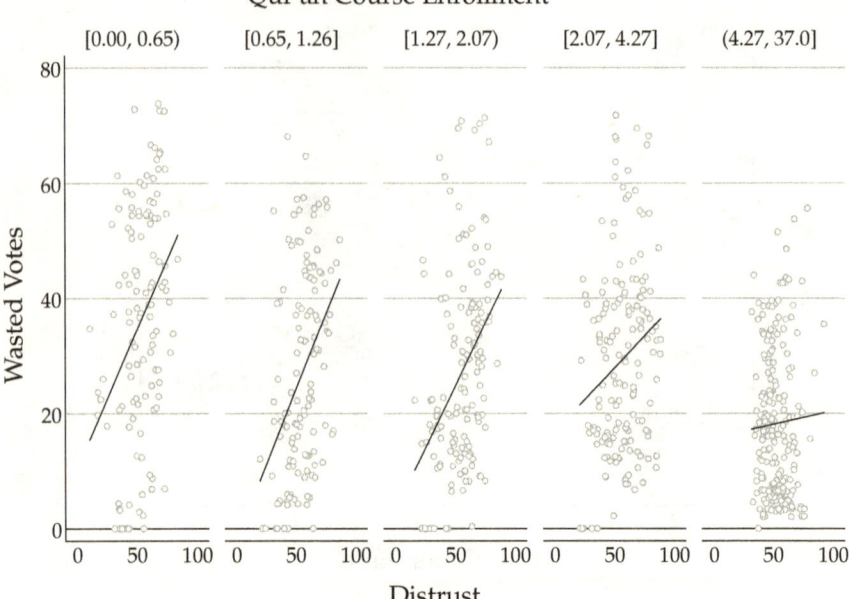

FIGURE 7.7 Distrust and Wasted Votes, across Levels of Islamic Identity
Notes: Wasted votes and distrust, across province election years (1983–2018), by level of enrollment in Qur'an courses (per capita). Black lines indicate linear trends.

I find further evidence of the substitution effect in interaction models in which the effect of distrust on wasted votes is allowed to vary depending on the level of local Islamic identity (see Online Appendix Table OA.31).[36] Even with the inclusion of province fixed effects and the full battery of controls – volatility in the previous election, district population and magnitude, illiteracy and unemployment rates – I find that the trust problem is significantly alleviated in the top two quintiles for both enrollment measures. An illustration of the estimated marginal effects of distrust on coordination failure across the different groups is available in Online Appendix Figure OA.14.

[36] The interaction model is $Wasted_{it} = \beta_0 + \beta_1 Distrust_{it} + \beta_2 Enrollment_{2it} + \beta_3 Enrollment_{3it} + \beta_4 Enrollment_{4it} + \beta_5 Enrollment_{5it} + \beta_6 Distrust_{it} \times Enrollment_{2it} + \beta_7 Distrust_{it} \times Enrollment_{3it} + \beta_8 Distrust_{it} \times Enrollment_{4it} + \beta_9 Distrust_{it} \times Enrollment_{5it} + X_{it} + \mu_i + \epsilon_i$, where $Wasted_{it}$ is the rate of wasted votes in electoral district (province) i in election-year t, $Distrust_{it}$ is the inverse measure of private savings deposits (as a percent of all deposits) in that province-year, $Enrollment_{2it}$ is a binary indicator of whether the enrollment rates in the province-year fell within the second quintile of all enrollment rates, $Distrust_{it} \times Enrollment_{2it}$ is the interaction between the two, X_{it} is a set of province-year characteristics, μ_i is a fixed-effect term for each province, and ϵ_i is the error term. I have hypothesized that the effect of distrust on coordination failures will be significantly negative ($\beta_1 < 0$) but that this effect will decrease across the frequency of religious school enrollment ($\beta_6 > 0$) so that the magnitude of the marginal effect of distrust on wasted votes ($\beta_1 + \beta_6 * Enrollment_{2=1}$) will be smaller than the direct effect (β_1), essentially that β_6 will be significantly negative.

Because the religious community never fills an entire electoral district, the best group-based trust is able to do is improve coordination and weaken the effect of distrust on wasted votes. For secular, distrusting voters, the coordination problem continues. But unlike some extant theories, which hold that identity-based vote behavior is essentially a numbers game (Chandra 2004) and which imply that coordination within groups would occur only when they represent a majority (or near majority) in the district, I find an almost linear effect of Islamic identity on coordination; and the substitution effect kicks in when the religious community represents a relatively small proportion of the district – far from a dominating majority.

There might be some concerns that the substitution effect I identify is actually an artifact of banking practices in more religious communities. If, for example, those in more religious districts deposit their savings in *sharī'ah*-compliant participation banks, these districts could *appear* to have less interpersonal trust because they have less money deposited in TBB member banks. Since formal bank deposits in these places would not actually reflect levels of interpersonal distrust, the relationship between banking and wasted votes could break down, even though the effect of distrust on coordination remains.

To assess this possibility, I begin by examining the relationship between religiosity and banking practices. Contrary to the concerns outlined above, I struggle to find a consistent relationship between religiosity and private savings in TBB member banks. The correlation between Qur'an course enrollment and deposits across 2,840 province-years is negative, but far from statistically significant; and the correlation between savings and *imam hatip* enrollment rates is positive although also not significant. Further, when I return to the survey-based measures of trust and Islamic identity and conduct a cross-sectional test, I find entirely consistent results: in the twenty-one provinces with below-average levels of mosque attendance, the correlation between wasted votes and distrust is positive, though not statistically significant at conventional levels ($r=0.185$); meanwhile, in the twenty-one provinces with above-average mosque attendance, the correlation barely registers above zero ($r=0.013$).

7.3.3 Explaining the Comparative Advantage of Islamic Parties

So far, I have found considerable support for the main expectations of my trust-based theory of voter coordination: fewer votes are wasted in electoral districts where trust is higher and where religious group identity is more salient. More specifically, the coordination advantage within Islamic communities is based on a substitution effect, wherein group-based trust is able to ameliorate the generalized trust problem. This occurs when Islamic-based parties are active and are able to effectively prime religious group identity via references to Islam.

The latter implies that religious voters do not inherently vote as a bloc, but that they enjoy a coordination advantage when they actively think of themselves as sharing a group identity. Although these voters will not necessarily coordinate their votes around an Islamic party, the fact that they and party leaders share this identity makes it more likely than not. That would imply a comparative advantage for an Islamic-based party, whose supporters – with their feelings of group-based trust – are likely to be more coordinated than others. This trust-based advantage would only be as large as the size of the underlying trust problem, so Islamic parties should be best off in distrusting, otherwise ill-coordinated districts.

To test this expectation, I first need to estimate the relationship between Islamic party vote share, on the one hand, and distrust and coordination failure, on the other; then, I need to see how these relationships compare to those between trust, coordination, and the popularity of other parties. Given that the vote shares of different parties in the same election year are inherently interrelated, standard OLS regression analysis is inappropriate. Instead, I employ seemingly unrelated regression (SUR) analysis, in which the vote shares of all parties are modeled simultaneously (Tomz, Tucker, and Wittenberg 2002). Given that so many parties enter and quickly exit the Turkish electoral system, I focus only on those that ran candidates in the majority of election-years between 1987 and 2002, the period in which both phenomena – the height of voter coordination failure and the rise of Islamic parties – came to a head.

As before, I identify party continuities that transcend name changes. In addition to the main independent variables – distrust, as bank savings, the share of wasted votes, and the Pedersen index of vote volatility – each model includes province fixed effects, as well as illiteracy and Qur'an course enrollment (per capita) in each province-year. The inclusion of the fixed effects again focuses the comparison on inter-temporal trends within each province, controlling for time-invariant characteristics that could produce both distrust (or coordination failure) and the success of a particular party. For their part, literacy and religious education reflect two rival explanations for the success of different parties: economic voting, on the one hand, and direct identity-based voting, on the other.

Across the panel, I find that the Islamic parties were indeed particularly successful in distrusting, uncoordinated districts (see Online Appendix Table OA.32). In terms of interpersonal trust, only they and the center-left (HP/SHP/CHP) were consistently popular in more distrusting districts. Similarly, only the Islamic parties and these center-left parties garnered support where vote volatility was higher. And while the Islamic-based parties were not consistently better off where the rate of wasted votes was higher, they were not significantly worse off, as the center-left tended to be. Remarkably, I also find no evidence that Turkey's Islamic parties enjoyed an advantage in the poorest districts – as the grievance theory would expect – nor in the most religious ones – as the faith-based theory implies. If anything, after taking their trust-based advantage into account, the Islamic parties' vote share was significantly *lower* in province-years with more illiteracy and higher rates of Qur'an course enrollment.

These results suggest that Turkey's Islamic-based parties enjoy more consistent levels of support than their secular (and secularist) rivals. Indeed, using transition matrices calculated at the district (*ilçe*) level, I find Islamic parties were able to hold onto a remarkable share of their support base from election to election.[37] While other parties tended to keep roughly 52.7 percent of their voters from year to year, Islamic parties averaged 80 percent in the elections in which they competed. RP/FP/AKP/SP consistency was especially high between 1995 and 2007, even as the movement grappled with multiple interventions by the Turkish military and Constitutional Court that directly threatened the movement's existence. Indeed, during those years, Islamic parties were unrivaled in their ability to maintain a loyal constituency. Only more recently has the AKP been surpassed by the Kurdish HDP and the center-left CHP.

Because of the many obstacles to coordinating and voting strategically in Turkish general elections, consistent support enjoyed by Islamic parties would make these parties an attractive target for strategic votes, especially from distrusting voters to the right of center, including those who are not particularly religious. More specifically, this consistency would provide distrusting voters with an alternative source of social information – past actions that credibly signal future vote intentions – to help them vote strategically. Consistency through the tumult of the mid-1990s would have been particularly impressive, lending an additional layer of credibility to this informative signal. This would help explain the particular timing of the AKP's rise to power in 2002: only after the "post-modern coup," the disbanding of the RP, and the subsequent elections in 1999 could distrusting but secular voters feel confident that they could predict how Islamic voters would act in future election years.

I am able to test these different expectations in a final set of models. Here, the outcome I am interested in explaining is the change in support for Islamic parties from year to year, calculating the percent change in their vote share since the previous election. My expectation is that their vote share will increase in districts where their support base had previously been most consistent. To capture consistency, I calculate the standard deviation of the parties' vote share in the previous two elections.[38] Because the standard deviation could also reflect the absolute vote share in either of the previous elections – larger values tend to have larger variances – I include these as controls in every specification. I also include Qur'an course enrollment and illiteracy rates to capture the two main competing explanations for the rise of the AKP (i.e., faith and grievances). And to focus the comparison on cross-temporal trends, I again add province-level fixed effects.

Using this modeling framework, I find that Islamic party vote share is indeed bolstered by consistent support in previous elections (see Online Appendix Table OA.33 for full results). Remarkably, I find no similar boost to any other party – if anything, for them, previous consistency has a negative effect on subsequent performance, as if their previous vote share is never a credible signal of what voters can expect in the future. And in line with my expectations,

---

[37] For an illustration see Online Appendix Figure OA.15.
[38] This method is preferable to estimates from a province-level transition matrix because Andreadis and Chadjipadelis warn against using these "division estimates" when modeling trends (2009, p. 217).

I see that the effect of consistency on Islamic party growth operates entirely in the post-2000 period (2002–2018), but not before (1987–1999). Across all models, neither religious education nor illiteracy rates explain cross-temporal trends in Islamic vote share within electoral districts. And rather than finding that Islamic parties are simply building on their previous wins, as opposed to their previous consistency, I find that their absolute vote share in the last election actually reduces their chances of enjoying a boost in subsequent years.

7.4 CONCLUSION

In this chapter, I have argued that much of the success of Islamic parties can be explained by the degree to which voters trust one another. This is because interpersonal trust impacts the extent to which they can successfully coordinate their individual votes in fractionalized, volatile party systems. In these settings, like in Turkey and in most developing Muslim democracies, where there are too many parties, with unclear, ever-changing, and/or overlapping platforms, there is considerable interdependence and uncertainty in individual vote choices. Because voters have instrumental and expressive incentives to cast their vote for a party that wins representation, their best choice may be strategic, rather than sincere: they should abandon parties unlikely to win sufficient support and vote for those more likely to gain representation. But identifying which party they should strategically support depends on what others are likely to do, and a large number of parties with undefined or overlapping positions means a huge set of possible outcomes. Further, incentives among voters to mislead one another about their intended vote choices, whether real or imagined, mean that voters must trust one another in order to coordinate successfully.

My trust-based theory of strategic voting helps to explain two trends in Turkish elections – a long history of vote volatility and wasted votes, on the one hand, and the rise of the AKP, on the other. I have demonstrated how low levels of generalized trust among most Turkish voters historically presented an obstacle to successful coordination, resulting in wasted votes and inconsistent election results. In stark contrast, feelings of group-based trust among voters in religious communities have been able to support consistency and coordination, resulting in a comparative advantage for Islamic-based parties in distrusting, ill-coordinated districts. This consistency, particularly through the tumultuous events of the late 1990s, made it easier for conservative *but secular* voters to use Islamic parties' past performance as a credible indication of how they would fare at the polls in future elections. As a result, many of these voters started strategically supporting the AKP beginning in 2002 as a way of ensuring that their votes would count. Overall, this has meant greater stability for the party system as a whole.

Unlike existing theories of vote behavior in Turkey, my focus on trust is able to explain Turkey's long history of electoral instability as well as why vote behavior finally began to stabilize, just as Islamic parties grew in popularity. Additionally, it addresses the growing appeal of the Islamic AKP among

7.4 Conclusion

decidedly secular Turkish voters. In presenting and testing my theory, I have also raised serious questions about existing views of Islamic politics, in Turkey and elsewhere, challenging theories of grievances and economic voting, on the one hand, and the presumed link between Islamic parties and a religiosity, on the other. The popularity of the AKP among secular voters in the Turkish case challenges the assumption that a religious resurgence can explain the success of other Islamic-based parties. I hope that this will encourage a more empirically sound approach to the study of Islam and Islamic-based voting going forward.

Rather than expecting Islamic parties to be most successful in more religious Muslim countries, my trust-based theory suggests that they are likely to be especially popular in fractionalized, ill-coordinated electoral environments where interpersonal trust is low. Among the democracies of the Muslim world, two of the most electorally volatile are also the most distrusting. Remarkably, in both Mali and Albania, Islamic parties have yet to compete. By my theory, were moderate, Islamic-based parties to enter the electoral landscape, they would perform quite well, winning considerable support even in Albania, where voters are comparatively secular. Even where the religious community is small, if their behavior is consistent enough, it could start a cascade, inducing distrusting but secular voters to strategically support an Islamic party. They would do so not because that party is their most-preferred one, but because they want to make their votes count, which is no easy task given the unpredictable electoral environment.

By the same logic, my theory implies significant opportunities for Islamic parties to succeed in not-yet-democratic contexts where generalized trust is low. Were countries such as Burkina Faso, Algeria, Malaysia or Kyrgyzstan to fully democratize, voters there would likely struggle to coordinate, opening up the possibility of a dominant Islamic-based party. This would be the case even though levels of religiosity in these different contexts vary considerably, higher in Burkina Faso and Malaysia, lower in Algeria and Kyrgyzstan. Further, the case of Algeria highlights the important but counter-intuitive role of state interference in the success of Islamic-based parties. If multiparty voting continues in the wake of anti-Islamist measures taken by the state, and if voters prove consistent in their support of Islamic parties despite these measures, the state's attempt to stem the rise of an Islamic political movement may backfire. By this logic, had multiparty elections continued in Algeria after military interference in 1991, the popularity of the FIS would likely have grown. Similarly, if competitive multiparty elections are held again in the Egyptian context, the Freedom and Justice Party (or its successor) could yet see electoral gains as a result of the state action against it.

Finally, my theory is able to explain the surprisingly poor performance of Islamic parties in some electoral contexts where religiosity is quite high, such as Indonesia (Liddle and Mujani 2007). In these cases, the popularity of Islamic-based parties is not limited by religiosity but by the absence of a significant trust problem among Indonesian voters. Whereas existing theories of identity-based voting would predict that religiosity would help Indonesian Islamists coordinate under any circumstances, by my theory, the extent of their comparative advantage depends on the size of the underlying trust problem. In a relatively trusting electoral environment, the coordination advantage of Islamist voters is inherently limited. By the same logic, the opening for Islamic politics would be more limited in not-yet-democratic Muslim countries where both trust and religiosity are high, such as Jordan and Yemen.

Returning to the Turkish case, while I have argued that feelings of trust among Islamist voters are key to explaining the popularity of Islamic-based parties, I do not mean to imply that the AKP will always dominate the electoral field. In fact, there are a number of factors perfectly consistent with my trust-based theory that could explain the party's eventual fall from power. First, although trust is indeed important for supporting voter coordination, policy still matters. Even when a party's support base is perfectly coordinated, unpopular policies and bad outcomes can still get incumbents thrown out of office. Indeed, the better coordinated the support base, the more swift the potential exit. Another factor to consider is fractionalization within the Islamist voting bloc. That voters with a more salient religious identity have an in-built solution to their coordination problem does not necessarily imply that they will always prefer the same party, and the Islamist bloc could be divided either by the introduction of other viable Islamic-based parties, or by the increasing competitiveness of non-Islamic parties on religious issues.[39]

Finally, since the AKP's advantage is only as large as the extent of the underlying trust problem among voters, any increases in interpersonal trust within Turkey could also undermine the party's popularity. Indeed, although generalized trust is recognized as a slow-moving phenomenon (Bjørnskov 2007), there is some evidence of a slight increase in trust in Turkey. According to waves of the EVS and WVS, average distrust came in at 94.5 percent in 1996, 93.2 percent in 2001, 95.2 percent in 2007, but was down to 87.6 percent in 2011. Similarly, savings-deposit rates have generally been increasing across Turkish provinces since 2003. It could even be argued that feelings of group-based trust could explain these changes in generalized trust: since an overwhelming majority of Turkish citizens are at least nominally (Sunni) Muslim and identify with their Islamic identity to some degree, feelings of group-based trust can plausibly be extended to "most people" if identity is consistently primed. If this is indeed the case, then the exact source of the AKP's electoral edge could eventually undermine its advantage at the polls.

---

[39] Although neither of Turkey's main opposition parties has been successful at chipping support away from the AKP, they have certainly tried, introducing religious language into their political appeals. For its part, the MHP has mixed nationalist messages with religious ones, holding mass prayer sessions (*cum* political rallies) at historical Armenian churches. Indeed, even the supposedly secularist CHP recently employed a religious pun, referring to the celebration of Ramadan, as part of its "No" campaign during the 2010 referendum: a commonly seen CHP advertisement wished everyone "*Hayır'lı Bayramlar!*," literally a "no-filled" holiday, playing off the common holiday greeting "*Hayırlı Bayramlar*" ("good/auspicious holiday").

8

The Quasi-Integration of Firms in an Islamic Community: The Case of MÜSİAD

> [A] Muslim must be very careful of the rights of his employees and those with whom he does business. He must know that any earnings gained by abusing others' rights will be harmful over the long run.
>
> MÜSİAD Bulletin (1997)

Until now, applications of my trust-based theory of the Islamic advantage have focused on the political sphere – participation in latent political activities, on the one hand, and voter coordination, on the other. In this third empirical application, I turn from the political to the economic. Across the Muslim world, references to Islam have been used to spur a variety of collective economic activities, including investment in conventional and *sharī'ah*-compliant financial institutions, Islamic-oriented consumerism, and inter-firm and international trade. Indeed, in many Muslim countries, a distinct Islamic economy has developed, populated by an Islamic-oriented business class, organized by a set of Islamic-based business associations, and supported by a growing network of Islamic banks and micro-lending organizations (Hosgör 2011; Kuran 1995, 2005).

The role of trust in supporting these types of collective economic activities is a bit different than how it bolsters political cooperation and coordination. In the practice of mass politics, what it means to be trustworthy is quite clear: to show up, as promised, if others do the same (i.e., the essence of conditional cooperation). Generalized trust is needed to support collective action of this type because participation remains largely anonymous, given the scale of the movement. In the case of voter coordination, trustworthiness is a bit different: a willingness to have an open and honest conversation with others, in order to reach the best collective outcome. Here, non-particularized trust is necessary because of the anonymity of voting and the size of the electoral district in which coordination takes place.

But in most economic exchanges, trustworthiness has yet another meaning. Since most exchanges occur between two parties – a buyer and a seller, a principal and an agent – the scale is considerably smaller. And yet, there are plenty of opportunities for trading partners to cheat one another. Even in one-shot transactions, few exchanges take place simultaneously, and informational asymmetries abound, creating openings for the second mover to renege or the agent to withhold valuable information. At the same time, in longer-term, iterated transactions, conditions often change to effect the bottom line of the original agreement, favoring one partner over the other. Most existing theories of generalized trust and economic exchange focus on the first case – one-off transactions with strangers – while longer-term relationships are assumed to be based on feelings of particularized trust, informed by direct previous experiences working together. But particularized trust has to start from somewhere, and even long-term partners were once strangers, meaning that the two types of trust may be more related than previously thought. Considering the interaction between particularized and generalized trust also reopens the question of how group identity supports economic cooperation, in both the short- and long-term.

In this chapter, I explore how Islamic identity and group-based trust have impacted the success of MÜSİAD (Müstakil Sanayici ve İşadamları Derneği), the Independent Industrialists' and Businessmen's Association, an Islamic-based group operating in Turkey. First founded in 1990, MÜSİAD was meant to represent the interests of politically and religiously conservative firms located far from the Turkish industrial epicenter in Istanbul. What began as an association of only thirteen members has grown steadily, and is now said to have more than 11,000 member firms, the great majority of which are best defined as small- or medium-sized enterprises (SMEs). Although Turkish SMEs have historically struggled to grow relative to larger, more diversified firms, this trend is said to have been reversed among MÜSİAD members.

The success of MÜSİAD and its member firms has piqued the interest of many, from journalists to politicians and scholars. Most explain the association's rise in terms of its connection to Islamic politicians or its ability to rely on Islamic-based micro-finance. The first implies that member firms would be best off under periods of Islamic-party rule, while the second holds that their comparative advantage depends on whether other forms of credit are more limited. To date, neither of these expectations has been effectively tested. Surprisingly little is known about patterns of MÜSİAD success or failure, over space or across time, owing mostly to the association's relative secrecy about its operations. Despite this paucity of data, theoretically speaking, I have my doubts about the two extant theories, both of which are tightly focused on the resources and opportunities that accrue to member firms individually. In line with my earlier critique, I would argue that these theories critically underestimate how relationships among member firms might factor into MÜSİAD's growing success.

This emphasis on inter-firm relations fits within a large existing literature on trade within identity-groups. In these models, economic exchange within groups is supported by a reputation mechanism, whereby group members share valuable information among themselves about which of them should be trusted. To function effectively, reputation mechanisms require relatively small, closed circles, where entry is limited and exit is costly. But using a first-of-its-kind dataset on MÜSİAD members from 1990 to 2013, I find tremendous turnover in its membership from year to year, far more than could plausibly sustain a well-functioning reputation mechanism. In place of reputation, I argue that group-based trust helps to support economic exchange among MÜSİAD member firms, new and old alike. As an organization, MÜSİAD invests considerable energy in creating a sense of group identity, founded around Islamic principles, and primes members to think of themselves and others as having a set of values and ideals. In so doing, it strengthens the salience of the shared identity, as well as the trust expectations that come along with it.

I argue that these feelings of non-particularized, group-based trust are used in the beginning of longer-term economic relationships, that build particularized trust "chains" between member firms. I expect these relationships to be especially valuable to smaller firms, particularly under conditions of macroeconomic volatility, because they absorb price shocks the way that vertical integration does for larger firms. But volatility also exacerbates the initial trust problem in forming these types of "quasi-integrative" relationships, giving a comparative advantage to firms that share a group identity and feelings of group-based trust. In the pages that follow, I articulate the trust problem in short- and long-term exchange, arguing that it is based on interdependence from asset specificity and uncertainty from macroeconomic volatility. Next, I define the advantage of MÜSİAD member firms in terms of quasi-integration, based on trust. Using data at the firm-level, I find that belonging to MÜSİAD has a similar "value" to member firms as vertical integration does for non-members. Both are most beneficial to firm sales and profits under conditions of volatility. Based on this, I unearth a remarkable and counter-intuitive pattern: that MÜSİAD firms have been comparatively worse off under AKP rule, owing to the stabilization of the Turkish economy since 2002.

8.1 THE TRUST PROBLEM IN ECONOMIC RELATIONS

Arrow (1972) was perhaps first to highlight the critical role of interpersonal trust in economic relations. Since then, numerous studies have found generalized trust to be strongly correlated with economic outcomes, including investment (Bottazzi, Rin, and Hellman 2016; Guiso, Sapienza, and Zingales 2004), trade (Guiso, Sapienza, and Zingales 2009), productivity (Bjørnskov and Méon 2010), and growth (Knack and Keefer 1997; Zak and Knack 2001). These studies focus on the need for non-particularized trust in one-shot transactions, which are dominant in most modern economies. Meanwhile, an additional strand of the literature emphasizes how particularized trust "chains" are able to support long-term partnerships and economic growth, in both developed and developing economies (Gulati 1995; Lorenz 1999). Until now, the two sets of theories have rarely interacted. But even long-term partners originally begin as strangers, meaning that the trust and trustworthiness they build between them has to start somewhere: from an initial willingness to trust, that is not based on a shared history.

A common replacement for particularized trust is reputation: individuals relay their personal experiences so that others may learn from them, developing an indirect sense of who should be trusted. But reputation mechanisms have lofty requirements: a shared sense of right and wrong, a solution to a second-order collective action problem, and a credible threat of sanctioning. As such, they work best in tight-knit groups with common cultural understandings. Outside of these conditions, where a reputation mechanism is not possible, another source of non-particularized trust will be needed to support economic exchange among strangers, including those who may eventually become friends. In the sections that follow, I define the scope of the trust problem in economic exchange: the sources of interdependence and uncertainty, with special reference to Turkey and MÜSİAD. I argue that group-based trust is a viable substitute for both generalized trust and a reputation mechanism, able to support the first in a long series of iterated transactions, even under conditions of macroeconomic volatility.

8.1.1 Generalized Trust in One-Off Exchanges

Interpersonal trust factors into almost every economic exchange because these transactions intrinsically entail both interdependence and uncertainty. The interdependence of economic agents is derived, first and foremost, from specialization, the hallmark of a modern economy. Specialization implies that no individual can independently produce everything he needs to survive. Instead, he sells whatever he produces but does not consume in order to purchase those things that he needs to consume but does not produce. This interdependence is further deepened by the existence of supply chains: in most cases, what one individual produces is largely derived from materials that others produce or requires tools that others create. For example, a furniture manufacturer must sell whatever furniture she does not personally need in order to be able afford both the food she needs to survive as well as the fabrics and other materials she uses in the furniture she makes. As a result, she is dependent not only on the farmers who grow her food but also on the artisans who weave her fabrics. And they, in turn, are dependent on her business so that they may be able to purchase the goods they need for both consumption and production.

The interdependence between producers and consumers within supply chains is deepened by asset specificity, when investments are made in the production of specialized goods rather than generic ones (Williamson 1985). Returning to the example of the furniture manufacturer, she may wish to find a fabric weaver willing to make custom patterns for her and may be willing to pay a premium for this customization. But in agreeing to produce this customized good, the weaver faces a risk: if the furniture manufacturer ends up not buying the pattern she ordered, he may not be able to sell it to another customer for the same price, losing the time and energy he spent creating the pattern for her. In most cases, he must decide whether he should invest

8.1 The Trust Problem in Economic Relations

resources in creating the customized pattern before she fully pays him for it. Once the investment is made, he remains extremely vulnerable to her: if she refuses to buy the fabric (or if she refuses to pay him the agreed-upon price), he may lose his investment, even if he is able to sell it to another customer.

In this way, "a situation of *ex ante* competitive supply, with a large number of subcontractors tendering bids for the contract, can be transformed into one of bilateral monopoly due to investment in specific assets" (Lorenz 2000, p. 200). Both sides stand to gain from investing in specific assets, but doing so substantially increases their interdependence. Supply chains and asset specificity tend to be most prevalent in the manufacturing sector, making it particularly acute in many Muslim-majority economies (Henry and Springborg 2010) and, within them, for small- and medium-sized enterprises (Taymaz 1997). And yet, these interdependencies on their own pose little threat to the development of cooperative inter-firm relationships. Interdependencies, broadly speaking, and asset specificity, in particular, only create obstacles to inter-firm cooperation "in the presence of uncertainty" (Williamson 1985, p. 56).

For its part, uncertainty in economic exchange stems from the fact that few transactions occur simultaneously. Often, one party is asked to make an investment long before that investment is repaid. The time lag between investment and payment creates incentives for the second-mover to act dishonestly and renege. Information asymmetries further complicate this situation by introducing moral hazard problems, in which the better-informed party is willing to take risks that the other party will be forced to bear. In either case, the potential for opportunism creates uncertainty about what others might do if given the chance, making it less likely that transactions occur in the first place.

Even when incentives are aligned in a way that limits opportunism, uncertainty remains: where incentives start off as aligned, changes in market conditions can shift to create opportunities for dishonesty. As Williamson explains, it is this second type of uncertainty that creates the real obstacles to economic cooperation:

To be sure, behavioral uncertainties would not pose contractual problems if transactions were *known* to be free from exogenous disturbances, since then there would be no occasion to adapt and unilateral efforts to alter contracts could and presumably would be voided by the courts or other third party appeal... . The ease of enforcing contracts vanishes, however, once the need for adaptation appears (or can plausibly be asserted). (1985, p. 59)

Uncertainty about future market conditions often revolve around questions of price variance and changing demand, both of which can fundamentally alter either party's incentives to abide by a previously made agreement (Klein, Crawford, and Alchian 1978).

Given both interdependence and uncertainty, trust becomes critical to economic exchange. As Edward Lorenz emphatically states, "If transaction costs are thought of as friction in the economy, then trust can be seen as an extremely effective lubricant" (2000, p. 198). More specifically, trust can be said to create "an open architecture of exchange which promotes the exchange of services that are critical for survival but difficult to price or specify contractually beforehand" (Uzzi 1996, p. 678). Even where pricing and contracting are possible, robust trust expectations among business associates save considerable time and resources by lessening the need for protracted bargaining, explicit contracting, and control mechanisms:

[U]nder conditions of high trust, transactors will spend less time on *ex ante* contracting because they are confident that payoffs will be fairly divided... In addition, negotiations will likely be more efficient because transactors will have greater confidence that information provided by the other [party] is not misrepresented (Dyer and Chu 2003, p. 59).

In developed economies where most exchanges are one-shot, between strangers, the most valuable form of trust is generalized, non-particularized trust. Indeed, there is a lengthy empirical literature that has found a robust effect of generalized trust on economic development, cross-nationally. And within Turkey, I see signs that the generalized distrust problem hinders economic exchange. A survey of Turkish businessmen conducted by USAID in the late 1960s found rampant interpersonal distrust that created a

reluctance to invest in another man's enterprise, or conversely, of the enterprise owner to accept outside financial participation... [as well as] a low degree of confidence on the part of businessmen, frequently justified, in the reliability of delivery schedules, quality of product delivered, or other promised conditions (Hopper and Levin 1968, p. 141).

Similarly, in my 2012 survey, I asked respondents about their willingness to consider loaning money to a family member, friend, or business partner. I find that generalized distrust is associated with significantly fewer loans to friends and business partners, an effect that is robust to the inclusion of demographic controls, that is, age, gender, education, and income (see Online Appendix Table OA.34). This basic trust problem is further complicated by the instability of the Turkish economy, which elevates uncertainty. Cross-national data on macroeconomic volatility is not easily available, but studies from Turkey (Celasun, Denizer, and He 1999; Kasman and Ayhan 2006) and the Muslim world (Mobarak 2005; Neaime 2005) indicate that these economies are comparatively unstable. On a smaller scale, in her study of Turkish SMEs, Gül Berna Özcan finds that "economic problems and high inflation rates create a low level of confidence and an insecure environment for business owners in the absence of organizational support" (1995, p. 280).

8.1.2 Particularized Trust in Long-Term Exchanges

The traditional solution to the trust problem under conditions of macroeconomic volatility is to align incentives under single ownership. The strategy of buying out upstream producers or downstream consumers is known as vertical integration. Originally, integration was assumed to be used to streamline technological inefficiencies by bringing production and manufacturing in-house;

but Williamson points out that it could help address other market-based inefficiencies, most notably asset specificity (i.e., interdependence) and uncertainty. He argues that "the substitution of internal organization for market exchange is attractive less on account of technological economies associated with production but because of what may be referred to broadly as 'transactional failures' in the operation of markets for intermediate goods" (1971, p. 112).

Larger Turkish firms have long accepted the wisdom of this prescription, opting to integrate and diversify in the hopes of protecting themselves from the uncertainty of the Turkish macroeconomy (Buğra 1994b; Gündüz and Tatoğlu 2003). Indeed, the tax code was rewritten in 1961 to support the growth of holding companies – large, diversified firms that have an active managerial role in a number of different enterprises. Since this legal change, holding companies have gained a dominant position in the Turkish economy; but as Ayşe Buğra explains, "while advantages stemming from the tax system have undoubtedly played a role in the increase in the number of holding companies, the possibility of the centralized management of physical and financial resources in highly diversified activities ... appears to have been equally important" (1994a, p. 44). When surveying Turkish businessmen about their reasons for diversifying, she also notes that "the answers were almost never formulated in terms of the possibility of using acquired expertise in one area in a different, yet related field of activity [but instead were] formulated with reference to risk-aversion" (p. 45). In other words, diversification and integration were intended to help ameliorate the uncertainties of the Turkish macroeconomy.

Although vertical integration helps address the twin challenges of distrust and volatility, not every firm is in a position to buy its suppliers. Integration is usually reserved for the largest firms, with sufficient capital available to invest; meanwhile, smaller firms, without said resources, remain more vulnerable to shifting market conditions. Indeed, the inability of Turkish SMEs to integrate and protect themselves from macroeconomic uncertainty has been cited as a key reason for their historical under-performance (Buğra 1994b, 1998). I can see evidence of this in a series of surveys of Turkish firms conducted by the World Bank. In these Enterprise Surveys, owners were asked whether their firms had recently acquired or merged with another business in the previous three years. A very small number self-reported having integrated with another firm (7.9 percent acquired, 1.6 percent merged), and those that did were significantly more likely to be large, with over 250 full-time employees.[1]

When small- and medium-sized Turkish firms are less likely to integrate vertically, they remain in a precarious position. To begin with, they are heavily dependent on credit: according to the Enterprise Surveys, medium-sized firms, in particular, sell a significantly larger share of their goods on credit.[2]

---

[1] While large firms make up only 9.3 percent of the entire survey sample in 2005, they comprise 27.3 percent of firms that report having recently merged with another firm and 15.8 percent of those that acquired one.

[2] While the average across all firms is 41.8 percent, medium-sized firms – with between 50 and 250 full-time employees – self-report selling as much as 53.9 percent of their goods on credit.

Moreover, these firms are aware of the challenges they face because of macroeconomic volatility. Across a set of twenty-one factors that could pose a threat to their success, macroeconomic volatility was the obstacle most cited by small- and medium-sized businesses.[3] To see why, consider how the business owners predicted their customers would react if they suddenly had to increase their prices by 10 percent. While fewer than 8 percent of large firm owners worried that they would lose their customers to one of their competitors, 16.4 percent of medium-sized and 22.4 percent of small-sized firms reported the same concern. Similarly, when the tables were turned, over 30 percent of SMEs said they would take their business elsewhere if their suppliers suddenly raised prices, while less than 15 percent of large firms said they would do the same. (For an illustration of these patterns, see Online Appendix Figure OA.16.)[4]

Under conditions of macroeconomic volatility, the best option for SMEs may be to mimic the benefits of vertical integration by entering into iterated, cooperative partnerships with other small firms. This "quasi-integration" allows "a firm to develop a relationship with some of its suppliers such that the advantages of vertical integration can be obtained without the normally associated disadvantages" (Blois 1972, p. 254). In order to best approximate vertical integration, quasi-integrative relationships must be long-term, flexible arrangements, with limited threat of opportunism and moral hazard. As parties emphasize long-term stability over opportunism, prices may be more loosely tied to market rates, and information related to research, development, and market dynamics may be shared rather than withheld.

Uncertainty from macroeconomic volatility represents a sizable obstacle to economic exchange and growth among members of MÜSİAD, Turkey's Islamic-based business association. The group was originally founded in 1990 to serve the interests of smaller firms, the majority of which were situated far from Istanbul, in smaller Anatolian cities. Member firms tend to be headed by more conservative owners and managers who lacked the financial resources and political connections usually needed to succeed in Turkey. Moreover, MÜSİAD includes large numbers of independent manufacturers, working in textiles, furniture, and wood-working (Buğra 1994a; Jang 2006).

---

[3] For their part, large and public firms were more likely to report high tax rates and uncertainty surrounding government regulation. Available "obstacles" included access to and the cost of financing, telecommunications, electricity, transportation, access to and ownership of land, tax rates and administration, the regulation of trade and labor, permitting, availability of skilled workers, corruption, petty and organized crime, the judicial system, anticompetitive practices, and contract violations. Interestingly, firms interviewed in 2005 Enterprise Survey, during a period when the Turkish economy was considerably more stable, were significantly less concerned about volatility than those interviewed in 2002, at the tail end of a more unstable period.

[4] The firms' expected behavior reflects not only their size but also the current economic environment: while 34.4 percent of firms interviewed in 2002 admitted that they would abandon a supplier if it suddenly raised its prices, only 25.3 percent of those interviewed in 2005, a less volatile period, said the same. Similarly, while 22.7 percent of respondents predicted that customers would opt to buy from a competitor in the face of raised prices in 2002, only 18.2 percent predicted the same outcome in 2005.

8.1 The Trust Problem in Economic Relations

So, in addition to being vulnerable to uncertainty from volatility, because of their size, member firms are also susceptible to interdependence due to supply chains and asset specificity. And without the resources to vertically integrate, the traditional solution to both problems is closed off to them. And yet, despite all of these obstacles, over the years, and with the association's help, MÜSİAD's member firms seem to have gone from marginalized and vulnerable to mainstream and stable, earning them the moniker of the "Anatolian Tigers."[5]

While some have suggested that MÜSİAD's success is based on privileged access to Islamic-based micro-credit (Hosgör 2011; Özcan and Çokgezen 2006), others focus on the political connections they have enjoyed since the rise of the AKP (Gumuscu and Sert 2009; Lorasdaği 2010; Meyersson 2011; Özel 2010). But even beyond these factors, a part of MÜSİAD's success lies in the cooperative "quasi-integrative" relationships it supports among its members. As Emin Adaş notes,

> networks and solidarity among [member] firms are more developed than others. They involve joint-investments, borrowing money from each other and joint-purchase of machinery, industrial inputs and other commodities in order to reduce costs and survive in a highly competitive globalized economy (2006, p. 123).

Similar types of flexible and cooperative transactions, within and between Islamic agents, have been cited in employee–employer relationships,[6] in the practice of micro-lending (Adaş 2006; Jenkins 2008), and even in international trade.[7] These are not the types of collaborative arrangements that traditional theories of economic relations would expect to see among independent economic agents. Still, MÜSİAD member firms regularly cooperate and collaborate over the long term, arguably to their benefit.[8] Yıldız Atasoy suggests that these quasi-integrative arrangements are intended "to create a

---

[5] Although data on MÜSİAD and its member firms have rarely been made public, there is a general sense that the association's economic presence is growing. Journalists and scholars alike note an increase in the number of local MÜSİAD branches (Çemrek 2002), in the number of international trade fairs the association sponsors (Doğruöz 2008), and in the number of its members listed among Turkey's top 500 firms, as identified annually by the Istanbul Chamber of Industry (Berberoğlu 2006).

[6] M. Hakan Yavuz describes a management style within Islamic firms that "is less rigid," where "contact between workers and management has become more personalized" (2003, p. 88). Alan Dubetsky (1976) highlights the importance of *dürüstlük* (honesty) in hiring decisions, which Buğra notes may become "more important than professional competence as a determinant of success in a managerial career" (1994, p. 214).

[7] MÜSİAD published a pamphlet in 1994 for its members titled "Economic Cooperation Among Islamic Countries" that explains how "contrary to what obtains in western societies, community [(*ummah* or *ümmet*)] in Islam is not considered as a group of people in a location or in a region but is described in a larger concept which exceeds regional and national boundaries" (p. 7).

[8] These types of relationships can become profitable for both parties. As Atasoy explains in the case of employer–employee relations, "In the face of economic hardship, trust networks invoke a strong cultural consensus: employers expect [employees] to work for lower wages without social-security provision; but labor is only wiling to do so in return for 'charity,' and the necessary support when needed" (2009, p. 133).

sense of unity among smaller groups to [resemble] larger companies capable of competing in external markets" (2009, p. 14). In other words, this type of cooperation helps these SMEs to compete against larger, more diversified Turkish firms.

For obvious reasons, starting and maintaining these quasi-integrative relationships requires that the underlying trust problem be addressed. And the question of trust is made considerably more complex whenever volatility (and uncertainty) is high. Still, as long as trust expectations are sufficiently strong, the exchange of transaction-specific assets in these quasi-integrative arrangements can be supported without the need for vertical integration (Chiles and McMackin 1996). Most existing research contends that the type of trust most beneficial to quasi-integration is particularized trust. Gulati argues that "interfirm trust is incrementally built as firms repeatedly interact" (1995, p. 92). Additionally, Lorenz suggests that with repeated interactions, feelings of trust will deepen and develop "through a learning process" (1999, p. 309). But if repeated interactions are required in order for trust to develop, what explains the first exchange?

8.1.3 The Role of Reputation in MÜSİAD

Islam plays a critical role in supporting the quasi-integrative relationships among MÜSİAD members. As Buğra notes, member firms' have "a shared understanding concerning business ethics, corporate responsibility, and commonality of interest" (1998, p. 529) all of which help to support cooperation among them. A prominent existing literature on identity-based trade specifies how group identity addresses the trust problems among members: it helps to support a reputation mechanisms wherein members report their dealings with one another, so that each can more easily determine who among them should be trusted (Carr and Landa 1983; Greif 1989, 1996; Landa 1994). In this way, particularized trust is extended so that group members all learn from each one's experiences.

For a reputation mechanism to work effectively, each member must faithfully report his experiences with others in the group, while committing not to do business with any who have wronged others in the past. In this way, "[b]y establishing *ex ante* a linkage between past conduct and a future utility stream, an agent [can] credibly commit himself *ex ante* not to breach a contract *ex post*" (Greif 1989, pp. 858–859). As a result, interdependence and uncertainty are fully addressed.

Timur Kuran makes a strong case for the relevance of reputations in Islamic-based economic exchange. While appreciating that particularized trust is best, Kuran points out that social mobility and migration make exchange based on first hand experience difficult: first-generation business owners and new arrivals to urban centers are disadvantaged because they do not have access to ready-made particularized trust networks. All they have are "networks built on ties of kinship and regional origin – networks whose members tend to be poor, inexperienced, and politically powerless" (2005, p. 51). Their main alternative

8.1 The Trust Problem in Economic Relations

is an Islamic-based network which will tend to be larger, more diverse, and within which "information about dishonest behavior spreads quickly" (Kuran 2005, p. 51).

In this model, a reputation mechanism explains how MÜSİAD member firms are able to cooperate, establishing long-term partnerships, to their comparative advantage relative to other SMEs. But for reputations to play such a role, the mechanism must operate effectively, and this requires that it meet a number of conditions. Specifically, it must be designed in a way that incentivizes members to share information honestly and that credibly threatens to sanction those who do not comply or who behave dishonestly. This requires that the group be relatively small. As Carr and Landa explain, "[t]oo large a group may imply too small an ability to impose sanctions on those who breach contracts" (1983, p. 152). Moreover, reputation mechanisms tend to operate best within minority communities: "If a religious organization is very large in relation to the potential trading population, then little economic advantage will be received by belonging to it" (1983, p. 152). Further, reputation mechanisms struggle to grow to include new group members: "Once a mechanism for information transmission through mutual acquaintances is established, the coalition that utilizes this mechanism will not expand" (Greif 1989, p. 878). Conversely, to insure that group-based sanctions are sufficiently costly, exit from the group should be difficult (Landa 1994).

From even a cursory look, MÜSİAD does not seem to meet all of these requirements. While reputation mechanisms operate best within small groups, MÜSİAD, with its thousands of members, spread across most of Anatolia, may be too large and too diverse. And while reputation mechanisms tend to be most effective within minority groups, MÜSİAD is an Islamic-based association operating in a country where Muslims comprise a supra-majority. Further, within Turkey, the association is particularly prominent in regions where the Islamic community is larger and Islamic group identity is more salient. But, even beyond all this, MÜSİAD's ability to support a reputation mechanism is challenged by how easily and regularly members enter and exit the organization. Until now, specific information about MÜSİAD membership has been limited, with little information available to the public. But using a first-of-its-kind dataset of annual MÜSİAD membership given to me by MÜSİAD officials, I am able to trace patterns of entry into and exit from the association.

Figure 8.1 illustrates the number of MÜSİAD member firms in each year (1990–2013) as well as the share of new members and exiting ones. While the number of firms rose steadily between 1992 and 1997, and again between 2003 and 2013, MÜSİAD lost a significant percentage of members in every year since 1994, when they lost 149 members (7.7%). The largest decline (654 members, or 27.6 percent) occurred in 1999, shortly after the post modern coup, when "the activities of business establishments with close links to [Islam] came under the increasing scrutiny of state agencies" (Öniş and Türem 2002, p. 448). But even ignoring this significant drop, the exit rate averaged just over 9.5 percent in every other year between 1994 and 2013, indicating that exit from the association was neither rare nor (apparently) costly. This pattern bolsters anecdotal

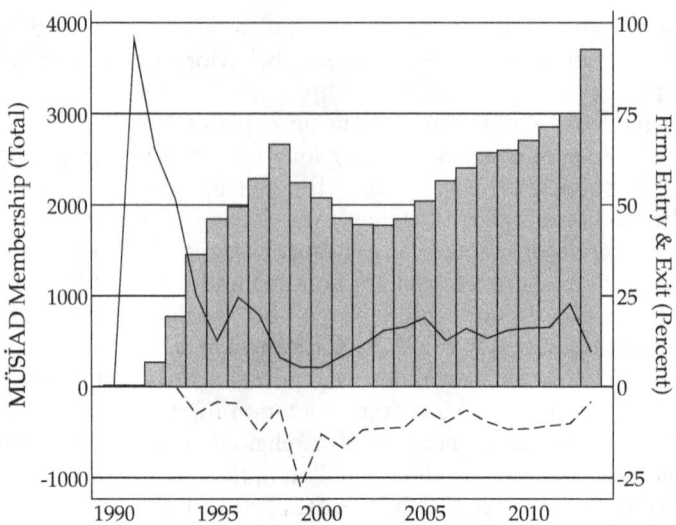

FIGURE 8.1 Changes in MÜSİAD Membership over Time
Notes: Total number of member firms per year indicated by bars. Percent new members indicated by solid black line and percent of members exiting, by dashed black line.

evidence collected by Özcan, indicating that "social networks [among Anatolian entrepreneurs] are not closed or isolated systems. New members can enter, old members can be 'expelled'" (1995, p. 279). It also supports analysis of survey data collected by Kurt et al. which finds that "there are no significant paths from length of membership... to network commitment" among Anatolian Tigers (2016, p. 694).

Given this, it seems unlikely that the strength of MÜSİAD as an organization rests in its ability to support a reputation mechanism. If member firms are indeed better off – more profitable than similar non-member firms, better able to enter into quasi-integrative agreements with one another – than the source of their comparative advantage must lie elsewhere. As previously mentioned, at least two alternative explanations for MÜSİAD's relative success already exist: one emphasizing its links to Islamic-based micro-credit, which help member firms bypass the conventional (and less reliable) Turkish credit system (Hosgör 2011; Jenkins 2008; Özcan and Çokgezen 2006); meanwhile, the other highlights the political connections between member firms and state officials during the AKP period (Gumuscu and Sert 2009; Lorasdaği 2010; Özel 2010). But I want to suggest a third option: that group-based trust among MÜSİAD members is key. Rather than reputation, this trust supports the first step in establishing quasi-integrative relationships among member firms.

8.1.4 Group-Based Trust in Economic Exchange

While reputation mechanisms help group members better identify who should be trusted, they are different from group-based trust in key ways. In the

8.1 The Trust Problem in Economic Relations

latter case, those with a shared group identity have an inherent tendency to expect reciprocal cooperation from one another. For their part, reputations are based on information relayed about others' personal experiences, producing something akin to particularized trust. Meanwhile, group-based trust remains strictly non-particularized: it is not based on any information other than group membership. For this reason, the conditions needed to develop and sustain group-based trust are different from what a reputation mechanism requires: so long as the group identity is common knowledge and made salient through priming, trust develops in large and small groups, among members of a minority and the majority, and even with fluctuating group boundaries.

Anecdotal evidence indicates that MÜSİAD takes great care in creating and maintaining a shared identity among members, defining this identity, in large part, in terms of how they should treat one another. More specifically, the organization has developed an image of its members as *Homo-Islamicus*, standing in contrast to *Homo-Economicus*, the free-riding "rational egoist," and *Homo-Traditionalus*, who is motivated by cultural norms. As Adaş explains, "unlike homo-economicus and homo-traditionalus, homo-Islamicus is said to be both entrepreneurial and moral" (2006, p. 127). The particular combination of traits is detailed in a letter from the MÜSİAD director in a 1997 newsletter, sent to all members:

[A] Muslim businessman should not produce or do business without limits, he should earn by means of effort and risk.... [A] Muslim must be very careful of the rights of his employees and those with whom he does business. He must know that any earnings gained by abusing others' rights will be harmful over the the long run... [A] Muslim businessman must never forget that his capital is a trust and that he must fulfill all his responsibilities toward it (p. 4, translated by Çemrek (2002)).

The clear expectation is that MÜSİAD members be trustworthy, guided by their religious convictions, as well as by their commitment to their community. Indeed, MÜSİAD is said to screen potential members for this quality and this quality only (Çemrek 2002; Özler 2001; Yavuz 2003).

These individual directives about what it means to be *Homo-Islamicus* become common knowledge through regular and ritualized meetings of MÜSİAD members. As Buğra explains:

MÜSİAD's special commissions and professional committees, the conferences it organizes around economic and political issues, and its other social activities [are significant] both for providing technology- and marketing-related information and for enhancing group cohesion and solidarity.... These activities play a very important role in fostering feelings of solidarity, especially because they take place in a cultural frame of reference where Islam significantly contributes to the establishment of a shared understanding... (1998, p. 529)

Çemrek echoes this description, arguing that "the association plays a very important role in network formation by fostering feelings of trust and solidarity both at local and at national levels by the periodical meeting of boards and professional committees in different cities" (2002, p. 196). The result is what Yavuz calls "social synergy ... . MÜSİAD members... are members of overlapping networks..., which are based on interpersonal trust and are derived from Islamic identity, [and which] help to promote work ethics and new channels of communication for collaborating and sharing business information" (2003, p. 94). The solidarity developed in official conferences is then maintained once members return home, where participation in religious group activities such as Friday prayer helps to "reinforce ties between workers and employers as they join the praying together" (Özcan 1995, p. 278).

In contrast to a reputation mechanism, which supports honesty through the credible threat of sanction, group-based trust bolsters cooperation through reciprocal (and therefore self-fulfilling) expectations of others. Each individual member is therefore charged with monitoring himself, to ensure that he upholds his commitments to others. When interviewing owners of Turkish SMEs, Selçuk Uygur observes this type of self-monitoring, done with direct reference to Islam. One business owner explained that he "can't cheat in trading as a person who does daily praying," while another argued that "religion controls the trade and industrialist... for example, the sample you show to your customer and the actual goods must be the same" (2009, p. 218). Key here is not that Islam influences business practices, but how it does so, via trust and honesty. This is echoed in a study of religiosity and business networks among some "Anatolian Tigers." Kurt et al. find that "trust operates as a mediating variable between spirituality and network commitment" (2016, p. 694). The significance of group-based trust – above and beyond personal piety – can also help explain how cooperation can be sustained even if individuals' "shared commitment to Islam [is] partly feigned," as Kuran has argued (2005, p. 51).

Based on this, I contend that group-based trust among MÜSİAD members plays an important role in explaining their comparative advantage. Specifically, this trust is used to start longer-term, flexible "quasi-integrative" relationships among them. I expect this to hold where there is distrust, generally, and when macroeconomic volatility complicates the trust problem by creating more uncertainty. Indeed, the comparative advantage of MÜSİAD members, based on their quasi-integration, should be largest during periods of volatility, when vertical integration is most valuable to non-members. I anticipate that the value of quasi-integration will outweigh the impact of credit markets and political connections on member success.

Given the connection between MÜSİAD's comparative advantage and macroeconomic volatility, I anticipate that member firms will fare poorly under AKP rule, since the Turkish economy stabilized after 2002. Indeed, during longer periods of stability, I suspect that quasi-integration may even hinder MÜSİAD member growth. This is because the methods by which long-term trading partners protect themselves from market dynamics during periods of volatility can weaken their market-driven motives and produce inefficiencies during quieter times. As Özcan explains, "in an inflationary and volatile economy, Turkish small firms survive by exploiting local ties and market niches at the expense of flexible specialization and innovation" (1995, p. 281). Taken together, these arguments imply that MÜSİAD's comparative advantage is considerably more limited than commonly presumed.

8.2 ESTIMATING MÜSİAD'S COMPARATIVE ADVANTAGE

I have argued that a shared group identity and group-based trust among MÜSİAD member firms support the establishment of long-term, flexible relationships among them. I suggest that this "quasi-integration" will be most valuable during periods of macroeconomic volatility, when it mimics the benefits of vertical integration for larger non-members. Outside of these unstable periods, I expect that MÜSİAD membership and quasi-integration may not be beneficial at all, possibly hindering member-firm growth.

Unfortunately, most of these hypotheses cannot be directly tested. MÜSİAD remains a relatively closed organization, and I have been unable to secure additional data from them beyond the membership lists introduced earlier. Further, I have been unable to carry out a systematic survey of MÜSİAD member firms to retrieve an unbiased sample. As such, I cannot directly measure members' group-based trust, nor the ways they interact with one another, as compared to non-members.

Already, I have presented some anecdotal and indirect evidence of the significant challenges posed by interdependence and uncertainty for Turkish firms, especially for the SMEs that comprise the bulk of MÜSİAD's membership. Using responses to my nationally representative survey, I have also shown how generalized distrust undermines Turks' willingness to make economic investments. I am also able to confirm that group-based trust increases their willingness to loan money to family and friends, in addition to business partners.[9] These lend some support to my assumptions, but none is a systematic test of my main hypothesis.

As an indirect test, I rely on panel data at the firm level, comparing the sales and profits of MÜSİAD member firms relative to similar non-members, as well as the growth of firms that are vertically integrated to those that are not. In both cases, I want to assess how the advantages of quasi- and vertical integration vary based on the level of volatility in the Turkish economy. I can compare these effects to other predictors of firm success, including variation in conventional credit and political connections. To use available data to test my hypotheses, I make some key assumptions: first, that MÜSİAD membership implies quasi-integration, based on group-based trust; and, second, that the degree of macroeconomic volatility reflects the scope of the trust problem that all firms must solve.

---

[9] While only 76.1 percent of those who distrust members of their religious in-group are willing to loan money to a family member, 81.5 percent of those with in-group trust are willing to do the same. The difference in loans to friends is 33.8 percent compared to 40.3 percent, while the difference in business loans is 13.4 percent vs. 16.3 percent. In regression analysis with demographic controls and province fixed effects, I confirm that the latter two differences are statistically significant at conventional levels.

8.2.1 Panel Data on Turkish Firms

To capture variation in the success of Turkish firms, I rely on a set of statistics published annually by the Istanbul Chamber of Industry (İstanbul Sanayi Odası, ISO), which includes the sales, assets, and profits of its 1,000 largest members. All Turkish firms headquartered or with any production facility in Istanbul are legally required to join the ISO and, if they are sufficiently large in a given year, they are included in the ISO list. This means that ISO members – particularly those that appear on the annual lists – are not representative of the average Turkish firm: they will tend to be larger and more profitable, and their presence in Istanbul indicates better access to national (and international) markets.

Although firms included on the ISO lists are not typical, I am less concerned about sampling bias because it tends to work against me: on the one hand, bigger, more geographically central firms should be better able to withstand economic volatility without needing to integrate, making it less likely that I find a significant benefit to integration; on the other, the largest MÜSİAD members should be least dependent on the association for their success, making it less likely that I find a significant benefit to membership.

Because the inclusion of a given firm on the ISO list in a given year depends on its most recent performance, data are not always available for each firm across all years. To minimize potential bias from firms repeatedly entering and exiting the dataset or from firms who make only a brief appearance, I restrict analysis to those that appear on the list for at least four years, three of which are consecutive. That leaves me with a total of 1,784 firms. For each of these, I use annual net sales and profits to capture variation in firm growth and success, taking the natural logarithm to correct for skewness in the raw numbers.

To facilitate a comparison between MÜSİAD members and non-members, I rely on internal MÜSİAD documents, given to me by officials from the Istanbul headquarters, that track which of its members appeared on the ISO lists in each year between 1990 and 2011.[10] I supplement these with annual MÜSİAD membership lists, indicating the year in which each member firm joined and, possibly, left the association. Using these, I create a bivariate indicator for each firm-year in the ISO data, indicating whether that firm is a current MÜSİAD member. Of the firms included in the ISO lists, 158 (8.9 percent) are or were members of MÜSİAD at one time. Combining information about MÜSİAD membership with other indicators from the ISO lists, I corroborate anecdotal observations made by Buğra (1994a, 1994b, 1998). MÜSİAD member firms are over-represented in manufacturing sectors: they tend to produce food,

---

[10] The availability of these internal MÜSİAD documents determines the time frame of the forthcoming analysis. While ISO lists have continued to be published in the years since, and I have MÜSİAD member lists through 2013, it would be difficult to correctly identify members through name-matching without introducing considerable measurement errors in these later years.

8.2 Estimating MÜSİAD's Comparative Advantage

furniture, and footwear, as well as manufacturing inputs, such as wood and plastic; meanwhile, members are under-represented in heavy machinery and mining. (For a break down across all sectors, see Online Appendix Figure OA.17.) MÜSİAD members also tend to be smaller, with an average of just over 520 wage employees, compared to an average of nearly 656 employees among non-members.

To assess whether firms on the ISO list are vertically integrated, I conducted a search of each in the Orbis database, published by Bureau van Dijk. Using information on whether a given firm is majority-owned by another company or is a subsidiary of one, I create a binary indicator of integration status. Unfortunately, the Orbis database only provides firm-level information in the year in which the search is conducted, and no other cross-temporal data source could be identified. As such, the indicator of vertical integration is cross-sectional, reflecting information available in Orbis in 2014. In line with Buğra's (1994) observation that large Turkish firms tend to be vertically integrated, I find that 860 (52.6 percent) of the firms on the ISO list are integrated.[11]

To estimate macroeconomic volatility in Turkey for each year, I use inflation statistics derived from monthly consumer price indices, calculating the standard deviation of monthly rates. Between 1990 and 2011, volatility averaged 1.60 (σ=1.21), with a high of 6.25 in 1994 and a low of 0.59 in 2005. I also capture alternative explanations for MÜSİAD member success: variation in the availability of conventional credit is measured using business-oriented loans distributed in each year by members of the Banks Association of Turkey (TBB); and variation in political connections is measured by Islamic party control at the local level. I do the latter in two ways, using Islamic party vote share in the most recent provincial council election and creating a binary indicator of whether an Islamic party was the single largest vote-getter in that election. I also assess variation in political connections at the national level, comparing trends in the pre-AKP period to those since 2002.

Because MÜSİAD member firms may be systematically different than non-member firms in ways that could impact their relative growth, I include a number of time-invariant controls. These include firm size, proxied by the number of wage employees in the firm's first appearance on the ISO list, and wealth, proxied by firm assets and sales (both logged) in that first year. I also include a binary indicator of whether the firm is majority publicly owned as well as fixed effects at the sector- and province-level. The inclusion of these fixed effects focuses the comparison between members and non-members from the same sector and location.[12] And while sales and profits do not increase

---

[11] Of these, 142 firms (8.7 percent) are subsidiaries of larger companies, 316 (19.3 percent) are parent companies with at least one subsidiary, and 402 (24.6 percent) are in the middle of an integrated chain.

[12] An attempt was made to match MÜSİAD member firms with similar non-members based on initial size and wealth, sector and province, but the successful match rate was low. Still, I use matched pair comparisons in some of the robustness checks below.

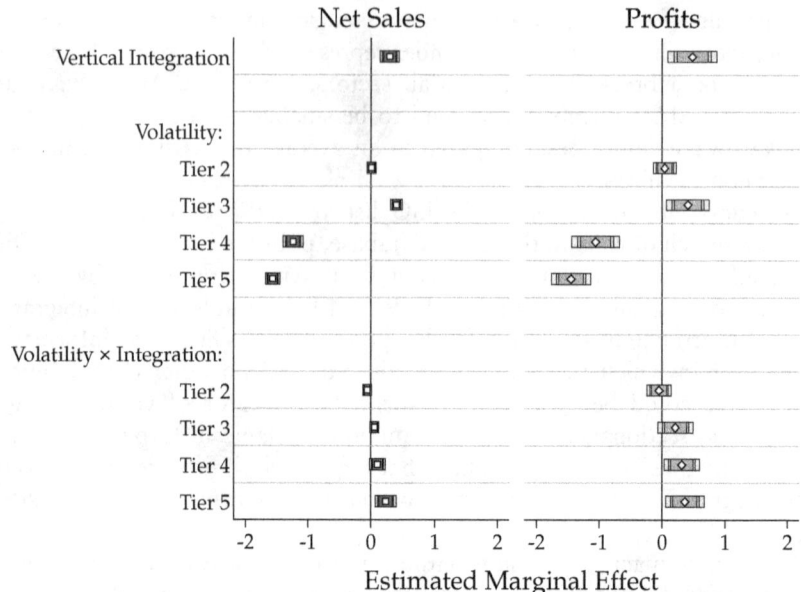

FIGURE 8.2 Marginal Effect of Vertical Integration, across Levels of Volatility
Notes: Estimated marginal effect of vertical integration on the sales and profits of Turkey's 1,000 largest firms, across levels of macroeconomic volatility. All models include the consumer price index in a given year, the firms' assets, sales, and number of employees in its first appearance on the ISO list, a binary indicator of whether it is a publicly owned firm, and both province and sector fixed effects, with standard errors clustered at the province level.

monotonically over time, I see an increase that roughly correlates with the inflation rate. As such, I use the annual consumer price index to correct for this trend.

8.2.2 The Value of Vertical and Quasi-Integration under Volatility

I have argued that group-based trust among MÜSİAD members supports their quasi-integration. This is expected to benefit them during periods of macroeconomic volatility, much in the same way as vertical integration does for larger firms. To test this hypothesis, I conduct a series of comparisons: first estimating the effects of vertical integration on firm growth, across levels of volatility; and then doing the same for the effect of MÜSİAD membership. Both require the estimation of interaction models. And given the important role played by statistical control in these models – focusing the comparison on firms of relatively similar size, operating in the same province and sector, and accounting for temporal trends in inflation – the raw data are less informative.

Given this, I jump straight into the statistical results. Before introducing the interaction, I find that vertically integrated firms are significantly better off and that volatility tends to hurt firm performance, in terms of both sales and profits. Once I interact integration and volatility, I find that the benefits to vertical

8.2 Estimating MÜSİAD's Comparative Advantage

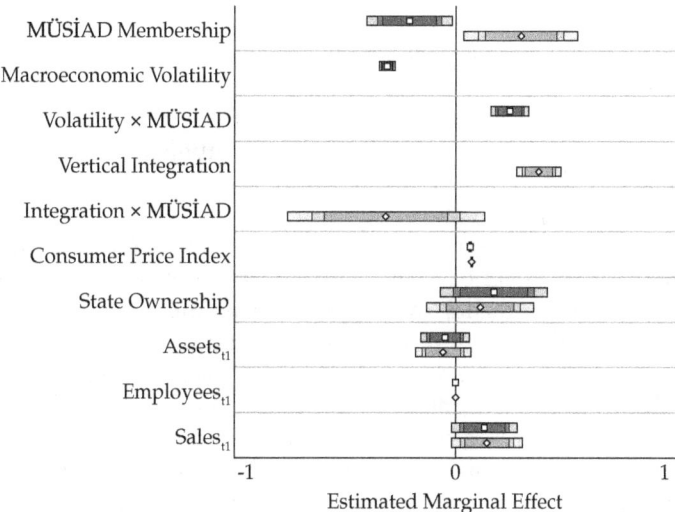

FIGURE 8.3 Marginal Effect of MÜSİAD Membership
Notes: Estimated marginal effect of MÜSİAD Membership on the firm sales, across levels of macroeconomic volatility and conditioned on whether firm is vertically integrated. All models include the consumer price index in a given year, the firms' assets, sales, and number of employees in its first appearance on the ISO list, a binary indicator of being publicly owned, and province and sector fixed effects, with standard errors clustered at the province level.

integration are even larger in volatile years.[13] The full results are available in Online Appendix Table OA.35, but an illustration of the coefficients is displayed in Figure 8.2. Here, I include binary indicators of volatility quintiles, and an interaction between each and the firm's integration status, calculating the marginal effects on both sales and profits. While the impact of volatility on firm performance is not strictly linear – middle levels of volatility actually appear to help firms grow – volatility at the highest levels is damaging to both firm sales and profits. And while integrated firms are better off in all years, as indicated by the positive coefficient on integration itself, their advantage is significantly larger at higher levels of volatility, as indicated by the positive coefficients on the interaction terms.

I estimate a similar model to assess the comparative advantage of MÜSİAD member firms, particularly in volatile periods (see Online Appendix Table OA.36). Before introducing the interaction between MÜSİAD membership and volatility, I continue to find a negative effect of volatility on firm growth but no comparative advantage for MÜSİAD firms. (If anything, they perform slightly

---

[13] The interaction model takes the form $Sales_{it} = \beta_0 + \beta_1 Volatility_t + \beta_2 Integration_i + \beta_3 Volatility_t \times Integration_i + X_{it} + \mu_i + \epsilon_i$, where $Sales_{it}$ is the natural logarithm of net sales of firm i in year t, $Volatility_t$ is the standard deviation of monthly inflation in year t, $Integration_i$ is a binary indicator of whether firm i is vertically integrated, $Volatility_t \times Integration_i$ is the interaction between the two, X_i is a set of firm-level characteristics, μ_p is a fixed-effect term for each province, and ϵ_i is the error term.

worse off than similar non-members when it comes to profits.) Only when I introduce the interaction term, do I find a significant difference: while volatility continues to depress sales and growth, this effect is significantly ameliorated for MÜSİAD members. Meanwhile, the direct effect of MÜSİAD membership is now significantly *negative* in most models, indicating that outside of its ability to counteract the negative impact of volatility, MÜSİAD does little to help its member firms grow.

An illustration of this pattern is presented as Figure 8.3. The darker bars define the marginal effect of MÜSİAD membership, vertical integration, and their interaction on net sales. While membership and volatility both exert a direct negative effect on sales, these are ameliorated when they interact, for member firms under volatile periods. Indeed, the magnitude of this interaction is larger than that between integration and volatility, meaning that MÜSİAD membership may go even further to protect firms from volatility than vertical integration does. I take this as evidence that MÜSİAD members successfully mimic the benefits of vertical integration, via quasi-integration. And since I identify this effect among the firms appearing on the ISO lists – the largest of MÜSİAD's members, and those for whom quasi-integration may be least valuable – it suggests that the benefits of these relationships are likely even stronger for the average member firm.

I can test the comparability of quasi- and vertical integration in a slightly different way, comparing the benefits of vertical integration for MÜSİAD members and non-members, using another interaction model.[14] The full results of the model are available in Online Appendix Table OA.37, and its main coefficients are displayed in Figure 8.3 in lighter gray. As expected, I find that both MÜSİAD membership and vertical integration bolster firm sales and profits, but that the positive effect of integration is reversed for MÜSİAD firms that are integrated. Similarly, the positive effect of MÜSİAD membership is negated for those members who are integrated. I interpret this as evidence of a substitution effect between integration and MÜSİAD membership, as I had hypothesized.

8.2.3 Alternative Interpretations of MÜSİAD's Advantage

The empirical results, thus far, point to an advantage for MÜSİAD members during volatile periods, but not necessarily at other times. An illustration of the cross-temporal pattern is displayed in Figure 8.4. Here, I take the results of the linear interaction model and predict the marginal effect of MÜSİAD membership in each year, based on its level of macroeconomic volatility. This helps identify the periods during which MÜSİAD members were comparatively

---

[14] This model takes the form $Sales_{it} = \beta_0 + \beta_1 MÜSİAD_{it} + \beta_2 Integration_i + \beta_3 MÜSİAD_{it} \times Integration_i + X_{it} + \mu_i + \epsilon_i$, where $Sales_{it}$ is the natural logarithm of net sales of firm i in year t, $MÜSİAD_{it}$ a binary indicator of firm i's membership status in year t, $Integration_i$ is a binary indicator of whether firm i is vertically integrated, $MÜSİAD_{it} \times Integration_i$ is the interaction between the two.

8.2 Estimating MÜSİAD's Comparative Advantage

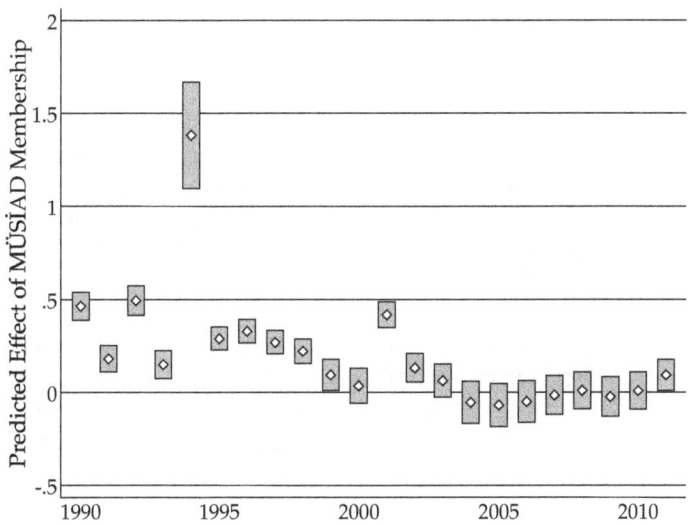

FIGURE 8.4 Effect of MÜSİAD Membership, by Level of Volatility
Notes: Predicted marginal effect of MÜSİAD membership on firm sales across levels of macroeconomic volatility (1990–2011).

advantaged: in the early to mid-1990s, and again in 2001. At other times, the benefits of membership were marginal, at best.

Of course, many factors correlate with macroeconomic volatility that could also explain variation in the MÜSİAD advantage. For example, credit is known to covary with volatility (Aghion et al. 2010a; Denizer and Iyigun 2002), and scholars have posited that MÜSİAD firms thrive when conventional credit markets are weakened, when they can rely on privileged access to Islamic-based microcredit (Demir, Acar, and Toprak 2004; Hosgör 2011; Özcan and Çokgezen 2006). Indeed, across years, I find that volatility and conventional business loans from TBB banks are negatively correlated, and significantly so.

To assess whether it is actually fluctuations in credit markets that explain the comparative advantage of MÜSİAD firms, I estimate yet another interaction model, this time gauging how the benefits of membership are impacted by variation in the availability of conventional loans. Before introducing the interaction term, I find that more business loans actually *suppress* the growth of ISO firms, measured in terms of net sales (see Online Appendix Table OA.38). This could be because more loans are issued during leaner periods, a possibility belied by the negative correlation between volatility and loans, or because the loans are given disproportionately to smaller firms, which then outpace the larger firms that appear on the annual ISO lists. Either way, it implies that all of the firms – MÜSİAD members and non-members, on average – are worse off when conventional credit is freely available.

With the inclusion of the interaction term, I see that MÜSİAD members are particularly disadvantaged by healthy credit markets. Indeed, when business loans are sufficiently large, the advantage of membership is entirely negated.

This pattern would seem to support the theory that MÜSİAD's advantage stems from its alternative source of credit. But recall that the conventional credit market is weaker in years with more volatility, an inter-temporal correlation that could produce a spurious result. For this reason, it is important to include volatility as an additional control, as well as a second interaction term between it and MÜSİAD membership. When I do this, I find that *both* effects are at work to explain the MÜSİAD advantage: member firms continue to do comparatively better during periods of volatility, while also doing comparatively worse than non-members when business loans are more freely available.

Another major existing theory for the MÜSİAD advantage is the association's close relationship with Islamic parties, particularly the AKP, which has singularly controlled the central government since 2002. Preferential access to state contracts and an inside track to regulators could plausibly privilege member firms relative to non-members. While the cross-temporal trend predicted above (Figure 8.4) seems to contradict this hypothesis, it is worth testing directly. I can assess "political connections" to Islamic parties in a number of different ways: comparing pre-AKP years to those after 2002 or, alternatively, focusing on local politics and leveraging variation in the home province of each firm.

Ultimately, no matter how I measure the political advantage, I find no evidence that it helps explain the success of MÜSİAD member firms (see Online Appendix Table OA.39). Using the vote share of Islamic parties in the most-recent provincial council election, I find that MÜSİAD members located in provinces that supported the RP, FP, and AKP tend to grow at slower rates than members in provinces where Islamic parties are less popular. Similarly, when restricting the analysis to provinces in which Islamic parties were the single largest vote-getter, I also find a disadvantage to MÜSİAD membership.[15] I also see that MÜSİAD members were worse off after 2002, under AKP rule, while being slightly better off in the years before.

Having evaluated two alternative theories of MÜSİAD's success, it is also worth considering plausible challenges to the causal claims I am making based on the evidence I have presented. If, for example, MÜSİAD is selecting its members based on their pre-existing ability to thrive under conditions of volatility, I would find the patterns I have uncovered here, but not because MÜSİAD membership, itself, helps to ameliorate the costs of volatility. Leveraging cross-temporal variation in MÜSİAD membership, I can test for this possibility, comparing current members to future ones. If members are indeed being selected based on their capacity to withstand macroeconomic volatility, then they should enjoy this comparative advantage even before they formally join the association.

---

[15] These patterns run counter to those identified by Meyersson (2011) in a similar, though smaller, set of ISO lists. While my indicator of MÜSİAD membership, based on the lists I acquired, is time-varying, Meyersson's is cross-sectional. This difference, I fear, may be biasing the results of his model.

Comparing current members and future members to non-members (the baseline), I assess how each is able to counteract the effects of volatility (see Online Appendix Table OA.40). As before, I find a negative direct effect of volatility on net sales, but one that is effectively ameliorated by current MÜSİAD members. For future members, however, a different pattern emerges: like other non-members, they suffer from volatility. Far from being handpicked to join MÜSİAD based on their ability to withstand volatile conditions, it seems more likely that these firms self-select into the association because its members are able to thrive under volatility.

Finally, I consider yet another rival interpretation of my main result: if the benefits of MÜSİAD membership are indeed based on better access to credit or to regulators, that is, anything that is distributed to members from the association itself, then those benefits should disappear whenever firms leave the organization. Alternatively, if the benefits of membership are based on a shared group identity and group-based trust, it is plausible that these should extend past firms' exit from MÜSİAD, so long as they continue to identify themselves as part of the community.

To assess this possibility, I again leverage cross-temporal variation in MÜSİAD membership, this time comparing non-members to current members and to *former* ones. The results of this analysis are also available in Online Appendix Table OA.40. They reveal that the benefits of membership (via volatility) extend to ex-members as well. Although the direct effect of former MÜSİAD membership on net sales is significant and negative – larger than the direct effect of current membership – its interaction with volatility remains significant and positive. In other words, while there are some real costs associated with leaving MÜSİAD, a key benefit is maintained. This could imply that the quasi-integrative relationships between current and former members might continue even after the latter have officially left the organization.

8.3 CONCLUSION

In this chapter, I have presented an amendment to existing scholarship on identity-based economic exchange. Rather than emphasizing how identity groups build reputation mechanisms to inform trust and encourage trade among members, I have argued that group-based trust can play a similar role. In the specific case of Turkey's MÜSİAD, an Islamic-based business association, I suggested that the group is too large, too diverse, and its membership too inconsistent to support a traditional reputation mechanism. But feelings of group-based trust, sustained through organized events that deepen members' sense of solidarity, are able to function similarly. Specifically, they help to establish the first link in a particularized trust chain that supports long-term, flexible business agreements between independent business owners. I argued that these quasi-integrative relationships are especially valuable under conditions of macroeconomic volatility because they mimic the benefits of vertical integration, absorbing price shocks. This is especially true for SMEs, who lack the resources to buy out their suppliers.

In my empirical analysis, using panel data at the firm level, I showed how the benefits MÜSİAD membership for firm growth indeed parallel those of vertical integration, ameliorating the negative effects of macroeconomic volatility to support both sales and profits. I interpreted this as evidence of MÜSİAD's trust-based advantage and showed how member firms' comparative advantage is largest under the most volatile economic conditions. Ironically, that means that MÜSİAD firms have been worse off since the Islamic-based AKP came to power and stabilized the Turkish economy.

Of course, these patterns reflect the growth of Turkey's larger firms, and it is not yet clear whether they would hold out-of-sample, especially among the SMEs that make up the majority of MÜSİAD's membership. Across the full sample of ISO firms, there are some indications that smaller firms have performed better than larger ones under AKP rule, and yet the benefits of MÜSİAD membership and quasi-integration have also declined over the same period. As such, it is difficult to form a clear expectation of what might be true for MÜSİAD's smaller members.

Still, the success of MÜSİAD member firms under conditions of economic uncertainty may bode well for other Islamic-based economic associations operating in volatile markets across the Muslim world. Consider the Islamic Economic Society (Masyarakat Ekonomi Syariah, MES) in Indonesia, the Moroccan Association for Islamic Economics (ASMECI), or the Muslim Corpers Association of Nigeria (MCAN), all attempting to support the development of the private sector in their respective countries, with specific reference to Islam. Each has to contend with considerable economic uncertainty in the form of inflation, capital flows, and inconsistent growth in national income. The results presented here would suggest that members of these associations would be able to establish quasi-integrative relationships among them that would help them to withstand at least some of the costs associated with economic volatility.

As in every case in which the benefits of Islam are primarily trust based, the benefits of quasi-integration within these Islamic-based business associations should be particularly significant where generalized trust expectations are low, as they are in Nigeria and, to some extent, in Morocco. Here, the ability of firms to establish long-term, flexible partnerships is likely to be severely limited without an alternative source of trust. This should serve to heighten the comparative advantage of MCAN members, as well as ASMECI's, relative to their secular competitors.

Beyond MÜSİAD, within the Turkish case, my trust-based theory of Islamic-based economics can be extended to explain the Islamic advantage in other organizations, from the Islamic-oriented İGİAD – the Turkish Entrepreneurship and Business Ethics Association (Türkiye İktisadi Girişim ve İş Ahlakıı Derneği) – to Hak-İş the Islamic-based confederation of trade unions. And even beyond formal organizations, the theory implies an advantage of Islamic-based economics whenever generalized trust is low and uncertainty is high. As described earlier, a wide number of economic activities are trust dependent in that they entail both interdependence and uncertainty. This includes

8.3 Conclusion

investment in large-scale (latent) financial institutions, from micro-credit agencies and savings clubs, to formal banks. Moreover, the need for trust to support these different types of activity is likely to arise as Muslim economies continue to modernize. As Pierre Bourdieu describes in the case of the Kabyle of Algeria, the introduction of capitalist market conditions can undermine traditional trust networks, while forcing individual traders to start engaging in one-shot transactions with strangers:

> In the age of credit... wretched indeed are those who can only appeal to the trust in which their parents were held. All that counts now is the goods you have immediately on hand. Everyone wants to be a market man. Everyone thinks he has a right to trust, so that there's no trust anywhere now (2013, p. 249).

In this vacuum, as suggested by Yavuz, "religious networks [may be] the only actors to provide much needed trust and information for the circulation of goods and ideas" (2009, p. 276).

PART III

CONCLUSION

9

Conclusion

In the preceding pages, I sought to explain the comparative advantage of political and economic groups that make explicit reference to Islam, relative to their secular counterparts. More specifically, I focused on the added value of Islamic-based appeals in encouraging participation and sustaining cooperation among average citizens. In contrast to existing theories of the Islamic advantage, emphasizing the importance of grievances, faith, and information, I argued that the success of Islamic-based political and economic groups in mobilizing supporters is largely about trust.

More specifically, Islamic references prime feelings of trust among those with a salient Islamic identity. I have conceptualized Islamic identity as something that may be related to one's personal faith, but something that remains nevertheless distinct, defined by an attachment to one's religious community. Like other group identities, Islamic identity generates reciprocal expectations of trust among group members whenever it is mutually recognized and salient, and this trust supports cooperation and coordination. I have suggested that the added value of group-based trust is in its ability to substitute for more generalized trust expectations – of most people – which are absent in many Muslim countries, including in Turkey. In this distrusting environment, without an alternative broad-based form of trust, political and economic groups struggle to support large-scale mobilization and cooperation. Meanwhile Islamic-based groups, with the feelings of group-based trust they inspire, thrive, to their comparative advantage.

Over the course of the book, I have defined a number of political and economic activities that are fundamentally trust-based and in which Islamic groups enjoy a particular advantage. Participation in everyday politics in the Muslim world depends on trust, much as it does in Western democratic contexts. But trust is also critical for strategic voting and in the formation of long-term economic partnerships. In all cases, I defined the trust problem in terms of interdependence and uncertainty in individual decision-making. And in each, I demonstrated how group-based trust underlies the success of Islamic-based groups relative to similar, but secular, ones. In testing my trust-based theory, I have leveraged variation across individual survey respondents, in a panel of district-level election results, and in the activities of Turkey's largest firms. While many of these tests focused on the Turkish case, I assessed their external validity whenever possible. In this way, what began as my explanation for a Turkish phenomenon has developed into a theory of Islamic-based politics and economics across the Muslim world.

While testing the main hypotheses of my trust-based theory, I defined a number of additional, often counterintuitive implications. I suggested that, because state repression of political activity exacerbates the trust problem, it can strengthen the Islamic mobilization advantage, even when it targets Islamic political groups. And the trust-based coordination advantage among religious voters helps to make Islamic parties an attractive target for strategic support from conservative secular voters, increasing their national support base. Finally, Islamic-oriented businesses are not always better off under Islamic party rule, especially when the party ushers in a period of economic stability. This is because stability undermines the comparative advantage of these businesses under volatility.

Alongside these results, my theory has challenged some existing assumptions about the relationship between Islam, on the one hand, and politics and economics, on the other, within the Muslim world. For example, scholars and pundits alike have worried that the popularity of Islamic parties threatens to undermine prospects for democracy in the region. Similarly, the rise of Islamic-based economic exchange is often assumed to undermine modernization and development. But I have demonstrated how appeals to Islam bolster two key components of a well-functioning democracy – political participation and vote coordination. At the same time, I have found that Islamic references support economic exchange and growth in the private sector. Indeed, by offering an alternative source of trust in an otherwise low-trust environment, Islamic-based groups can bolster both democracy and development, which tend to be stunted by high levels of distrust.

That Islam has the potential to bolster democracy and development does not imply that Islamic-based movements are necessarily good for political and economic development. In highlighting how Islamic-based groups, like the AKP and MÜSİAD, have been pro-democratic or pro-growth in certain contexts, I do not mean to diminish the many ways in which some have curtailed the spread of both democracy and development, including President Erdoğan's recent autocratic turn. Indeed, it could be argued that Erdoğan has leveraged his supporters' coordination at the polls and in the streets to push through constitutional reforms, tightening his grip on power. In this way, the Islamic advantage, while helping make Turkish elections more representative, has been used by the AKP leadership to limit the overall quality of Turkey's democracy.

Conclusion

INTERNAL AND EXTERNAL VALIDITY

Throughout this book, I have brought a number of data sources to bear on the question of political and economic mobilization, whether Islamic-based or otherwise. I have mixed quantitative datasets with observations from long periods of fieldwork in Turkey and anecdotal evidence from secondary sources. Using these, I have conducted tests of my hypotheses, leveraging variation across different dimensions and addressing additional empirical implications. And yet, I have been unable to conduct a perfect test, one which would assess the theory directly, identifying the causal effects of trust and identity on politics and economics. It might be possible to design such a test in a lab, creating fictitious groups, priming identity and trust, and noting their effects on decision-making in stylized interactions. But such an experiment is beyond the scope of this book, which has focused on political and economic realities in the Muslim world, built around a real-world Islamic identity.

Without a definitive test, I am unable to fully address concerns about reverse causality, spuriousness, and omitted variable bias, although I have assessed these whenever possible using my observational data. Where available, I have also cited evidence presented by other scholars, including their experimental results. While used to support some of my theoretical assumptions, these other works have helped establish the generalizability of my theory and its broader empirical implications. And yet, some questions undoubtedly remain. For example, while I have revealed the dimensionality of Islam, operating as both a faith and an identity, it is not yet clear whether other religions operate similarly. Understanding which religions can function as group identities should help to define the scope conditions of my theory: whether it applies to religion, in general, Islam, specifically, or something in between.

Based on a distinction introduced in Chapter 5, egalitarian or congregational religions should be more likely to function as a group identity. This is because hierarchical religions create vertical ties between clergy and adherents, limiting horizontal bonds between congregants. This implies that Catholicism, the exemplar hierarchical religion, and Eastern Orthodox denominations should struggle to function as group identities, meaning that some key religious minorities in the Muslim world would not enjoy a trust-based mobilization advantage.[1] Meanwhile, Judaism, Protestantism, Buddhism, and Hinduism, as more egalitarian faiths, should be more likely to have the dimensionality of Islam.

I am able to explore the dimensionality of other religions in two ways. I begin by repeating the principal component factor analysis from Chapter 5, using the same five indicators of religion for each religious group represented in the cross-national survey dataset: Muslims, but also Jews, Catholics, the Eastern Orthodox, other Christians, Buddhists, Hindus, Pagans/Animists,

---

[1] For example, the Coptic Church in Egypt mimics the vertical structure of Eastern Orthodoxy, and the Maronite Church in Lebanon takes after Eastern Catholicism.

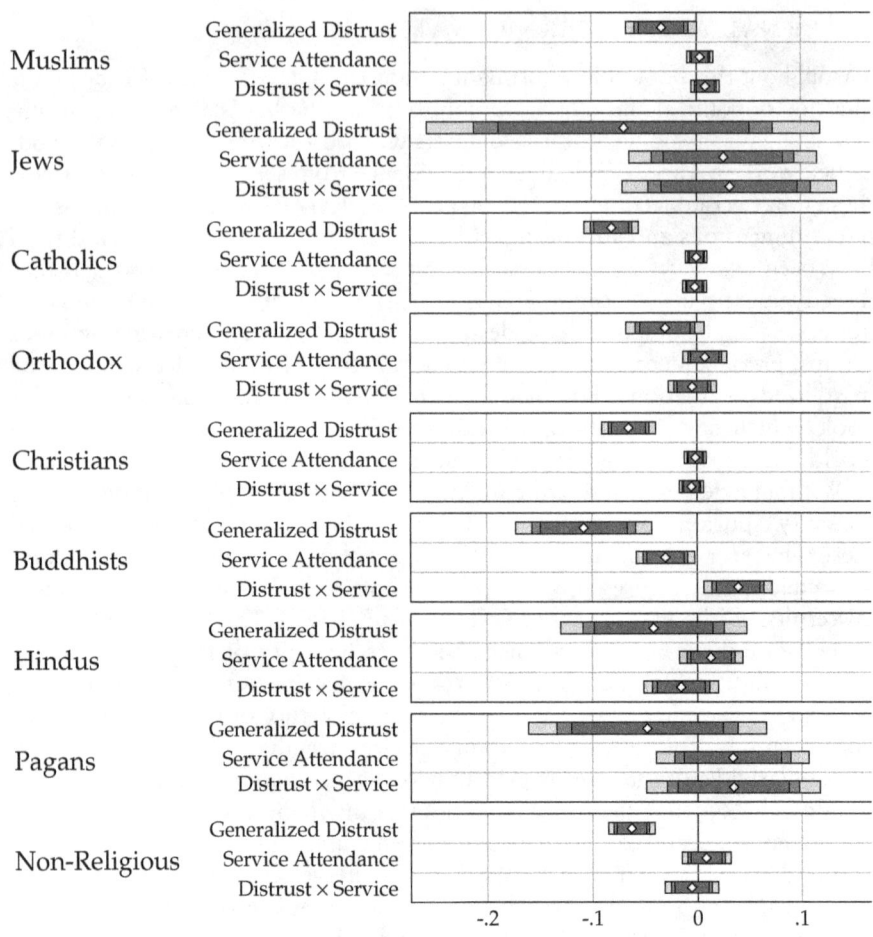

Marginal Effect on Political Participation

FIGURE 9.1 The Substitution Effect across Religious Denominations
Notes: Estimated marginal effect of generalized distrust, religious service attendance, and their interaction on a composite index of political participation. All models include age, gender, education, and country fixed effects.

and the non-religious.[2] Remarkably, the multi-dimensionality of religion that I found among Muslims turns out to be relatively rare, shared only by Jews, and

---

[2] While the original analysis focused on self-identified Muslims living in Muslim countries, these models ignore factors at the country level and rely on how individual respondents identify themselves. Across the 345,974 respondents for whom I have all five indicators, the largest share (32.2%) self-identify as Catholic, while 18.3 percent identify as Christian and 14.3 as Orthodox. A similar share (14.9%) identify as Muslim, while 12.3 percent define themselves as having no religion. The rest of the groups are relatively small: 2.8 percent Hindu; 2.4 percent Buddhist; 0.5 percent Pagan or Animist; and 0.3 percent Jewish. The Sikh share (less than 0.1 percent, just 126 respondents) was simply too small to include in the analysis.

Hindus, relatively egalitarian faiths, as well to the Eastern Orthodox, a more hierarchical one.[3]

In my conceptualization of religious identity, it is able to produce group-based trust to effectively substitute for generalized trust, supporting collective action even among those who distrust most people. In Chapter 6, without a direct measure of group identity, I relied on religious group activities as a proxy, estimating how religious service attendance interacted with distrust to lessen the latter's effect on political participation. I am able to estimate the same models for individuals ascribing to each of the major religions (see Figure 9.1, with full results available in Online Appendix Table OA.41). As earlier, I find that religious group activities among Muslims effectively substitute for generalized trust, to support participation; but, again, this turns out to be a relatively rare phenomenon. Nearly all of the groups face a significant trust problem when it comes to political activity, but religious service attendance only ameliorates this problem for Buddhists and, in some respects, Jews, although the small number of Jewish respondents means that none of the effects are statistically significant.

Taken together, these two sets of results raise questions about the generalizability of religious group identity, as a concept. In addition to Islam, possibly only Judaism, Buddhism, and Hinduism function as both a faith and an identity, with group-based trust that can address different trust problems. Further work will be required to confirm this. Different data may yet reveal that other faiths function as religious identities. At the very least, additional tests should try to confirm (and expand upon) my preliminary results among Jewish respondents, since they were the group most similar to Muslims across the two tests.

In addition to assessing the generalizability of religious group identity, as a concept, I am interested in examining the external validity of a key trust problem I identified. In Chapter 7, I found that interpersonal distrust undermines successful coordination among Turkish voters, as evidenced in higher levels of wasted votes and vote volatility in electoral districts where trust is low. Does generalized distrust hinder coordination among voters elsewhere? Because panel measures of trust are hard to come by, it is difficult to repeat the subnational analysis from Turkey in another country; but I am able to use survey-based measures to conduct a cross-national comparison. When comparing levels of coordination failure across countries, wasted votes may not be the ideal measure because of differences in electoral institutions. But cross-sectional models of vote volatility are relatively common (Birnir 2007; Roberts and Wibbels 1999). And so I turn to assessing how generalized distrust

---

[3] For Jews, Hindus, and the Eastern Orthodox, as with Muslims, I find that all five indicators load positively onto the first "personal religiosity" factor, while only religious service attendance and associational membership load onto the second "religious identity" one. When I distinguish between mainstream Protestants and a catch-all "other Christians" category, I find that this second group (a mere 4,800 respondents) also appears to have a religious identity, distinct from its personal faith.

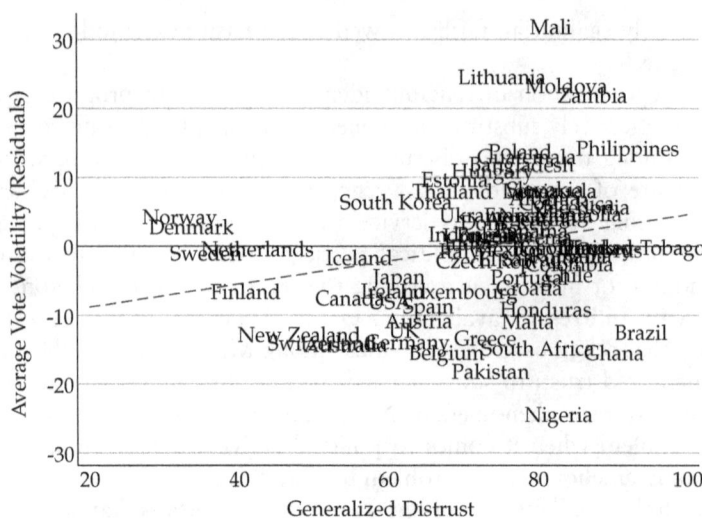

FIGURE 9.2 Generalized Distrust and Vote Volatility, across Countries

Notes: Average vote volatility in democratic elections (1975–2010) across levels of generalized distrust, using residuals from a model of volatility with growth in GDP per capita, inflation, ethno-linguistic diversity, party system fractionalization, political distrust, and region fixed effects.

impacts levels of vote volatility, leveraging variation across all countries that have conducted at least two democratic elections between 1975 and 2010.[4] In all but three cases, volatility is based on the results of national legislative elections.[5] To trace the performance of parties from year to year, I account for party mergers and splits, estimating a lower bound on volatility.[6] After calculating volatility in each democratic election year, I average these to create a single observation for each case.

The bivariate correlation between average volatility and generalized distrust is statistically significant, but because there are many factors that affect volatility and may also impact generalized trust – from economic development, to ethnic diversity and political distrust – I take the analysis a step further, plotting the residuals from a model of volatility, across estimates of distrust (Figure 9.2). In this analysis, I control for the average growth in GDP per capita and inflation across democratic years, the level of ethno-linguistic diversity and the

---

[4] I identified every country-election-year between 1975 and 2010 that was democratic, with a Polity score of at least six. For each, I collected electoral results, using a variety of (mostly internet) sources, including websites of local Electoral Commissions, the International Foundation for Electoral Systems' Election Guide, and Psephos.

[5] In the United States, presidential election results are a better indicator of national-level vote instability; and in Mali and Kenya, the quality of data was far superior for presidential election results.

[6] A newly merged party's vote share is compared to the vote share of the largest member party in the previous election; and a recently split party is compared to the largest offshoot party in the next election. Alliances are treated similarly.

Conclusion

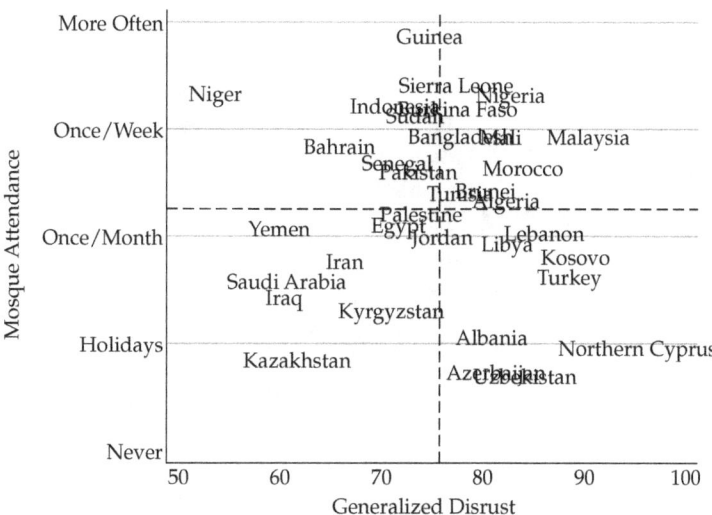

FIGURE 9.3 Generalized Distrust and Islamic Group Identity, across the Muslim World
Notes: Generalized distrust and mosque attendance across Muslim countries. Dashed lines indicate averages in the Muslim world.

average party system fractionalization, as well as political distrust.[7] Here, and in regression analysis (Online Appendix Table OA.42) I continue to find a significant effect of distrust on volatility, wherein more of the former increases the latter. Remarkably, it far outweighs the effect of either economics or party system fractionalization on volatility. I take this as preliminary support for my theory's generalizability, although additional analysis at the subnational level, beyond the Turkish case, would be valuable.

UNDERSTANDING THE SOURCE OF THE TRUST PROBLEM

In arguing that the Islamic advantage rests heavily on trust, I have implied that the success of Islamic-based politics and economics parallels the size of the generalized trust problem. Islamic groups should be more popular in places where people tend to distrust "most others" and under conditions that exacerbate either interdependence or uncertainty. The Islamic advantage may also reflect the salience of Islamic group identity in a given time and place, although, as I demonstrated in Chapter 7, one does not always follow from the other.

Figure 9.3 identifies the countries where Islamic-based political and economic groups stand the best chances of succeeding. While most Muslim countries are above the global average in generalized distrust (just under

---

[7] Annual growth and inflation rates are taken from the World Bank, while ethnic diversity is from Alesina et al. (2003). Party system fractionalization from Beck et al. (2001), is averaged across democratic years. Political distrust is the first principal component factor of distrust of government, parliament, political parties, and the justice system, averaged across all surveys.

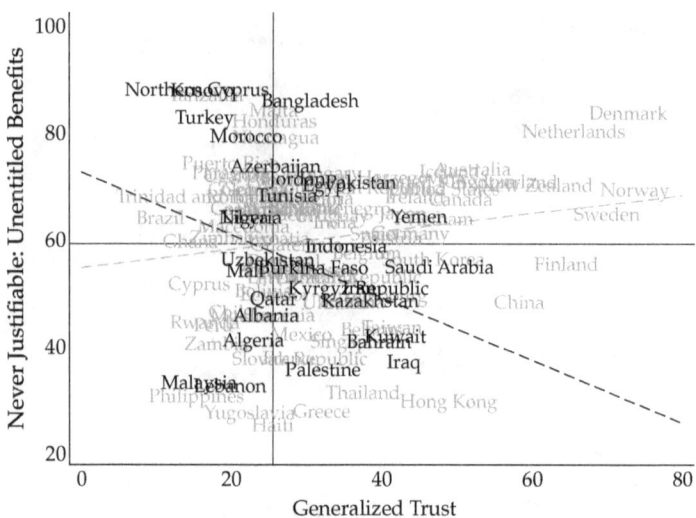

FIGURE 9.4 Trust and Honesty, across Countries
Notes: Generalized trust and honesty, measured as share of respondents who say that receiving unentitled government benefits is "never justifiable." Muslim countries indicated in black and the bivariate relationship in these countries indicated by the dashed black line.

75 percent), I have identified which have above-average distrust within the Muslim world, to the right of the dashed vertical line. When these countries are arranged according to the salience of Islamic identity among Muslims living there, in terms of the frequency of mosque attendance, those in the upper right-hand corner stand out as having the highest potential for Islamic-based activity. Some of these are in sub-Saharan Africa, a region which has not seen the universal popularity of Islamic-based political movements (Bleck and Patel 2011); but others are in South and Southeast Asia and in the Middle East. Not all currently have active Islamic-based groups, but many do.

Anticipating where Islamic organizations and activities might succeed, based on underlying levels of distrust, also raises important questions about the trust problem itself. While I find that generalized trust tends to be lower in Muslim countries, I have not yet offered an explanation for this difference. Indeed, in Chapter 4, I find that no existing cross-national trust-covariates could account for the trust deficit in the Muslim world. But analysis of migrants from the region also indicates that distrust is not static and can be updated. As such, if we can identify the source(s) of the Muslim world's trust deficit, we may be able to help improve it.

As a first step, I suggest returning to a puzzle I uncovered earlier: those who live in Muslim countries have significantly lower levels of generalized trust, but they are no less trustworthy. In fact, they are significantly more honest. It is possible that the existing literature is wrong about the association between aggregate trust and trustworthiness, but when I look at the cross-sectional correlation between the two (Figure 9.4), I find that there is a positive association

Conclusion

in non-Muslim countries ($N=86$, $r=0.170$). It is only among the Muslim countries that the relationship is reversed, with a statistically significant negative correlation ($r=-0.331$, $N=30$).[8]

To me, this systematic mismatch between trust (low) and honesty (high) speaks to an information problem: most people in the Muslim world should be trusted, but their compatriots do not know it. If information is the culprit, how might generalized trust expectations be better informed?[9] The majority of the existing literature expects trust to be stable, based on historical factors such as religion, language, or climate (Bergh and Bjørnskov 2011; Durante 2009; La Porta et al. 1997). But individuals should be able to roughly estimate the number of trustworthy types in their community in real time, especially if honest people can be clearly distinguished from those who should not be trusted. Such a separating equilibrium is possible given the heterogeneity of preferences between trustworthy and untrustworthy types, especially when the differences between them can be exaggerated through incentive structures that are consistently applied across individuals and over time. This would imply a role for institutions, particularly formal ones, established and maintained by an authority, like the state.[10]

A variety of institutions could plausibly play this informative role, helping distinguish between honest and dishonest types, on a scale large enough for individuals to gauge the relative share of each and determine whether "most" are trustworthy. But in this preliminary investigation, I borrow from the work of George Akerlof (1970) in arguing that the regulation of entry can thusly inform trust. Akerlof theorized that high quality (trustworthy) producers would be willing to invest some resources to be officially labeled as such, as long as low-quality (untrustworthy) types would not enjoy the same privilege. If entry was appropriately regulated, only they would go through the process of joining the formal economy, leaving the others to operate in the informal ("shadow") one.[11] For the regulation of entry to support a separating

---

[8] In this comparison, I rely on the honesty question with the broadest coverage (i.e., the justifiability of receiving government benefits to which one is not legally entitled). The results are broadly similar when using the principal component factor of all three justifiability questions, although the sample is considerably smaller.

[9] There might appear to be a contradiction between my focus on information and the fact that generalized trust is non-particularized. But I see no such contradiction: just because trust expectations are not based on first hand experience with a given individual does not mean that they cannot be more or less right, based on whether one has a better or worse sense of what to expect from the average person or "most people."

[10] North defines institutions as "humanly devised constraints that structure political, economic and social interactions" (1991, p. 97). In focusing on how institutions help inform generalized trust, I stand apart from existing theories of institutions and trust. While some of these argue that institutions boost trust directly (Aghion et al. 2010b), others suggest that interventions crowd trust out (Frey 1994). But I am suggesting not that institutions improve or undermine trust, rather that they help to make it a more accurate reflection of whether most people can, in fact, be trusted.

[11] In this model, the regulation of entry has a preventative role, keeping dishonest types from entering the formal economy; but it also has the ability to inform: if it works as intended, the

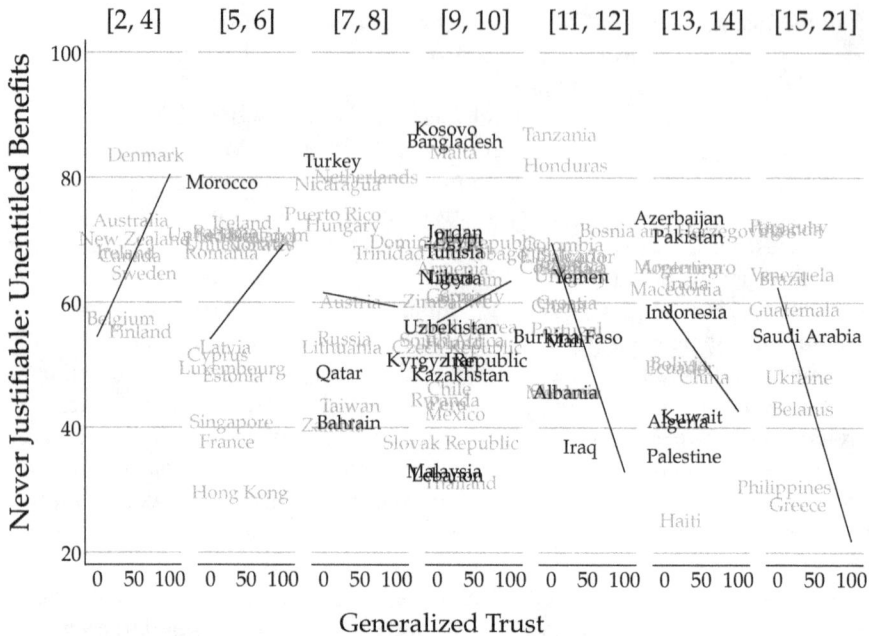

FIGURE 9.5 Trust and Honesty, across Levels of Regulation
Notes: Generalized trust and honesty, across the number of procedures required to register a new business, averaged across all survey years.

equilibrium, the procedure for entering the formal economy cannot be so burdensome as to discourage honest types from going through it; at the same time, the barriers to entry must be high enough to keep the untrustworthy types out. The expectation, therefore, is that the relationship between trust and aggregate honesty should follow an inverted U-shaped pattern based on the number of entry procedures: no relationship between the two at too-low and too-high levels of regulation, but a positive correlation when regulation is moderate.

To test for this, I use information about the regulation of entry from the World Bank's Doing Business Project. Using the average number of entry procedures across all survey years, I divide the 113 countries in my sample into seven, roughly even groups.[12] In each, I assess the correlation between trust and honesty (Figure 9.5). As expected, I find that the relationship between trust and honesty varies considerably across groups. Without any unregulated

---

distinction between the formal and informal economy should map perfectly on to the difference between honest and dishonest types.

[12] Ten countries averaged between two and four entry procedures, twenty-four with five or six procedures, thirty-one with seven or eight, fifty with nine or ten, thirty-six with eleven or twelve, twenty-five with thirteen or fourteen, and the remaining fourteen with between fifteen and twenty-one procedures.

countries, the first part of the inverted-U is not visible in my sample, but the second bend is clear: in countries with fewer regulations, there tends to be a positive correlation between trust and honesty; but in heavily regulated countries, the relationship breaks down, even becoming negative. Moreover, Muslim countries – indicated in black – tend to cluster towards the more-regulated side, with many more entry procedures than needed to inform generalized trust expectations.

While affected by the scope of institutions, the relationship between trust and honesty should also depend on how these institutions are perceived. If, for example, individuals see the state as corrupt, they might expect regulators would accept bribes and let untrustworthy types enter the formal economy. This would undermine the separating equilibrium and dilute its ability to inform trust, even if the number of regulations is moderate. And indeed I find that the relationship between trust and honesty hinges on both the extent of regulations and their perceived quality: the positive correlation between trust and honesty is restricted to well-regulated countries (below the global mean) where trust in government is above average. Overall, political distrust seems to be a deciding factor, reversing the relationship between trust and honesty in well regulated and over-regulated countries, alike.[13]

For their part, Muslim states tend to over-regulate, but are trusted, so regulation alone would seem to be the main obstacle to better-informed trust expectations. Were states such as Azerbaijan and Pakistan to improve their regulatory practices – reducing the number of entry procedures and supporting a separating equilibrium – generalized trust expectations might improve, to better reflect the healthy levels of honesty there. Meanwhile, governments in Turkey, Morocco, Tunisia, and Nigeria, which regulate effectively but which are distrusted, will have to work to earn the confidence of their citizens in order for trust expectations to be appropriately updated.

EXPLAINING THE END OF THE ISLAMIC ADVANTAGE

If generalized trust expectations were to improve in these Muslim countries, the advantage of Islamic-based groups should largely disappear. But even if the trust deficit persists, there are plenty of reasons, consistent with my trust-based theory, to explain the collapse of Islamic politics and economics. To begin with, Islamic groups could face a formidable challenge from other identity-based groups. Recall that my theory applies to any group identity – all should be able to leverage feelings of group-based trust. And there is nothing to stop another group from mobilizing in this low-trust environment. Rival movements could be based on a shared ethnicity, among the Kurds of Turkey, Iraq, Iran, or Syria, the Berbers of Algeria or Morocco, or within an ethnic supra-majority.

[13] Among well-regulated countries with ample political trust, the correlation between trust and honesty is 0.426, but in similarly regulated countries without trust, the correlation drops to −0.281, stronger even than the correlation in over-regulated countries that are trusted (−0.027) or distrusted (−0.175).

Alternatively, the rival identity could be pan-ethnic, similar to Pan-Arabism under Nasser or Pan-Turkism as promoted by Ziya Gökalp. Or staying within the realm of religion, Islamic groups could face a challenge from other religious identities, including from within their own community, whether Sunni, Shi'a, Alevi, etc.

Aside from rival identity-based groups, the largest obstacle to the continued success of Islamic-based movements in the Muslim World may well be their internal cohesion. Although feelings of trust are a necessary condition for collective mobilization, they are hardly sufficient. For members of a religious community to successfully collaborate and cooperate, they must believe that they are working towards a shared goal, and this requires them to have reasonably similar preferences over outcomes. When there are competing visions about what it means to be Muslim in a given society, religious communities can easily fracture, and the splinter movements that emerge will each be able to leverage the same feelings of group-based trust. In this way, competing Islamic-based movements can become arch rivals: competing for the support of the same constituency, enjoying the same trust-based advantage. In Turkey, while the AKP has been successful at absorbing other Islamic parties, others may yet emerge to divide and, eventually, conquer the party.

NEXT STEPS

Throughout this book, I have tried to showcase the importance of the comparative method: the process of defining falsifiable hypotheses, based on a well-specified theory, and then leveraging variation in outcomes to effectively test them. I have used this method to question and then upend some widely held assumptions about Islam and the practice of Islamic politics and economics. More specifically, I have tested existing explanations for the Islamic advantage and challenged the view that the success of these groups is based on grievances, faith, or information. In place of these theories, I have offered my own, focused on the importance of generalized and group-based trust.

Given my focus on the advantage of Islamic appeals for mobilizing individuals into latent activities, there are a number of important questions, beyond the scope of this book, that have not been addressed. First and foremost, there is the important question of timing: Why did Islamic-based groups rise to prominence towards the end of the twentieth century, growing in popularity in the early part of the twenty-first? While I offered a partial answer in the specific case of Turkey's AKP, I have not sought to explain why the Islamic Revolution took place in Iran in 1979, or why Ennahda rose to victory in Tunisia after Arab Spring of 2011.

Similar to the question of timing, I have not been able to explain why Islam, in particular, is the group identity at the heart of so many political and economic movements today. Indeed, my trust-based theory applies to any group identity, and there are countless rivals poised to challenge the dominance of Islamic groups, going forward. Looking back at the histories of many of Muslim countries, one sees that Islam is hardly the first group identity used to

Conclusion

mobilize individuals towards political or economic ends. In the Middle East in particular, Islamic politics followed class-based movements, which, themselves, followed nationalist ones. The question of why Islam (and not ethnicity, regionalism, gender) was next in line has been posed by other scholars, but a definitive answer has yet to be offered.

While I have focused in on the Turkish case and then examined broad trends across the Muslim world, I have tended to overlook variation *within* the region. There are obvious differences across Muslim countries, as well as within countries, over time. But there are also threads that run through the region that deserve exploration in future work. At the very least, the unity of Islam, as a concept, needs to be reconsidered. For example, when it comes to trust, I would expect to see differences between Sunni communities, which tend to be more decentralized, and Shi'a groups, which are more hierarchical, as well as within each denomination, where there is interesting variation across schools (*madāhib*) and branches.

Finally, in my emphasis on the process of mobilization from the bottom up, I have had far less to say about the leaders of Islamic-based organizations. It is important to ask whether leaders recognize how trust plays into their successes, and whether they use Islamic references for this particular reason. And while the focus of the book has been about interpersonal trust, there are key questions to raise about the interplay between social and political trust. Since the leadership is also part of the identity group, feelings of trust among group members should also be extended to these individuals. But is there no limit to this association, wherein the leader is inherently trusted as an in-group member under all conditions? In the specific case of Turkey, one wonders how the country's recent autocratic turn could impact the credibility of Erdoğan as a trusted representative of the broader Islamic political movement.

Appendix

For additional tables and figures, see the Online Appendix at http://www.alivny.com.

Appendix

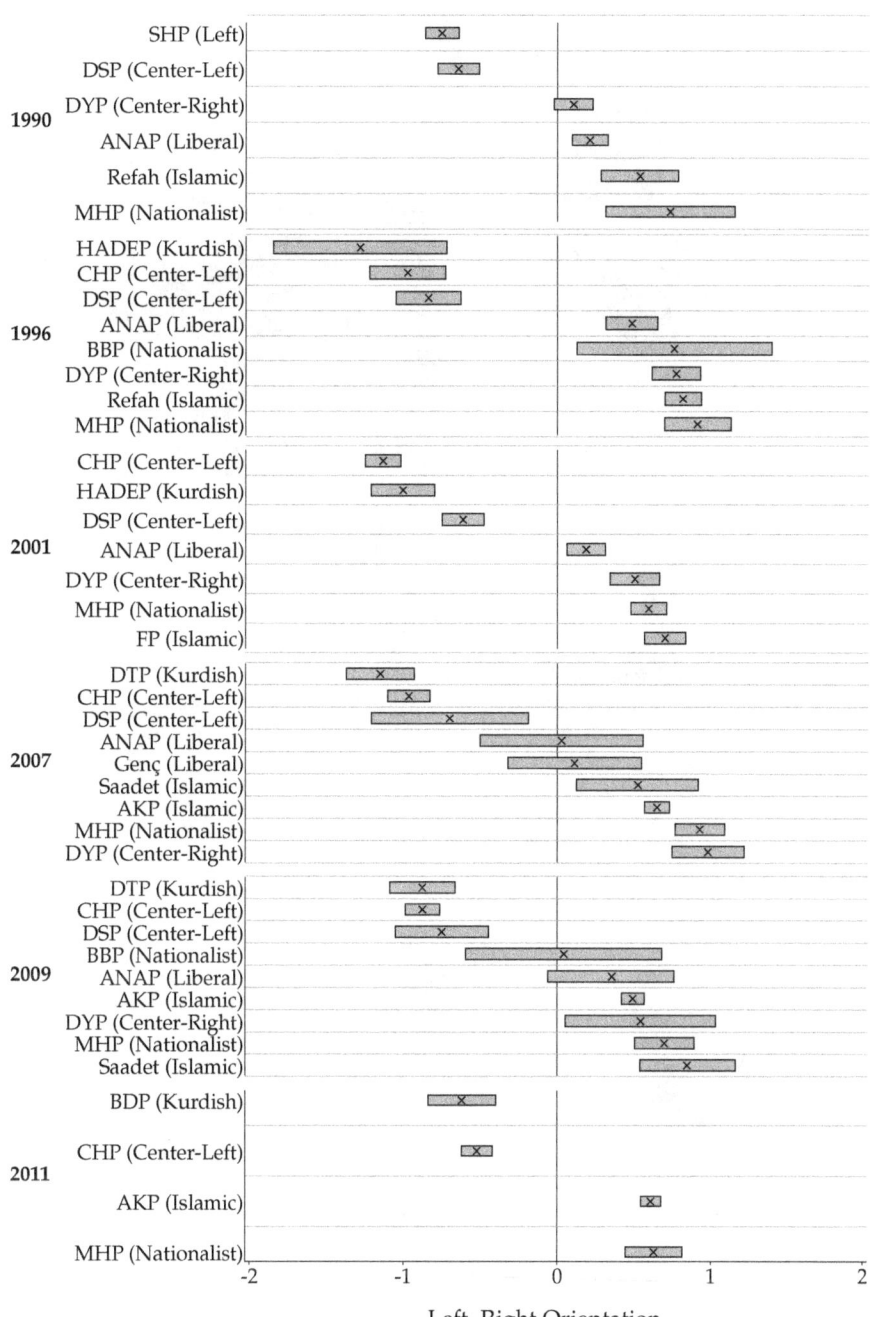

FIGURE A6.1 Turkish Parties' Left–Right Orientation, over Time
Notes: The left–right orientation of Turkey's largest parties, estimated using supporters' positioning on a (standardized) left–right spectrum. Bars indicate 95 percent confidence intervals around each mean.

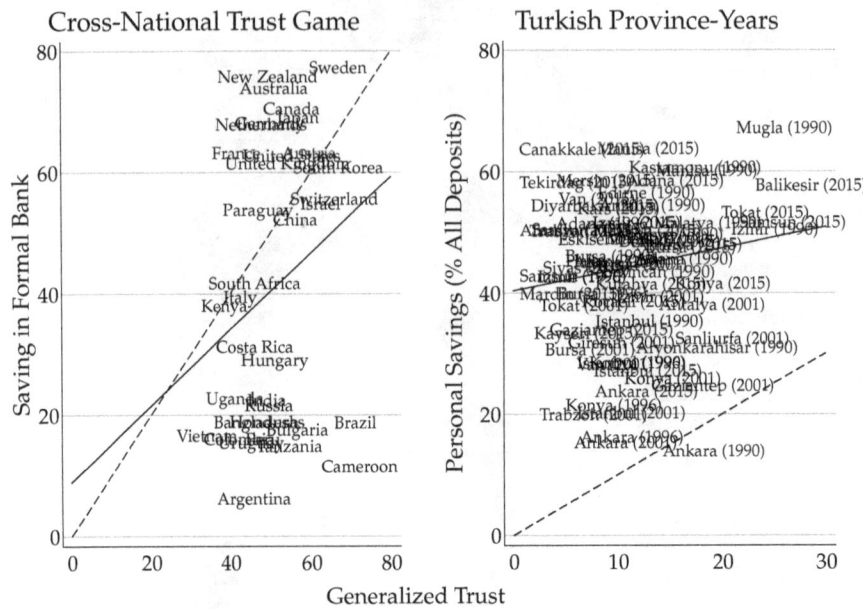

FIGURE A6.2 Bank Savings as Trust Proxy
Notes: Average generalized trust and percent who save in formal banks, across 135 countries; and generalized trust and personal savings deposits, across eighty-two Turkish province-years.

Bibliography

Abou-Youssef, Mariam Mourad Hussein, Wael Kortam, Ehab Abou-Aish, and Noha El-Bassiouny. 2015. "Effects of Religiosity on Consumer Attitudes toward Islamic Banking in Egypt." *International Journal of Bank Marketing* 33 (6): 786–807.
Achen, Christopher H. 2002. "Toward a New Political Methodology: Microfoundations and ART." *Annual Review of Political Science* 5: 423–450.
Adaş, Emin Baki. 2006. "The Making of Entrepreneurial Islam and the Islamic Spirit of Capitalism." *Journal for Cultural Research* 10 (2): 113–137.
Aghion, Philippe, George-Marios Angeletos, Abhijit Banerjee, and Kalina Manova. 2010a. "Volatility and Growth: Credit Constraints and the Composition of Investment." *Journal of Monetary Economics* 57: 246–265.
Aghion, Phillipe, Yann Algan, Pierrce Cahuc, and Andrei Shleifer. 2010b. "Regulation and Distrust." *Quarterly Journal of Economics* 125 (3): 1015–1049.
Ahn, T. K., Elinor Ostrom, and James M. Walker. 2003. "Heterogeneous Preferences and Collective Action." *Public Choice* 117 (3–4): 295–314.
Ajami, Fouad. 1991. *The Arab Predicament: Arab Political Thought and Practice since 1967*. Cambridge University Press.
Akarca, Ali T. 2008. "Inter-Party Vote Movements in Turkey between 1999 and 2002: A Statistical Analysis Using Cross-Provincial Election Data." MPRA Paper No. 927. http://mpra.ub.uni-muenchen.de/9627/.
Akarca, Ali T., and Cem Başlevent. 2010a. "Inter-Party Vote Movements in Turkey: The Sources of AKP Votes in 2007." Economic Research Forum, Working Paper No. 509.
Akarca, Ali T., and Cem Başlevent. 2010b. "The Region-of-Origin Effect on Voting Behavior: The Case of Turkey's Internal Migrants." *İktisat İşletme ve Finans* 25: 9–36.
Akarca, Ali T., and Aysit Tansel. 2006. "Economic Performance and Political Outcomes: An Analysis of the Turkish Parliamentary and Local Election Results between 1950 and 2004." *Public Choice* 129: 77–105.
Akay, Alpaslan, Gokhan Karabulut, and Peter Martinsson. 2015. "Cooperation and Punishment: The Effect of Religiosity and Religious Festival." *Economics Letters*.
Akerlof, George A. 1970. "The Market for 'Lemons': Quality Uncertainty and the Market Mechanism." *Quarterly Journal of Economics* 84 (3): 488–500.
Why Turks Don't Smile. 2012. www.hurriyetdailynews.com/opinion/mustafa-akyol/why-turks-dont-smile-17310.
Alesina, Alberto, Reza Baqir, and William Easterly. 1999. "Public Goods and Ethnic Divisions." *The Quarterly Journal of Economics* 114 (4): 1243–1284.

Alesina, Alberto, Arnaud Devleeschauwer, William Easterly, Sergio Kurlat, and Romain Wacziarg. 2003. "Fractionalization." *Journal of Economic Growth* 8 (2): 155–194.

Alesina, Alberto, and Eliana La Ferrara. 2002. "Who Trusts Others?" *Journal of Public Economics* 85: 207–234.

Alexander, Christopher. 2000. "Opportunities, Organizations, and Ideas: Islamists and Workers in Tunisia and Algeria." *International Journal of Middle East Studies* 32: 465–490.

Algan, Yann, and Pierrce Cahuc. 2010. "Inherited Trust and Growth." *American Economic Review* 100 (5): 2060–2092.

Algan, Yann, Pierrce Cahuc, and Marc Sangnier. 2011. "Efficient and Inefficient Welfare States" IZA Discussion Paper Series No. 5445.

Allport, Gordon W., and J. Michael Ross. 1967. "Personal Religious Orientation and Prejudice." *Journal of Personality and Social Psychology* 5 (4): 432–443.

Almond, Gabriel A., and Sidney Verba. 1963. *The Civic Culture: Political Attitudes and Democracy in Five Nations*. Princeton University Press.

Alvarez, R. Michael, and Jonathan Nagler. 2000. "A New Approach for Modeling Strategic Voting in Multiparty Elections." *British Journal of Political Science* 30 (1): 57–75.

Anderson, Benedict. 2006. *Imagined Communities: Reflections on the Origin and Spread of Nationalism*. Verso.

Anderson, Lisa. 1987. "The State in the Middle East and North Africa." *Comparative Politics* 20 (1): 1–18.

Anderson, Lisa R., Jennifer M. Mellor, and Jeffrey Milyo. 2004. "Social Capital and Contributions in a Public-Goods Experiment." *American Economic Review* 94 (2): 373–376.

Andonie, Costel, and Christoph Kuzmics. 2012. "Pre-Election Polls as Strategic Coordination Devices." *Journal of Economic Behavior and Organization* 84: 681–700.

Andreadis, Ioannis, and Theodore Chadjipadelis. 2009. "A Method for the Estimation of Voter Transition Rates." *Journal of Elections, Public Opinion and Parties* 19 (2): 203–218.

Andreoni, James. 1990. "Impure Altruism and Donations to Public Goods: A Theory of Warm-Glow Giving." *The Economic Journal* 100 (401): 464–477.

Ansolabehere, Stephen, Jonathan A. Rodden, and James M. Snyder Jr. 2008. "The Strength of Issues: Using Multiple Measures to Gauge Preference Stability, Ideological Constraint, and Issue Voting." *American Political Science Review* 102 (2): 215–232.

Arikan, Gizem, and Pazit Ben-Nun Bloom. 2018. "Religion and Political Protest: A Cross-Country Analysis." *Comparative Political Studies* 52 (2): 246–276.

Armbrust, Walter. 2006. "Synchronizing Watches: The State, the Consumer, and Sacred Time in Ramadan Television" In *Religion, Media, and the Public Sphere*, edited by Birgit Meyer and Annelies Moors, 207–226. Indiana University Press.

Arrow, Kenneth J. 1972. "Gifts and Exchanges." *Philosophy and Public Affairs* 1 (4): 343–362.

Ascher, William, and Sidney Tarrow. 1975. "The Stability of Communist Electorates: Evidence from a Longitudinal Analysis of French and Italian Aggregate Data." *American Journal of Political Science* 19 (3): 475–499.

Ashmore, Richard D., Kay Deaux, and Tracy McLaughlin-Volpe. 2004. "An Organizing Framework for Collective Identity: Articulation and Significance of Multidimensionality." *Psychological Bulletin* 130 (1): 80–114.

Ashraf, Nava, Iris Bohnet, and Nikita Piankov. 2006. "Decomposing Trust and Trustworthiness." *Experimental Economics* 9: 193–208.

AsiaBarometer Project. 2009. "AsiaBarometer Survey Data: 2003, 2004, 2005, 2006, 2007, 2008." www.asiabarometer.org.
Aslam, Ali. 2017. "Salat-al-Juma: Organizing the Public in Tahrir Square." *Social Movement Studies* 16 (3): 297–308.
Atasoy, Yildiz. 2009. *Turkey, Islamists and Democracy: Transition and Globalization in a Muslim State*. I. B. Tauris.
Atkinson, Quentin D., and Pierrick Bourrat. 2011. "Beliefs About God, the Afterlife and Morality Support the Role of Supernatural Policing in Human Cooperation." *Evolution and Human Behavior* 32: 41–49.
Ayubi, Nazih. 1991. *Political Islam: Religion and Politics in the Arab World*. Routledge.
Bäck, Maria, and Henrik Serup Christensen. 2016. "When Trust Matters: A Multilevel Analysis of the Effect of Generalized Trust on Political Participation in 25 European Democracies." *Journal of Civil Society* 12 (2): 178–197.
Başlevent, Cem, Hasan Kirmanoğlu, and Burhan Şenatalar. 2005. "Empirical Investigation of Party Preferences and Economic Voting in Turkey." *European Journal of Political Research* 44: 547–562.
Başlevent, Cem, Hasan Kirmanoğlu, and Burhan Şenatalar. 2009. "Party Preferences and Economic Voting in Turkey (Now That the Crisis is Over)." *Party Politics* 15 (3): 377–391.
Badimon, Montserrat Emperador. 2011. "Unemployed Moroccan University Graduates and Strategies for 'Apolitical' Mobilization." Chap. 11 in *Social Movements, Mobilization, and Contestation in the Middle East and North Africa*, edited by Joel Beinin and Frederic Vairel, 217–235. Stanford University Press.
Balliet, Daniel, and Paul A. M. van Lange. 2013. "Trust, Punishment, and Cooperation across 18 Societies: A Meta-Analysis." *Perspectives on Psychological Science* 8 (4): 363–379.
Banks Association of Turkey. 2018. "The Banking System in Turkey: Savings and Loans Activity by Provinces and Regions." www.tbb.org.tr/en/banks-and-banking-sector-information/statistical-reports/20.
Bardakci, Mehmet. 2016. "2015 Parliamentary Elections in Turkey: Demise and Revival of AKP's Single-Party Rule." *Turkish Studies* 17 (1): 4–18.
Barfield, Thomas. 2005. "An Islamic State Is a State Run by Good Muslims: Religion as a Way of Life and Not an Ideology in Afghanistan." Chap. 9 in *Remaking Muslim Politics: Pluralism, Contestation, Democratization*, edited by Robert W. Hefner, 213–239. Princeton University Press.
Barry, Brian. 1978. *Sociologists, Economists, and Democracy*. University of Chicago Press.
Bayat, Asef. 2010. *Life as Politics: How Ordinary People Change the Middle East*. Amsterdam University Press.
Beall, Jo. 1995. "Social Security and Social Networks among the Urban Poor in Pakistan." *Habitat International* 19 (4): 427–445.
Beck, Thorsten, George Clarke, Alberto Groff, Philip Keefer, and Patrick Walsh. 2001. "New Tools in Comparative Political Economy: The Database of Political Institutions." *World Bank Economic Review* 15 (1): 165–176.
Beinin, Joel. 2005. "Political Islam and the New Global Economy: The Political Economy of an Egyptian Social Movement." *CR: The New Centennial Review* 5 (1): 111–139.
Beinin, Joel, and Frédéric Vairel. 2011. "Popular Uprisings in Tunisia and Egypt." Chap. 12 in *Social Movements, Mobilization, and Contestation in the Middle East*

and North Africa, edited by Joel Beinin and Frederic Vairel, 237–254. Stanford University Press.

Bendor, Jonathan, Daniel Diermeier, David A. Siegel, and Michael M. Ting. 2011. *A Behavioral Theory of Elections*. Princeton University Press.

Benoit, Kenneth, and Michael Laver. 2006. *Party Policy in Modern Democracies*. Routledge.

Benson, Michelle, and Thomas R. Rochon. 2004. "Interpersonal Trust and the Magnitude of Protest: A Micro and Macro Level Approach." *Comparative Political Studies* 37 (435–437).

Berberoğlu, Enis. 2006. "Is TÜSİAD Bigger or MÜSİAD? (*TÜSİAD mıBüyük Yoksa MÜSİAD mı?*)." *Hürriyet Daily News*.

Berg, Joyce, John Dickhaut, and Kevin A. McCabe. 1995. "Trust, Reciprocity, and Social History." *Games and Economic Behavior* 10 (1): 122–142.

Berggren, Niclas, and Henrik Jordahl. 2006. "Free to Trust: Economic Freedom and Social Capital." *Kyklos* 59 (2): 141–169.

Bergh, Andreas, and Christian Bjørnskov. 2011. "Historical Trust Levels Predict the Current Size of the Welfare State." *Kyklos* 64 (1): 1–19.

Berkes, Niyazi. 1998. The *Development of Secularism in Turkey*. Routledge.

Berman, Eli, and David D. Laitin. 2008. "Religion, Terrorism, and Public Goods: Testing the Club Model." *Journal of Public Economics* 92: 1942–1967.

Besley, Timothy, Stephen Coate, and Glenn Loury. 1993. "The Economics of Rotating Savings and Credit Associations." *American Economic Review* 83 (4): 792–810.

Billig, Michael. 1973. "Normative Communication in a Minimal Intergroup Situation." *European Journal of Social Psychology* 3 (3): 339–343.

Binzel, Christine, and Jean-Paul Carvalho. 2016. "Education, Social Mobility and Religious Movements: The Islamic Revival in Egypt." *The Economic Journal* 127: 2553–2580.

Binzel, Christine, and Dietmar Fehr. 2013. "Social Distance and Trust: Experimental Evidence from a Slum in Cairo." *Journal of Development Economics* 103: 99–106.

Birnir, Jóhanna Kristín. 2007. *Ethnicity and Electoral Politics*. Cambridge University Press.

Bisin, Alberto, and Thierry Verdier. 2001. "The Economics of Cultural Transmission and the Dynamics of Preferences." *Journal of Economic Theory* 97 (2): 298–319.

Bjørnskov, Christian. 2006. "The Multiple Facets of Social Capital." *European Journal of Political Economy* 22: 22–40.

Bjørnskov, Christian. 2007. "Determinants of Generalized Trust: A Cross-Country Comparison." *Public Choice* 130: 1–21.

Bjørnskov, Christian. 2009. "Social Trust and the Growth of Schooling." *Economics of Education Review* 28: 249–257.

Bjørnskov, Christian. 2012. "How Does Social Trust Affect Economic Growth?" *Southern Economic Journal* 78 (4): 1346–1368.

Bjørnskov, Christian, and Pierre-Guillaume Méon. 2010. "The Productivity of Trust." *CEB Working Paper* No. 10/042.

Black, Antony. 2011. The *History of Islamic Political Thought: From the Prophet to the Present*. 2nd ed. Edinburgh University Press.

Blais, André, Cengiz Erisen, and Ludovic Rheault. 2014. "Strategic Voting and Coordination Problems in Proportional Systems: An Experimental Study." *Political Research Quarterly* 67 (2): 386–397.

Blaydes, Lisa. 2011. *Elections and Distributive Politics in Mubarak's Egypt*. Cambridge University Press.

Bleck, Jaimie, and David Siddhartha Patel. 2011. "Out of Africa: Electoral Failure and the Future of Political Islam in West Africa." Presented at the APSA Annual Meeting.
Blois, K. J. 1972. "Vertical Quasi-Integration." *The Journal of Industrial Economics* 20 (3): 253–272.
Bloom, Pazit Ben-Nun, Gizem Arikan, and Marie Courtemanche. 2015. "Religious Social Identity, Religious Belief, and Anti-Immigration Sentiment." *American Political Science Review* 109 (2): 203–221.
Bohnet, Iris, Fiona Greig, Benedikt Herrmann, and Richard Zeckhauser. 2008. "Betrayal Aversion: Evidence from Brazil, China, Oman, Switzerland, Turkey, and the United States." *American Economic Review* 98 (1): 294–310.
Bohnet, Iris, Benedikt Herrmann, and Richard Zeckhauser. 2010. "Trust and the Reference Points for Trustworthiness in Gulf and Western Countries." *The Quarterly Journal of Economics* 125 (2): 811–228.
Bottazzi, Laura, Marco Da Rin, and Thomas F. Hellman. 2016. "The Importance of Trust for Investment: Evidence from Venture Capital." *Review of Financial Studies* 29 (9): 2283–2318.
Bourdieu, Pierre. 2013. *Outline of a Theory of Practice*. Cambridge University Press.
Bowen, John R. 1986. "On the Political Construction of Tradition: Gotong Royong in Indonesia." *The Journal of Asian Studies* 45 (3): 545–561.
Bowles, Samuel, and Herbert Gintis. 2004. "The Evolution of Strong Reciprocity: Cooperation in Heterogeneous Populations." *Theoretical Population Biology* 65: 17–28.
Boyd, Robert, Herbert Gintis, Samuel Bowles, and Peter J. Richerson. 2003. "The Evolution of Altruistic Punishment." *Proceedings of the National Academy of Sciences (PNAS)* 100 (6): 3531–3535.
Brady, Henry E., Sidney Verba, and Kay Lehman Schlozman. 1995. "Beyond SES: A Resource Model of Political Participation." *American Political Science Review* 89 (2): 271–294.
Brambor, Thomas, William Roberts Clark, and Matt Golder. 2006. "Understanding Interaction Models: Improving Empirical Analysis." *Political Analysis* 14 (1): 63–82.
Brams, Steven J., and Frank C. Zagare. 1977. "Deception in Simple Voting Games." *Social Science Research* 6: 257–272.
Bratton, Michael, E. Gyimah-Boadi, and Robert Mattes. 2000. "Compilation of Afrobarometer Round 1 Survey in 12 Countries: Botswana, Ghana, Lesotho, Malawi, Mali, Namibia, Nigeria, South Africa, Tanzania, Uganda, Zambia, and Zimbabwe, 1999–2001." www.afrobarometer.org.
Bratton, Michael, E. Gyimah-Boadi, and Robert Mattes. 2007. "Afrobarometer Round 3: The Quality of Democracy and Governance in 18 African Countries, 2005–2006." www.afrobarometer.org.
Brewer, Marilynn B. 2007. "The Importance of Being We: Human Nature and Intergroup Relations." *American Psychologist*: 728–738.
Brewer, Marilynn B. 2008. "Depersonalized Trust and Ingroup Cooperation" In *Rationality and Social Responsibility: Essays in Honor of Robyn Mason Dawes*, edited by Joachim I. Krueger, 215–232. Taylor Francis.
Brewer, Marilynn B., and Roderick M. Kramer. 1986. "Choice Behavior in Social Dilemmas: Effects of Social Identity, Group Size, and Decision Framing." *Journal of Personality and Social Psychology* 50 (3): 543–549.
Brewer, Mark D., Rogan Kersh, and R. Eric Petersen. 2003. "Assessing Conventional Wisdom about Religion and Politics." *Journal for the Scientific Study of Religion* 42 (1): 125–136.

Bringa, Tone. 1995. *Being Muslim the Bosnian Way: Identity and Community in a Central Bosnian Village.* Princeton University Press.

Brooke, Steven. 2017. "From Medicine to Mobilization: Social Service Provision and the Islamist Reputational Advantage." *Perspectives on Politics* 15 (1): 42–61.

Buchan, Nancy R., Eric J. Johnson, and Rachel T. A. Croson. 2006. "Let's Get Personal: An International Examination of the Influence of Communication, Culture and Social Distance on Other Regarding Preferences." *Journal of Economic Behavior and Organization* 60 (3): 373–398.

Bureau van Dijk. 2013. "BankScope: Bank and Financial Institution Information Worldwide."

Bureau van Dijk. 2014. "Orbis: Company Information Across the Globe."

Buğra, Ayşe. 1994a. "Political and Institutional Context of Business Activity in Turkey." In *Developmentalism and Beyond: Society and Politics in Egypt and Turkey*, edited by A. Öncü and Ç. Keyder, 233–255. American University in Cairo Press.

Buğra, Ayşe. 1994b. *State and Business in Modern Turkey: A Comparative Study.* State University of New York Press.

Buğra, Ayşe. 1998. "Class, Culture, and State: An Analysis of Interest Representation by Two Turkish Business Associations." *International Journal of Middle East Studies* 30 (4): 521–539.

Cammett, Melani, and Pauline Jones Luong. 2014. "Is There an Islamist Political Advantage?" *Annual Review of Political Science* 17: 187–206.

Carlsson, Fredrik, Olof Johansson-Stenman, and Pham Khanh Nam. 2014. "Social Preferences Are Stable Over Long Periods of Time." *Journal of Public Economics* 117: 104–1014.

Carr, Adam. 2011. "Psephos." http://psephos.adam-carr.net.

Carr, Jack L., and Janet T. Landa. 1983. "The Economics of Symbols, Clan Names, and Religion." *Journal of Legal Studies* 12: 135–156.

Carvalho, Jean-Paul. 2016. "Identity-Based Organizations." *American Economic Review* 106 (5): 410–414.

Caucasus Research Resource Centers. 2018. "Caucasus Barometer 2008-2017." www.crrccenters.org/caucasusbarometer/.

Çarkoğlu, Ali. 1998. "The Turkish Party System in Transition: Party Performance and Agenda Change." *Political Studies* 46: 544–571.

Çarkoğlu, Ali. 2009. "Women's Choices of Head Cover in Turkey: An Empirical Assessment." *Comparative Studies of South Asia, Africa and the Middle East* 29 (3): 450–467.

Çarkoğlu, Ali, and Ersin Kalaycıoğlu. 2007. *Turkish Democracy Today: Elections, Protest and Stability in an Islamic Society.* I. B. Tauris.

Çarkoğlu, Ali, and Ersin Kalaycıoğlu. 2009. *The Rising Tide of Conservatism in Turkey.* Palgrave Macmillan.

Çarkoğlu, Ali, and Binnaz Toprak. 2000. *Religion, Society and Politics in Turkey (TUrkiye'de Din, Toplum ve Siyaset).* TESEV Publications.

Çarkoğlu, Ali, and Binnaz Toprak. 2007. *Religion, Society and Politics in a Changing Turkey.* TESEV Publications.

Çarkoğlu, Ali, and Kerem Yıldırım. 2015. "Election Storm in Turkey: What Do the Results of June and November 2015 Elections Tell Us?" *Insight Turkey* 17 (4): 57–79.

Çağaptay, Soner. 2006. *Islam, Secularism, and Nationalism in Modern Turkey: Who Is a Turk?* Routledge.

Çavdar, Gamze. 2006. "Islamist *New Thinking* in Turkey: A Model for Political Learning?" *Political Science Quarterly* 121 (3): 477–497.
Çemrek, Murat. 2002. "Formation and Representation of Interests in Turkey Political Economy: The Case of MÜSİAD." PhD diss., Bilkent University, Institute of Economics and Social Sciences.
Celasun, Oya, Cevdet Denizer, and Dong He. 1999. "Capital Flows, Macroeconomic Management, and the Financial System: Turkey, 1989–97." World Bank Policy Research Working Paper No. 2141.
Chandra, Kanchan. 2004. *Why Ethnic Parties Succeed*. Cambridge University Press.
Chandra, Kanchan. 2006. "What Is Ethnic Identity and Does It Matter?" *Annual Review of Political Science* 9: 397–424.
Charness, Gary, Luca Rigotti, and Aldo Rustichini. 2007. "Individual Behavior and Group Membership." *American Economic Review* 97 (4): 1340–1352.
Charnysh, Volha, Christopher Lucas, and Prerna Singh. 2015. "The Ties That Bind: National Identity Salience and Pro-Social Behavior toward the Ethnic Other." *Comparative Political Studies* 48 (3): 267–300.
Chavez, Maria L., Brian Wampler, and Ross E. Burkhart. 2006. "Left Out: Trust and Social Capital Among Migrant Seasonal Farmworkers." *Social Science Quarterly* 87 (5): 1012–1029.
Chen, Roy, and Yan Chen. 2011. "The Potential of Social Identity for Equilibrium Selection." *American Economic Review* 101: 2562–2589.
Cherry, Todd, David M. McEvoy, and Håkon Sælen. 2017. "Conditional Cooperation and Cultural Worldviews." *Economics Letters* 158: 51–53.
Chiles, Todd H., and John F. McMackin. 1996. "Integrating Variable Risk Preferences, Trust, and Transaction Cost Economics." *Academy of Management Review* 21 (1): 73–99.
Chong, Dennis. 1991. *Collective Action and the Civil Rights Movement*. University of Chicago Press.
Chong, Dennis. 1993. "Coordinating Demands for Social Change." *The Annals of the American Academy of Political and Social Science* 528 (1): 126–141.
Christensen, Christian. 2005. "Pocketbooks or Prayer Beads? U.S./U.K. Newspaper Coverage of the 2002 Turkish Elections." *Press/Politics* 10 (1): 109–128.
Chuah, Swee-Hoon, Reema Fahoum, and Robert Hoffmann. 2013. "Fractionalization and Trust in India: A Field-Experiment." *Economics Letters* 119: 191–194.
Chuah, Swee-Hoon, Robert Hoffmann, Bala Ramasamy, and Jonathan H. W. Tan. 2014. "Religion, Ethnicity, and Cooperation: An Experimental Study." *Journal of Economic Psychology* 45 (33–43).
Chwe, Michael Suk-Young. 2003. *Rational Ritual: Culture, Coordination, and Common Knowledge*. Princeton University Press.
Cingranelli, David L., and David L. Richards. 2010. "The Cingranelli-Richards (CIRI) Human Rights Dataset v. 2010.08.15." www.humanrightsdata.org/.
Citizen Action Monitor. 2011. "Defiant, Inspiring Voices from Tahrir Square." https://citizenactionmonitor.wordpress.com/2011/11/29/.
Clark, Janine A. 2004a. *Islam, Charity, and Activism: Middle-Class Networks and Social Welfare in Egypt, Jordan, and Yemen*. Indiana University Press.
Clark, Janine A. 2004b. "Social Movement Theory and Patron-Clientelism: Islamic Social Institutions and the Middle Class in Egypt, Jordan, and Yemen." *Comparative Political Studies* 37 (8): 941–468.
Clark, Janine A. 2006. "Field Research Methods in the Middle East." *Political Studies* 39 (3): 417–424.

Cohen, Adam B., Daniel E. Hall, Harold G. Koenig, and Keith G. Meador. 2005. "Social Versus Individual Motivation: Implications for Normative Definitions of Religious Orientation." *Personality and Social Psychology Review* 9 (1): 48–61.

Commission of the European Communities. 1988. "Eurobarometer 25: Holiday Travel and Environmental Problems, April 1986." GESIS Data Archive. ZA1543 Data file Version 1.0.1. doi:10.4232/1.10882.

Commission of the European Communities. 2004. "Eurobarometer 62.2: Agricultural Policy, Development Aid, Social Capital and Information and Communication Technology, November-December 2004." GESIS Data Archive. ZA4231 Data file Version 1.1.0. doi:10.4232/1.10964.

Condra, Luke N., Mohammad Isaqzadeh, and Sera Linardi. 2017. "Clerics and Scriptures: Experimentally Disentangling the Influence of Religious Authority in Afghanistan." *British Journal of Political Science* 49: 401–419.

Conroy-Krutz, Jeffrey, Devra C. Moehler, and Rosario Aguilar. 2016. "Partisan Cues and Vote Choice in New Multiparty Systems." *Comparative Political Studies* 49 (1): 3–35.

Cook, Steven A., *Turkey's Elections: Partially Free, Fair, and Fake*. 2018. www.cfr.org/blog/turkeys-elections-partially-free-fair-and-fake.

Cox, Gary W. 1994. "Strategic Voting Equilibria Under the Single Nontransferable Vote." *American Political Science Review* 88 (3): 608–621.

Cox, Gary W. 1997. *Making Votes Count: Strategic Coordination in the World's Electoral Systems.* Cambridge University Press.

Craig, Stephen C., Richard G. Niemi, and Glenn E. Silver. 1990. "Political Efficacy and Trust: A Report on the NES Pilot Study Items." *Political Behavior* 12 (3): 289–314.

Crisp, Brian F., Santiago Olivella, and Joshua D. Potter. 2011. "Electoral Contexts that Impede Voter Coordination." *Electoral Studies* 30: 1–16.

Croson, Rachel T. A., and Nancy R. Buchan. 1999. "Gender and Culture: International Experimental Evidence from Trust Games." *American Economic Review* 89 (2): 386–391.

Davis, Eric. 1984. "Ideology, Social Class and Islamic Radicalism in Modern Egypt." In *From Nationalism to Revolutionary Islam*, edited by Saïd Amir Arjomand. State University of New York Press.

Dawes, Robyn M., Alphons J. C. Van de Kragt, and John M. Orbell. 1988. "Not Me or Thee but We: The Importance of Group Identity in Eliciting Cooperation in Dilemma Situations: Experimental Manipulations." *Acta Pyschologica* 68: 83–97.

Dawes, Robyn M., Jeanne McTavish, and Harriet Shaklee. 1977. "Behavior, Communication, and Assumptions about Other People's Behavior in a Commons Dilemma Situation." *Journal of Personality and Social Psychology* 35 (1): 1–11.

De La O, Ana, and Jonathan A. Rodden. 2008. "Does Religion Distract the Poor? Income and Issue Voting Around the World." *Comparative Political Studies* 41: 437–476.

Deeb, Lara. 2006. *An Enchanted Modern: Gender and Public Piety in Shi'i Lebanon.* Princeton University Press.

Delaney, Carol. 1993. "Traditional Modes of Authority and Co-operation." In *Culture and Economy: Changes in Turkish Villages.* Eothen Press.

Delhey, Jan, and Kenneth Newton. 2005. "Predicting Cross-National Levels of Social Trust: Global Pattern or Nordic Exceptionalism?" *European Sociological Review* 21 (4): 311–327.

Delhey, Jan, Kenneth Newton, and Christian Welzel. 2011. "How General Is Trust in 'Most People'? Solving the Radius of Trust Problem." *American Sociological Review* 76 (5): 786–807.

Demir, Ömer, Mustafa Acar, and Metin Toprak. 2004. "Anatolian Tigers or Islamic Capital: Prospects and Challenges." *Middle Eastern Studies* 40 (6): 166–188.

Demirgüç-Kunt, Asli, Baybars Karacaovali, and Luc A. Laeven. 2005. "Deposit Insurance around the World: A Comprehensive Database." World Bank Policy Research Working Paper No. 3628.

Demirgüç-Kunt, Asli, and Leora Klapper. 2012. "Measuring Financial Inclusion: The Global Index." http://go.worldbank.org/1F2V9ZK8Co.

Demirgüç-Kunt, Asli, Leora Klapper, and Douglas Randall. 2013. "Islamic Finance and Financial Inclusion: Measuring Use of and Demand for Formal Financial Services among Muslim Adults." World Bank Development Research Group, Policy Research Working Paper No. 6642.

Demirgüç-Kunt, Asli, Leora Klapper, Dorothe Singer, and Peter Van Oudheusden. 2014. "The GlobalFindex Database 2014: Measuring Financial Inclusion around the World." http://microdata.worldbank.org/index.php/catalog/global-findex/about.

Denizer, Cevdet A., and Murat F. Iyigun. 2002. "Finance and Macroeconomic Volatility." *Contributions to Macroeconomics* 2 (1).

Djupe, Paul A., and Christopher P. Gilbert. 2006. "The Resourceful Believer: Generating Civic Skills in Church." *Journal of Politics* 68 (1): 116–127.

Djupe, Paul A., and J. Robin Grant. 2002. "Religious Institutions and Political Participation in America." *Journal for the Scientific Study of Religion* 40 (2): 303–314.

Doğruöz, Hakan. 2008. "Muslim Entrepreneurs and Alternative Modernities: The Case of MÜSİAD." Master's Thesis, Central European University, Department of Sociology and Social Anthropology.

Downs, Anthony. 1957. *An Economic Theory of Democracy*. Harper.

Driskell, Robyn, Elizabeth Embry, and Larry Lyon. 2008. "Faith and Politics: The Influence of Religious Beliefs on Political Participation." *Social Science Quarterly* 89 (2): 294–314.

Dubetsky, Alan. 1976. "Kinship, Primordial Ties, and Factory Organization in Turkey: An Anthropological View." *International Journal of Middle East Studies* 7 (3): 433–451.

Duch, Raymong M., and Harvey D. Palmer. 2002. "Strategic Voting in Post-Communist Democracy?" *British Journal of Political Science* 32 (1): 63–91.

Dündar, Fuat. 2000. *Minorities in the Turkish Census (Türkiye Nüfus Sayimlarinda Azinlıklar)*. Çiviyazıları.

Durante, Ruben. 2009. "Risk, Cooperation and the Economic Origins of Trust: An Empirical Investigation." http://ssrn.com/abstract=1576774.

Durkheim, Emile. 1973. *On Morality and Society*. University of Chicago Press.

Duverger, Maurice. 1963. *Political Parties: Their Organization and Activity in the Modern State*. Wiley.

Dyer, Jeffrey H., and Wujin Chu. 2003. "The Role of Trustworthiness in Reducing Transaction Costs and Improving Performance: Empirical Evidence from the United States, Japan, and Korea." *Organization Science* 14 (1): 57–68.

Dzutsati, Valery, David Siroky, and Khasan Dzutsev. 2016. "The Political Economy of Support for Sharia: Evidence from the Russian North Caucasus." *Politics and Religion* 9: 695–719.

Easterly, William, and Ross Levine. 1997. "Africa's Growth Tragedy: Policies and Ethnic Divisions" *The Quarterly Journal of Economics* 112 (4): 1203–1250.

Eligur, Banu. 2010. *The Mobilization of Political Islam in Turkey*. Cambridge University Press.

Ellemers, Naomi, Russell Spears, and Bertjan Doosje. 2002. "Self and Social Identity." *Annual Review of Psychology* 53: 161–186.

Elster, Jon. 1985. "Rationality, Morality, and Collective Action." *Ethics* 96 (1): 136–155.

Eltantawy, Nahed, and Julie B. Wiest. 2011. "Social Media in the Egyptian Revolution: Reconsidering Resource Mobilization Theory." *International Journal of Communication* 5: 1207–1224.

Ersoy, Melih. 1992. "Relations Between Central and Local Governments in Turkey: An Historical Perspective." *Public Administration and Development* 12: 325–341.

Esen, Berk, and Sinan Ciddi. 2011. "Turkey's 2011 Elections: An Emerging Dominant Party System?" https://www.questia.com/library/journal/1P3-2580366111/turkey-s-2011-elections-an-emerging-dominant-party

Esfandiari, Golnaz. 2010. "The Twitter Devolution." *Foreign Policy*.

Esmer, Yılmaz, and Thorleif Pettersson. 2007. "The Effects of Religion and Religiosity on Voting Behavior" In *The Oxford Handbook of Political Behavior*, edited by Russell J. Dalton and Hans-Dieter Klingemann, 481–503. Oxford University Press.

Esposito, John L., and John O. Voll. 1996. *Islam and Democracy*. Oxford University Press.

Eugster, Beatrix, Rafael Levine, Andreas Steinhauer, and Josef Zweimüeller. 2011. "The Demand for Social Insurance: Does Culture Matter?" *The Economic Journal* 121 (556): F413–448.

European Values Project. 2011. "European Values Study 1981–2008, Longitudinal Data File." www.europeanvaluesstudy.eu/evs/surveys/.

Falk, Carl F., Steven J. Heine, and Kosuke Takemura. 2014. "Cultural Variation in the Minimal Group Effect." *Journal of Cross-Cultural Psychology* 45 (2): 265–281.

Fearon, James D. 1999. "What is Identity (as We Now Use the Word)?" Unpublished manuscript, Stanford University, California (1999).

Fehr, Ernst, and Urs Fischbacher. 2002. "Why Social Preferences Matter: The Impact of Non-Selfish Motives on Competition, Cooperation and Incentives." *The Economic Journal* 112: C1–C33.

Fehr, Ernst, and Urs Fischbacher. 2003. "The Nature of Human Altruism." *Nature* 425: 785–791.

Fehr, Ernst, Urs Fischbacher, Bernhard von Rosenbladt, Jürgen Schupp, and Gert G. Wagner. 2003. "A Nation-Wide Laboratory: Examining Trust and Trustworthiness by Integrating Behavioral Experiments into Representative Surveys." IZA Discussion paper series No. 715.

Fennema, Meindert, and Jean Tillie. 1999. "Political Participation and Political Trust in Amsterdam: Civic Communities and Ethnic Networks." *Journal of Ethnic and Migration Studies* 25 (4): 703–726.

Finkel, Steven E. 1985. "Reciprocal Effects of Participation and Political Efficacy: A Panel Analysis." *American Journal of Political Science* 29 (4): 891–913.

Fischbacher, Urs, Simon Gächter, and Ernst Fehr. 2001. "Are People Conditionally Cooperative? Evidence from a Public Goods Experiment." *Economics Letters* 71: 397–404.

Fish, M. Steven. 2002. "Islam and Authoritarianism." *World Politics* 55 (1): 4–37.

Fish, M. Steven. 2011. *Are Muslims Distinctive? A Look at the Evidence*. Oxford University Press.
Fisher, Robert J. 1993. "Social Desirability Bias and the Validity of Indirect Questioning." *Journal of Consumer Research* 20 (2): 303–315.
Fisher, Stephen D. 2004. "Definition and Measurement of Tactical Voting: The Role of Rational Choice." *British Journal of Political Science* 34 (1): 152–166.
Fisman, Raymond, and Tarun Khanna. 1999. "Is Trust a Historical Residue? Information Flows and Trust Levels." *Journal of Economic Behavior and Organization* 38 (1): 79–92.
Foddy, Margaret, and Robyn Dawes. 2008. "Group-Based Trust in Social Dilemmas." Chap. 5 in *New Issues and Paradigms in Research on Social Dilemmas*, edited by Anders Biel, Daniel Eek and Tommy Gärling, and Mathias Gustafsson, 57–71. Springer.
Forsythe, Robert, Roger B. Myerson, Thomas A. Rietz, and Robert J. Weber. 1993. "An Experiment on Coordination in Multi-Candidate Elections: The Importance of Polls and Election Histories." *Social Choice and Welfare* 10 (3): 223–247.
Fowler, James H., and Cindy D. Kam. 2007. "Beyond the Self: Social Identity, Altruism, and Political Participation." *The Journal of Politics* 69 (3): 813–827.
Frey, Bruno S. 1994. "How Intrinsic Motivation Is Crowded Out and In." *Rationality and Society* 6 (3): 334–352.
Gächter, Simon, Benedikt Herrmann, and Christian Thöni. 2004. "Trust, Voluntary Cooperation, and Socio-Economic Background: Survey and Experimental Evidence." *Journal of Economic Behavior and Organization* 55: 505–531.
Gallego, Aina. 2007. "Unequal Political Participation in Europe." *International Journal of Sociology* 37 (4): 10–25.
Gallup. 2015. "Gallup World Poll."
García-Rivero, Carlos, and Hennie Kotzé. 2007. "Electoral Support for Islamic Parties in the Middle East and North Africa." *Party Politics* 13 (5): 611–636.
Geddes, Barbara. 1990. "How the Cases You Choose Affect the Answers You Get: Selection Bias in Comparative Politics." *Political Analysis* 2: 131–150.
Geddes, Barbara. 2003. *Paradigms and Sand Castles: Theory Building and Research Design in Comparative Politics*. University of Michigan Press.
Geertz, Clifford, Hildred Geertz, and Lawrence Rosen. 1979. *Meaning and Order in Moroccan Society: Three Essays in Cultural Analysis*. Cambridge University Press.
Gellner, Ernest. 2000. "Trust, Cohesion, and the Social Order." In *Trust: Making and Breaking Cooperative Relations*, edited by D. Gambetta, 142–157. Oxford University Press.
Gelman, Andrew, and Jennifer Hill. 2007. *Data Analysis Using Regression and Multilevel/Hierarchical Models*. Cambridge University Press.
Gerber, Alan S., Gregory A. Huber, David Doherty, Conor M. Dowling, and Seth J. Hill. 2013. "Who Wants to Discuss Vote Choices with Others? Polarization in Preferences for Deliberation." *Public Opinion Quarterly* 77 (2): 474–496.
Ghonim, Wael. 2012. *Revolution 2.0: The Power of the People is Greater than the People in Power*. Houghton Mufflin Harcourt.
Glaeser, Edward L., David I. Laibson, Jose A. Scheinkman, and Christine L. Soutter. 2000. "Measuring Trust." *Quarterly Journal of Economics* 115 (3): 811–846.
Goette, Lorenz, David Huffman, and Stephan Meier. 2006. "The Impact of Group Membership on Cooperation and Norm Enforcement: Evidence Using Random Assignment to Real Social Groups." *American Economic Review* 96 (2): 212–216.

Gorman, Brandon. 2018. "The Myth of the Secular-Islamist Divide in Muslim Politics: Evidence from Tunisia." *Current Sociology* 66 (1): 145–164.

Graham, Jesse, and Jonathan Haidt. 2010. "Beyond Beliefs: Religions Bind Individuals Into Moral Communities." *Personality and Social Psychology Review* 14 (1): 140–150.

Greenaway, Katharine H., Tegan Cruwys, S. Alexander Haslam, and Jolanda Jetten. 2016. "Social Identities Promote Well-Being Because They Satisfy Global Psychology Needs." *European Journal of Social Psychology* 46: 294–307.

Greif, Avner. 1989. "Reputation and Coalitions in Medieval Trade: Evidence on the Maghribi Traders." *Journal of Economic History* 49 (4): 857–882.

Greif, Avner. 1996. "Cultural Beliefs and the Organization of Society." *Journal of Political Economy* 102 (5): 912–950.

Guiso, Luigi, Paola Sapienza, and Luigi Zingales. 2004. "The Role of Social Capital in Financial Development." *American Economic Review* 94 (3): 526–556.

Guiso, Luigi, Paola Sapienza, and Luigi Zingales. 2006. "Does Culture Affect Economic Outcomes?" *Journal of Economic Perspectives* 20 (2): 23–48.

Guiso, Luigi, Paola Sapienza, and Luigi Zingales. 2009. "Cultural Biases in Economic Exchange." *Quarterly Journal of Economics* 124: 1095–1031.

Guiso, Luigi, Paola Sapienza, and Luigi Zingales. 2011. "Civic Capital as the Missing Link." In *Handbook of Social Economics*, edited by Jess Benhabib, Alberto Bisin, and Matthew O. Jackson, vol. 1A, 417–480. Elsevier.

Gulati, Ranjay. 1995. "Does Familiarity Breed Trust? Implications of Repeated Ties for Contractual Choice in Alliances." *The Academy of Management Journal* 38 (1): 85–112.

Gumuscu, Sebnem, and Deniz Sert. 2009. "The Power of the Devout Bourgeoisie: The Case of the Justice and Development Party in Turkey." *Middle Eastern Studies* 45 (6): 953–968.

Gündüz, Lokman, and Ekrem Tatoğlu. 2003. "A Comparison of the Financial Characteristics of Group-Affiliated and Independent Firms in Turkey." *European Business Review* 15 (1): 48–54.

Gürpinar, Doğan, and Ceren Kenar. 2016. "The Nation and its Sermons: Islam, Kemalism and the Presidency of Religious Affairs in Turkey." *Middle Eastern Studies* 52 (1): 60–78.

Gurses, Mehmet. 2014. "Islamists, Democracy and Turkey: A Test of the Inclusion-Moderation Hypothesis." *Party Politics* 20 (4): 646–653.

Habyarimana, James, Macartan Humphreys, Daniel N. Posner, and Jeremy M. Weinstein. 2007. "Why Does Ethnic Diversity Undermine Public Goods Provision?" *American Political Science Review* 101 (4): 709–725.

Habyarimana, James, Macartan Humphreys, Daniel N. Posner, and Jeremy M. Weinstein. 2009. *Coethnicity: Diversity and Dilemmas of Collective Action*. Russell Sage Foundation.

Hafez, Mohammed M. 2003. *Why Muslims Rebel: Repression and Resistance in the Islamic World*. Lynne Rienner Publishers, Inc.

Hafez, Mohammed M., and Quintan Wiktorowicz. 2004. "Violence as Contention in the Egyptian Islamic Movement." In *Islamic Activism: A Social Movement Theory Approach*, edited by Q. Wiktorowicz. Indiana University Press.

Hall, Peter A. 1999. "Social Capital in Britain." *British Journal of Political Science* 29 (3): 417–461.

Hamayotsu, Kikue. 2011. "Beyond Faith and Identity: Mobilizing Islamic Youth in Democratic Indonesia." *The Pacific Review* 24 (2): 225–247.

Hardin, Russell. 1971. "Collective Action as an Agreeable n-Prisoners' Dilemma." *Behavioral Sciences* 16 (5): 472–481.
Hardin, Russell. 1982. *Collective Action*. Johns Hopkins University Press.
Hardin, Russell. 2002. *Trust and Trustworthiness*. Russell Sage Foundation.
Harris, Frederick C. 1994. "Something Within: Religion as a Mobilizer of African-American Political Activism." *The Journal of Politics* 56 (1): 42–68.
Hassan, Sharifah Zaleha Syed. 1997. "Constructions of Islamic Identities in a Suburban Community in Malaysia." *Southeast Asian Journal of Social Science* 25 (2): 25–38.
Hazama, Yasushi. 2004. "Electoral Volatility in Turkey." PhD diss., Bilkent University.
Hazama, Yasushi. 2007. "Electoral Volatility in Turkey: Cleavages vs. the Economy." I.D.E. Occasional Papers Series No. 41.
Hazama, Yasushi. 2009. "Economic Voting and Electoral Volatility in Turkish Provinces." IDE Discussion Paper No. 2020.
Heath, Anthony, Stephen Fisher, and Shawna Smith. 2005. "The Globalization of Public Opinion Research." *Annual Review of Political Science* 8: 297–333.
Helble, Matthias. 2007. "Is God Good for Trade?" *Kyklos* 60 (3): 385–413.
Helliwell, John F. 2003. "How's Life? Combining Individual and National Variables to Explain Subjective Well-Being." *Economic Modelling* 20: 331–360.
Helliwell, John F., and Robert D. Putnam. 2004. "The Social Context of Well-Being." *Philosophical Transactions of the Royal Society B: Biological Sciences* 359 (1449): 1435–1446.
Henderson, J. Vernon, and Ari Kuncoro. 2011. "Corruption and Local Democratization in Indonesia: The Role of Islamic Parties." *Journal of Development Economics* 94: 164–180.
Henry, Clement Moore, and Robert Springborg. 2010. *Globalization and the Politics of Development in the Middle East*. Cambridge University Press.
Herrmann, Benedikt, Christian Thöni, and Simon Gächter. 2008. "Antisocial Punishment across Societies." *Science* 319: 1362–1367.
Hertel, Guido, and Norbert L. Kerr. 2001. "Priming In-Group Favoritism: The Impact of Normative Scripts in the Minimal Group Paradigm." *Journal of Experimental Social Psychology* 37: 316–324.
Hewstone, Miles, Mir Rabiul Islam, and Charles M. Judd. 1993. "Models of Crossed Categorization and Intergroup Relations." *Journal of Personality and Social Psychology* 64 (5): 77–93.
Hicks, Jacqueline. 2012. "The Missing Link: Explaining the Political Mobilization of Islam in Indonesia." *Journal of Contemporary Asia* 42 (1): 39–66.
Hoffman, Michael T., and Elizabeth R. Nugent. 2017. "Communal Religious Practice and Support for Armed Parties: Evidence from Lebanon." *Journal of Conflict Resolution* 61 (4): 869–902.
Hopper, Jerry R., and Richard I. Levin. 1968. *The Turkish Administrator: A Cultural Survey*. Public Administration Division, US AID.
Hosgör, Evren. 2011. "Islamic Capital/Anatolian Tigers: Past and Present." *Middle Eastern Studies* 47 (2): 343–360.
Howe, Marvine. 2005. *Morocco: The Islamist Awakening and Other Challenges*. Oxford University Press.
Hu, Fu, and Yun-Han Chu. 2018. "East Asian Barometer Survey Data Release: Waves I-IV." www.asianbarometer.org.
Hürriyet Daily News. 2019. "People's Alliance Holds Massive Rallies in Istanbul, Ankara." *Hurriyet Daily News*.

Iannaccone, Laurence R. 1992. "Sacrifice and Stigma: Reducing Free-Riding in Cults, Communes, and Other Collectives." *Journal of Political Economy* 100 (2): 271–291.
Iannaccone, Laurence R. 1998. "Introduction to the Economics of Religion." *Journal of Economic Literature* 36 (3): 1465–1495.
Ibrahim, Saad Eddin. 1980. "Anatomy of Egypt's Militant Islamic Groups: Methodological Note and Preliminary Findings." *International Journal of Middle East Studies* 12 (4): 423–453.
Ibrahim, Saad Eddin. 1998. "The Troubled Triangle: Populism, Islam and Civil Society in the Arab World." *International Political Science Review* 19 (4): 373–385.
Idle, Nadia, and Alex Nunns, eds. 2011. *Tweets from Tahrir: Egypt's Revolution as it Unfolded, in the Words of the People Who Made It*. OR Books.
Inglehart, Ronald. 1977. *The Silent Revolution: Changing Values and Political Styles Among Western Publics*. Princeton University Press.
Inglehart, Ronald. 1999. "Trust, Well-Being and Democracy." In *Democracy and Trust*, edited by M. E. Warren. Cambridge University Press.
International Foundation for Electoral Systems. 2011. "Election Guide." www.electionguide.org.
Irwin, Galen A., and Joop J. M. Van Holsteyn. 2008. "What Are They Waiting For? Strategic Information for Late Deciding Voters." *International Journal of Public Opinion Research* 20 (4): 483–493.
Ismail, Salwa. 2004. "Being Muslim: Islam, Islamism, and Identity Politics." *Government and Opposition* 39 (4): 614–631.
Ismail, Salwa. 2006. *Political Life in Cairo's New garters: Encountering the Everyday State*. University of Minnesota Press.
Istanbul Chamber of Industry. 2014. "500 Large Industrial Organizations of Turkey (*Türkiye'nin 500 Büyük Sanayi Kuruluşu*)." www.iso.org.tr/projeler/turkiyenin-500-buyuk-sanayi-kurulusu.
Iyer, Sriya. 2016. "The New Economics of Religion." *Journal of Economic Literature* 54 (2): 395–441.
Jamal, Amaney. 2005. "The Political Participation and Engagement of Muslim Americans." *American Politics Research* 33: 521–544.
Jamal, Amaney. 2007. "When is Social Trust a Desirable Outcome? Examining Levels of Trust in the Arab World." *Comparative Political Studies* 40: 1328–1349.
Jamal, Amaney, Bassma Kodmani, Khalil Shikaki, Mark Tessler, and Michael Robbins. 2014. "Arab Barometer: Public Opinion Survey Conducted in Algeria, Egypt, Jordan, Lebanon, Morocco, Palestine, and Tunisia 2016–2017." www.arabbarometer.org/.
Jamal, Amaney, and Irfan Nooruddin. 2010. "The Democratic Utility of Trust: A Cross-National Analysis." *The Journal of Politics* 72 (1): 45–69.
Jamal, Amaney, Mark Tessler, Khalil Shikaki, Mohammad Almasri, Michael Robbins, Abdenasser al Jabi, Jamal Abdul Jawad, et al. 2012. "Arab Barometer: Public Opinion Survey Conducted in Algeria, Egypt, Iraq, Jordan, Lebanon, Palestine, Saudi Arabia, Sudan, Tunisia, and Yemen, 2010–2011" www.arabbarometer.org/.
Jang, Ji-Hyang. 2006. "On the Road to Moderation: The Role of Islamic Business in Transforming Political Islamists in Turkey." *Journal of International and Area Studies* 13 (2): 97–112.
Jenkins, Gareth. 2008. *Political Islam in Turkey: Running West, Heading East*. Palgrave Macmillan.
Jensen, Niels Holm, Michael Bang Petersen, Henrik Høgh-Olesen, and Michael Ejstrup. 2015. "Testing Theories about Ethnic Markers: Ingroup Accent Facilitates Coordination, Not Cooperation." *Human Nature* 26: 210–234.

Jin, Nobuhito, and Toshio Yamagishi. 1997. "Group Heuristics in Social Dilemma." *Japanese Journal of Social Psychology* 12 (3): 190–198.

Jin, Nobuhito, Toshio Yamagishi, and Toko Kiyonari. 1996. "Bilateral Dependency and the Minimal Group Paradigm." *The Japanese Journal of Psychology* 67: 77–85.

Johansson-Stenman, Olof, Minhaj Mahmud, and Peter Martinsson. 2013. "Trust, Trust Games and Stated Trust: Evidence from Rural Bangladesh." *Journal of Economic Behavior and Organization* 95: 286–298.

Johnson, Noel D., and Alexandra A. Mislin. 2011. "Trust Games: A Meta-Analysis." *Journal of Economic Psychology* 32: 865–889.

Johnson, Noel D., and Alexandra A. Mislin. 2012. "How Much Should We Trust the World Values Survey Trust Question?" *Economics Letters* 116:210–212.

Jolliffe, I. T. 2002. *Principal Component Analysis*. Springer.

Jones-Correa, Michael A., and David L. Leal. 2001. "Political Participation: Does Religion Matter?" *Political Research Quarterly* 54: 751–70.

Jusko, Karen Long, and W. Phillips Shively. 2005. "Applying a Two-Step Strategy to the Analysis of Cross-National Public Opinion Data." *Political Analysis* 13 (4): 327–343.

Kaabachi, Souheila, and Hassan Obeid. 2016. "Determinants of Islamic Banking Adoption in Tunisia: Empirical Analysis." *International Journal of Bank Marketing* 34 (7): 1069–1091.

Kaase, Max. 1999. "Interpersonal Trust, Political Trust and Non-Institutionalized Political Participation in Western Europe." *West European Politics* 22 (3): 1–21.

Kaase, Max, and Alan Marsh. 1979. "Political Action: A Theoretical Perspective." In *Political Action: Mass Participation in Five Western Democracies*, edited by Samuel H. Barnes and Max Kaase, 27–56. SAGE Publications.

Kalaycıoğlu, Ersin. 2012. "Kulturkampf in Turkey: The Constitutional Referendum of 12 September 2010." *South European Society and Politics* 17 (1): 1–22.

Kaplan, Sam. 2006. *The Pedagogical State: Education and the Politics of National Culture in Post-1980 Turkey*. Stanford University Press.

Karpat, Kemal H. 2009. *The Gecekondu: Rural Migration and Urbanization*. Cambridge University Press.

Kasman, Saadet, and Duygu Ayhan. 2006. "Macreconomic Volatility under Alternative Exchange Rate Regimes in Turkey." *Central Bank Review* 2: 37–58.

Kaufmann, Daniel, Aart Kraay, and Massimo Mastruzzi. 2012. "Worldwide Governance Indicators" www.govindicators.org.

Kawachi, Ichiro, S. V. Subramanian, and Daniel Kim. 2008. "Social Capital and Health: A Decade of Progress and Beyond." In *Social Capital and Health*, edited by Ichiro Kawachi, S. V. Subramanian, and Daniel Kim, 1–28. Springer.

Kemahlıoğlu, Özge. 2015. "Winds of Change? The June 2015 Parliamentary Election in Turkey." *South European Society and Politics* 20 (4): 445–464.

Kepel, Gilles. 2003. *Muslim Extremism in Egypt: The Prophet and Pharaoh*. University of California Press.

Kern, Anna, Sofie Marien, and Marc Hooghe. 2015. "Economic Crisis and Levels of Political Participation in Europe (2002–2010): The Role of Resources and Grievances." *West European Politics* 38 (3): 465–490.

Kerr, Norbert L., and Cynthia M. Kaufman-Gilliland. 1994. "Communication, Commitment, and Cooperation in Social Dilemmas." *Journal of Personality and Social Psychology* 66 (3): 513–529.

Khalili, Laleh, and Jillian Schwedler, eds. 2010. *Policing and Prisons in the Middle East*. Columbia University Press.

Khan, Sammyh S., Nick Hopkins, Stephen Reicher, Shruti Tewari, Narayanan Srinivasan, and Clifford Stevenson. 2016. "How Collective Participation Impacts Social Identity: A Longitudinal Study from India." *Political Psychology* 37 (3): 309–325.

King, Gary, Robert O. Keohane, and Sidney Verba. 1994. *Designing Social Inquiry: Scientific Inference in Qualitative Research*. Princeton University Press.

King, Gary, Ori Rosen, and Martin A. Tanner, eds. 2004. *Ecological Inference: New Methodological Strategies*. Cambridge University Press.

Kirkpatrick, David D. 2012. "In Egypt Race, Battle Is Joined on Islam's Role." *New York Times*.

Klein, Benjamin, Robert G. Crawford, and Armen A. Alchian. 1978. "Vertical Integration, Appropriable Rents, and the Competitive Contracting Process." *Journal of Law and Economics* 21 (2): 297–326.

Knack, Stephen. 1992. "Civic Norms, Social Sanctions, and Voter Turnout." *Rationality and Society* 4 (2): 133–156.

Knack, Stephen. 2001. "Trust, Associational Life, and Economic Performance" MPRA Paper No. 27247. http://mpra.ub.uni-muenchen.de/27247/.

Knack, Stephen. 2002. "Social Capital and the Quality of Government: Evidence from the US States." *American Journal of Political Science* 46: 772–85.

Knack, Stephen, and Philip Keefer. 1997. "Does Social Capital Have an Economic Payoff? A Cross-Country Investigation." *Quarterly Journal of Economics* 112: 1251–1288.

Knack, Stephen, and Paul J. Zak. 2003. "Building Trust: Public Policy, Interpersonal Trust, and Economic Development." *Supreme Court Economic Review* 10: 91–107.

Knight, Jack. 2001. "Social Norms and the Rule of Law: Fostering Trust in a Socially Diverse Society." In *Trust in Society*, edited by K. S. Cook. Russell Sage Foundation.

Kocher, Martin G., Todd Cherry, Stephan Kroll, and Robert J. Netzer adn Matthias Sutter. 2008. "Conditional Cooperation on Three Continents." *Economics Letters* 101: 175–178.

KONDA Research and Consultancy. 2012. "KONDA Barometer."

KONDA Research and Consultancy. 2015. "KONDA Barometer."

Korkmaz, Özgür. 2015. "'Marginal Atheists' Fighting Turkey's Kurdish Peace Process." *Hurriyet Daily News*.

Kramer, Roderick M., and Marilynn B. Brewer. 1984. "Effects of Group Identity on Resource Use in a Simulated Commons Dilemma." *Journal of Personality and Social Psychology* 46 (5): 1044–1057.

Kreps, David M., Paul Milgrom, John Roberts, and Robert Wilson. 1982. "Rational Cooperation in the Finitely Repeated Prisoners' Dilemma." *Journal of Economic Theory* 27 (2): 245–252.

Krosnick, Jon A. 1991. "Response Strategies for Coping with the Cognitive Demands of Attitude Measures in Surveys." *Applied Cognitive Psychology* 5: 213–236.

Krosnick, Jon A., Allyson L. Holbrook, Matthew K. Berent, Richard T. Carson, W. Michael Hanemann, Raymond J. Kopp, Robert Cameron Mitchell, et al. 2002. "The Impact of 'No Opinion' Response Options on Data Quality: Non Attitude Reduction or an Invitation to Satisfice?" *Public Opinion Quarterly* 66 (3): 371–403.

Kunce, Mitch. 2001. "Pre-Election Polling and the Rational Voter: Evidence from State Panel Data (1986–1998)." *Public Choice* 107: 21–34.

Kuran, Timur. 1991. "Now Out of Never: The Element of Surprise in the East European Revolution of 1989." *World Politics* 44 (1): 7–48.

Kuran, Timur. 1995. "Islamic Economics and the Islamic Subeconomy." *The Journal of Economic Perspectives* 9 (4): 155–173.
Kuran, Timur. 2005. *Islam and Mammon: The Economic Predicaments of Islamism*. Princeton University Press.
Kurt, Yusuf, Mo Yamin, Noemi Sinkovics, and Rudolf R. Sinkovics. 2016. "Spirituality as an Antecedent of Trust and Network Commitment: The Case of Anatolian Tigers." *European Management Journal* 34: 686–700.
Kuru, Ahmet T. 2009. *Secularism and State Policies Towards Religion: The United States, France, and Turkey*. Cambridge University Press.
Kurzman, Charles, and Ijlal Naqvi. 2010a. "Do Muslims Vote Islamic?" *Journal of Democracy* 21 (2): 50–63.
Kurzman, Charles, and Syed Ijlal Hussain Naqvi. 2010b. "Who Are the Islamists?" In *Rethinking Islamic Studies: From Orientalism to Cosmopolitanism*, edited by Carl W. Ernst and Richard C. Martin. University of South Carolina Press.
Kwak, Nojin, Dhavan V. Shah, and R. Lance Holbert. 2004. "Connecting, Trusting, and Participating: The Direct and Interactive Effects of Social Associations." *American Economic Review* 87 (2): 643–662.
La Porta, Rafael, Florencio Lopez de Silanes, Andrei Shleifer, and Robert W. Vishny. 1997. "Trust in Large Organizations." *American Economic Review* 137 (2): 333–338.
La Porta, Rafael, Florencio Lopez de Silanes, Andrei Shleifer, and Robert W. Vishny. 1999. "The Quality of Government." *Journal of Law, Economics and Organization* 15 (1): 222–279.
Laakso, Markku, and Rein Taagepera. 1979. "'Effective' Number of Parties: A Measure with Application to Western Europe." *Comparative Political Studies* 12 (1): 3–27.
Labonne, Julien, and Robert S. Chase. 2010. "A Road to Trust." *Journal of Economic Behavior and Organization* 74 (3): 253–261.
Landa, Janet T. 1994. *Trust, Ethnicity, and Identity: Beyond the New Institutional Economics of Ethnic Trade Networks, Contract Law, and Gift Exchange*. University of Michigan Press.
Latinobarómetro Corporation. 2018. "Latinobarometro, 1995–2018." www.latinobarometro.org/lat.jsp.
Lawrence, Adria K. 2016. "Repression and Activism among the Arab Spring's First Movers: Evidence from Morocco's February 20th Movement." *British Journal of Political Science* 47: 699–718.
Leite, Carlos A., and Jens Weidmann. 1999. "Does Mother Nature Corrupt? Natural Resources, Corruption, and Economic Growth." IMF Working Paper No. 99/85.
Letki, Natalia. 2006. "Investigating the Roots of Civic Morality: Trust, Social Capital, and Institutional Performance." *Political Behavior* 28: 305–325.
Levi, Margaret. 1996. "Social and Unsocial Capital: A Review Essay of Robert Putnam's Making Democracy Work." *Politics and Society* 24 (1): 45–55.
Levi, Margaret, and Laura Stoker. 2000. "Political Trust and Trustworthiness." *Annual Review of Political Science* 3 (475–507).
Levine, Daniel H. 1986. "Religion, the Poor, and Politics in Latin America Today." In *Religion and Political Conflict in Latin America*, edited by Daniel H. Levine.
Lewer, Joshua J., and Hendrik Van den Berg. 2007. "Estimating the Institutional and Network Effects of Religious Cultures on International Trade." *Kyklos* 60: 255–277.
Lewis-Beck, Michael S. 1999. *Economics and Elections: The Major Western Democracies*. University of Michigan Press.

Lia, Brynjar, and Jamal al Banna. 1998. *The Society of the Muslim Brothers in Egypt: The Rise of an Islamic Mass Movement, 1928–1942*. Ithaca Press.

Liddle, R. William, and Saiful Mujani. 2007. "Leadership, Party, and Religion: Explaining Voting Behavior in Indonesia." *Comparative Political Studies* 40 (7): 832–857.

Lohmann, Susanne. 1994. "The Dynamics of Informational Cascades: The Monday Demonstrations in Leipzig, East German, 1989–91." *World Politics* 47 (1): 42–101.

Lorasdağı, Berrin Koyuncu. 2010. "The Relationship between Islam and Globalization in Turkey in the Post-1990 Turkey: The Case of MÜSİAD." *Bilig* 52: 105–28.

Lorenz, Edward. 1999. "Trust, Contract and Economic Cooperation." *Cambridge Journal of Economics* 23: 301–315.

Lorenz, Edward H. 2000. "Neither Friends nor Strangers: Informal Networks of Subcontracting in French Industry." In *Trust: Making and Breaking Cooperative Relations*, edited by Diego Gambetta. Basil Blackwell Ltd.

Louw, Maria Elisabeth. 2007. *Everyday Islam in Post-Soviet Central Asia*. Routledge.

Lupu, Noam, and Kristin Michelitch. 2018. "Advances in Survey Methods for the Developing World." *Annual Review of Political Science* 21: 195–214.

Lussier, Danielle N. 2019. "Mosques, Churches, and Civic Skill Opportunities in Indonesia." *Journal for the Scientific Study of Religion*.

Luttmer, Erzo F. P., and Monica Singhal. 2011. "Culture, Context, and the Taste for Redistribution." *American Economic Journal: Economic Policy* 3 (1): 157–179.

Lynch, Marc. 2011. "After Egypt: The Limits and Promise of Online Challenges to the Authoritarian Arab State." *Perspectives on Politics* 9 (2): 301–310.

Maccoby, Eleanor M., and Nathan Maccoby. 1954. "The Interview: A Tool of Social Science." In *Handbook of Social Psychology*, edited by Gardiner Lindzey, 1:449–487. Addison-Wesley.

Magaloni, Beatriz. 2006. *Voting for Autocracy: Hegemonic Party Survival and its Demise in Mexico*. Cambridge University Press.

Mahmood, Saba. 2001. "Rehearsed Spontaneity and the Conventionality of Ritual: Disciplines of Ṣalāt." *American Ethnologist* 28 (4): 826–853.

Marlow, Louise. 1997. *Hierarchy and Egalitarianism in Islamic Thought*. Cambridge University Press.

Masoud, Tarek. 2014. *Counting Islam: Religion, Class, and Elections in Egypt*. Cambridge University Press.

Mattes, Robert, E. Gyimah-Boadi, and Michael Bratton. 2014. "Afrobarometer Round 5: The Quality of Democracy and Governance in 34 African Countries, 2011–2013." www.afrobarometer.org.

Mattes, Robert, E. Gyimah-Boadi, and Michael Bratton. 2016. "Afrobarometer Round 6: The Quality of Democracy and Governance in 36 Countries, 2016." www.afrobarometer.org.

McKelvey, Richard D., and Peter C. Ordeshook. 1972. "A General Theory of the Calculus of Voting." In *Mathematical Applications in Political Science*, edited by J. Herndon and J. L. Bernd, 32–78. University Press of Virginia.

Mecham, R. Quinn. 2004. "From the Ashes of Virtue, a Promise of Light: The Transformation of Political Islam in Turkey." *Third World Quarterly* 25 (2): 339–358.

Menoret, Pascal. 2011. "Leaving Islamic Activism Behind: Ambiguous Disengagement in Saudi Arabia." Chap. 2 in *Social Movements, Mobilization, and Contestation in the Middle East and North Africa*, edited by Joel Beinin and Frédéric Vairel, 43–60. Stanford University Press.

Meyersson, Erik. 2011. "'Turkish Tigers' and Political Change."
Miguel, Edward, and Mary Kay Gugerty. 2005. "Ethnic Diversity, Social Sanctions, and Public Goods in Kenya." *Journal of Public Economics* 89 (11–12): 2325–2368.
Mobarak, Ahmed Mushfiq. 2005. "Democracy, Volatility, and Economic Development." *The Review of Economics and Statistics* 87 (2): 348–361.
Mufti, Malik. 1999. "Elite Bargains and the Outset of Political Liberalization in Jordan." *Comparative Political Studies* 32: 100–129.
Müftüler-Baç, Meltem, and E. Fuat Keyman. 2012. "The Era of Dominant-Party Politics." *The Journal of Democracy* 23 (1): 85–99.
Mujani, Saiful. 2003. "Religious Democrats: Democratic Culture and Muslim Political Participation in Post-Suharto Indonesia." PhD diss., The Ohio State University.
MÜSİAD. 1994. *Economic Cooperation Among Islamic Countries.* MÜSİAD Research Reports 8.
Mutlu, Servet. 1996. "Ethnic Kurds in Turkey: A Demographic Study." *International Journal of Middle East Studies* 28 (4): 517–541.
Myatt, David P. 2007. "On the Theory of Strategic Voting." *Review of Economic Studies* 74: 255–281.
Myatt, David P., and Stephen D. Fisher. 2002. "Tactical Coordination in Plurality Electoral Systems." *Oxford Review of Economic Policy* 18 (4): 504–522.
Myerson, Roger B., and Robert J. Weber. 1993. "A Theory of Voting Equilibria." *American Political Science Review* 87 (1): 102–114.
Nannestad, Peter. 2008. "What Have We Learned About Generalized Trust, If Anything?" *Annual Review of Political Science* 11: 413–436.
Naser, Kamal, Jamal Ahmad, and Khalid Al-Khatib. 1999. "Islamic Banking: A Study of Customer Satisfaction and Preferences in Jordan." *The International Journal of Bank Marketing* 17 (3): 135–151.
Nasr, Seyyed Vali Reza. 2005. "The Rise of 'Muslim Democracy'." *Journal of Democracy* 16 (2): 13–27.
Navaro-Yashin, Yael. 2002. *Faces of the State: Secularism and Public Life in Turkey.* Princeton University Press.
Neaime, Simon. 2005. "Financial Market Integration and Macroeconomic Volatility in the MENA Region: An Empirical Investigation." *Review of Middle East Economics and Finance* 3 (3): 231–255.
Niemi, Richard G., Stephen C. Craig, and Franco Mattei. 1991. "Measuring Internal Political Efficacy in the 1988 National Election Study." *American Political Science Review* 85 (4): 1407–1413.
Norenzayan, Ara, and Azim F. Shariff. 2008. "The Origin and Evolution of Religious Prosociality." *Science* 322: 58–62.
Norris, Pippa. 2009. "Democracy Time-Series Dataset." www.pippanorris.com.
Norris, Pippa, and Ronald Inglehart. 2004. *Sacred and Secular: Religion and Politics Worldwide.* Cambridge University Press.
North, Douglass C. 1991. "Institutions." *Journal of Economic Perspectives* 5 (1): 97–112.
Norwegian Centre for Research Data. 2018. "European Social Survey Cumulative File, ESS 1-8." Data file edition 1.0. www.europeansocialsurvey.org/.
Noussair, Charles N., Stefan T. Trautmann, Gijs van de Kuilen, and Nathanael Vellekoop. 2013. "Risk Aversion and Religion." *Journal of Risk and Uncertainty* 47 (2): 165–183.

Nugroho, Anton Priyo, Anas Hidayat, and Hadri Kusuma. 2017. "The Influence of Religiosity and Self-Efficacy on the Saving Behavior of the Islamic Banks." *Banks and Bank Systems* 12 (3): 35–47.

Ocaklı, Feryaz. 2015. "Notable Networks: Elite Recruitment, Organizational Cohesiveness, and Islamist Electoral Success in Turkey." *Politics and Society* 43 (4): 385–413.

Office of Religious Affairs (*Diyanet İşleri Başkanlıgı*). 2017. "Religious Statistics in Turkey (*Din İstatistikleri*)." http://stratejigelistirme.diyanet.gov.tr/sayfa/57/istatistikler.

Olson, Mancur. 2002. *The Logic of Collective Action: Public Goods and the Theory of Groups*. Harvard University Press.

Öniş, Ziya, and Umut Türem. 2002. "Entrepreneurs, Democracy, and Citizenship in Turkey." *Comparative Politics* 34 (4): 439–456.

Önver, Defne, and Başak Taraktaş. 2017. "When Does Repression Trigger Mass Protest? The 2013 Gezi Protests." In *Non-State Violent Actors and Social Movement Organizations: Influence, Adaptation, and Change*, edited by Julie M. Mazzei, 205–239. Emerald Publishing.

Orbell, John M., Marion Goldman, Matthew Mulford, and Robyn M. Dawes. 1992. "Religion, Context, and Constraint toward Strangers." *Rationality and Society* 4 (3): 291–307.

Orbell, John M., Alphons J. C. Van de Kragt, and Robyn M. Dawes. 1988. "Explaining Discussion-Induced Cooperation." *Journal of Personality and Social Psychology* 54 (5): 811–819.

Ostrom, Elinor. 1998. "A Behavioral Approach to the Rational Choice Theory of Collective Action: Presidential Address." *American Political Science Review* 92 (1): 1–22.

Ostrom, Elinor. 2000. "Collective Action and the Evolution of Social Norms." *The Journal of Economic Perspectives* 14 (3): 137–158.

Özaloğlu, Serpil, and Meltem Ö. Gürel. 2011. "Designing Mosques for Secular Congregations: Transformations of the Mosque as a Social Space in Turkey." *Journal of Architectural and Planning Research* 28 (4): 336–358.

Özcan, Gül Berna. 1995. "Small Business Networks and Local Ties in Turkey." *Entrepreneurship and Regional Development* 7 (3): 265–284.

Özcan, Gül Berna, and Murat Çokgezen. 2006. "Trusted Markets: The Exchanges of Islamic Companies." *Comparative Economic Studies* 48: 132–155.

Özcan, Yusuf Ziya. 1990. "A Quantitative Study of Mosques in Turkey (*Ülkemizdeki Cami Sayilari Üzerine Sayisal bir İnceleme*)." Journal of Islamic Research 4 (1): 5–20.

Özdalga, Elizabeth. 1999. "Education in the Name of 'Order and Progress': Reflections on the Recent Rise of Eight Year Obligatory School Reform in Turkey." *The Muslim World* 89 (3–4): 414–438.

Özel, Işık. 2010. "Political Islam and Islamic Capital: The Case of Turkey." In *Religion and Politics in Europe, the Middle East and North Africa*, edited by Jeff Haynes. Routledge.

Özler, Hayrettin. 2001. "State and Business in Turkey: Issues of Collective Action with Special Reference to MÜSİAD." PhD diss., University of Strathclyde.

Özyürek, Esra. 2006. *Nostalgia for the Modern: State Secularism and Everyday Politics in Turkey*. Duke University Press.

Páez, Dario, Bernard Rimé, Nekane Basabe, and Anna Wlodarczyk. 2015. "Psychosocial Effects of Perceived Emotional Synchrony in Collective Gatherings." *Journal of Personality and Social Psychology* 108 (5): 711–729.

Pak, Soon-Young. 2004. "Articulating the Boundary between Secularism and Islamism: The Imam-Hatip Schools of Turkey." *Anthropology and Education Quarterly* 35 (3): 324–344.
Pamuk, Orhan. 2004. *Istanbul: Memories and the City*. Vintage Books.
Pamuk, Orhan. 2005. *Snow*. Vintage Books.
Patel, David Siddhartha. 2007. "Islam, Information, and Social Order: The Strategic Role of Religion in Muslim Societies." PhD diss., Stanford University.
Pechar, Emily, and Rachel Kranton. 2017. "Moderators of Intergroup Discrimination in the Minimal Group Paradigm: A Meta-Analysis." https://pdfs .semanticscholar.org/0a1f/7c2330ae9c85ad13b2a374c0ed21e4ace4d3.pdf.
Pedersen, Mogens N. 1979. "The Dynamics of European Party Systems: Changing Patterns of Electoral Volatility." *European Journal of Political Research* 7 (1): 1–26.
Pepinsky, Thomas B. 2013. "Development, Social Change, and Islamic Finance in Contemporary Indonesia." *World Development* 41: 157–167.
Pepinsky, Thomas B. 2016. "Measuring Piety in Indonesia." For presentation at the 2016 AALIMS Conferences on the Political Economy of Islam and Muslim Societies.
Pepinsky, Thomas B., R. William Liddle, and Saiful Mujani. 2012. "Testing Islam's Political Advantage: Evidence from Indonesia." *American Journal of Political Science* 56 (3): 584–600.
Pepinsky, Thomas B., R. William Liddle, and Saiful Mujani. 2018. *Piety and Public Opinion: Understanding Indonesian Islam*. Oxford University Press.
Persson, Mikael, and Maria Solevid. 2014. "Measuring Political Participation: Testing Social Desirability Bias in a Web-Survey Experiment." *International Journal of Public Opinion Research* 26 (1): 98–112.
Pew Research Center. 2015. "The Future of World Religions: Population Growth Projections, 2010–2050."
Platow, Michael J., Margaret Foddy, Toshio Yamagishi, Li Lim, and Aurore Chow. 2012. "Two Experimental Tests of Trust in In-Group Strangers: The Moderating Role of Common Knowledge of Group Membership." *European Journal of Social Psychology* 42: 30–35.
Polity IV Project. 2010. "Political Regime Characteristics and Transitions, 1800–2010."
Poortinga, Wouter. 2006. "Social Capital: An Individual or Collective Resource for Health?" *Social Science and Medicine* 62 (6): 292–302.
Przeworski, Adam. 1975. "Institutionalization of Voting Patterns, or is Mobilization the Source of Decay?" *American Political Science Review* 69 (1): 49–67.
Putnam, Robert D. 1993. *Making Democracy Work: Civic Traditions in Modern Italy*. Princeton University Press.
Quintelier, Ellen, and Andre Blais. 2016. "Intended and Reported Political Participation." *International Journal of Public Opinion Research* 28 (1): 117–128.
Rashkova, Ekaterina R. 2010. "Political Learning and the Number of Parties: Why Age Matters." PhD diss., University of Pittsburgh.
Riker, William H. 1982. *Liberalism against Populism: A Confrontation between the Theory of Democracy and the Theory of Social Choice*. W. H. Freeman.
Roberts, Kenneth M., and Erik Wibbels. 1999. "Party Systems and Electoral Volatility in Latin America: A Test of Economic, Institutional, and Structural Explanations." *American Political Science Review* 93: 575–590.
Robinson, Amanda Lea. 2016. "Nationalism and Ethnic-Based Trust: Evidence From an African Border Region." *Comparative Political Studies* 49 (14): 1819–1854.

Roháč, Dalibor. 2013. "Religion as a Commitment Device: The Economics of Political Islam." *Kyklos* 66 (2): 256–274.

Rosen, Lawrence. 2000. *The Justice of Islam: Comparative Perspectives on Islamic Law and Society*. Oxford University Press.

Rothstein, Bo, and Dietlind Stolle. 2008. "The State and Social Capital: An Institutional Theory of Generalized Trust." *Comparative Politics* 40 (4): 441–459.

Rousseau, Denise M., Sim B. Sitkin, Ronald S. Burt, and Colin F. Camerer. 1998. "Not So Different After All: A Cross-Discipline View of Trust." *Academy of Management Review* 23 (3): 393–404.

Roy, Olivier. 2012. "The Transformation of the Arab World." *Journal of Democracy* 23 (2): 5–18.

Rozenas, Arturas, and Anoop Sadanandan. 2018. "Literacy, Information, and Party System Fragmentation in India." *Comparative Political Studies* 51 (5): 555–586.

Ruffle, Bradley J., and Richard Sosis. 2007. "Does it Pay to Pray? Costly Ritual and Cooperation." *The B.E. Journal of Economic Analysis and Policy* 7 (1): 1–37.

Saher, Noreen, Muhammad Amanullah Khan, and Muhammad Bashir Khan. 2012. "Social Networks and Its Role in Contemporary Organizations: An Exploratory Research." *Interdisciplinary Journal of Contemporary Research in Business* 3 (12): 41–50.

Salvatore, Armando, and Dale F. Eickelman, eds. 2004. *Public Islam and the Common Good*. Brill.

Samuri, Mohd Al Adib, and Peter Hopkins. 2017. "Voices of Islamic Authorities: Friday Khutba in Malaysian Mosques." *Islam and Christian-Muslim Relations* 28 (1): 47–67.

Sapiro, Virginia, and W. Phillips Shively. 2018. "Comparative Study of Electoral Systems." www.cses.org/.

Sapsford, Roger, and Pamela Abbott. 2006. "Trust, Confidence and Social Environment in Post-Communist Societies." *Communist and Post-Communist Studies* 39 (1): 59–71.

Saroglou, Vassilis. 2011. "Believing, Bonding, Behaving, and Belonging: The Big Four Religious Dimensions and Cultural Variation." *Journal of Cross-Cultural Psychology* 42 (8): 1320–1340.

Schmidmayr, Michael. 2010. "Islamist Engagement in Contentious Politics: Kuwait and Bahrain." Chap. 8 in *Contentious Politics in the Middle East: Political Opposition under Authoritarianism*, edited by Holger Albrecht, 156–177. University Press of Florida.

Schofield, Norman, Maria Gallego, Uğur Ozdemir, and Alexei Zakharov. 2011. "Competition for Popular Support: A Valence Model of Elections in Turkey." *Social Choice and Welfare* 36: 451–482.

Schwedler, Jillian. 2006. *Faith in Moderation: Islamist Parties in Jordan and Yemen*. Cambridge University Press.

Seawright, Jason, and John Gerring. 2008. "Case Selection Techniques in Case Study Research: A Menu of Qualitative and Quantitative Options." *Political Research Quarterly* 61 (2): 294–308.

Selb, Peter, and Simon Munzert. 2013. "Voter Overrepresentation, Vote Misreporting, and Turnout Bias in Postelection Surveys." *Electoral Studies* 32: 186–196.

Shadmehr, Mehdi, and Dan Bernhardt. 2011. "Collective Action with Uncertain Payoffs: Coordination, Public Signals, and Punishment Dilemmas." *American Political Science Review* 105 (4): 829–851.

Shariff, Azim F., Aiyana K. Willard, Teresa Andersen, and Ara Norenzayan. 2016. "Religious Priming: A Meta-Analysis With a Focus on Prosociality." *Personality and Social Psychology Review* 20 (1): 27–48.

Shehata, Samer S. 2009. *Shop Floor Culture and Politics in Egypt*. State University of New York Press.

Shively, Kim. 2008. "Taming Islam: Studying Religion in Secular Turkey." *Anthropological Quarterly* 81 (3): 683–711.

Singerman, Diane. 1996. *Avenues of Participation-Family Politics, and Networks in Urban Quarters of Cairo*. Princeton University Press.

Singerman, Diane. 2004. "The Networked World of Islamist Social Movements." In *Islamic Activism: A Social Movement Theory Approach*, edited by Q. Wiktorowicz, 143–163. Indiana University Press.

Smith, Adam. 1986. "An Inquiry into the Nature and Causes of the Wealth of Nations." In *The Essential Adam Smith*, edited by Robert L. Heilbroner. W. W. Norton & Company.

Springborg, Robert. 1989. *Mubarak's Egypt: Fragmentation of the Political Order*. Westview Press.

Starrett, Gregory. 1995. "The Hexis of Interpretation: Islam and the Body in the Egyptian Popular School." *American Ethnologist* 22 (4): 953–969.

Stirling, Paul. 1998. *The Nature of Human Society: Turkish Village*. Centre for Social Anthropology / Computing.

Sullivan, Denis J. 1994. *Private Voluntary Organizations in Egypt: Islamic Development, Private Initiative, and State Control*. University Press of Florida.

Sutter, Matthias, and Martin G. Kocher. 2007. "Trust and Trustworthiness across Different Age Groups." *Games and Economic Behavior* 59: 364–382.

Sztompka, Piotr. 1998. "Trust, Distrust and Two Paradoxes of Democracy." *European Journal of Social Theory* 1 (1): 19–32.

Tajfel, Henri. 1974. "Social Identity and Intergroup Behavior." *Social Science Information* 13 (2): 65–93.

Tajfel, Henri, M. G. Billig, R. P. Bundy, and Claude Flament. 1971. "Social Categorization and Intergroup Behavior." *European Journal of Social Psychology* 1 (2): 149–178.

Tan, Jonathan H. W. 2006. "Religion and Social Preferences: An Experimental Study." *Economics Letters* 90: 60–67.

Tan, Jonathan H. W., and Claudia Vogel. 2008. "Religion and Trust: An Experimental Study." *Journal of Economic Psychology* 29 (6): 832–848.

Tavits, Margit. 2005. "The Development of Stable Party Support: Electoral Dynamics in Postcommunist Europe." *American Journal of Political Science* 49 (2): 283–298.

Tavits, Margit, and Taavi Annus. 2006. "Learning to Make Votes Count: The Role of Democratic Experience." *Electoral Studies* 25: 72–90.

Taymaz, Erol. 1997. *Small and Medium-Sized Industry in Turkey*. State Institute of Statistics.

Tepe, Sultan. 2005. "Turkey's AKP: A Model 'Muslim-Democratic' Party?" *Journal of Democracy* 16 (3): 69–82.

Tessler, Mark, Amaney Jamal, Abdallah Bedaida, Mhammed Abderebbi, Khalil Shikaki, Fares Braizat, Justin Gengler, and Michael Robbins. 2009. "Arab Barometer: Public Opinion Survey Conducted in Algeria, Morocco, Jordan, Lebanon, Palestine, Yemen, and Bahrain 2006–2009." www.arabbarometer.org/.

Tessler, Mark, Amaney Jamal, Musa Shteiwi, Khalil Shikaki, Michael Robbins, Rabih Hamami, Hesham Gaafar, et al. 2014. "Arab Barometer: Public Opinion Survey

Conducted in Algeria, Egypt, Iraq, Jordan, Kuwait, Lebanon, Libya, Morocco, Palestine, Sudan, Tunisia, and Yemen, 2012–2014.' www.arabbarometer.org/.
Tezcür, Güneş Murat. 2010. "The Moderation Theory Revisited: The Case of Islamic Political Actors." *Party Politics* 16 (1): 69–88.
Thompson, Bruce. 2004. *Exploratory and Confirmatory Factor Analysis: Understanding Concepts and Applications*. American Psychological Association.
Tomz, Mike, Joshua A. Tucker, and Jason Wittenberg. 2002. "An Easy and Accurate Regression Model for Multiparty Electoral Data." *Political Analysis* 10 (1): 66–83.
Toprak, Binnaz, İrfan Bozan, Tan Morgül, and Nedim Şener. 2009. "Being Different in Turkey: Religious, Conservatism and Otherization." Research Report on Neighborhood Pressure.
Torelli, Stefano Maria. 2012. "The 'AKP Model' and Tunisia's al-Nahda: From Convergence to Competition?" *Insight Turkey* 14 (3): 65–83.
Tsfati, Yariv. 2001. "Why Do People Trust Media Pre-Election Polls? Evidence from the Israel 1996 Elections." *International Journal of Public Opinion Research* 13 (4): 433–441.
Tufekci, Zeynep, and Christopher Wilson. 2012. "Social Media and the Decision to Participate in Political Protest: Observations from Tahrir Square." *Journal of Communication* 62 (2): 363–379.
Turam, Berna. 2007. *Between Islam and the State: The Politics of Engagement*. Stanford University Press.
Turan, Ömer. 2008. "The Turkish *Diyanet* Foundation." *The Muslim World* 98 (2–3): 370–384.
Turkish Institute of Statistics (*Türikye İstatistik Kurumu* TÜİK). 2003. "Census of Population (*Genel Nüfus Sayımı*)." https://biruni.tuik.gov.tr/nufusmenuapp/menu.zul.
Turkish Institute of Statistics. 2006. "Budgets: Municipalities, Provincial Special Administrations, and Villages (*Bütçeler: Belediyeler, İl Özel İdareler ve Köyler*)."
Turkish Institute of Statistics. 2013a. "Cultural Statistics (*Kültür İstatistikleri*)." https://biruni.tuik.gov.tr/kulturmedyadagitimapp/medya.zul.
Turkish Institute of Statistics. 2013b. "National Education Statistics: Informal Education (*Millî Eğitim İstatistikleri: Yaygin Eğitim*)." https://sgb.meb.gov.tr/www/resmi-istatistikler/icerik/64.
Turkish Institute of Statistics. 2014a. "Consumer Price Index (*Tüketici Fiyat Endeksi*)." https://biruni.tuik.gov.tr/medas/?kn=84&locale=tr.
Turkish Institute of Statistics. 2014b. "Local Administration Election Statistics (*Mahalli İdareler Seçim İstatistikleri*)." https://biruni.tuik.gov.tr/secimdagitimapp/menuyerel.zul.
Turkish Institute of Statistics. 2017. "Economic Indicators (*Ekonomik Göstergeler*)." https://biruni.tuik.gov.tr/medas/?kn=116.
Turkish Institute of Statistics. 2018a. "Address Based Population Registration System (*Adrese Dayalı Nüfus Kayıt Sistemi* (ADNKS))." https://biruni.tuik.gov.tr/medas/?kn=95.
Turkish Institute of Statistics. 2018b. "General Election Statistics (*Milletvekili Seçim İstatistikleri*)." https://biruni.tuik.gov.tr/secimdagitimapp/menusecim.zul.
Turkish Institute of Statistics. 2018c. "International Standard Book Number Statistics (*Uluslararasi Standart Kitap Numarasi İstatistikleri*)." www.turkstat.gov.tr.
Turkish Institute of Statistics. 2018d. "National Education Statistics: Formal Education (*Millî Eğitim İstatistikleri: Örgün Eğitim*)." https://sgb.meb.gov.tr/www/resmi-istatistikler/icerik/64.

Tusa, Felix. 2013. "How Social Media Can Shape a Protest Movement: The Cases of Egypt in 2011 and Iran in 2009." *Arab Media and Society* 17.
Tuğal, Cihan Z. 2009. "Transforming Everyday Life: Islamism and Social Movement Theory." *Theory and Society* 38: 423–458.
Tuğal, Cihan Z. 2016. *The Fall of the Turkish Model: How the Arab Uprisings Brought Down Liberalism*. Verso.
United Nations University. 2010. "UNU-WIDER World Income Inequality Database." www.wider.unu.edu.
Uslaner, Eric M. 2002. *The Moral Foundations of Trust*. Cambridge University Press.
Uslaner, Eric M. 2008. "Where You Stand Depends Upon Where Your Grandparents Sat." *Public Opinion Quarterly* 72 (4): 725–740.
Uygur, Selçuk. 2009. "The İslamic Work Ethic and the Emergence of Turkish SME Owner-Managers." *Journal of Business Ethics* 88: 211–25.
Uzzi, Brian. 1996. "The Sources and Consequences of Embeddedness for the Economic Performance of Organizations: The Network Effect." *American Sociological Review* 61 (4): 674–698.
van Elk, Michiel, Dora Matzke, Quentin F. Gronau, Maime Guan, Joachim Vandekerckhove, and Eric-Jan Wagenmakers. 2015. "Meta-Analyses are No Substitute for Registered Replications: A Skeptical Perspective on Religious Priming." *Frontiers in Psychology* 6.
Verba, Sidney, Nancy Burns, and Kay Lehman Schlozman. 1997. "Knowing and Caring about Politics: Gender and Political Engagement." *The Journal of Politics* 59 (4): 1051–1072.
Verba, Sidney, Kay Lehman Schlozman, and Henry E. Brady. 1995. *Voice and Equality: Civic Voluntarism in American Politics*. Harvard University Press.
Volkens, Andrea, Pola Lehmann, Theres Matthieß, Nicolas Merz, Sven Regel, and Bernhard Weßels. 2018. "The Manifesto Data Collection." Version 2018a. https://doi.org/10.25522/manifesto.mpds.2018a.
Wald, Kenneth D., Dennis E. Owen, and Samuel S. Hill Jr. 1988. "Churches as Political Communities." *American Political Science Review* 82 (2): 531–548.
Weber, Eugen. 1976. *Peasants into Frenchmen: The Modernization of Rural France, 1870–1914*. Stanford University Press.
Weber, Max. 1922. *The Sociology of Religion*. Beacon Press.
Westfall, Aubrey, Özge Çelik Russell, Bozena C. Welborne, and Sarah Tobin. 2017. "Islamic Headcovering and Political Engagement: The Power of Social Networks." *Politics and Religion* 10: 3–30.
White, Jenny. 2002. *Islamist Mobilization in Turkey: A Study in Vernacular Politics*. University of Washington Press.
White, Jenny. 2012. *Muslim Nationalism and the New Turks*. Princeton University Press.
Whitt, Sam, and Rick K. Wilson. 2007. "The Dictator Game, Fairness and Ethnicity in Postwar Bosnia." *American Journal of Political Science* 51 (3): 655–668.
Wickham, Carrie Rosefsky. 2002. *Mobilizing Islam: Religion, Activism, and Political Change in Egypt*. Columbia University Press.
Wickham, Carrie Rosefsky. 2004. "Interests, Ideas, and Islamist Outreach in Egypt." In *Islamic Activism: A Social Movement Theory Approach*, edited by Q. Wiktorowicz. Indiana University Press.
Wiktorowicz, Quintan. 1999. "State Power and the Regulation of Islam in Jordan." *Journal of Church and State* 41 (4): 677–696.

Wiktorowicz, Quintan, and Karl Kaltenhaler. 2006. "The Rationality of Radical Islam." *Political Science Quarterly* 121 (2): 295–319.
Wilcox, Clyde, Kenneth D. Wald, and Ted G. Jelen. 2008. "Religious Preferences and Social Science: A Second Look." *Journal of Politics* 70 (3): 874–879.
Williamson, Oliver E. 1971. "The Vertical Integration of Production: Market Failure Considerations." *American Economic Review* 61 (2): 112–123.
Williamson, Oliver E. 1985. *The Economic Institutions of Capitalism: Firms, Markets, Relational Contracting.* The Free Press.
Wilson, Rick K. 2018. "Trust Experiments, Trust Games, and Surveys." Chap. 13 in *The Oxford Handbook of Social and Political Trust*, edited by Eric M. Uslaner, 279–304. Oxford University Press.
Wit, Arjaan, and Henk A. M. Wilke. 1992. "The Effect of Social Categorization on Cooperation in Three Types of Social Dilemmas." *Journal of Economic Psychology* 13 (1): 135–151.
World Bank. 2005a. "Doing Business in 2005." www.doingbusiness.org/.
World Bank. 2005b. "Turkey – Enterprise Survey." www.enterprisesurveys.org/.
World Bank. 2014. "World Development Indicators, 2014." http://data.worldbank.org/data-catalog/world-development-indicators/.
World Values Survey Association. 2018. "World Values Survey 1981–2014 Longitudinal Aggregate." V.20150418. www.worldvaluessurvey.org/.
Yamagishi, Toshio, Nobuhito Jin, and Toko Kiyonari. 1999. "Bounded Generalized Reciprocity: In-Group Boasting and In-Group Favoritism." *Advances in Group Processes* 16: 161–197.
Yamagishi, Toshio, and Toko Kiyonari. 2000. "The Group as the Container of Generalized Reciprocity." *Social Psychology Quarterly* 63 (2): 116–132.
Yavuz, M. Hakan. 2003. *Islamic Political Identity in Turkey.* Oxford University Press.
Yavuz, M. Hakan. 2004. "Opportunity Spaces, Identity, and Islamic Meaning in Turkey." In *Islamic Activism: A Social Movement Theory Approach*, edited by Q. Wiktorowicz. Indiana University Press.
Yavuz, M. Hakan. 2009. *Secularism and Muslim Democracy in Turkey.* Cambridge University Press.
Yeşilada, Birol A., and Peter Noordijk. 2010. "Changing Values in Turkey: Religiosity and Tolerance in Comparative Perspective." *Turkish Studies* 11 (1): 9–27.
Yılmaz, İhsan, and James Barry. 2018. "Instrumentalizing Islam in a 'Secular' State: Turkey's Diyanet and Interfaith Dialogue." *Journal of Balkan and Near Eastern Studies.*
Yılmaz, Serdar, and Ayşe Güner. 2013. "Local Government Discretion and Accountability in Turkey." *Public Administration and Development* 33: 125–142.
Yousef, Tarik M. 2004. "Development, Growth and Policy Reform in the Middle East and North Africa since 1950." *Journal of Economic Perspectives* 18 (3): 91–116.
Zak, Paul J., and Stephen Knack. 2001. "Trust and Growth." *The Economic Journal* 111: 295–321.
Zand, Dale E. 1972. "Trust and Managerial Problem Solving." *Administrative Science Quarterly* 17 (2): 229–239.
Zubaida, Sami. 1989. *Islam, the People and the State.* I. B. Tauris.

Index

Address-Based Population Registration System (*Adrese Dayalı Nüfus Kayıt Sistemi*, ADKS), 113, 169
Afghanistan, 33, 53
Afrobarometer, 25, 26, 40, 81, 86, 115, 116
age, 3, 26, 28, 43, 83, 87, 113, 120, 133, 138, 143
Albania, 48, 60, 179
Algeria, 28, 50, 57, 141, 179, 205, 219
altruism, 7, 72–73, 104, 104–129
Ankara, 66, 113, 162
apathy, 31, 35, 39, 41, 43
Arab Barometer, 26, 40, 63, 81, 86, 91
Arab Spring, 8, 28, 66, 69, 71, 127, 220
AsiaBarometer, 25, 49, 81, 86, 115
assumption, 5, 35, 51, 54, 63, 68, 72, 77, 84, 85, 88, 128, 195
Atatürk, Mustafa Kemal, 1, 2, 4, 151
autocracy, 24, 46, 210, 221
Azerbaijan, 219

Bahrain, 28, 50, 52, 128
Bangladesh, 52, 57, 80, 98, 142, 145
banking, 24, 26–29, 33, 40, 44, 48–49, 51–54, 65, 69, 76, 92, 167–168, 181, 201–202
   Islamic, 4, 21–23, 29, 51–54, 175, 181, 182, 189, 192
   micro-financing, 11, 21, 101, 181, 205
Berbers, 146, 219
Bosnia, 77, 98, 99
Buddhism, 211, 213
Burkina Faso, 48, 179
business associations, 4, 5, 16, 22, 93, 181

case study, 12, 35, 37, 45, 51
Catholicism, 83, 85, 211
Caucasus Barometer, 26, 39, 79, 115

Chad, 53
charity
   Islamic (*zakat*), 4, 30
Christianity, 83, 85, 211, 213
   Coptic, 146, 211
   Maronite, 211
church, 10, 112, 118, 147, 180
class, *see* income
collective action
   problem, *see* free-rider problem
collective action, 6, 14, 26, 68
common knowledge, 9, 66, 70, 73, 95, 101–103, 110–111, 130, 161, 193
comparative method, 3, 6, 12, 35, 37, 45, 220
Comparative Study of Electoral Systems (CSES), 60, 62
comparison
   cross-sectional, 4, 12–14, 25, 24–28, 40–42, 46–49, 52–54, 54, 56–63, 63, 79–83, 91, 155, 168
   cross-temporal, 2, 4, 12–14, 56–57, 81, 148, 151–154, 160, 173
   individual, 13, 42–44, 49–51, 54, 86–89, 91, 120–121, 132, 164, 165
conceptualization, 49, 67–68, 74, 84, 102, 106–108
Constitutional Court of Turkey (Anayasa Mahkemesi), 5, 141, 149, 152, 156–157
cooperation, 6, 7, 10, 13, 97–99
   conditional, 7, 15, 72–74, 105, 129, 142
coordination, 6, 10, 62
   voting, 16, 70, 75, 93, 105, 161, 148–162, 166, 180, 213–215
corruption, 34, 78, 158
credibility, *see* honesty
credit, *see* banking

culture, 75, 84–85, 88, 131

data
  census, 2, 50, 55, 169, 171
  interpolation, 169
  official statistics, 2, 4, 55–56, 171
  panel, 3, 16, 166, 195
  polling, 162–164
  survey, 4, 13, 16, 25, 27, 39, 49, 56, 60, 61, 63, 76, 78, 80–81, 113, 115, 119, 160, 163, 165, 167, 172, 186
democracy, 4, 24, 26, 46, 47, 54, 57, 76, 82, 148, 210, 214
Demographic and Health Survey (DHS), 171

East Asia Barometer, 25, 26, 40, 42, 81, 86, 115
economic transactions, 6, 8, 14, 16, 22, 24, 29, 33, 46, 69–71, 75–77, 92, 101, 102, 181–205
  identity-based, 182, 190–191
  iterated, 182, 188
  one-shot, 182, 186, 205
economics
  behavioral, 9, 72, 73, 95
  evolutionary, 98
  political, 14, 88
  religion, of, 107
education, 3, 21, 22, 26, 28, 43, 56, 82, 83, 87, 113, 120, 133, 138, 143, 162, 169
  religious, 4, 54, 55, 109, 111, 121, 171, 172
efficacy, 118–119, 163
Egypt, 1, 28, 29, 33, 34, 50–52, 66, 69, 71–72, 77, 98, 99, 101, 106, 111, 127, 131, 141, 146, 179, 211, 220
elections, 4, 21
  general, 1, 16, 21, 22, 54–56, 113, 156–157, 169
  local, 21
  referendum, 21, 22, 152
electoral districts, 12, 16, 75, 155, 161, 167
electoral threshold, 149, 155, 159, 167
empirical implications, *see* hypothesis
employment, 11, 21, 31, 169
Erbakan, Necmettin, 156
Erdoğan, Recep Tayyip, 1, 146, 157, 210, 221
Eurobarometer (EB), 40, 81, 86
Europe, 13, 33, 88–91
European Social Survey (ESS), 88
European Values Study (EVS), 25, 39, 40, 49, 52, 61, 63, 79, 81, 86, 115, 119, 167
external validity, 14, 35, 37, 45, 51, 57–59, 88, 132, 167–168, 204, 211–215

faith-based theory, 13–15, 31–33, 35, 38, 45, 59
firms, 13, 14, 16, 22, 40, 105, 181, 196
  manufacturing, 185, 196
  small- and medium-sized, 6, 22, 182, 185, 187–189, 197, 204
fractionalization
  ethno-linguistic, 82–84, 98, 111, 214
  party system, 1, 8, 70, 93, 149, 151–152, 154–155, 157, 159, 215
free-rider problem, 7, 67, 71–72, 129

game
  coordination, 129
  dictator, 104
  public goods, 72, 129
  theory, 36, 70, 88
  trust, 80–81, 133, 168
gender, 11, 26, 28, 43, 83, 87, 90, 111, 113, 120, 125, 133, 137, 143, 221
Gezi Park, 8, 22, 66, 127
Global Financial Inclusion (Findex) Database, 27, 40, 44, 48, 51, 52, 168
Green Movement, 66, 129
grievance theory, 11, 13, 15, 30–31, 35, 38–45
Gül, Abdullah, 157
Gülen, Fethullah, 22, 146

health, 11, 21, 22, 31, 76
Hinduism, 211, 213
honesty, 7, 13, 65, 68, 73–75, 77–80, 162, 216–219
hypothesis, 10, 15, 16, 31, 33–35, 37, 39, 42, 49, 51, 59, 77, 86, 88, 92, 93, 105, 118, 121, 131, 164, 194

identity, 14, 107–108
  ethnic, 9, 11, 98, 99, 104, 111, 146, 219, 221
  group, 9, 14, 15, 23, 95, 97–98, 104, 105, 107, 171, 183
  national, 11, 221
  partisan, 154
  personal, 98, 103
  religious, 9, 10, 16, 99, 106–109, 112–117, 130, 136–138, 164–165, 171–175, 211–213
imam hatip schools, 55, 171, 172
income, 28, 30–32, 35, 38, 39, 42–44, 76, 82–84, 98, 135, 168, 169, 171, 183, 186, 197, 204, 214
Independent Industrialists' and Businessmen's Association (Müstakil Sanayici ve İşadamları Derneği, MÜSİAD), 4, 6,

Index

16, 17, 22, 182, 190, 191–192, 196–197, 199–203
Indonesia, 12, 33, 34, 51, 52, 57, 98, 111, 112, 117, 118, 142, 145, 179, 204
inefficiency, 14, 17
inequality, 82–84
inference
   causal, 35, 37, 56, 80, 82, 86, 132, 136, 168, 197, 201–203, 211
   ecological, 168
inflation, 197, 198, 204, 214
information, 8, 10–13, 15, 34–35, 38, 59–64, 66, 74, 112, 135, 140, 149, 161, 163, 164, 169, 185, 217
   political, 38, 59, 149, 160
   social, 149, 161–164
institutions, 46, 47, 82–84, 86, 136, 170, 217–219
integration
   "quasi"-, 13, 16, 17, 188–190
   vertical, 17, 186–187, 189, 197–200
interdependence, 7, 14, 15, 36, 66, 68–70, 72–73, 128–129, 142, 158–161, 184–185, 189
investment, *see* banking
Iran, 29, 52, 66, 70, 129, 219, 220
Iraq, 29, 52, 57, 63, 142, 145, 219
Islam, 85–87, 99, 107, 109–110
   Alevi, 146, 220
   Shi'a, 85, 86, 220, 221
   Sufi, 85
   Sunni, 85, 86, 220, 221
Istanbul, 12, 22, 76, 98, 101, 113, 125, 196
Istanbul Chamber of Industry (İstanbul Sanayi Odası, İSO), 189, 196

Jordan, 52, 57, 58, 63, 64, 112, 142, 145, 180
Judaism, 211–213

Kazakhstan, 77
KONDA Research and Consultancy, 113, 160, 171
Kurds, 1, 23, 146, 170, 171, 219
Kuwait, 50, 52, 128
Kyrgyzstan, 60, 77, 179

laiklik, *see* secularism
Latinobarómetro, 25, 26, 39, 40, 79, 81, 86
Lebanon, 110, 118, 211
Libya, 57, 58

Malaysia, 1, 28, 52, 57, 98, 99, 108, 111, 112, 142, 145, 179
Maldives, 52

Mali, 12, 48, 142, 145, 179
Mauritania, 52
measurement, 10, 24–25, 27, 39–40, 42, 46–47, 49, 51–52, 54–58, 60–61, 63, 78–81, 83, 86, 88, 89, 113–115, 133, 136–137, 140, 152, 166–169, 171–172, 177, 196–198, 214
   error, 3, 5, 25, 26, 50, 52, 79, 81, 90–91, 120, 132
media, 2, 55
   social, 66, 69–71, 162
Middle East and North Africa (MENA), 30, 38
migration, 13, 76, 84, 88–91, 99, 170, 190
military, 5, 141, 146, 151
   coup, 153, 155, 156, 166, 177, 191
mobilization, 6, 24–28
model
   club goods, 7, 32, 109
   hierarchical, 26, 28, 43, 51, 54, 79, 83, 87, 89, 132
   interaction, 87, 89, 138, 144, 174, 198, 200, 201
   multinomial, 133
   regression, 44, 87, 91, 120, 169, 172, 215
   seemingly unrelated, 176
   tipping, 127
moderation, 29, 57, 157
monitoring, 98, 100, 194
Morocco, 28, 57, 58, 77, 101, 128, 142, 145, 204, 219
mosque, 9, 54, 55, 107, 109–112, 114, 115, 117, 121, 137, 171
motivation, 8, 10, 11, 15, 31, 35, 38, 39, 41, 66, 74, 112, 135, 140, 163, 169
movements
   "latent", 7, 8, 24, 67, 96, 126–127
   Islamic-based, 1, 22, 125
Muslim Brotherhood, 1, 29, 33, 34, 111, 141, 146, 179
Muslim world, 12, 23, 47

networks, 11, 34
Niger, 53
Nigeria, 142, 145, 204, 219

Office of Religious Affairs (Diyanet İşleri Başkanlığı, Diyanet), 55, 112, 172
operationalization, *see* measurement
organization, 4, 6, 34

Pakistan, 52, 57, 58, 99, 142, 145, 219
Palestine, 28, 52, 57, 58, 63, 64
parties, 21, 60, 125

center-left, 61, 62
center-right, 2, 4, 6, 61, 155, 165
Islamic, 1, 4, 6, 12, 14–16, 23, 28, 34, 54–59, 93, 148, 156–157, 165–166, 173, 176–178, 182, 189, 192, 194, 202
Kurdish, 22, 61, 155, 177
nationalist, 61, 62
Party
  Democratic Left (Demokratik Sol Parti, DSP), 61, 155
  Democratic People's (Demokratik Halk Partisi, DEHAP), 22, 61
  Felicity (Saadet Partisi, SP), 54, 63, 152, 157, 164
  Freedom and Justice (Ḥizb al-Ḥurriyyah wa al-ʿAdala), see Muslim Brotherhood
  Justice and Development (Adalet ve Kalkınma Partisi, AKP), 1–5, 16, 17, 22, 28, 33, 54, 61, 56–63, 148, 153, 157–158, 171, 180
  Motherland (Anavatan Partisi, ANAP), 61, 62, 153, 155, 159
  National Salvation (Millî Selamet Partisi, MSP), 54, 152, 156
  Nationalist Action (Milliyetçi Hareket Partisi, MHP), 61, 152, 180
  People's Democratic (Halkların Demokratik Partisi, HDP), 22, 63, 152
  People's Voice (Halkın Sesi Partisi, HAS), 54
  Prosperous Justice (Partai Keadilan Sejahtera, PKS), 33, 57, 111
  Republican People's (Cumhuriyet Halk Partisi, CHP), 61, 63, 151, 152, 154, 159, 176, 177, 180
  True Path (Doğru Yol Partisi, DYP), 61, 152
  Virtue (Fazilet Partisi, FP), 54, 152, 157
  Welfare (Refah Partisi, RP), 54, 141, 152, 156, 159
policy positions, 2, 11, 34, 35, 61–63, 155, 157
  economic, 34, 61, 62, 158
  social, 61, 62
political participation, 6, 8, 13, 16, 21, 24–26, 35, 42–43, 48–51, 65, 67, 69, 75, 76, 92, 104, 105, 112, 125–147
poverty, see income
prayer, 9, 22, 107, 109
preferences, 7, 15, 72, 82, 100, 180
priming, 9, 10, 14, 15, 95, 101–103, 132, 165, 173
principal component factor analysis, 42, 61, 79, 113, 117, 135, 137, 211
prosociality, 111, 119, 139
protest, see political participation
psychology, 9, 95, 98, 105, 110

public goods, 21, 22, 34, 65, 67, 71, 76, 98

Qatar, 50, 52
Qur'an
  reading groups, 54, 56, 101, 109, 111, 172

rational choice, 33, 35, 45, 68, 69
rational egoism, 7, 72, 71–72, 72, 73, 100, 105, 129, 142
reciprocity, 7, 68, 70, 73, 100
regulation, see institutions
religion, 96, 211–213
  egalitarian, 85–86, 96, 211
religiosity
  personal, 2–3, 5, 10–16, 32, 35, 38, 49–57, 96, 106–109, 112–117, 131
religious group activities, 10, 14, 16, 109–112, 131, 136, 171
repression, 14, 16, 45–47, 71–72, 93, 131, 141–145
reputation, 11, 16, 34, 35, 63–64, 75, 98, 109, 182, 190–191
risk, 11, 14, 15, 24, 31, 33, 35, 38, 45–47, 69, 71–72, 128, 141
robustness, 24, 26, 28, 42–43, 46, 50–51, 54, 79–80, 87, 89–90, 135–136, 139–140, 170–171, 175

salience, 9, 10, 14, 95, 101–103, 105, 110, 130, 164
Saudi Arabia, 52, 101
savings
  bank, see banking
  household, 23, 27–28, 44
secularism, 2–4, 16, 30, 125, 148
selective incentives, 11, 12, 31, 38, 39, 42
  spiritual, 11, 32, 33
social capital, 82, 131
sociology, 107
state, 14, 16, 21, 30, 46, 141, 179, 197
statistical
  correlation, 114–116, 169, 172, 216
  partial, 143, 214
  distribution, 60, 157, 177
  significance, 3, 25, 28, 41, 46, 47, 54, 79, 80, 82, 83, 87, 89, 120, 134, 138, 168
substitution, 10, 14, 15, 95, 97, 104–105, 131, 138, 164–165, 173–174
Sudan, 52
Syria, 52, 219

trade, see economic transactions
transition matrix, 154, 169, 176, 177
transvaluation theory, see faith-based theory

Index

trust, 7–10, 14, 15, 67, 67, 74, 67–78, 163, 130–163, 185–186
  generalized, 7, 10, 13, 15, 67, 68, 74–76, 80–83, 87, 100, 103–105, 119, 130, 133–135, 164, 167–171, 176, 180, 182, 183, 186–187, 216–219
  group-based, 9, 10, 14–16, 23, 95, 97, 100, 99–105, 107–108, 119, 120, 130, 164–165, 180, 183, 192–194
  institutional, 40, 50, 82
  particularized, 7, 8, 74–75, 88, 130, 182, 190
  political, 7, 34, 63, 64, 67, 118, 135, 158, 169, 170, 215, 219, 221
trustworthiness, *see* honesty
Tunisia, 13, 28, 51, 52, 57, 58, 127, 219, 220
Turkey, 4, 1–5, 5, 12–14, 16, 22–25, 27, 28, 33, 52, 54–57, 60–64, 75–77, 89, 91, 93, 95, 98, 99, 101, 102, 105, 108, 109, 111–113, 125, 131, 141, 142, 148, 150–159, 163, 165, 186–187, 219, 220
Turkish Statistical Institute (Türkiye İstatistik Kurumu, TÜİK), 55

uncertainty, 7, 13, 15, 68, 72, 70–72, 74, 129–130, 142, 161–163, 185
United Arab Emirates (UAE), 52
Uzbekistan, 77, 142, 145

veiling, 3, 108, 109, 113
volatility
  economic, 8, 13, 14, 17, 67
  electoral, 2, 149, 152–155, 158, 161–162, 167, 176, 213–215
  macroeconomic, 186–188, 197–200
voting, 8, 24, 33, 65, 69, 70
  economic, 154, 164, 170, 176
  mandatory, 159
  strategic, 8, 13, 14, 16, 67, 70, 71, 149, 159–160
  turnout, 21, 26, 92
  wasted, 13, 16, 149, 155–156, 158, 160–162, 167, 169–174, 176

World Bank Enterprise Survey, 187
World Values Survey (WVS), 25, 26, 39, 40, 49, 50, 52, 61, 63, 79, 81, 86, 114–116, 119, 167, 172

Yemen, 52, 57, 58, 142, 180

CPSIA information can be obtained
at www.ICGtesting.com
Printed in the USA
BVHW031744050422
633465BV00002B/34